March 19–22, 2017
Portland, OR, USA

**Association for
Computing Machinery**

Advancing Computing as a Science & Profession

ISPD'17

Proceedings of the 2017 ACM
International Symposium on Physical Design

Sponsored by:
ACM SIGDA

Technical Co-sponsor:
IEEE Circuits and Systems Society

Supported by:
***Cadence, IBM Research, Intel, Mentor Graphics, NEC, Oracle,
Synopsys, TSMC, & Xilinx***

**Association for
Computing Machinery**

Advancing Computing as a Science & Profession

The Association for Computing Machinery
2 Penn Plaza, Suite 701
New York, New York 10121-0701

Notice to Past Authors of ACM-Published Articles

ISBN: 978-1-4503-4696-2 (Digital)

ISBN: 978-1-4503-5449-3 (Print)

Additional copies may be ordered prepaid from:

ACM Order Department
PO Box 30777
New York, NY 10087-0777, USA

Phone: 1-800-342-6626 (USA and Canada)
+1-212-626-0500 (Global)
Fax: +1-212-944-1318
E-mail: acmhelp@acm.org
Hours of Operation: 8:30 am – 4:30 pm ET

Printed in the USA

Foreword

On behalf of the organizing committee, we are delighted to welcome you to the 2017 ACM International Symposium on Physical Design (ISPD), held at Portland-Lake Oswego, Oregon. Continuing the great tradition established by its twenty-five predecessors, which includes a series of five ACM/SIGDA Physical Design Workshops held intermittently in 1987-1996 and twenty editions of ISPD in the current form since 1997, the 2017 ISPD provides a premier forum to present leading-edge research results, exchange ideas, and promote research on critical areas related to the physical design of VLSI and other related systems.

The regular papers in the ISPD 2017 program were selected after a rigorous, month-long, double-blind review process and a face-to-face meeting by the Technical Program Committee (TPC) members. The papers selected exhibit latest advancements in a variety of topics in physical design, including emerging challenges for current and future process technologies, FPGA layout, clock construction and timing analysis, and application of machine-learning based techniques to physical design.

The ISPD 2017 program is complemented by three keynote addresses, fourteen invited talks and a tribute session, all of which are delivered by distinguished researchers from both industry and academia. Two of the keynote speeches are on Monday. In the morning, Dr. Ian Young, senior fellow of Intel Corporation, will talk about technology options for beyond CMOS. In the afternoon, Dr. Ivo Bolsens, CTO and senior VP of Xilinx, will talk about the transition from FPGA to the All Programmable Platform. In the third keynote speech on Tuesday, Dr. Lee-Chung Lu, senior director and fellow of TSMC, will present the physical design challenges and innovations to meet the power, speed, and area scaling trends. A commemorative session on Tuesday afternoon will pay tribute to Professor Satoshi Goto. His collaborators will share with us Dr. Goto's exceptional contributions to research in physical design and VLSI applications, including his influential work on placement tools. There will be other invited talks interspersed with the presentations of the regular papers. The topics of the invited papers range from clock construction, physical optimization, machine learning in EDA, security-aware physical design, in-memory computing, and FPGA EDA.

Since 2005, the ISPD has organized highly competitive contests to promote and advance research in placement, global routing, clock network synthesis, discrete gate sizing, and detailed routing-driven placement. The contest this year, organized by Xilinx, is on FPGA placement. Different from last year's contest, which was also on FPGA placement, this year's contest focuses on the placement of clocking components. Continuing the tradition of all the past contests, a new large-scale real-world benchmark suite for FPGA circuits based on an advanced heterogeneous FPGA architecture will be released in the ISPD website (http://www.ispd.cc). The contest evaluates the quality of an FPGA placement with an advanced commercial FPGA routing tool making the problem even more challenging and practical. It is expected to lead and motivate more research and contributions on FPGA physical design.

We would like to take this chance to express our gratitude to the authors, the presenters, the keynote/invited speakers for contributing to the high-quality program, and the session chairs for moderating the sessions. We would like to thank our program committee and external reviewers, who provided insightful constructive comments and detailed reviews to the authors. We greatly appreciate the exceptional set of invited talks put together by the Steering Committee, which is chaired by Evangeline Young. We also thank the Steering Committee for selecting the best paper.

Special thanks go to the Publications Chair Ismail Bustany and the Publicity Chair Bill Swartz for their tremendous services. We would like to acknowledge the team organizing the contest led by Stephen Yang. We are also grateful to our sponsors. The symposium is sponsored by the ACM SIGDA (Special Interest Group on Design Automation) with technical co-sponsorship from the IEEE Circuits and Systems Society. Generous financial contributions have also been provided by (in alphabetical order): Cadence, IBM, Intel Corporation, Mentor Graphics, NEC, Oracle, Synopsys, TSMC, and Xilinx. Last but not least, we thank Lisa Tolles and others from Sheridan Communications for their expertise and enormous patience during the production of the proceedings.

The organizing committee hopes that you will enjoy ISPD. We look forward to seeing you again in future editions of ISPD.

Mustafa Ozdal
ISPD 2017 General Chair

Chris Chu
Technical Program Chair

Table of Contents

Welcome and Keynote Address

Machine Learning in EDA

Monday Afternoon Keynote

Invited Poster Presentation

Nontraditional Physical Design Challenges

Tuesday Keynote Address

Clock and Timing

Routability Considerations

Commemoration for Professor Satoshi Goto

Optimization and Placement

FPGA CAD and Contest

ISPD 2017 Organization

General Chair: Mustafa Ozdal (Bilkent University)

Past Chair/Steering Committee Chair: Evangeline Young (Chinese University of Hong Kong)

Technical Committee Chair: Chris Chu (Iowa State University)

Publications Chair: Ismail Bustany (Mentor Graphics)

Publicity Chair: William Swartz (TimberWolf Systems and University of Texas at Dallas)

Contest Chair: Stephen Xiaojian Yang (Xilinx)

Steering Committee:
Chuck Alpert (Cadence)
Yao-Wen Chang (National Taiwan University)
Azadeh Davoodi (Univerity of Wisconsin)
Patrick Groeneveld (Synopsys)
Jiang Hu (University of Texas A & M)
Noel Menezes (Intel)
David Pan (University of Texas at Austin)
Martin Wong (University of Illinois at Urbana-Champaign)
Evangeline Young –Chair (Chinese University of Hong Kong)

Technical Program Committee:
Youngchan Ban (GlobalFoundries)
Ismail Bustany (Mentor Graphics)
Salim Chowdhury (self)
Chris Chu – Chair (Iowa State University)
Sabya Das (Xilinx)
Sheqin Dong (Tsinghua University)
Mahesh Iyer (Intel)
Iris Hui-Ru Jiang (National Chiao Tung University)
Jens Lienig (Technische Universitat Dresden)
Mark Po-Hung Lin (National Chung Cheng University)
Wen-Hao Liu (Cadence)
David Newmark (AMD)
Ulf Schlichtmann (Technische Universitat Munchen)
Yasuhiro Takashima (University of Kitakyushu)
Hua Xiang (IBM)
Gary Yeap (Synopsys)
Bei Yu (Chinese University of Hong Kong)

Additional reviewers:

Kostas Adam
Saurabh Adya
Gregg Baeckler
Johathan Bishop
Anja Boos
Mark Bourgeault
Kalen Brunham
David Chinnery
Alex Choong
Shounak Dhar
Yixiao Ding
Carl Ebeling
Mike Hutton
Oleg Levitsky
Bing Li
Matt Liberty
Yibo Lin
Bao Liu

Yuzhe Ma
Wai-Kei Mak
Larry McMurchie
Chak-Wa Pui
Subhendu Roy
Nilolay Rubanov
Eric Sather
Shveta Sharma
Joseph Shinnerl
Love Singhal
Nish Sinnadurai
Tom Spyrou
Babette Van Antwerpen
Alexander Volkov
Scott Weber
Xiaoqing Xu
Wei Yei
Li Zhang

ISPD 2017 Sponsor & Supporters

Sponsor:

Supporters:

Technology Options for Beyond-CMOS

Ian A. Young
Senior Fellow and Director of Exploratory Integrated Circuits,
Components Research,
Intel Corporation, Hillsboro, Oregon

CMOS integrated circuit technology for computation is at an inflexion point. Although this is the technology which has enabled the semiconductor industry to make vast progress over the past 30-plus years, it is expected to see challenges going beyond the ten year horizon, particularly from an energy efficiency point of view. Thus it is extremely important for the semiconductor industry to discover a new integrated circuit technology which can carry us to the beyond CMOS era, so that the power-performance of computing can continue to improve. Currently, researchers are exploring novel device concepts and new information tokens as an alternative for CMOS technology. Examples of areas being actively researched are; quantum electronic devices, such as the tunneling field-effect transistor (TFET), and devices based on electron spin and nano-magnetics (spintronics). It is clear that choices will need to be made in the next 10 years to identify viable alternatives for CMOS by 2025. To prioritize and guide the research exploration in materials, devices and circuits, benchmarking methodology and metrics are being used.

This talk will give an overview of the beyond CMOS device research horizon and the benchmarking of these devices for computation. A more detailed investigation of circuits based upon some promising beyond-CMOS devices will follow.

Biography:
Ian Young is a Senior Fellow and director of Exploratory Integrated Circuits in the Technology and Manufacturing Group of Intel Corporation. He joined Intel in 1983 and his technical contributions have been in the design of DRAMs, SRAMs, microprocessor circuit design, Phase Locked Loops and microprocessor clocking, mixed-signal

circuits for microprocessor high speed I/O links, RF CMOS circuits for wireless transceivers, and research for chip to chip optical I/O. He has also contributed to the definition and development of Intel's process technologies.

He now leads a research group exploring the future options for the integrated circuit in the beyond CMOS era. Recent work has developed a uniform benchmarking to identify the technology options in spintronics, tunneling junction field-effect and photonics devices.

Ian Young received the Bachelor of Electrical Engineering and the Master Eng. Science, Microwave Communications, from the University of Melbourne, Australia. He received the PhD in Electrical Engineering from the University of California, Berkeley. He is the recipient of the 2009 International Solid-State Circuits Conference's Jack Raper Award for Outstanding Technology Directions paper. He is a Fellow of the IEEE.

ISPD'17, March 19–22, 2017, Portland, OR, USA.
ACM. ISBN 978-1-4503-4696-2/17/03.
DOI: http://dx.doi.org/10.1145/3036669.3041225

The Quest for the Ultimate Learning Machine

Pradeep Dubey
Parallel Computing Lab, Intel Corporation
Santa Clara, CA
corina.rios@intel.com

ABSTRACT

Traditionally, there has been a division of labor between computers and humans where all forms of number crunching and bit manipulations are left to computers; whereas, intelligent decision-making is left to us humans. We are now at the cusp of a major transformation that can disrupt this balance. There are two triggers for this: firstly, trillions of connected devices (the "Internet of Things") that have begun to sense and transform the large untapped analog world around us to a digital world, and secondly, (thanks to Moore's Law) beyond-exaflop levels of compute, making a large class of structure learning and decision-making problems now computationally tractable. In this talk, I plan to discuss real challenges and amazing opportunities ahead of us for enabling a new class of applications and services, "Machine Intelligence Led Services." These services are distinguished by machines being in the 'lead' for tasks that were traditionally human-led, simply because computer-led implementations are about to reach and even surpass the quality metrics of current human-led offerings.

Author Keywords

Learning Machine

BIOGRAPHY

Dr. Pradeep Dubey is an Intel Fellow and Director of Parallel Computing Lab (PCL), part of Intel Labs. His research focus is computer architectures to efficiently handle new compute-intensive application paradigms for the future computing environment. He previously worked at IBM's T.J. Watson Research Center, and Broadcom Corporation. He has made contributions to the design, architecture, and application-performance of various microprocessors, including IBM(R) Power PC, Intel(R) i386TM, i486TM, Pentium(R) Xeon(R), and the Xeon Phi(tm) line of processors. He holds over 36 patents, has published over 100 technical papers, won the Intel Achievement Award in 2012 for Breakthrough Parallel Computing Research, and was honored with Outstanding Electrical and Computer Engineer Award from Purdue University in 2014. Dr. Dubey received a PhD in electrical engineering from Purdue University. He is a Fellow of IEEE.

ISPD'17, March 19–22, 2017, Portland, OR, USA.
ACM. ISBN 978-1-4503-4696-2/17/03.
http://dx.doi.org/10.1145/3036669.3038247

Deep Learning in the Enhanced Cloud

Eric Chung
Microsoft Corporation
erchung@microsoft.com

Abstract:

Deep Learning has emerged as a singularly critical technology for enabling human-like intelligence in online services such as Azure, Office 365, Bing, Cortana, Skype, and other high-valued scenarios at Microsoft. While Deep Neural Networks (DNNs) have enabled state-of-the-art accuracy in many intelligence tasks, they are notoriously expensive and difficult to deploy in hyperscale datacenters constrained by power, cost, and latency. Furthermore, the escalating (and insatiable) demand for DNNs comes at an inopportune time as ideal silicon scaling (Moore's Law) comes to a diminishing end.

At Microsoft, we have developed a new cloud architecture that's enhanced using FPGA (Field Programmable Gate Array). FPGAs can be viewed as programmable silicon and are being deployed into each and every new server in Microsoft's hyperscale infrastructure. The flexibility of FPGAs combined with a novel Hardware-as-a-Service (HaaS) architecture unlocks the full potential of a completely programmable hardware and software acceleration plane.

In this talk, I'll give a history and overview of the project, discuss the key enabling technologies behind our enhanced cloud, present opportunities to harness this technology for accelerated deep learning, and conclude with directions for future work.

Keywords: deep learning; clould; haas; hardware-as-a-service; hyperscale

Bio:

Eric Chung is a researcher and technical lead at MSR-NExT, working on hardware specialization and deep learning. Eric has been a core member of the Microsoft Catapult project since its incubation and contributed to the research, piloting, and production deployment of FPGAs at hyperscale. Eric is broadly interested in the intersection of hardware and software. He has worked and published in the areas of computer architecture, datacenter and cloud architectures, hardware-accelerated machine learning, domain-specific high-level synthesis, FPGA-based simulation methodologies, heterogeneous multicore analytical modeling, and hardware design automation. In addition, Eric has contributed as a reviewer and committee member for major conferences such as ASPLOS, ISCA, MICRO, HPCA, IISWC, FPGA, and FCCM. He received his Ph.D. at Carnegie Mellon University in 2011 and a B.S. from UC Berkeley in EECS in 2004. Previously, Eric led the CoRAM and ProtoFlex projects at CMU.

ISPD'17, March 19–22, 2017, Portland, OR, USA.
ACM. ISBN 978-1-4503-4696-2/17/03.
http://dx.doi.org/10.1145/3036669.3038243

Bilinear Lithography Hotspot Detection *

Hang Zhang, Fengyuan Zhu, Haocheng Li, Evangeline F. Y. Young, and Bei Yu
Department of Computer Science and Engineering
The Chinese University of Hong Kong
Shatin N.T., Hong Kong
{hzhang,fyzhu,hcli,fyyoung,byu}@cse.cuhk.edu.hk

ABSTRACT

Advanced semiconductor process technologies are producing various circuit layout patterns, and it is essential to detect and eliminate problematic ones, which are called lithography hotspots. These hotspots are formed due to light diffraction and interference, which induces complex intrinsic structures within the formation process. Though various machine learning based methods have been proposed for this problem, most of them cannot capture the intrinsic structure of each data. In this paper, we propose a novel feature extraction by representing each data sample in matrix form. We argue that this method can well preserve the intrinsic feature of each sample, leading to better performance. We then further propose a *bilinear lithography hotspot detector*, which can tackle data in matrix form directly to preserve the hidden structural correlations in the lithography process. Experimental results show that the proposed method outperforms state-of-the-art ones with remarkably large margin in both false alarms and runtime, with 98.16% detection accuracy.

1. INTRODUCTIONS

Today, we witness various design for manufacturing (DFM) technologies to tackle problems caused by shrinking feature device size. However, the existence of hotspots after DFM process remains to be a problem, and the issue of hotspot detection is important to ensure high manufacturability. Although full-chip lithography simulation can achieve very satisfactory performance, it is extremely computationally expensive. Thus, it is imperative to derive a fast and accurate hotspot detection method.

Besides full-chip lithography simulation, pattern matching (PM) [1–4] and machine learning (ML) [5–10] based methods are playing an increasingly important role in DFM due to their high performance in detecting hotspots. Particularly, ML based methods show their superiority of detecting unseen layout patterns, which are used more widely than PM based

*The work described in this paper was partially supported by a grant from the Research Grants Council of the Hong Kong Special Administrative Region, China (Project No. 14209214).

ISPD '17, March 19-22, 2017, Portland, OR, USA
© 2017 ACM. ISBN 978-1-4503-4696-2/17/03. . . $15.00
DOI: http://dx.doi.org/10.1145/3036669.3036673

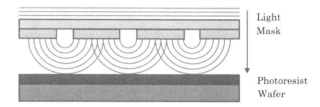

Figure 1: Phenomenon of light propagation, diffraction and interference in lithography process.

methods. These ML methods are mainly guided by supervised learning algorithms, such as Support Vector Machine (SVM) [8, 11], boosting classifier [9, 10, 12] and Deep Neural Network (DNN) [13, 14]. However, the performance of these methods is not satisfactory empirically.

One reason is that those endeavors have not fully utilized the hidden information of circuit layout patterns. Conventional PM and ML based hotspot detectors are designed for layout pattern data in vector form. However, circuit layout patterns are intrinsically in matrix form, which can be represented as layout images in nanometer level. When using traditional PM and ML methods to process the layout patterns, we have to reshape data into vectors, resulting in destroying the hidden structural information, such as light propagation and interference between different layout features, and the spatial relationship of nearby pixels within a circuit layout image. Moreover, the dimensionality of each reshaped vector can be rather high and this may cause the problem of over-fitting in ML when the number of available data samples is limited. Therefore, the following two challenges should be well considered to develop more effective hotspot detection approaches: 1) the preservation of intrinsic structures for each layout pattern data in matrix form when training classifiers; 2) the over-fitting issue with limited number of high dimensional data samples.

Several methods [15–17] have been proposed to perform direct matrix classification and preserve the hidden structure of each data. The over-fitting issue can also be handled for these approaches with constrains on model parameters. The paper [15] uses the sum of k rank-one orthogonal matrices to model the classifier matrix, and the paper [16] assumes the rank of classifier matrix to be k. Both methods describe the correlation of the data in different ways, but they require the rank k to be pre-specified. The paper [17] proposes a spectral elastic net penalty into the model to determine the rank automatically, which intends to capture the grouping effect property of the data. However, it assigns same weights to all singular values when using nuclear norm penalty, resulting in the ignorance of important issue that hotspots are formed by the sum of light influence in the neighboring layout and larger singular values should be shrunk less to preserve the major influential components. Also, lithography process does not have the grouping effects as stated in [17], because layout polygons from different distances to one point may produce various light intensities to that point due to light diffraction. More importantly, the labeling process of layout patterns consists of manually set parameters, which may introduce label noises into the data sample. Therefore, it is important to derive a new model to capture such hidden structural information induced by the lithography process.

To tackle the above problems, we propose a bilinear lithography hotspot detection (BL-HSD) framework, taking the advantages of both hinge loss [18] and weighted nuclear norm [19]. In lithography manufacturing, the wave-length of the current lithography technique (usually $193nm$) is much larger than the feature size of the layout polygons (we use $28nm$ and $32nm$ for evaluation). Therefore, light diffraction and interference, as shown in Fig. 1, will occur under such conditions and cause problematic layout patterns. Since hotspot is formed by light passing through the polygon masks and causing interference with each other, intuitively, there exist structural correlations among the contributions of each layout feature to hotspot formation, and we aim at developing a learning model that can find out these correlations. Based on the above issues of exsiting models and the mechanism of lithography process, we adopt weighted nuclear norm penalty into our model. In addition, as mentioned, the procedure of labeling hotspot and non-hotspot is complicated, and there may exist some noises on labels; thus, we use hinge loss for its robustness and sparseness.

Another important issue for ML based hotspot detection is the feature extraction procedure. Current approaches [4, 9, 10, 20] for hospot detection are all designed to extract vector-form features, which cannot capture the hidden structural correlations induced by the lithography process. Although the paper [10] proposed an maximal circular mutual information (MCMI) scheme for feature optimization with a specifically designed Naive Bayes classifier to capture such correlations, it can only preserve the local correlations instead of global correlations, because it assumes that the sampling points on the same circle are dependent but different circles are independent. To tackle this issue, we propose a simple matrix based concentric circle sampling (MCCS) method. This method extracts features in matrix form, which can preserve the hidden structural information among data and serve for the bilinear machine learning model. More importantly, with the simplicity of MCCS, through appropriate use of parallel programming techniques, we achieve high efficiency in the feature extraction procedure, resulting in an acceleration of the whole framework.

We also conduct extensive empirical experiments. Our proposed BL-HSD framework can outperform current state-of-the-art methods, and achieve satisfactory performance in accuracy, false alarms and runtime. The key contributions of our paper can be summarized as follows.

- A novel matrix based concentric circle sampling method for feature extraction is proposed.

- A novel bilinear machine learning model is constructed to solve hotspot detection problem, which is the first such model.

- Efficient proximal algorithms are derived for model training.

- The excess risk bound of our proposed bilinear model is theoretically analyzed.

- Only $18s$ is needed on average to perform the whole detection process.

The rest of this paper is organized as follows. In Section 2 and 3, we describe the notations for our model, metrics for evaluations, and problem formulations. In Section 4, we derive the bilinear machine learning model and its numerical solver. Section 6 presents the experimental results, followed by a conclusion in Section 7.

2. PRELIMINARIES

We first define two terminologies to quantify the performance of our proposed BL-HSD framework as follows.

Definition 1 (Accuracy). *The rate of correctly predicted hotspots among the set of actual hotspots.*

Definition 2 (False Alarm). *Non-hotspot that is incorrectly predicted.*

We then give notations for our optimization framework. We present the scalar values with lower case letters (e.g., x); vectors by bold lower case letters (e.g., $\mathbf{x}$); and matrix by bold upper case letters (e.g., $\mathbf{X}$). For a matrix $\mathbf{X} \in \mathbb{R}^{p \times q}$ of rank r where $r \leq \min(p, q)$, its (i, j)-entity is represented as $\mathbf{X}_{i,j}$. $\mathrm{tr}(\cdot)$ denotes the trace of a matrix, $(a)_+ = \max(0, a)$ and $\langle A, B \rangle = \sum_{i,j} A_{i,j} \cdot B_{i,j}$ is the element-wise multiplication for matrices . We further set $||\mathbf{X}||_F$ and $||\mathbf{X}||_*$ as the Frobenius norm and nuclear norm of a matrix $\mathbf{X}$, respectively, where $||\mathbf{X}||_F = \sqrt{\sum_{i,j} X_{i,j}^2}$ and $||\mathbf{X}||_* = \sum_{i=1}^n \sigma_i$ (σ_i is the ith singular value for matrix $\mathbf{X}$). Weighted nuclear norm is defined as $||\mathbf{X}||_{\mathcal{W},*} = \sum_i^n w_i \sigma_i$, where $\mathcal{W} = [w_1, w_2, ..., w_n]$ and w_i is a non-negative weight for σ_i. For a given norm $||\cdot||$ on $\mathbb{R}^n$, the dual norm, denoted $||\cdot||^*$ is the function from $\mathbb{R}^n$ to $\mathbb{R}$ with values $||\mathbf{y}|| = \sup_{\mathbf{x}} \mathbf{x}^\top \mathbf{y}$, s.t. $||\mathbf{x}|| \leq 1$. The dual norm of the nuclear norm and the weighted nuclear norm are denoted as $||\mathbf{X}||_*^*$ and $||\mathbf{X}||_{\mathcal{W},*}^*$.

3. LAYOUT FEATURE EXTRACTION

In this section, we will tackle the issue of layout feature extraction, which plays an important role in keeping layout pattern information. Only with well preserved pattern information can machine learning model get a good performance. Current feature extraction methods [4, 9, 10, 20] encode layout clips into feature vectors that contains geometrical information, such as density, shape and polygon topology. However, none of the existing methods takes the physical essentials, such as light propagation, diffraction, and interference of the lithography process into consideration, resulting in loss of pattern information. Empirically, as shown in Fig. 1, problematic layout patterns are caused by light passing through the photo masks, and these diffracted lights interfere with each other. Therefore, it is imperative to derive a feature extraction method that can efficiently capture the physical phenomenon of light propagation and interference.

Recently, besides the hotspot detection problem, machine learning methods have also been used in optical proximity correction (OPC) works [21, 22] and show reasonably good performance. The paper [21] proposes a concentric square sampling (CSS) method to model OPC, but this method only samples squares on layout clips, which ignores the information of light propagation. The paper [22] addresses this issue by

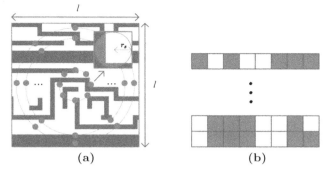

(a)   **(b)**

Figure 2: Examples of CCAS and MCCS feature. (a) Illustration of concentric circle area sampling. (b) The feature matrix of our proposed matrix based concentric circle sampling.

introducing the concentric circle area sampling (CCAS) methods. Although CCAS considers light propagation and shows its superiority in OPC regression work compared to CSS, it still ignores the important information of light interference. Inspired from the fact that OPC work involves a lithography process similar to hotspot detection, the paper [10] proposes an MCMI scheme to perform circle selection with reasonable good result. However, this feature extraction method [10] can only preserve light interference in a local manner, and ignores important global information, and it also required expensive time cost to perform the circle selection procedure. To tackle the above issue, we propose a novel layout feature extraction method, matrix based concentric circle sampling (MCCS), to preserve the structural correlations and serve for the bilinear machine learning model. In the following two sub-sections, we first review the process of CCAS and then we present our MCCS.

3.1 Concentric Circles with Area Sampling

CCAS [22] is proposed to train a Hierarchical Bayesian Model (HBM) for OPC regression. It extracts sub-sampled pixel values on concentric circles and forms a feature vector $\mathbf{x}$. The basic concept of CCAS is shown in Fig. 2(a), where the clip sample is taken from the ICCAD benchmark suite [23]. Parameters of the CCAS feature extraction method consist of the total size of the clip l (indicated in Fig. 2(a)), r_{in} and r_s. Each circle of CCAS has 8 sampling points, and each point stands for a circular sampling area (see Fig. 2(a)) with radius r_s (we would get the sum of the red area). r_{in} is the the sampling density controlling parameter, where we sample circles up to radius r_{in} in increments of 10 and further up to radius $\frac{l}{2}$ using increments of 20. Under the conditions that the clip size $l = 1200nm$, and $r_{in} = 60nm$, the dimension of each feature vector $\mathbf{x}$ should be 265 ($265 = 1 + (6+27) \times 8$). Although CCAS can correctly preserve layout pattern information that affects propagation of diffracted light from a mask pattern, it is not able to preserve the most important information in the lithography process, light interference, as CCAS destroys the structural correlation by forming the feature in vector form.

3.2 Matrix based Concentric Circle Sampling

We then describe our proposed MCCS feature extraction method. Intuitively, the light intensity induced by each sampling point on a certain circle should have proportional influence to the hotspot formation. Therefore, we concatenate sampling point values within one circle, putting them into a vector forming one row of our feature matrix, as shown in

Fig. 2(b). The center point of a clip is the place where hotspot forms, and statistically the layout feature at this point does not contribute to the hotspot formation. Hence, we will ignore the value of the center point in MCCS. From inner to outer circles, values on one circle form one row of the feature matrix from bottom to top and one example is shown in Fig. 2(a) and Fig. 2(b). We also denote the vector form of MCCS feature as vector based concentric circle sampling (VCCS), where each instance is represented as a vector instead of a matrix. Besides the parameters in CCAS, l, r_{in}, r_s, we add a new parameter n_p, which is the number of sampling points on a circle. For some complicated layout designs, it would be more accurate to use more sampling points to represent the layout patterns.

Under the conditions that $l = 1200nm$, $r_{in} = 60nm$ and $n_p = 16$, the dimension of each feature matrix $\mathbf{X}$ is 33×16 ($33 = 6 + 27$). Each row of the feature matrix consists of sampling point values on a circle, which affects the phenomenon of light propagation, and each entry in the matrix is a continuous number ranging from zero to the maximal value of the sampling area (e.g, when $r_s = 2$, the maximal value is 4π). With the data in matrix form, our bilinear learning model (described in Section 4) can capture the correlations among these rows and columns, which affects the phenomenon of light interference. Although MCCS is still an approximation of the original layout pattern, we achieve satisfactory performance by utilizing the information of hidden structural correlations.

4. BILINEAR CLASSIFIER

In this section, we introduce our proposed bilinear classifier to address hotspot detection problem. Then an efficient Alternating Directional Method of Multipliers (ADMM) algorithm will be proposed for model training.

4.1 Model

In lithography hotspot detection with MCCS feature extraction, it is essential to efficiently handle feature matrices while preserving the hidden topological structures of the layout patterns. However, using traditional linear or non-linear classification methods directly requires to reorganize matrices into vectors, which may destroy the hidden structures. To tackle this issue, we propose a bilinear classifier that can process the data matrices directly with their hidden structures preserved. The procedure of labeling layout patterns consists of multiple lithography processes, which may bring noises into pattern labels. To tackle this issue, an intuitive idea is to model the loss of each instance within a margin, where loss means the training error. Therefore, we consider the hinge loss for our model fitting due to its robustness and sparseness, and the loss for each instance $\mathbf{X}_i$ is defined as follows

$$h_i(\mathbf{W}, b) = \{1 - y_i[\mathrm{tr}(\mathbf{W}^\top \mathbf{X}_i) + b]\}_+, \qquad (1)$$

where $\mathbf{W}$ is the classifier matrix, b is the bias, $\mathbf{X}_i$ is the feature matrix of the ith instance and y_i is the label of the ith instance ($\mathbf{W} \in \mathbb{R}^{p \times q}$, $\mathbf{X}_i \in \mathbb{R}^{p \times q}$).

When learning the classifier matrix, another important issue is to take the structural correlation among each data matrix into consideration. Clearly, methods like SVM [24] cannot handle this issue though the hinge loss is also adopted, as it can only handle data in vector form. The Bilinear SVM proposed in [16] factorized a classifier matrix into two low rank matrices, but it is needed to indicate the rank before the optimization. Recently, machine learning models apply nuclear norm for low-rank modeling and obtain reasonable good result. The paper [17] considers the grouping effects of features and treat each singular value of the classifier matrix equally. However, because of light diffraction, layout features from different places within a clip may impose different light intensities to the clip center and thus the grouping effect considered in [17] may not be consistent with our lithography process.

Another important issue is that, singular values corresponding to the subspaces of the classifier matrix have clear physical meanings in certain applications. In our hotspot detection problem, since the mask is exposed to parallel lights during the lithography process, intuitively, layout feature from different places contributes inequally to the hotspot formation. As a result, it would be better to treat each singular value differently and shrink more the smaller singular values, which contributes less to the hotspot formation. When learning the classifier matrix, we apply weighted nuclear norm regularization and assign different weights to different singular values to keep the physical property.

The work [19] has discussed different weighting schemes for the weighted nuclear norm, such as the weights in non-ascending order, in arbitrary order and in non-descending order. The non-ascending order can ensure the convexity of the optimization problem empirically. However, it does not help to preserve the physical property for this problem. Therefore, for hotspot detection, we apply weights in the non-descending order meaning that we will shrink less those larger singular values of the classifier matrix in weighted nuclear norm minimization. Although weights in a non-descending order does not guarantee the convexity of the objective function, we still can get a fixed point solution in an analytical form, which will be discussed later.

The optimization problem for our proposed bilinear classifier is defined as follows. It is specifically designed for this hotspot detection problem and is different from all previous bilinear classifiers to the best of our knowledge,

$$\arg\min_{\mathbf{W},b} \ \lambda||\mathbf{W}||_{\mathcal{W},*} + C\sum_i^n \{1 - y_i[\mathrm{tr}(\mathbf{W}^\top\mathbf{X}_i) + b]\}_+. \quad (2)$$

The first term in Eq. (2) represents a weighted nuclear norm penalty, which considers the importances of different singular values of $\mathbf{W}$ and is the key term to capture the inherent structure of the lithography layout patterns. The second term denotes the hinge loss.

4.2 Solver

Since the objective function in Eq. (2) contains both hinge loss and weighted nuclear norm, traditional methods such as the Nesterov method used in [25] is not applicable here. However, observing the structure of our objective function, we derive an efficient learning algorithm based on ADMM [26] with the restart rule [27] for numerical optimization, which can achieve relatively faster training speed compared to other machine learning methods used in hotspot detection. The optimization problem defined in Eq. (2) can be equivalently written as follows,

$$\arg\min_{\mathbf{W},b,\mathbf{S}} \ \lambda||\mathbf{S}||_{\mathcal{W},*} + C\sum_i^n \{1 - y_i[\mathrm{tr}(\mathbf{W}^\top\mathbf{X}_i) + b]\}_+, \quad (3)$$

$$\text{s.t.} \ \mathbf{S} - \mathbf{W} = 0,$$

In this way, the original optimization problem is split into

two sub-problems with respect to $\{\mathbf{W}, b\}$ and the auxiliary variable $\mathbf{S}$. Then we apply Augmented Lagrangian Multiplier to develop an efficient ADMM method as follows:

$$L(\mathbf{W}, b, \mathbf{S}, \mathbf{\Lambda}) = \lambda||\mathbf{S}||_{\mathcal{W},*} + C\sum_i^n \{1 - y_i[\mathrm{tr}(\mathbf{W}^\top\mathbf{X}_i) + b]\}_+$$
$$+ \mathrm{tr}[\mathbf{\Lambda}^\top(\mathbf{S} - \mathbf{W})] + \frac{\rho}{2}||\mathbf{S} - \mathbf{W}||_F^2, \quad (4)$$

where $\rho > 0$ is a coefficient parameter and $\mathbf{\Lambda}$ is a Lagrangian multiplier matrix.

The algorithm flow of using ADMM to solve the problem is summarized in Algorithm 1. Take $\mathbf{W}$ as an example, in the kth iteration, variable obtained before the restart rule is denoted as $\mathbf{W}^{(k)}$ and variable obtained in the restart rule is denoted as $\widehat{\mathbf{W}}^{(k)}$. The key steps of Algorithm 1 are the computations of $\mathbf{S}^{(k)}$ and $(\mathbf{W}^{(k)}, b^{(k)})$, we will derive them in the coming sections.

4.2.1 Weighted Nuclear Norm Minimization

Following the work [19], we discuss the weighted nuclear norm minimization. Without loss of generality, the general weighted nuclear norm minimization problem can be written as follows:

$$\min_{\mathbf{X}} \frac{1}{2}||\mathbf{Y} - \mathbf{X}||_F^2 + \lambda||\mathbf{X}||_{\mathcal{W},*}. \quad (5)$$

where $\mathbf{X}$ and $\mathbf{Y}$ are matrices, $\mathcal{W}$ is the weight vector.

The analytical solution for weights in non-descending order [19] is

$$\hat{\mathbf{X}} = \mathbf{U}\mathcal{D}_{\mathcal{W},\lambda}(\mathbf{\Sigma})\mathbf{V}^\top, \quad (6)$$

where $\mathbf{Y} = \mathbf{U}\mathbf{\Sigma}\mathbf{V}^\top$ is the Singular Value Decomposition (SVD) of $\mathbf{Y}$, and $\mathcal{D}_{\mathcal{W},\lambda}$ is the generalized soft-thresholding operator with weight vector $\mathcal{W}$ and $\mathcal{D}_{\mathcal{W},\lambda}(\mathbf{\Sigma})$ is a diagonal matrix with

$$\mathcal{D}_{\mathcal{W},\lambda}(\mathbf{\Sigma})_{ii} = \max(\mathbf{\Sigma}_{ii} - \lambda w_i, 0). \quad (7)$$

4.2.2 Optimization for Auxiliary Variable

We first derive the optimization method for solving the auxiliary variable $\mathbf{S}$. The first subproblem for solving $\mathbf{S}$ in Eq. (4) can be equivalently written as follows

$$\arg\min_{\mathbf{S}} \ \lambda||\mathbf{S}||_{\mathcal{W},*} + \mathrm{tr}(\widehat{\mathbf{\Lambda}}^{(k)\top}\mathbf{S}) + \frac{\rho}{2}||\mathbf{W}^{(k)} - \mathbf{S}||_F^2. \quad (8)$$

Then we can get $\mathbf{S}^{(k)}$ in the kth iteration by solving the problem in Eq. (8). We can get a equation with structure similar to Eq. (5) by simple equation transformation, which is shown as follows. The optimizatiopn problem Eq. 8 is equivalent to

$$\arg\min_{\mathbf{S}} \ \lambda||\mathbf{S}||_{\mathcal{W},*} + \frac{\rho}{2}||(\mathbf{W}^{(k)} - \mathbf{S} - \frac{\mathbf{\Lambda}^{(k)}}{\rho})||_F^2, \quad (9)$$

which can be further transformed into

$$\arg\min_{\mathbf{S}} \ \lambda||\rho\mathbf{S}||_{\mathcal{W},*} + \frac{1}{2}||(\rho\mathbf{W}^{(k)} - \mathbf{\Lambda}^{(k)}) - \rho\mathbf{S}||_F^2. \quad (10)$$

Thus, we can get the fixed point solution of Eq. (10) by applying Eq. (6), which is

$$\mathbf{S}^{(k)} = \mathbf{U}\mathcal{D}_{\mathcal{W},\lambda}(\rho\mathbf{W}^{(k)} - \mathbf{\Lambda}^{(k)})\mathbf{V}^\top, \quad (11)$$

where $\mathbf{U}\mathbf{\Sigma}\mathbf{V}^\top = \rho\mathbf{W}^{(k)} - \mathbf{\Lambda}^{(k)}$.

4.2.3 Optimization for Classifier Matrix and Bias

We first derive the subproblem for solving $(\mathbf{W}^{(k)}, b^{(k)})$ as follows.

$$\arg\min_{\mathbf{W},b} \quad C\sum_{i}^{n}\{1 - y_i[\mathrm{tr}(\mathbf{W}^\top \mathbf{X}_i) + b]\}_+$$
$$+ \mathrm{tr}[\mathbf{\Lambda}^\top(\mathbf{S} - \mathbf{W})] + \frac{\rho}{2}||\mathbf{S} - \mathbf{W}||_F^2, \quad (12)$$

Following the derivation in the work [17], the optimal values of $(\mathbf{W}^{(k)}, b^{(k)})$ are:

$$\mathbf{W}^* = \frac{1}{\rho}(\sum_{i=1}^{N}\alpha_i^* y_i \mathbf{X}_i + \mathbf{\Lambda} + \rho\mathbf{S}) \quad (13)$$
$$b^* = \frac{1}{|\mathcal{I}^*|}\sum_{i\in\mathcal{I}^*}\{y_i - \mathrm{tr}[(\mathbf{W}^*)^\top \mathbf{X}_i]\},$$

where $\mathcal{I}^* = \{i : 0 < \alpha_i^* < C\}$, and $\alpha^* \in \mathbb{R}^n$ is the solution of the following box constraint quadratic programming problem.

$$\arg\min_{\alpha} \quad \frac{1}{2}\alpha^\top \mathbf{K}\alpha - \mathbf{q}^\top \alpha, \quad (14)$$
$$s.t \quad \mathbf{0} \leq \alpha \leq C\mathbf{1}_n,$$
$$\sum_{i=1}^{n}\alpha_i y_i = 0.$$

Here $\mathbf{K} \in \mathbb{R}^{n\times n}$ and $\mathbf{q} \in \mathbb{R}^n$ are coefficient matrix and coefficient vector for variable α; specifically,

$$K_{ij} = y_i y_j \frac{\mathrm{tr}(\mathbf{X}_i^\top \mathbf{X}_j)}{\rho},$$
$$q_i = 1 - \frac{\mathrm{tr}[(\mathbf{\Lambda} + \rho\mathbf{S})^\top \mathbf{X}_i]}{\rho}.$$

Several methods can be used to solve the optimization problem in Eq. (14), such as the sequential minimization optimization algorithm [28, 29]. With the derivation of above problems and optimization algorithms, we can update $(\mathbf{W}^{(k)}, b^{(k)})$.

4.2.4 Summary

We have presented the key steps for solving the problem in Eq. (4), where the classifier parameters $(\mathbf{W}, b)$ and the auxiliary variable $\mathbf{S}$ are solved in an iterative manner. In addition, we also need to update the Lagrangian parameter $\mathbf{\Lambda}$. Here we update $\mathbf{\Lambda}$ in a single gradient step as follows.

$$\mathbf{\Lambda} = \widehat{\mathbf{\Lambda}}^{(k)} - \rho(\mathbf{W}^{(k)} - \mathbf{S}^{(k)}). \quad (15)$$

Then we summarize the whole flow in Algorithm 1, where ADMM [26] with the restart rule [27] is applied here.

5. THEORETICAL JUSTIFICATIONS

Now we analyze the excess risk of the proposed bilinear classifier theoretically. Excess risk means the difference between the empirical risk (see Definition 3) and the expected risk (see Definition 4). In our theoretical analysis, we assume that each entry of a feature matrix follows unit Gaussian distribution.

The proposed optimization problem as defined in Eq. 2 can be reformulated as follows

$$\arg\min_{\mathbf{W},b} \quad \sum_{i=1}^{n} h(\mathbf{W}, b, \mathbf{X}_i, y_i), \quad (16)$$
$$s.t. \quad ||\mathbf{W}||_{\mathcal{W},*} \leq B,$$

Algorithm 1 ADMM for problem in Eq. (4)

1: Initialize $\mathbf{S}^{(-1)} = \widehat{\mathbf{S}}^{(0)} \in \mathbb{R}^{p\times q}$, $\mathbf{\Lambda}^{(-1)} = \widehat{\mathbf{\Lambda}} \in \mathbb{R}^{p\times q}$, $\rho > 0$, $t^{(1)} = 1$, $\eta \in (0,1)$.
2: **for** $k = 0, 1, 2, 3...$ **do**
3: $\quad (\mathbf{W}^{(k)}, b^{(k)}) = \arg\min_{\mathbf{W},b} C\sum_i^n\{1 - y_i[\mathrm{tr}(\mathbf{W}^\top \mathbf{X}_i) + b]\}_+ + \mathrm{tr}[\widehat{\mathbf{\Lambda}}^{(k)\top}(\widehat{\mathbf{S}}^{(k)} - \mathbf{W})] + \frac{\rho}{2}||\widehat{\mathbf{S}}^{(k)} - \mathbf{W}||_F^2$
4: $\quad \mathbf{S}^{(k)} = \arg\min_{\mathbf{S}} \lambda||\mathbf{S}||_{\mathcal{W},*} + \mathrm{tr}(\widehat{\mathbf{\Lambda}}^{(k)\top}\mathbf{S}) + \frac{\rho}{2}||\mathbf{W}^{(k)} - \mathbf{S}||_F^2$
5: $\quad \mathbf{\Lambda}^{(k)} = \widehat{\mathbf{\Lambda}}^{(k)} - \rho(\mathbf{W}^{(k)} - \mathbf{S}^{(k)})$
6: $\quad c^{(k)} = \rho^{-1}||\mathbf{\Lambda}^{(k)} - \widehat{\mathbf{\Lambda}}^{(k)}||_F^2 + \rho||\mathbf{S}^{(k)} - \widehat{\mathbf{S}}^{(k)}||_F^2$
7: $\quad$ **if** $c^{(k)} < \eta c^{(k-1)}$ **then**
8: $\quad\quad t^{(k+1)} = \frac{1 + \sqrt{1 + 4t^{(k)2}}}{2}$
9: $\quad\quad \widehat{\mathbf{S}}^{(k+1)} = \mathbf{S}^{(k)} + \frac{t^{(k)} - 1}{t^{(k+1)}}(\mathbf{S}^{(k)} - \mathbf{S}^{(k)-1})$
10: $\quad\quad \widehat{\mathbf{\Lambda}}^{(k+1)} = \mathbf{\Lambda}^{(k)} + \frac{t^{(k)} - 1}{t^{(k+1)}}(\mathbf{\Lambda}^{(k)} - \mathbf{\Lambda}^{(k)-1})$
11: $\quad$ **else**
12: $\quad\quad t^{(k+1)} = 1$
13: $\quad\quad \widehat{\mathbf{S}}^{(k+1)} = \mathbf{S}^{(k-1)}$
14: $\quad\quad \widehat{\mathbf{\Lambda}}^{(k+1)} = \mathbf{\Lambda}^{(k-1)}$
15: $\quad\quad c^{(k)} = \eta^{-1}c^{(k-1)}$
16: $\quad$ **end if**
17: **end for**

---

where B is a constant value, and $h(\mathbf{W}, b, \mathbf{X}_i, y_i) = \{1 - y_i[\mathrm{tr}(\mathbf{W}^\top \mathbf{X}_i) + b]\}_+$ is the hinge loss function. The loss function can be easily rewritten as follows with respect to $\mathbf{W}$ given the relation between $\mathbf{W}$ and b as in Eq. 13

$$\hat{h}(\mathbf{W}, \mathbf{X}_i, y_i) = \{1 - y_i[\mathrm{tr}(\mathbf{W}^\top(\hat{\mathbf{X}}_i))]\} + c. \quad (17)$$

The loss function is L-Lipschitz continuous with c as a constant, and $\hat{\mathbf{X}}_i = \mathbf{X}_i - \frac{1}{n}\sum_{j=1}^{n}\mathbf{X}_j$, where the second term is the empirical expectation of each data and the value of each entry should tend to be zero when n is large, thus by removing empirical expectation of each data, we do not need to consider the bias b.

Before defining and proposing the excess risk bound, we first derive the dual norm of our weighted nuclear norm in Lemma 1, which will be used to derive inequalities later. To the best of our knowledge, this is the first time that the dual norm of the weighted nuclear norm is analyzed.

Lemma 1. *The dual norm of the weighted nuclear norm* $||\mathbf{W}||_{\mathcal{W},*}$ *is*

$$||\mathbf{W}||_{\mathcal{W},*}^* = \max_i \frac{1}{w_i}\mathbf{\Sigma}_{ii} \quad (18)$$

where $\mathbf{W} = \mathbf{U}\mathbf{\Sigma}\mathbf{V}^\top$ through SVD.

Proof. Following the definition of dual norm, we need to prove the following equation:

$$\sup_{||\mathbf{Q}||_{\mathcal{W},*}^* \leq 1} \langle \mathbf{Q}, \mathbf{A} \rangle = \sup_{||\mathbf{Q}||_{\mathcal{W},*}^* \leq 1} \mathrm{tr}(\mathbf{Q}^\top \mathbf{A}) = ||\mathbf{A}||_{\mathcal{W},*}. \quad (19)$$

To prove this, let $\mathbf{A} = \mathbf{U}\mathbf{\Sigma}\mathbf{V}^\top$ through the SVD, with $\mathbf{\Sigma}$ containing d singular values. Then, we can simply set $\mathbf{Q}$ with $\mathbf{Q} = \mathbf{U}\mathbf{Z}\mathbf{V}^\top$ through SVD, where $\mathbf{Z}$ is diagonal matrix with $\mathbf{Z}_{ii} = w_i$, and the constrain that $||\mathbf{Q}||_{\mathcal{W},*}^* \leq 1$ can be naturally satisfied. In this case, we have

$$\langle \mathbf{Q}, \mathbf{A} \rangle = \langle \mathbf{U}\mathbf{Z}\mathbf{V}^\top, \mathbf{U}\mathbf{\Sigma}\mathbf{V}^\top \rangle$$
$$= \mathrm{tr}(\mathbf{Z}\mathbf{\Sigma}) \quad (20)$$
$$= ||\mathbf{A}||_{\mathcal{W},*}.$$

In this way, we have $\sup_{||\mathbf{Q}||^*_{\mathcal{W},*} \leq 1} \langle \mathbf{Q}, \mathbf{A} \rangle \geq ||\mathbf{A}||_{\mathcal{W},*}$. Now, we further show the other direction of the inequality. Let $\mathbf{u}_i$ and $\mathbf{v}_i$ be the ith column vector respectively, we have

$$
\begin{aligned}
\sup_{||\mathbf{Q}||^*_{\mathcal{W},*} \leq 1} \langle \mathbf{Q}, \mathbf{A} \rangle &= \sup_{||\mathbf{Q}||^*_{\mathcal{W},*} \leq 1} \mathrm{tr}(\mathbf{Q}^\top \mathbf{U}\boldsymbol{\Sigma}\mathbf{V}^\top) \\
&= \sup_{||\mathbf{Q}||^*_{\mathcal{W},*} \leq 1} \sum_{i=1}^{d} w_i \boldsymbol{\Sigma}_{ii} \frac{1}{w_i} \mathbf{u}_i \mathbf{Q}\mathbf{v}_i^\top \\
&\leq \sup_{||\mathbf{Q}||^*_{\mathcal{W},*} \leq 1} \sum_{i=1}^{d} w_i \boldsymbol{\Sigma}_{ii} ||\mathbf{Q}||^*_{\mathcal{W},*} \\
&= ||\mathbf{A}||_{\mathcal{W},*}
\end{aligned}
\tag{21}
$$

Combining both Eq. 20 and Eq. 21, we have proved Eq. 19. Then following the definition of dual norm, we finish the proof of Lemma 1. $\qquad\square$

We further provide the definition of empirical and expected risks with respect to our loss function following [30].

Definition 3. *The standard form of empirical risk without bias term for loss function* $\hat{h}(\mathbf{W}, \mathbf{X}_i, y_i)$ *can be formulated as*

$$
\hat{R}(\mathbf{W}) = \frac{1}{n} \sum_{i=1}^{n} \hat{h}(\mathbf{W}, \mathbf{X}_i, y_i). \tag{22}
$$

Definition 4. *The standard form of expected risk without bias term for loss function* $\hat{h}(\mathbf{W}, \mathbf{X}_i, y_i)$ *can be formulated as*

$$
R(\mathbf{W}) = \mathbb{E}_{(\mathbf{X}_i, y_i) \sim \mu} \hat{h}(\mathbf{W}, \mathbf{X}_i, y_i), \tag{23}
$$

with $\mathbb{E}$ *as the expectation operator, and* μ *as the probability distribution that each pair of* $\{\mathbf{X}_i, y_i\}$ *is sampled.*

Here, we set $\mathbf{W}^o$ as the optimal solution with respect to the expected risk with

$$
\mathbf{W}^o = \arg\min_{\mathbf{W}} R(\mathbf{W}), \qquad \text{s.t. } ||\mathbf{W}||_{\mathcal{W},*} \leq B, \tag{24}
$$

and $\hat{\mathbf{W}}$ as the optimal solution with respect to the empirical risk with

$$
\hat{\mathbf{W}} = \arg\min_{\mathbf{W}} \hat{R}(\mathbf{W}), \qquad \text{s.t. } ||\mathbf{W}||_{\mathcal{W},*} \leq B. \tag{25}
$$

Then we can provide the upper bound of the excess risk of our method in the following theorem.

Theorem 1: *With probability at least* $1 - \delta$*, the excess risk of our method, for each data* $\mathbf{X}_i \in \mathbb{R}^{d_1 \times d_2}$*, is bounded as*

$$
\begin{aligned}
R(\hat{\mathbf{W}}) - R(\mathbf{W}^o) &\leq \frac{2BL}{\sqrt{n}} \max_i(\frac{1}{w_i}) \\
&\cdot (\sqrt{d_1} + \sqrt{d_2}) + \sqrt{\frac{\ln(1/\delta)}{2n}}.
\end{aligned}
\tag{26}
$$

Proof. Following the proof in the paper [30], we can first reformulate the excess risk with respect to $\mathbf{W}^o$ and $\hat{\mathbf{W}}$ as follows

$$
\begin{aligned}
R(\hat{\mathbf{W}}) - R(\mathbf{W}^o) &= [R(\hat{\mathbf{W}}) - \hat{R}(\hat{\mathbf{W}})] \\
&+ [\hat{R}(\hat{\mathbf{W}}) - \hat{R}(\mathbf{W}^o)] + [\hat{R}(\mathbf{W}^o) - R(\mathbf{W}^o)]
\end{aligned}
\tag{27}
$$

Here, the second term is negative naturally. Following the *Hoeffding's inequality*, the third one can be bounded as $\sqrt{\ln(1/\delta)/2n}$, with probability $1 - \delta/2$.

Different from the paper [30], our derivation of Eq. (30) and Eq. (31) follows the *L-Lipschitz* continuous property of the loss function and Lemma 1. For the first term, it is shown in [30] that

$$
R(\hat{\mathbf{W}}) - \hat{R}(\hat{\mathbf{W}}) \leq \sup_{||\mathbf{W}||^*_{\mathcal{W},*} \leq B} [R(\mathbf{W}) - \hat{R}(\mathbf{W})]. \tag{28}
$$

Further using the *McDiarmid's inequality*, we can obtain the *Rademacher complexity* with probability $1 - \delta$, with

$$
\mathcal{R} = \frac{2}{n} \mathbb{E} \sup_{||\mathbf{W}||_{\mathcal{W},*} \leq B} \sum_{i=1}^{n} \sigma_i \hat{h}(\mathbf{W}, \mathbf{X}_i, y_i), \tag{29}
$$

where $\sigma_i \in \{-1, 1\}$ represents the *Rademacher variables*. Let $\hat{\mathbf{M}} = \sum_{i=1}^{n} \sigma_i \hat{\mathbf{X}}_i$, and following that our loss function is *L-Lipschitz* continuous, we can obtain the upper bound of $R(\hat{\mathbf{W}}) - \hat{R}(\hat{\mathbf{W}})$ as follows

$$
\begin{aligned}
R(\hat{\mathbf{W}}) - \hat{R}(\hat{\mathbf{W}}) &\leq \mathcal{R} \\
&\leq \frac{2L}{n} \mathbb{E} \sup_{||\mathbf{W}||_{\mathcal{W},*} \leq B} \sum_{i=1}^{n} \sigma_i \mathrm{tr}(\mathbf{W}\hat{\mathbf{X}}_i) \\
&= \frac{2L}{n} \mathbb{E} \sup_{||\mathbf{W}||_{\mathcal{W},*} \leq B} \mathrm{tr}(\mathbf{W}\hat{\mathbf{M}}).
\end{aligned}
\tag{30}
$$

Further applying the *Hölder's inequality* and Lemma 1, we have

$$
\begin{aligned}
R(\hat{\mathbf{W}}) - \hat{R}(\hat{\mathbf{W}}) &\leq \frac{2L}{n} \mathbb{E} \sup_{||\mathbf{W}||_{\mathcal{W},*} \leq B} ||\hat{\mathbf{M}}||_{\mathcal{W},*} ||\mathbf{W}||^*_{\mathcal{W},*} \\
&\leq \frac{2LB}{n} \mathbb{E} ||\hat{\mathbf{M}}||^*_{\mathcal{W},*}.
\end{aligned}
\tag{31}
$$

Since $\hat{\mathbf{M}}$ is the sum of random variables, it should tend to be normal distributed with the *Central Limit Theorem*, with variance equal to $\max_i(\frac{1}{w_i})\sqrt{n}$. Thus, following [30], with the *Gordan's theorem*, we have

$$
\mathbb{E}||\hat{\mathbf{M}}||^*_{\mathcal{W},*} \leq \max_i(\frac{1}{w_i})\sqrt{n}(\sqrt{d_1} + \sqrt{d_2}). \tag{32}
$$

Combining all the above together, we can obtain the upper bound of the excess risk with probability at least $1 - \delta$ as follows

$$
\begin{aligned}
R(\hat{\mathbf{W}}) - R(\mathbf{W}^o) &\leq \frac{2BL}{\sqrt{n}} \max_i(\frac{1}{w_i}) \\
&\cdot (\sqrt{d_1} + \sqrt{d_2}) + \sqrt{\frac{\ln(1/\delta)}{2n}}.
\end{aligned}
\tag{33}
$$

$\qquad\square$

6. EXPERIMENTAL RESULTS

We implement our MCCS feature extraction method in the programming language `Python`, whose speed is further accelerated by `Cython`. In addition, we utilize the advantages of matrix calculation of `Matlab`, and implement our proposed bilinear classifier in `Matlab`. We executed the program on a machine with Quad Intel Xeon E7-4830 v2 CPUs and 1TB memory. Experiments are conducted on 5 industrial circuit layout designs, which consists of one $32nm$ and four $28nm$ circuit layouts. These circuit designs are released by [23], the details of which can be found in the paper [10]. In the experiments, all the coefficient parameters are selected via cross validation. The weight vector of weighted nuclear norm is set

Table 1: Comparisons with three classical methods

	VCCS-SVM			VCCS-Adaboost			DBF-Adaboost [9]			Ours			
	M-CPU(s)	Accuracy	FA#	M-CPU(s)	Accuracy	FA#	CPU(s)	Accuracy	FA#	CPU(s)	M-CPU(s)	Accuracy	FA#
Case 1	1.09	100.00%	0	1.37	99.55%	1	7.00	100%	0	2.09	0.20	100.00%	0
Case 2	1.81	94.78%	4	5.44	96.78%	0	351.00	98.60%	0	10.70	0.33	99.40%	0
Case 3	3.26	95.52%	94	4.73	97.62%	4	297.00	97.20%	0	20.56	2.34	97.78%	2
Case 4	1.74	80.23%	31	9.45	84.10%	0	170.00	87.01%	1	8.09	0.38	96.05%	0
Case 5	1.30	95.12%	0	2.27	97.56%	0	69.00	92.86%	0	5.84	0.49	97.56%	0
avg.	1.84	93.13%	25.8	4.65	95.12%	1.00	178.80	95.13%	0.20	9.45	0.75	98.16%	0.40
ratio	2.46	-	-	6.21	-	-	18.92	-	-	1.0	1.0	-	-

Table 2: Comparisons with three state-of-the-art hotspot detectors [4, 10, 20]

	TCAD'14 [1]			TCAD'15 [20]			ICCAD'16 [10]			Ours		
	CPU(s)	Accuracy	FA#	CPU(s)	Accuracy	FA#	CPU(s)	Accuracy	FA#	CPU(s)	Accuracy	FA#
Case 1	11	100.00%	1714	38	94.69%	1493	10	100.00%	788	4	100.00%	783
Case 2	287	99.80%	4058	234	98.20%	11834	103	99.40%	544	17	99.40%	700
Case 3	417	93.80%	9486	778	91.88%	13850	110	97.51%	2052	49	97.78%	2166
Case 4	102	91.00%	1120	356	85.94%	3664	69	97.74%	3341	14	96.05%	2132
Case 5	49	87.80%	199	20	92.86%	1205	41	95.12%	94	9	97.56%	52
avg.	173.2	94.48%	3315.4	285.2	92.71%	6409.2	66.6	97.95%	1363.8	18.4	98.16%	1166.6
ratio	9.40	-	2.84	15.50	-	5.49	3.62	-	1.17	1.0	-	1.0

as $w_i = 2^{i-1}$. For each test case, a set of training data are used to construct our bilinear classifier, while another set of data are used to evaluate the performance of the classifier. Since the feature extraction for each clip is a separate procedure, we use multi-core processing techniques to accelerate the feature extraction step.

6.1 Performance Comparison with Classical Classifiers

In the first experiment, we compare our proposed BL-HSD framework with other classical hotspot detection frameworks. SVM [11] and Adaboost [11] classifiers are widely used in many applications, which also demonstrate their superiority in hotspot detection [8, 9]. Thus in this experiment, we investigate the performance of our BL-HSD with two classical classifiers and one recent work: 1) VCCS feature + SVM classifier (denoted as VCCS-SVM); 2) VCCS feature + Adaboost classifier (denoted as VCCS-Adaboost); 3) Density based feature + Adaboost classifier (denoted as DBF-Adaboost) [9]. Note that during the testing layout scanning in the detector of [9], only the core area of each clip will be verified. In order to have a fair comparison, our BL-HSD framework also scans the core area.

A detailed comparison of our BL-HSD and other classical classifiers are shown in Table 1. For each method in the Table 1, Columns "**M-CPU(s)**", "**CPU(s)**", "**Accuracy**" and "**FA#**" list the runtime of the model in seconds (sum of training and testing time of the model), the runtime of the overall flow in seconds (including the feature extraction time, and model training and testing time), the accuracy of the method, and the number of false alarms. We can see from Table 1 that our BL-HSD method outperforms all the other three classical methods in terms of accuracy, false alarm number and runtime performance. Particularly, comparing with both VCCS-SVM and VCCS-adaboost, our framework can achieve at least 2× speed-up in model CPU performance and can increase detection accuracy from 95.12% to 98.16%. In addition, our method also outperforms the recent hotspot detector [9], where our approach achieves 19× speed-up in the overall CPU performance and improves the accuracy by

3.03%. Meanwhile, for all five test cases, only 2 false alarms are reported in our framework.

Our framework achieves extremely fast speed in model runtime (only model training and testing time, denoted as M-CPU(s)) compared to other classical methods, which may be related to the proposed bilinear classifier, where the model complexity is reduced by incorporating weighted nuclear norm penalty.

6.2 Performance Comparison with state-of-the-art methods

In the second experiment, we further compare our framework with three state-of-the-art hotspot detection frameworks [4, 10, 20]. The details of comparisons are listed in Table 2, and for each detector, columns "**CPU(s)**", "**Accuracy**" and "**FA#**" are the same as those in Table 1. In this experiment, we first decompose the layout designs of each test case of the ICCAD-2012 benchmark suite [23] into a set of independent clips, whose size is the same as the core area in the training layout. We then scan all grids and verify their labels in our BL-HSD hotspot detector.

It can be observed from Table 2 that our method outperforms all other state-of-the-art methods in terms of runtime, accuracy and the number of false alarms on average. Our method achieves around 9× better running time performance comparing to [4], 15× comparing to [20], and 4× comparing to [10]. The superiority of the runtime performance is related to the simplicity of both the MCCS feature which only samples several points from the layout, and bilinear classifier which achieves faster convergence speed by discovering structural correlations and reducing model complexity. Besides, our method improves the accuracy by 3.68%, 5.45% and 0.21% on average compared with [4], [20] and [10]. We also achieve around 3× and 5× reduction in false alarms compared with [4] and [20] respectively. Although the work [10] performs feature optimization in the hotspot detection framework, it only put local correlation in the layout patterns into consideration; hence, we still on average reduce around 200 false alarms compared to [10]. Our method considers the global correlations of different points and circles during feature extraction and classifier construction, which allows us to capture the hidden structural information in lithography process. It can be observed that our method is more efficient compared to other state-of-the-art methods.

7. CONCLUSION

In this paper, we propose a novel BL-HSD hotspot detection framework, which incorporates a novel MCCS feature extraction method and an efficient bilinear machine learning model. With MCCS feature, the hidden structural information of the circuit layout patterns is well preserved. With bilinear machine learning model, the hidden information that comes from light propagation and interference can be efficiently and accurately captured. In addition, we proved the excess risk bound of the bilinear model theoretically. More importantly, our framework outperform state-of-the-art methods in all evaluation terms on average. With accurate capture of lithography process phenomenon, our method can be widely used not only in the hotspot detection problem, but also in other research problem in DFM which involves lithography process, such as OPC, SRAF insertion and EPE value prediction.

8. REFERENCES

[1] Jingyu Xu, Subarna Sinha, and Charles C. Chiang. Accurate detection for process-hotspots with vias and incomplete specification. In *IEEE/ACM International Conference on Computer-Aided Design (ICCAD)*, pages 839–846, 2007.

[2] Yen-Ting Yu, Ya-Chung Chan, Subarna Sinha, Iris Hui-Ru Jiang, and Charles Chiang. Accurate process-hotspot detection using critical design rule extraction. In *ACM/IEEE Design Automation Conference (DAC)*, pages 1167–1172, 2012.

[3] Sheng-Yuan Lin, Jing-Yi Chen, Jin-Cheng Li, Wan-Yu Wen, and Shih-Chieh Chang. A novel fuzzy matching model for lithography hotspot detection. In *ACM/IEEE Design Automation Conference (DAC)*, pages 68:1–68:6, 2013.

[4] Wan-Yu Wen, Jin-Cheng Li, Sheng-Yuan Lin, Jing-Yi Chen, and Shih-Chieh Chang. A fuzzy-matching model with grid reduction for lithography hotspot detection. *IEEE Transactions on Computer-Aided Design of Integrated Circuits and Systems (TCAD)*, 33(11):1671–1680, 2014.

[5] Dragoljub G. Drmanac, Frank Liu, and Li-C. Wang. Predicting variability in nanoscale lithography processes. In *ACM/IEEE Design Automation Conference (DAC)*, pages 545–550, 2009.

[6] Duo Ding, J. Andres Torres, and David Z. Pan. High performance lithography hotspot detection with successively refined pattern identifications and machine learning. *IEEE Transactions on Computer-Aided Design of Integrated Circuits and Systems (TCAD)*, 30(11):1621–1634, 2011.

[7] Duo Ding, Bei Yu, Joydeep Ghosh, and David Z. Pan. EPIC: Efficient prediction of IC manufacturing hotspots with a unified meta-classification formulation. In *IEEE/ACM Asia and South Pacific Design Automation Conference (ASPDAC)*, pages 263–270, 2012.

[8] Yen-Ting Yu, Geng-He Lin, Iris Hui-Ru Jiang, and Charles Chiang. Machine-learning-based hotspot detection using topological classification and critical feature extraction. In *ACM/IEEE Design Automation Conference (DAC)*, pages 671–676, 2013.

[9] Tetsuaki Matsunawa, Jhih-Rong Gao, Bei Yu, and David Z. Pan. A new lithography hotspot detection framework based on AdaBoost classifier and simplified feature extraction. In *Proceedings of SPIE*, volume 9427, 2015.

[10] Hang Zhang, Bei Yu, and Evangeline FY Young. Enabling online learning in lithography hotspot detection with information-theoretic feature optimization. In *Proc. IEEE/ACM International Conference on Computer-Aided Design*, 2016.

[11] Bernhard Scholkopf and Alexander J. Smola. *Learning with Kernels: Support Vector Machines, Regularization, Optimization, and Beyond*. MIT press, 2001.

[12] Jerome Friedman, Trevor Hastie, Robert Tibshirani, et al. Additive logistic regression: a statistical view of boosting (with discussion and a rejoinder by the authors). 28(2):337–407, 2000.

[13] Geoffrey E Hinton and Ruslan R Salakhutdinov. Reducing the dimensionality of data with neural networks. *Science*, 313(5786):504–507, 2006.

[14] Tetsuaki Matsunawa, Shigeki Nojima, and Toshiya Kotani. Automatic layout feature extraction for lithography hotspot detection based on deep neural network. In *SPIE Advanced Lithography*, pages 97810H–97810H. International Society for Optics and Photonics, 2016.

[15] Lior Wolf, Hueihan Jhuang, and Tamir Hazan. Modeling appearances with low-rank svm. In *2007 IEEE Conference on Computer Vision and Pattern Recognition*, pages 1–6. IEEE, 2007.

[16] Hamed Pirsiavash, Deva Ramanan, and Charless C Fowlkes. Bilinear classifiers for visual recognition. In *Advances in neural information processing systems*, pages 1482–1490, 2009.

[17] Luo Luo, Yubo Xie, Zhihua Zhang, and Wu-Jun Li. Support matrix machines. In *International Conference on Machine Learning (ICML)*, 2015.

[18] Alex J Smola and Bernhard Schölkopf. A tutorial on support vector regression. *Statistics and computing*, 14(3):199–222, 2004.

[19] Shuhang Gu, Qi Xie, Deyu Meng, Wangmeng Zuo, Xiangchu Feng, and Lei Zhang. Weighted nuclear norm minimization and its applications to low level vision. *International Journal of Computer Vision*, pages 1–26, 2016.

[20] Yen-Ting Yu, Geng-He Lin, Iris Hui-Ru Jiang, and Charles Chiang. Machine-learning-based hotspot detection using topological classification and critical feature extraction. *IEEE Transactions on Computer-Aided Design of Integrated Circuits and Systems (TCAD)*, 34(3):460–470, 2015.

[21] Allan Gu and Avideh Zakhor. Optical proximity correction with linear regression. *IEEE Transactions on Semiconductor Manufacturing (TSM)*, 21(2):263–271, 2008.

[22] Tetsuaki Matsunawa, Bei Yu, and David Z. Pan. Optical proximity correction with hierarchical bayes model. In *Proceedings of SPIE*, volume 9426, 2015.

[23] Andres J. Torres. ICCAD-2012 CAD contest in fuzzy pattern matching for physical verification and benchmark suite. In *IEEE/ACM International Conference on Computer-Aided Design (ICCAD)*, pages 349–350, 2012.

[24] Alexander J Smola. *Advances in large margin classifiers*. MIT press, 2000.

[25] Hua Zhou and Lexin Li. Regularized matrix regression. *Journal of the Royal Statistical Society: Series B (Statistical Methodology)*, 76(2):463–483, 2014.

[26] Stephen Boyd, Neal Parikh, Eric Chu, Borja Peleato, and Jonathan Eckstein. Distributed optimization and statistical learning via the alternating direction method of multipliers. *Foundations and Trends® in Machine Learning*, 3(1):1–122, 2011.

[27] Tom Goldstein, Brendan O'Donoghue, Simon Setzer, and Richard Baraniuk. Fast alternating direction optimization methods. *SIAM Journal on Imaging Sciences*, 7(3):1588–1623, 2014.

[28] John Platt et al. Sequential minimal optimization: A fast algorithm for training support vector machines. 1998.

[29] S. Sathiya Keerthi and Elmer G Gilbert. Convergence of a generalized smo algorithm for svm classifier design. *Machine Learning*, 46(1-3):351–360, 2002.

[30] Andreas Maurer and Massimiliano Pontil. Excess risk bounds for multitask learning with trace norm regularization. In *Conference on Learning Theory (COLT)*, volume 30, pages 55–76, 2013.

Routability Optimization for Industrial Designs at Sub-14nm Process Nodes Using Machine Learning

Wei-Ting J. Chan[2], Pei-Hsin Ho[3], Andrew B. Kahng[1,2] and Prashant Saxena[3]
[1]CSE and [2]ECE Departments, UC San Diego, La Jolla, CA 92093
[3]Synopsys Inc., Hillsboro, OR 97124
{wechan, abk}@ucsd.edu, {pei-hsin.ho, prashant.saxena}@synopsys.com

ABSTRACT

Design rule check (DRC) violations after detailed routing prevent a design from being taped out. To solve this problem, state-of-the-art commercial EDA tools global-route the design to produce a global-route congestion map; this map is used by the placer to optimize the placement of the design to reduce detailed-route DRC violations. However, in sub-14nm processes and beyond, DRCs arising from multiple patterning and pin-access constraints drastically weaken the correlation between global-route congestion and detailed-route DRC violations. Hence, the placer—based on the global-route congestion map—may leave too many detailed-route DRC violations to be fixed manually by designers. In this paper, we present a method that employs (1) machine-learning techniques to effectively predict detailed-route DRC violations after global routing and (2) detailed placement techniques to effectively reduce detailed-route DRC violations. We demonstrate on several layouts of a sub-14nm industrial design that this method predicts the locations of 74% of the detailed-route DRCs (with false positive prediction rate below 0.2%) and automatically reduces the number of detailed-route DRC violations by up to 5×. Whereas previous works on machine learning for routability [30] [4] have focused on routability prediction at the floorplanning and placement stages, ours is the first paper that not only predicts the actual locations of detailed-route DRC violations but furthermore optimizes the design to significantly reduce such violations.

1. INTRODUCTION

As semiconductor technology advances, the EDA and design communities have seen increasing unpredictability in the IC implementation flow. In particular, design tapeouts are increasingly placed at risk by the inability of the router to complete the routing successfully. Historically, any risk of unroutability could be identified prior to the runtime-intensive detailed route (DR) stage, based on congestion maps generated using global routing (GR). How-

*This work was performed while W.-T. J. Chan was with Synopsys, Inc., Hillsboro, OR.

ISPD '17, March 19–22, 2017, Portland, OR, USA.
© 2017 ACM. ISBN 978-1-4503-4696-2/17/03...$15.00
DOI: http://dx.doi.org/10.1145/3036669.3036681

ever, the miscorrelation between these congestion maps and the actual routing design rule check (DRC) violation maps has increased significantly at current process nodes due to the many new, complicated design rules defined at these nodes. This unpredictability causes added iterations (and consequent schedule slippage) during design implementation, sometimes endangering the design tapeout itself.

1.1 Motivation

At advanced process nodes, GR-based congestion maps do not correlate well with DRC violation maps obtained at the end of detailed routing. This is a consequence of the numerous complicated design rules imposed upon design layouts to ensure viable fabrication; these DRCs, most of which are not visible in the GR routing model, constrain the detailed router significantly. (The study of Han et al. [6] quantifies wirelength overheads due to increasing numbers of design rules.) As a result, GR-based congestion maps are no longer good predictors either for evaluating overall design routability or for identifying potential DRC violation hotspots prior to detailed routing. Therefore, they can easily mislead any routability optimization engines that rely on these maps, resulting in poor effectiveness at resolving routability problems, even as they sacrifice timing and area metrics to ameliorate spurious congestion problems. Figure 1 shows an example of such a miscorrelation on a sub-14nm design. The figure compares a map of actual DRC violations with a map of congestion hotspots obtained by running a state-of-the-art industrial global router on the same layout; an overlay of these two maps is also shown. The GR-based congestion map is thresholded so that both maps display the same number of violating grid cells.[1]

The miscorrelation between the congestion map and the actual DRC hotspot map demonstrates why the routability improvement techniques traditionally employed during physical synthesis are not very effective at advanced process nodes (since they are driven by GR-based congestion maps). At the same time, it is critical to model and optimize routability during the physical synthesis stage, since the netlist and layout transforms that are permissible during routing-based optimization—when the DRC violations actually manifest themselves—are very limited in scope. This motivates the study of better DRC hotspot prediction tech-

---

[1]We use the GR-based congestion map as the reference because this is still the most common way to estimate routability in industrial physical implementation tools and flows. We generate the congestion maps by summing up numbers of overflows on each metal layer.

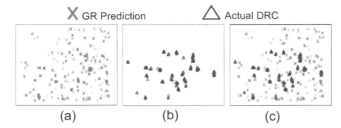

Figure 1: Comparison between the GR-based congestion map and the actual DRC violations (gcells with DRCs) on a sub-14nm design. (a) Overflows extracted from GR-based congestion map (per gcell). (b) DRC violations after detailed routing. (c) An overlay of the GR-predicted overflows and actual DRCs, highlighting the numerous false positive and false negative predictions. The placer and global router are from a state-of-the-art industrial physical design platform.

niques and their use for routability improvement without hurting the timing convergence of the design. In this paper, we describe a new algorithm that employs machine learning to accurately identify and optimize routability hotspots during physical synthesis without any timing or area overhead; furthermore, we demonstrate the effectiveness of our approach on industrial benchmarks in a sub-14nm process node from a leading foundry.

1.2 Related Work

Ensuring the routability of designs has always been a central challenge in IC implementation. Attempts to address this problem are usually most effective at the physical synthesis stage. In parallel, the problem of routability misprediction has also attracted interest in the EDA research community. We categorize and summarize previous works in these domains as follows.

Congestion predictors. Taghavi et al. [24] propose *MILOR* to identify local routing hotspots by examining pin-shape layouts and their densities or proximities within the placed design. Chan et al. [4] propose a learning-based methodology to predict the overall routability of a design by using placement information. Zhou et al. [30] use MARS to model DR congestion.

Routability-aware global routing. Qi et al. [20] improve the DR model from [30] to guide the global router. Wang et al. [26] and Zhong et al. [29] also propose the use of DR model-guided global routers. However, such works typically apply only to the routing stage, during which the allowed netlist and layout transforms are limited.

Congestion-aware placement. There has been significant work on congestion-aware placement in both industrial and academic coarse placers. For example, [12] [10] [8] [15] [16] [17] [19] [14] use global routers to predict congestion and feed the information back to the placer in order to improve routability. The works [3] [25] [9] [22] [13] [21] [27] use spreading regions, densities of nets, or routing patterns to estimate congestion and guide placement. However, such works are typically limited by their reliance on GR-based congestion maps.

White space optimization. When the pin accessibility problem dominates the DRCs, it is effective to use cell inflation during placement to improve the routability. Sadakane et al. [23] first addressed pin accessibility in the context of metal gate arrays, using a simulated annealing approach. [11] and [2] incorporate empirical heuristics to guide cell inflation in two academic placers to improve the routability. Instead of considering added space as attachments to (bloated) cells, [28] [18] [5] [1] handle the white space as separate components in placement, which enables more proactive control of white space to improve routability. However, the introduction of white space typically involves a timing and area overhead, especially when it is conservatively driven by poor routability predictor metrics such as GR-based congestion maps.

Our work is different from the previous works in several significant ways. (1) Rather than merely predicting routability, we show how to use machine learning to automatically *improve* the routability of the design. (2) Our engine focuses on improving route completion at the detailed routing stage, rather than optimizing GR congestion (and, does so without hurting the timing closure of the design). (3) Rather than merely predicting whether the overall design is routable or not, we use learning to predict the actual locations of the DRC hotspots. (4) Our predictor comprehends global routing, netlist structure, and cell-layout level information to capture routability risks due to both routing resource shortage and complicated design rules.

1.3 Overview of Our Work

In order to overcome the miscorrelation between the GR-based congestion map and the actual DRC map, we use machine learning to improve the accuracy of our identification of potential DRC hotspots. We model this prediction problem as a supervised classification problem. We label DRC-violating gcells in our training set of IC layouts with true labels, and cleanly-routed gcells with false labels. We then extract various parameters from the training netlists and layouts and use them to build an accurate predictor. Using this predictor, we propose an engine that minimally perturbs the converged physical synthesis netlist in a way that surgically redistributes the white space in the vicinity of the predicted DRC hotspots so as to ameliorate those hotspots without hurting timing, area or wirelength. We demonstrate the effectiveness of this approach on several layouts at a sub-14nm process node from a leading foundry. Our results show that we can reduce DRC violations by up to 76.8% and by an average of 20.6%, without hurting design convergence.

The key contributions of our work are as follows.

1. We present the first application of the machine learning paradigm to actually *optimize* design routability (in contrast to *predicting* routability, as in [4]).

2. We quantify the miscorrelation between a GR-based congestion map and the actual DRC map in designs at a sub-14nm process node.

3. We use machine learning to predict actual DRC locations in a design layout and use the prediction to improve post-placement routability. This is a significantly more difficult problem than the binary predic-

tion made in [4] on whether the overall design would be routable or not.

4. We develop an engine that employs our new learning-based predictor of DRC hotspots to ameliorate these hotspots without hurting timing, area or wirelength.

2. OUR APPROACH

We use machine learning to generate a model to close the gap between DRC hotspot prediction using congestion map and actual DRC violations located after detail routing. To enable accurate predictions, our model incorporates diverse parameters that we describe in Section 2.1.

With the help of this robust and accurate predictor, we are able to guide the optimization effectively to improve design routability. We design an algorithm that can leverage this predictor to ameliorate the DRC hotspots with minimal layout perturbation, thus avoiding timing or area penalties. This algorithm is described in more detail in Section 2.2.

2.1 Predictor Design

We use *hotspots to* refer to gcells with DRCs. The objective of our predictor is to separate hotspot gcells from non-hotspot gcells. In order to analyze the root causes of routability problems, we first partition training layouts into small grids on top of gcells (we use the term *local windows*[2] for these grids) to generate training data. We extract numerous netlist and layout parameters for each local window. These parameters include:

- **Density parameters** such as local pin density and local cell density;

- **GR parameters** obtained from a global routing invocation, such as local overflow, demand and capacity of each metal layer and via layer;

- **Pin proximity** measuring the average and minimum spacings between pins in each local window (proposed in [4]);

- **"Unfriendly" cells**, which are library cells that occur in the DRC hotspots (local windows with more than one DRC) at a rate significantly higher than their overall rate of incidence in the netlist;

- **Multi-height and sequential cells** and parameters relating to their fanins, fanouts, and occurrence frequencies in local windows;

- **Connectivity parameters** such as the number of buried nets completely enclosed inside the local windows, the number of non-buried nets crossing these window boundaries [4], and the number of connected pins lying outside the windows; and

- **Structural parameters** such as the number and depth of fanin and fanout logic stages in paths crossing local windows.

Multi-height cells are cells with heights greater than that of a single cell row, which are typically sequential cells in this technology. Fanin or fanout numbers refer to the numbers of sequential cells transitively connected (incident or outgoing, respectively) to the cells within the current local window. The intuition of "structural parameters" is to evaluate the likelihood of cells to be placed around the sequential cells. The sequential cells are especially of interest because they have lower pin densities and different track heights.

We then go through an iterative process of training the predictor model using our parameter list. The iterative process contains both layout observation and evaluation of statistical significance.[3] In each iteration, we measure the statistical significance of the various parameters, and analyze the locations of both false-positive and false-negative predictions, in order to refine the parameter list and identify additional predictive features of the design. This process is repeated with several mathematical models of machine learning, *viz.*, linear regression, logistic regression, and support vector machines (SVM) [7] with various kernel choices.[4] As an illustration of the physical analysis involved in this iterative process, consider the following example.

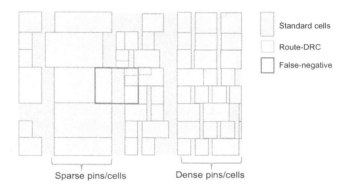

Standard cells

Route-DRC

False-negative

Sparse pins/cells   Dense pins/cells

Figure 2: An example of the analysis of a false negative prediction.

Figure 2 shows an example of a DRC hotspot that was predicted to be DRC-clean in one of our earlier predictor models.[5] In our manual analysis of this hotspot, we find that the red false-negative region itself has low pin and cell density but is located close to a region with higher pin and cell density. We capture this anomaly (caused by the tendency of the router to introduce small detours around

---

[2]We use two sizes of local windows, including 1×1 (gcell itself) and 3×3 windows (including a central gcell and the surrounding gcells). The 3×3 local windows have overlapping regions. Overlapping regions capture the influence among gcells in the DRC prediction.

[3]For the layout observation, we check the DRC locations and the cell placements. We also examine the false-positive and false-negative rates and the p-values (derived from the confusion matrices) after adding the parameters. We keep parameters that contribute to accuracy improvement in the process.
[4]We test among linear, polynomial, and radial basis function (RBF) kernels. We apply different weights to the DRC-violating gcells during model training and evaluate the model accuracy with testing gcells. RBF shows the best true-positive rate with similar false-positive rate with the first few parameters (density and GR). We choose RBF for our main experiments reported here.
[5]This reference predictor model has only basic parameters (density, GR overflow, etc.) and uses a single size (1×1) of local windows. The mathematical model for prediction is SVM.

DRC hotspots) in our predictor model by using larger local windows for such parameters, and by distinguishing between the parameter values inside a gcell, and the parameter values in a larger window that is centered on the gcell.

Besides incorporating different parameters to improve the prediction accuracy, we apply the following approaches to improve the accuracy and robustness of our local hotspot predictor. (1) Since the majority of the gcells in a typical layout do not have DRC violations, the training of the predictor is easily misguided by the biased distribution of the few DRC-violating gcells and the many DRC-clean gcells. We address this problem by emphasizing the DRC-violating gcells, increasing their weights[6] during the training stage. (2) Given that there are very few real-world sub-14nm designs and layouts available at this time, it becomes important to choose the training methodology carefully so as to avoid overfitting. We do this by randomly choosing 20% of the gcells from the layout to be the training data set and use the remaining 80% for testing. We repeat this randomized 20%-80% evaluation 12 times and use the average and distribution of the prediction accuracy from these 12 runs[7] to draw any conclusions about the tested parameter set and mathematical prediction model (*viz.*, linear regression, logistic regression, or SVM). (3) In order to take the neighborhood effect into consideration, we use both small and large local windows to annotate the central gcells. In addition to the multiple local window sizes, we also annotate the central gcell of each window with the extremal (i.e., maximum and minimum) values of selected parameters within the *expanded observation windows*.[8]

We use the R [31] statistical analysis package to prototype our predictor. As an illustration, the average true-positive and false-negative rates (over the 12 evaluations) for a series of evolving parameter sets are reported in Figure 3. We incrementally update the parameter set and mathematical model from predictor P1 through to predictor P9 based on our physical and statistical analysis of each of these predictors.

We use true-positive rate and false-negative rate to evaluate the statistical significance of prediction results. We compare the true-positive rates among combinations of different weighting[9] and the 12 evaluations for P{i} with or without a new set of parameters (unfriendly cells, sequential cells, etc.) If improvement is observed in the true-positive rate with the same false-positive rate constraint (typically, 0.5%), we accept the P{i} with new parameters as the P{i+1} predictor.

In Figure 3, P1 is the baseline set of predictors with 1×1 local windows, including pin density, cell density, and per-

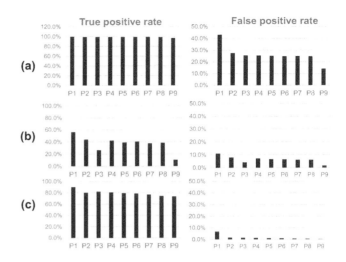

Figure 3: Accuracy comparisons between different parameter sets and mathematical models. (a) Linear regression; (b) logistic regression; (c) SVM classifier.

layer (metals and vias) GR capacity, demand, and overflow. P2 to P3 are variations of P1 with 3×3 windows and combinations of 1×1 and 3×3 windows.[10] P4 to P8 are the baseline predictors, combined with pin proximity, number of multi-height cells, number of unfriendly cells, connectivity parameters, and structural parameters. P9 uses the *Leaps* [32] package in R to pick predictors with high correlation to DRCs.[11]

We observe significant improvements in the prediction accuracy, especially in the false-positive rate, across this series. These plots also show that SVM (with a RBF kernel) can provide better separation between DRC gcells and non-DRC gcells than linear or logistic regression models. We also plot the predicted DRC hotspots (red squares) and actual DRC hotspots (blue squares) in Figure 4. The contrast with the corresponding figure (Figure 1) for GR-based predictions is readily apparent.[12] Our learning-based predictor provides a significantly more accurate prediction of the DRC hotspots, achieving 74% true-positive rate with a false-positive rate less than 0.2% (see Table 1). This is in contrast to a true-positive rate of 24% and a false-positive rate of 0.5% obtained from the GR-based predictor (Figure 1), as shown in Table 2.

2.2 Predictor-guided Routability Optimization

We present an optimization engine to improve the routability of a converged netlist with minimal perturbation of the layout. This algorithm is summarized in Figure 5. Given

---

[6]The DRC-clean cells are always weighted with one. We swept the weight of DRC-violated gcells with {2, 3, 4, 5,.... 10, 20, 30, 40, 50}.

[7]We pick 12 evaluations (larger than two times of 100%/20%) to avoid overfitting on specific training sets since we can only access one design in this technology.

[8]Two types of windows are mentioned in our discussion. The first type is the local window with two sizes (1×1 and 3×3 gcells) to extract per-layer GR information and other parameters. The second type is the expanded observation window with four sizes (3×3, 5×5, 7×7, 9×9) to keep track of max/min values within a certain range.

[9]We then choose the weight according to the true-positive rate for those runs with false-positive rates lower than a certain threshold (typically 0.5%).

[10]P1 to P3 are the same predictors with different local window sizes. We observe significant false-positive rate improvement when we compare P2 and P3 with P1 ($\sim$ 1% vs. > 6%), due to different local window sizes.

[11]Note that P1 essentially uses only cell and pin density parameters from global routing and thus has a high false-positive rate even if SVM is used ($\sim$6%). This again indicates that global routing is not sufficient to predict DRC hotspots.

[12]Note that the learning-based model has an advantage over GR-based congestion map because it generates proper thresholds (i.e., support vectors) in the training stage.

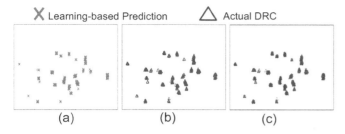

X Learning-based Prediction △ Actual DRC

(a)   (b)   (c)

Figure 4: Comparison between our learning-based DRC hotspot map and the actual DRC violations (gcells with DRCs) on a sub-14nm design. (a) DRC hotspots predicted by our learning-based model. (b) Actual DRC violations after detailed routing (note that this is the same as Figure 1(b) presented earlier, and is reproduced here merely for comparison with the predicted map in (a)). (c) An overlay of the predicted and actual DRCs.

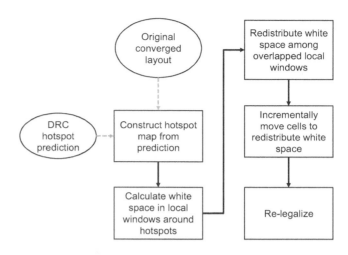

Figure 5: The predictor-guided routability optimization algorithm.

| | | Actual | |
		FALSE	TRUE
Prediction	FALSE	98571	117
	TRUE	170	344

Table 1: Learning-based prediction: confusion matrix of our learning-based predictor. True-positive rate = 74% and false-positive rate = 0.2%.

| | | Actual | |
		FALSE	TRUE
Prediction	FALSE	98260	350
	TRUE	481	111

Table 2: GR-based prediction: confusion matrix of prediction by GR shown in Figure 1. True-positive rate = 24% and false-positive rate = 0.5%.

the placement of a timing-converged netlist, we first use our DRC prediction model to identify the potential DRC hotspots in that layout. We have developed a local white space optimization engine that redistributes the white space already present in the neighborhood of the predicted DRC hotspots in a way that improves the routability of these hotspots. Real-world physical implementation flows are almost invariably run under some form of local cell density constraints in order to improve the flow convergence. Such constraints ensure the existence of white space everywhere in the layout when measured at some level of spatial granularity. However, this granularity is typically much larger than that of individual cells; therefore, this default white space distribution is not always able to resolve detailed routing DRC problems. This shortcoming is addressed effectively in our work by introducing a new, detailed white space redistribution stage that relies on our hotspot prediction model to minimize the perturbation to the layout while maximizing the routability impact of the redistribution.

The spreading is constructed based on the legalizer. First, the available whitespace size is collected in a given window. Then, we distribute a certain fraction of the available whitespace by adding small temporary keepout regions adjacent to the cells in the window, and run the legalizer to increase the cell spacing. This step incrementally moves the cells from the initial locations obtained from the original converged layout. The legalizer tends to abut the cells in order to

minimize the routed wirelength; the temporary keepouts help counter this behavior by introducing porosity in order to improve routability.

During the whitespace redistribution process, we first mark out local windows around each hotspot, and calculate the amount of white space available in these windows in order to compute a local white space budget (splitting overlapping windows appropriately during this process). We then incrementally distribute this budget among the cells in a row-major scanning sequence by gradually adding the aforementioned keepout region instances within the windows until the space budget is used up.

Subsequent to this white space redistribution step, the detailed routing engine can use the newly introduced space between problematic cell instances to handle the complicated design rules. This approach of applying redistribution to only the potential DRC hotspots and avoiding the introduction of any new white space there, while leaving the rest of the layout untouched, minimizes the perturbation to the already-converged layout, which in turn minimizes the likelihood of incurring any significant timing penalty. Indeed, our experimental results (discussed in Section 3) demonstrate large routability improvements from the application of this algorithm, without hurting timing.

3. EXPERIMENTAL RESULTS

In this section, we describe the experimental methodology that we have used to evaluate the effectiveness of our predictor-guided routability optimization algorithm. We then present the results of this evaluation.

Our experimental methodology is shown in Figure 6. Our routability optimization engine is implemented in $C++$ as part of a state-of-the-art industrial physical implementation platform. The predictor model generation code is implemented using scriptware in the R [31] statistical analysis package.[13] We evaluate our algorithm using an industrial benchmark design at a sub-14nm process node from a leading foundry. Given the difficulty of obtaining additional real-world sub-14nm benchmarks at this time, we gener-

---

[13]The extraction and training scriptware is split across several machines to reduce turnaround time.

Table 3: Comparisons between the default and the learning-optimized layouts. There are under one million instances in this design.

	#DRCs			Wirelength			TNS (ns)			#FEPs		
	Base	Test	%Change	Base	Test	%Change	Base	Test	%Change	Base	Test	%Change
eg1	8478	1964	-76.8%	1742804	1747685	0.3%	-153.43	-158.4	3.2%	7289	7352	0.86%
eg2	1502	927	-38.3%	1750698	1753047	0.1%	-168.23	-163.5	-2.8%	7406	7374	-0.43%
eg3	2017	1819	-9.8%	1772889	1773701	0.0%	-215.75	-213.6	-1.0%	7817	7751	-0.84%
eg4	2026	1780	-12.1%	1735185	1735227	0.0%	-151.36	-149.6	-1.2%	7195	7143	-0.72%
eg5	4252	4255	0.1%	1831492	1836060	0.2%	-264.34	-275.6	4.3%	7865	7975	1.40%
eg6	3440	3891	13.1%	1790059	1794184	0.2%	-195.65	-203.5	4.0%	7587	7562	-0.33%
		Avg	-20.6%		Avg	0.2%		Avg	1.1%		Avg	-0.01%
		Max	13.1%		Max	0.3%		Max	4.3%		Max	1.40%
		Min	-76.8%		Min	0.0%		Min	-2.8%		Min	-0.84%

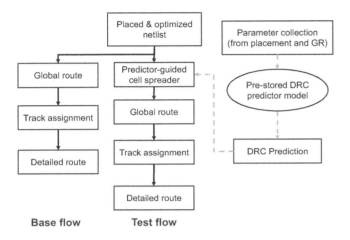

Base flow   Test flow

Figure 6: The experimental methodology used to evaluate the proposed predictor-guided routability optimization algorithm.

ate multiple widely-differing netlists and layouts from our benchmark design by running the design through an industrial congestion-aware physical synthesis flow with different (but still realistic) placement and optimization settings.

The input to our evaluation is an optimized netlist and a legalized placed layout obtained from the physical synthesis flow as described above. The layout has already been optimized using traditional congestion alleviation techniques during physical synthesis. Our base flow is the typical physical implementation flow that takes netlist and layout through standard global routing, track assignment and detailed routing using the state-of-the-art router embedded in our industrial physical implementation platform. For our test flow, we first use the pre-stored predictor to predict DRC hotspots in our starting layout. This prediction is then used by our routability optimization engine for localized white space redistribution, followed by legalization. The resulting layout is fed to the same router as in the base flow.

We report the number of DRC violations, total negative timing slack (TNS), wirelength, and number of failing timing endpoints (#FEP) at the end of detailed routing in the base and test flows. The results are shown in Table 3.[14] In this table, negative values in the "%Change" columns refer to

improvements achieved in the test flow (relative to the base flow), and positive values in these columns refer to degradations. As is evident from this data, we achieve significant reduction of the DRC count in the test flow. Moreover, these routability improvements are obtained without any significant impact on design closure: the timing and wirelength impacts are neutral, and the design area is unchanged. More specifically, we see that the number of DRC violations reduces by an average of 20.6% and a maximum of 76.8%, with TNS degrading by an average of 1.1%, and the number of failing timing endpoints improving by an average of 0.01%, and wirelength degrading by an average of 0.2%.

4. CONCLUSIONS

In this paper, we have addressed the route completion problem for designs at advanced process nodes. We make the case that traditional routability amelioration approaches that rely on GR-based congestion maps during physical synthesis are no longer effective at these advanced nodes due to the complexity of the design rules. We quantify this difficulty by measuring the accuracy of a GR-based prediction of routability hotspots. We then propose a machine learning based algorithm to automatically improve the routability of these designs without hurting timing convergence. We evaluate the effectiveness of this algorithm on design layouts at a sub-14nm process node from a leading foundry, using an industrial physical implementation platform. Our experiments show that we are able to reduce the number of DRC violations by an average of 20.6% and a maximum of 76.8%, with no adverse impact on design closure. Our future works include (1) improving the prediction accuracy and spreading results, (2) guiding the routability optimization by applying the machine learning model to coarse placement, and (3) applying our methodology to other advanced node technologies.

5. ACKNOWLEDGMENTS

We would like to express our gratitude to T. Andersen, B. Gregory, S. Nath, W. Naylor and J. Wong for a number of valuable discussions, and to J. Wong for helping us set up the experimental framework.

6. REFERENCES

[1] S. N. Adya, I. L. Markov and P. G. Villarrubia, "On Whitespace and Stability in Mixed-Size Placement

---

[14]In our experiments, we do not retrain the model for these regenerated layouts.

and Physical Synthesis" *Integration, the VLSI Journal* 39(4) (2008), pp. 340-362.

[2] U. Brenner and A. Rohe, "An Effective Congestion Driven Placement Framework", *Proc. ISPD*, 2002, pp. 6-11.

[3] A. E. Caldwell, A. B. Kahng, S. Mantik, I. L. Markov and A. Zelikovsky, "On Wirelength Estimations for Row-based Placement" *IEEE Trans. on CAD* 18(9) (1999), pp. 1265-1278.

[4] W.-T. J. Chan, Y. Du, A. B. Kahng, S. Nath and K. Samadi, "BEOL Stack-Aware Routability Prediction from Placement Using Data Mining Techniques", *Proc. ICCD*, 2016, pp. 41-48.

[5] A. E. Caldwell, A. B. Kahng and I. L. Markov, "Hierarchical Whitespace Allocation in Top-down Placement" *IEEE Trans. on CAD* 22(11) (2003), pp. 1550-1556.

[6] K. Han, A. B. Kahng and H. Lee, "Evaluation of BEOL Design Rule Impacts Using an Optimal ILP-Based Detailed Router", *Proc. DAC*, 2015, pp. 68:1-68:6.

[7] T. Hastie, R. Tibshirani and J. Friedman, *The Elements of Statistical Learning: Data Mining, Inference, and Prediction*, Springer, 2009.

[8] X. He, T. Huang, W.-K. Chow, J. Kuang, K.-C. Lam, W. Cai and E. F. Y. Young, "Ripple 2.0: High Quality Routability-Driven Placement via Global Router Integration", *Proc. DAC*, 2013, pp. 1-6.

[9] X. He, T. Huang, L. Xiao, H. Tian, G. Cui and E. F. Young, "Ripple: An Effective Routability-Driven Placer by Iterative Cell Movement", *Proc. ICCAD*, 2011, pp. 74-79.

[10] M.-K. Hsu, S. Chou, T.-H. Lin and Y.-W. Chang, "Routability-Driven Analytical Placement for Mixed-Size Circuit Designs", *Proc. ICCAD*, 2011, pp. 80-84.

[11] W. Hou, H. Yu, X. Hong, Y. Cai, W. Wu, J. Gu and W. H. Kao, "A New Congestion-Driven Placement Algorithm Based on Cell Inflation", *Proc. ASP-DAC*, 2001, pp. 606-608.

[12] Z.-W. Jiang, B.-Y. Su and Y.-W. Chang, "Routability-Driven Analytical Placement by Net Overlapping Removal for Large-scale Mixed-Size Designs", *Proc. DAC*, 2008, pp. 167-172.

[13] A. B. Kahng and X. Xu, "Accurate Pseudo-Constructive Wirelength and Congestion Estimation", *Proc. SLIP*, 2003, pp. 61-68.

[14] M.-C. Kim, J. Hu, D.-J. Lee and I. L. Markov, "A SimPLR Method for Routability-Driven Placement", *Proc. ICCAD*, 2011, pp. 67-73.

[15] W.-H. Liu, T.-K. Chien and T.-C. Wang, "A Study on Unroutable Placement Recognition", *Proc. ISPD*, 2014, pp. 19-26.

[16] W.-H. Liu, T.-K. Chien and T.-C. Wang, "Region-Based and Panel-Based Algorithms for Unroutable Placement Recognition" *IEEE Trans. on CAD* 34(4) (2015), pp. 502-514.

[17] W.-H. Liu, Y.-L. Li and C.-K. Koh, "A Fast Maze-Free Routing Congestion Estimator with Hybrid Unilateral Monotonic Routing", *Proc. ICCAD*, 2012, pp. 713-719.

[18] C. Li, M. Xie, C.-K. Koh, J. Cong and P. H. Madden, "Routability-Driven Placement and White Space Allocation", *Proc. ICCAD*, 2004, pp. 394-401.

[19] M. Pan and C. Chu, "IPR: An Integrated Placement and Routing Algorithm", *Proc. DAC*, 2007, pp. 59-62.

[20] Z. Qi, Y. Cai and Q. Zhou, "Accurate Prediction of Detailed Routing Congestion using Supervised Data Learning", *Proc. ICCD*, 2014, pp. 97-103.

[21] J. A. Roy and I. L. Markov, "Seeing the Forest and the Trees: Steiner Wirelength Optimization in Placement" *IEEE Trans. on CAD* 23(4) (2007), pp. 632-644.

[22] P. Spindler and F. M. Johannes, "Fast and Accurate Routing Demand Estimation for Efficient Routability-Driven Placement", *Proc. DATE*, 2007, pp. 1226-1231.

[23] T. Sadakane, H. Shirota, K. Takahashi, M. Terai and K. Okazaki, "A Congestion-Driven Placement Improvement Algorithm for Large Scale Sea-of-gates Arrays", *Proc. CICC*, 1997, pp. 573-576.

[24] T. Taghavi, C. J. Alpert, A. Huber, Z. Li, G.-J. Nam and S. Ramji, "New Placement Prediction and Mitigation Techniques for Local Routing Congestion", *Proc. ICCAD*, 2010, pp. 621-624.

[25] K. Tsota, C.-K. Koh and V. Balakrishnan, "Guiding Global Placement with Wire Density", *Proc. ICCAD*, 2008, pp. 212-217.

[26] M. Wang, X. Yang, K. Eguro and M. Sarrafzadeh, "Multicenter Congestion Estimation and Minimization during Placement", *Proc. ISPD*, 2000, pp. 147-152.

[27] J. Westra, C. Bartels and P. Groeneveld, "Probabilistic Congestion Prediction", *Proc. ISPD*, 2004, pp. 204-209.

[28] X. Yang, B.-K. Choi and M. Sarrafzadeh, "Routability-Driven White Space Allocation for Fixed-Die Standard-Cell Placement" *IEEE Trans. on CAD* 22(4) (2003), pp. 410-419.

[29] K. Zhong and S. Dutt, "Algorithms for Simultaneous Satisfaction of Multiple Constraints and Objective Optimization in a Placement Flow with Application to Congestion Control", *Proc. DAC*, 2002, pp. 854-859.

[30] Q. Zhou, X. Wang, Z. Qi, Z. Chen, Q. Zhou and Y. Cai, "An Accurate Detailed Routing Routability Prediction Model in Placement", *Proc. ASQED*, 2015, pp. 119-122.

[31] The R Project for Statistical Computing, https://www.r-project.org/

[32] Leaps package, https://cran.r-project.org/web/packages/leaps/

Pushing the Boundaries of Moore's Law to Transition from FPGA to All Programmable Platform

Ivo Bolsens
Xilinx Inc.
San Jose, CA
ivo@xilinx.com

ABSTRACT

Since their inception, FPGAs have changed significantly in their capacity and architecture. The devices we use today are called upon to solve problems in mixed-signal, high-speed communications, signal processing and compute acceleration that early devices could not address. The architecture has evolved towards an 'All Programmable' platform that immerses multiple programmable technologies into a complex interconnect infrastructure that, today, spans the boundary of multiple dies in one package. As the devices continue to grow in capability and complexity , new design tools and methodologies are being proposed. We will discuss future technology challenges that need to be solved in order to continue pushing the boundary of integration.

Author Keywords

FPGA; All Programmable Platform

BIOGRAPHY

Dr. Ivo Bolsens is senior vice president and chief technology officer (CTO) at Xilinx, with responsibility for advanced technology development, Xilinx research laboratories (XRL) and Xilinx university program (XUP). He came to Xilinx in June 2001 from the Belgium-based research center IMEC, where he was vice president of information and communication systems. His research included the development of knowledge-based verification for VLSI circuits, design of digital signal processing applications, and wireless communication terminals. He also headed the research on design technology for high-level synthesis of DSP hardware, HW/SW co-design and system-on-chip design. He holds a PhD in applied science and an MSEE from the Catholic University of Leuven in Belgium.

ISPD'17, March 19–22, 2017, Portland, OR, USA.
ACM. ISBN 978-1-4503-4696-2/17/03.
http://dx.doi.org/10.1145/3036669.3041226

How Game Engines Can Inspire EDA Tools Development: A use case for an open-source physical design library

Tiago Fontana, Renan Netto, Vinicius Livramento, Chrystian Guth,
Sheiny Almeida, Laércio Pilla, José Luís Güntzel
Embedded Computing Lab, Federal University of Santa Catarina, Brazil
{tiago.fontana, renan.netto}@posgrad.ufsc.br

ABSTRACT

Similarly to game engines, physical design tools must handle huge amounts of data. Although the game industry has been employing modern software development concepts such as data-oriented design, most physical design tools still relies on object-oriented design. Differently from object-oriented design, data-oriented design focuses on how data is organized in memory and can be used to solve typical object-oriented design problems. However, its adoption is not trivial because most software developers are used to think about objects' relationships rather than data organization. The entity-component design pattern can be used as an efficient alternative. It consists in decomposing a problem into a set of entities and their components (properties). This paper discusses the main data-oriented design concepts, how they improve software quality and how they can be used in the context of physical design problems. In order to evaluate this programming model, we implemented an entity-component system using the open-source library Ophidian. Experimental results for two physical design tasks show that data-oriented design is much faster than object-oriented design for problems with good data locality, while been only sightly slower for other kinds of problems.

1. INTRODUCTION

Modern game engines must efficiently handle huge amounts of data to render 3D graphics for very-high resolution images, model realistic physical systems, and also process complex artificial intelligence systems. To fulfill such requirements, several concepts and design patterns are applied during the game development to take advantage of modern computer architectures, where the memory represents the main bottleneck. One of the most important concepts employed during the development of game engines is the so-called data-oriented design (DOD). Unlike the traditional object-oriented design (OOD), which focuses on how objects represent problem entities, DOD focuses on how data will be organized in memory. This programming model may reduce the software complexity and aims for a more efficient processing, exploiting the available computer resources such as the memory subsystem and multithreading capabilities.

Traditional OOD makes heavy use of inheritance which tends to create complex class hierarchies, making the software difficult to maintain [10]. Although DOD can alleviate this limitation, the modeling of complex structures and relationships is not as natural as it is in OOD. Therefore, a design pattern called entity-component system is widely adopted in game engines to efficiently handle the creation and destruction of entities, and also to manage their underlying data (properties). The entity-component system can also replace inheritance trees by lightweight relations, like aggregation and composition, to build a more robust and modular software.

Similarly to game engines, electronic design automation (EDA) tools must be able to handle a high volume of data with very tight runtime budgets. Therefore, this work focuses on the discussion and application of these modern software concepts targeting the development of physical design tools. To discuss the related concepts we employ an open-source library for physical design as use case.

Since the early 2000's, there have been some efforts in the physical design community to create academic open-source databases and standardization, such as the works from [2], [3], [8] and [7]. However, few of the current projects are fully open source. For example, the Open Access project from [2] requires approved registration in order to be used, while the open database from [7] provides only binaries, and not the tools' source code. Even the truly open source initiatives, such as the open timer from [6], are mainly constructed using objected-oriented programming concepts, and therefore, might be improved.

In this direction, this work adopts as use case Ophidian, an Open-Source Library for Physical Design Research and Teaching [1], implemented by us, which is available through the collaborative GitHub platform. This library aims to fill the shortage of open source code for basic underlying infrastructure to facilitate research and teaching in the field. In Ophidian, we employed software development concepts borrowed from the game industry to handle large-scale designs. This way, Ophidian is used to explain and discuss how to take benefit from DOD to model circuit cells, pins, interconnections, and their respective properties.

Besides improving the software quality by overcoming the design problems of OOD, experimental results show that the DOD programming model is about 90% faster in a scenario that fully explores data locality, and it is only 6% slower in a

ISPD '17, March 19-22, 2017, Portland, OR, USA

© 2017 ACM. ISBN 978-1-4503-4696-2/17/03. . . $15.00

DOI: http://dx.doi.org/10.1145/3036669.3038248

scenario with bad data locality. Such results show that this programming model can be efficiently used to solve physical design problems.

The rest of this paper is organized as follows. Section 2 presents the main characteristics and limitations of the OOD and DOD programming models. Section 3 details the entity-component system design pattern. Section 4 presents the experimental results and finally, Section 5 draws the conclusions.

2. OBJECT-ORIENTED DESIGN VS. DATA-ORIENTED DESIGN

This section discusses the use of OOD and DOD for software development. First, Section 2.1 shows a few limitations of OOD that make it difficult the development of software. Then Section 2.2 describes how the adoption of DOD may overcome shortcomings limitations, making also possible to improve memory access and program execution time.

2.1 Object-oriented design (OOD)

Typically, physical design tools are built using the OOD model, which decomposes a problem into objects. These objects are accessed through a well-defined interface, and their relations are represented through hierarchy, composition and aggregation [4]. The OOD programming model is popular because there is usually a one-to-one mapping between the real world objects and their corresponding objects in the program.

To illustrate the OOD basic concepts, suppose we are developing a physical design library to be used to solve different physical design problems. Then let us assume that a software developer wants to use such library to build a tool for estimating circuit interconnection wirelength. Figure 1 shows an example of a digital circuit containing four nets and eight pins. An interconnection wirelength estimator must get access to the information of which pins belong to each net, as well as to the pins' positions within the circuit layout.

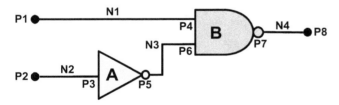

Figure 1: Combinational circuit portion with two logic gates (A and B), four nets (N1 to N4), and eight pins (P1 to P8).

Figure 2 illustrates a possible decomposition for the wirelength estimation problem by using OOD consisting of two modules: *netlist* and *placement*. The *netlist* module employs two classes, *net* and *pin*, to describe the circuit nets and the associated pins. For the *pin* class, this module characterizes only the name of the pin and the net such pin belongs to, without any placement information. The *placement* module, by its turn, describes the pins' positions. The diamond-end arrow between *pin* and *net* classes represents an aggregation relationship, which means that net has a reference to its pins, while a pin has a reference to its owner net. The

triangle-end arrow between the two *pin* classes represents a hierarchy relationship, meaning that the *pin* class from the *placement* module extends the attributes from the *pin* class in the *netlist* module.

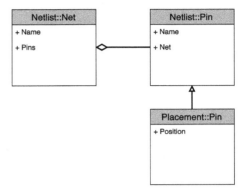

Figure 2: Class diagram to model wirelength estimation problem with OOD approach.

Although it may be easy to decompose a problem using OOD, building software based only on this programming model may lead to an overly complex class hierarchy. This issue is particularly critical in the development of a software library, because it is hard to predict, during the library design, how it will be actually used. For example, suppose that another problem requires pin timing information for the circuit of Figure 1. Then by using OOD, such information could be naturally added by creating a new module called *timing* and a new *pin* class (with pin timing attributes) in this module, which also extends the *pin* class from the *netlist* module. This new decomposition results in the class hierarchy shown in Figure 3.

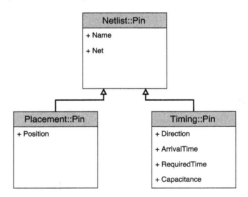

Figure 3: Class diagram to model when pin timing information is added.

Now suppose that another developer wants to use our physical design library to implement a timing-driven placement (ITDP) algorithm. In order to do that, she/he needs a new *pin* class with both placement and timing information. In OOD, this can be accomplished through multiple inheritance, where this new *pin* class extends the *pin* classes from *placement* and *timing* modules. However, multiple inheritance is not supported by all programming languages, and even when supported, it is not recommended because it may lead to design problems [10].

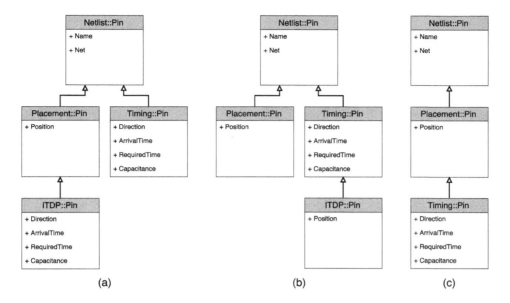

Figure 4: Possible class hierarchy to support information of *Timing* and *Placement* for a timing-driven placement algorithm following OOD approach.

Without resorting to multiple inheritance, the solution consists on creating a new *pin* class that extends the one from either the *placement* or the *timing* module, and repeating the code from the other class (that was not extended). Figures 4 (a) and (b) show these two solutions. Anyway, there is no clean manner of reusing placement and timing information without replicating code. The only remaining option is to push everything up in the *pin* class from the *timing* module by making it to extend the one from the *placement* module. This solution is illustrated in Figure 4 (c). However, it is not always necessary to have placement information in the *timing* module. For instance, a static timing analysis tool might not need placement information during early design steps. Therefore, adopting the latter solution would lead to memory waste, since unnecessary information would be stored.

2.2 Data-oriented design (DOD)

DOD may be used to overcome the previously mentioned limitations of OOD. This concept was first introduced in the work by Sharp [11], whose objective was to improve processing time and memory efficiency. Differently from OOD, the DOD programming model represents the problem objects, such as nets and pins, by indexes that are used to access their properties. The properties, by their turn, are contiguously stored in memory as data arrays. Figure 5 shows how we can model the same circuit from Figure 1 by following the DOD approach. The first two arrays describe the circuit's nets and pins as indexes. The remaining arrays describe their properties (equivalent to the attributes in OOD), which are accessed using the nets' and pins' indexes.

By doing so, the properties are not tied to objects, making it possible to add only the properties that are necessary for a given algorithm. For example, suppose an algorithm requires only placement information (as in global placement algorithms). In this case, the timing information is not necessary and the algorithm can include only the netlist and placement modules, resulting in the model shown in Figure

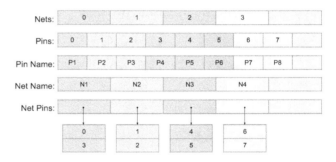

Figure 5: Modeling a combinational circuit with DOD approach. The lines represent arrays to describe nets and pins properties.

6 (a). On the other hand, if an algorithm needs only timing information (for example, for a static timing analysis performed before placement), it can include only the netlist and timing modules, resulting in the model in Figure 6 (b). Finally, for the implementation of an incremental timing-driven placement tool, the algorithm should include all the three modules (netlist, placement and timing), resulting in the model in Figure 6 (c). Notice that such programming model enables developers to employ only the piece of data required for their algorithms, thus avoiding memory waste. In addition, by storing the arrays of properties contiguously in memory, a more efficient use of the memory hierarchy is enabled.

Although DOD can simplify the class hierarchy, its concept is not trivial to adopt, since most software developers are used to think about objects' relationships rather than data organization. In order to efficiently use this programming model, it is necessary to manage the arrays of properties to ensure they remain contiguous as new data is added and removed. A design pattern called **entity-component**

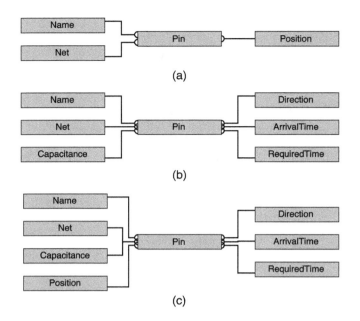

(a)

(b)

(c)

Figure 6: Properties of a pin using the DOD approach: pins have only placement information (a), pins have only timing information (b), pins have both information (c).

system can be used to handle such problem [10], as will be presented in Section 3.

3. THE ENTITY-COMPONENT SYSTEM DESIGN PATTERN

This section introduces the concepts of the entity-component system design pattern. First, Section 3.1 presents the concepts of entity and component. Then Section 3.2 shows how the entity system manages these concepts. Finally, Section 3.3 explains how to implement relationships between entities using this design pattern.

3.1 Entities and components

The entity-component system design pattern consists on decomposing a problem into a set of entities and their components [10]. The entities are analogous to the objects in OOD, while the components correspond to their properties (or attributes). Hereafter, we refer to components as properties to adhere to the context of this work. Differently from objects, entities are not complex structures, but only unique identifiers (ids). Each property, by its turn, is represented using an array of data. The entity id is used to access its properties in those arrays. For instance, Figure 7 illustrates an entity with five properties, where each property corresponds to an array, and the entity id is used to access all arrays for a given index. Similarly to the properties, each one of these entities is stored in a contiguous array.

In order to decompose the wirelength estimation problem mentioned in Section 2 using the entity-component system pattern, the circuit nets and pins could be modeled as entities as follows. For each net, the properties would be the net name and its pins, while for each pin, the properties would be the pin name, its position and its net. Figure 8 illustra-

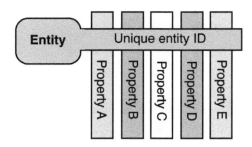

Figure 7: Example of entity with five properties. The entity id is used to access the information of all properties.

tes a possible pin representation using the entity-component system design pattern.

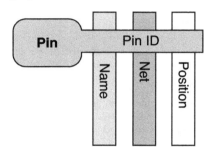

Figure 8: Possible representation of a pin using the entity-component system design pattern.

3.2 The Entity system

An entity system is necessary to properly access entities and their properties. The entity system is responsible for creating and destroying entities, as well as managing the arrays of properties when changing the number of entities. For example, if an entity is created or destroyed, the entity system must efficiently ensure that all arrays remain contiguous in memory.

Besides managing the creation and destruction of entities, the entity system must provide an interface to access entities and properties with constant time complexity. In order to present the entity system algorithms, we are going to use the notation described in Table 1. Observe that E_S and P are arrays, and therefore, their values can be accessed through the corresponding indexes. For example, $E_S(i)$ represents the entity in the ith position of the array of entities.

Table 1: Main notation.

Symbol	Meaning
S	An entity system
e	entity e
id_e	id of entity e
E_S	array of entities belonging to an entity system S
$E_S(i)$	entity stored in the ith position of the array E
$\mathcal{P}_S$	set of properties associated to an entity system S
P	array of property P
$P(j)$	value stored in the jth position of a property array P

Algorithm 1 describes how the entity system creates new

entities. When a new entity e is created (line 1), the entity system assigns to e an identifier id_e equivalent to the size of the entities array E_S (line 2). Then e is inserted in the end of the entities array E_S, by calling the $PUSH\_BACK$ function (line 3). Finally, for each property associated to the entity system S, a default value is added for the new entity e (lines 4-6). Notice that the identifier of e (id_e) is used as an index to access the arrays of properties.

Algorithm 1: ENTITY_CREATE

Input : Entity system S
Output: New entity e
1   $e \leftarrow$ new entity;
2   $id_e \leftarrow |E_S|$;
3   $PUSH\_BACK(E_S, e)$;
4   **foreach** $P \in \mathcal{P}_S$ **do**
5 | $P(id_e) \leftarrow$ default value;
6   **end**
7   **return** e;

Algorithm 2 presents the entity destruction steps. Given an entity e to be destroyed, the entity system could simply remove it from the entities array. However, removing an element from the middle of a contiguous array has a time complexity of $\mathcal{O}(n)$, with n being the number of entities. Another option would be to assign the entity e as invalid, instead of removing it from the array. Nonetheless, this approach would leave holes in the entities array, which could hinder the entity system's performance.

Instead of removing the entity e from the array or assigning it as invalid, the entity system replaces it with the last entity e' from the entities array (lines 1-4). Then the last element of this array is removed by calling the POP_BACK function (line 5). This way, the entities array remains contiguous in memory and the destroy operation is performed in $\mathcal{O}(1)$. After replacing e by e', the entity system does the same for the arrays of properties, replacing the values associated to entity e by the ones from entity e' (lines 6-9).

Algorithm 2: ENTITY_DESTROY

Input : Entity system S, and entity e to destroy
Output: Entity system S without e
1   $n \leftarrow |E_S|$;
2   $e' \leftarrow E_S(n-1)$;
3   $E_S(id_e) \leftarrow e'$;
4   $id_{e'} \leftarrow id_e$;
5   $POP\_BACK(E_S)$;
6   **foreach** $P \in \mathcal{P}_S$ **do**
7 | $P(id_e) \leftarrow P(n-1)$;
8 | $POP\_BACK(P)$;
9   **end**
10   **return** S;

3.3   Relationships between entities

Instead of heavily using hierarchical relationships (like OOD), the entity-component system design pattern represents relations between entities using mainly composition and aggregation. A composition represents an ownership relationship. An aggregation, by its turn, is simply an association between different entities, without ownership [5]. For example, a circuit cell is composed of pins, which means that when the cell is destroyed all its pins must be destroyed too. On the other hand, the relationship between a net and its pins is simply an aggregation. As consequence, if a net is destroyed, the relationship is also destroyed, but all pins remain alive in the entity system.

Such relationships can be added to the entity system implementation (Algorithms 1 and 2) as special properties. This way, when the property is removed from the array of properties (line 8 from Algorithm 2), it automatically destroys the relationship. In addition, if the property is a composition, it also destroys the related entities.

4.   EXPERIMENTAL RESULTS

In order to evaluate the impact of using either OOD or DOD on software performance, thus establishing a comparison between those programming models, we have implemented software prototypes for solving two physical design problems. Then those prototypes were run using the experimental infrastructure presented in Section 4.1. Then Section 4.2 describes the evaluated physical design problems, whereas Sections 4.3 and 4.4 present the experimental results for each problem.

4.1   Experimental infrastructure

We generated experimental results for the 8 circuits available from the ICCAD 2015 Contest (problem C: Incremental Timing-Driven Placement) [9]. These circuits were derived from industrial designs having from 768k to 1.93M cells. We performed all experiments in a Linux workstation whose architecture is depicted in Figure 9. This machine has an Intel® Core® i5-4460 CPU running at 3.20 GHz, 32GB RAM (4 × 8GB DDR3 at 1600MHz), and three levels of cache. All results presented in this section represent the average of 30 executions to ensure a small confidence interval.

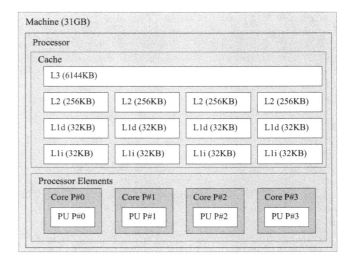

Figure 9: Architecture of workstation.

4.2 Evaluated physical design problems

We implemented the entity-component system design pattern described in Section 3 in the Ophidian library [1]. Ophidian is an open-source library developed by us for physical design teaching and research. It is composed of independent modules and implements the DOD concepts presented in Section 2. In addition, Ophidian supports industrial formats, such as Verilog, DEF, LEF and Liberty, so that it can be used by other research groups.

Then we used Ophidian to implement software prototypes for the following physical design problems:

- Problem A: verifying if all circuit cells' positions lie within the circuit's physical boundaries. In this scenario only one property is necessary for each entity (cell position), so it fully explores the data locality provided by DOD.

- Problem B: estimating the interconnection wirelength for all circuit nets. This scenario accesses different properties of different entities. Therefore, it cannot efficiently explore the data locality provided by DOD, since the properties of the pins in a single net may not be contiguous in memory, unless the property array is previously sorted.

For each problem, two versions of prototypes were developed: one with the DOD model (using the entity-component system design pattern) and another with the OOD model. Therefore, in the next sections we compare the runtime and the number of cache misses for each programming model.

The experiments are available in the Ophidian GitHub repository [1], so that they can be easily reproduced[1].

4.3 Experimental results for Problem A

Figure 10 presents the average runtime results (y axis) for each circuit (x axis) in the problem A scenario. For all figures in this section, blue bars identify the DOD results whereas red bars denote the OOD results. The runtimes of the DOD version were between $4ms$ and $12ms$, whereas the runtimes of OOD were between $74ms$ and $186ms$. Therefore, for problem A, DOD is on average 94% ($16\times$) faster than OOD. The shorter runtime achieved by DOD is due to the fact that problem A uses only one entity-component system and only one property. This is the best scenario for DOD because it fully benefits from the cache hierarchy due to its spatial locality. Exploiting data locality reduces the time to access the main memory, which represents the main bottleneck.

To illustrate the superior cache locality of DOD, Figure 11 shows the number of cache misses (y axis) resulted by solving problem A using both programming models. The number of cache misses includes both instruction and data caches, and all three levels of cache available in the workstation. The number of cache misses for DOD (from $0.5M$ to $1.4M$) was, on average, one-tenth of those achieved by OOD (from $5.4M$ to $13.7M$). These results explain the much lower runtime of DOD for problem A.

---

[1]The sources are available in the *ISPD2017* branch of the GitHub repository (https://github.com/eclufsc/ophidian/blob/ISPD2017/test/ispd/main.cpp).

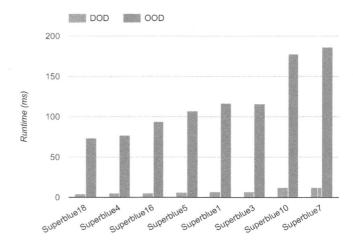

Figure 10: Runtime results for the two prototypes of problem A.

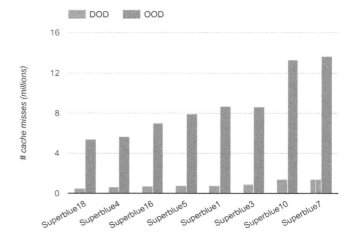

Figure 11: Cache miss results for the two prototypes of problem A.

4.4 Experimental results for Problem B

Figure 12 presents the average runtime results for problem B. The runtimes of DOD were between $3497ms$ and $10300ms$, while the runtimes of OOD were between $3306ms$ and $9654ms$. Differently from problem A, in order to solve problem B, the program employing the DOD programming model needs to access different entity-component systems (nets and pins) and multiple properties. In addition, the pins belonging to each net may not be contiguous in memory, which affects performance. As consequence, for problem B, OOD is on average 6% faster than DOD.

In order to verify the impact of the worse data locality of problem B, Figure 13 shows the number of cache misses resulted from each programming model. Observe that the number of cache misses of DOD (from $253M$ to $819M$) was, on average, 10% greater than those obtained by OOD (from $231M$ to $749M$). The higher number of cache misses from OOD resulted in the lower performance for problem B. However, DOD still provides software engineering advantages by overcoming the limitations of OOD presented in Section 2.1. In addition, the performance difference in pro-

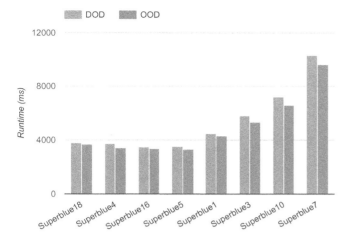

Figure 12: Runtime results for the two prototypes of problem B.

blem B (when DOD is slower) is much lower than that in problem A (when DOD is faster).

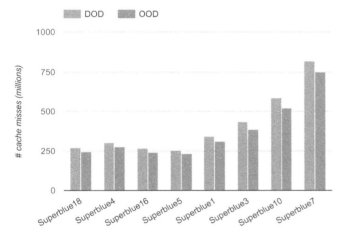

Figure 13: Cache miss results for the two prototypes of problem B.

5. CONCLUSIONS

Inspired software development concepts employed by game industry, the DOD programming model (along with the entity-component design pattern) can be used to overcome limitations of OOD in software implementation. This work discussed DOD concepts in the context of physical design problems, and presented an entity-component system implementation for such problems. The entity-component system design pattern was implemented in an open-source physical library called Ophidian.

The experimental results showed that the DOD programming model can reduce the program runtime by 94% on average, in a scenario that fully exploits data locality. These results are consequence of a lower number of cache misses provided by this programming model (90% reduction). On the other hand, in a scenario with worse data locality, using the OOD programming model resulted, on average, in a 6%

faster solution. However, this faster runtime achieved by OOD in the second scenario does not compensate for its much slower performance in the first scenario. In addition, employing DOD solves some typical design limitations resulted from OOD, thus resulting in software quality improvements.

As future work, we intend to investigate the limitations of the DOD programming model in scenarios with worse cache locality. A possible technique to improve the data locality, therefore making possible to improve the performance of DOD, consists in sorting the arrays of properties in order to group values that should be accessed in sequence. In addition, we intend to investigate the parallelism potential of DOD. For problems with good data locality, the DOD programming model improves the memory access and, consequently, may increase the speedup of a parallel solution.

6. ACKNOWLEDGMENTS

This work was partially supported by Brazilian agencies CAPES, through M.Sc. grants, and CNPq, through Project Universal (457174/2014-5) and PQ grant 310341/2015-9.

7. REFERENCES

[1] Embedded Computing Lab, Federal University of Santa Catarina, "Ophidian: an open source library for physical design research and teaching". https://github.com/eclufsc/ophidian.

[2] Silicon integration initiative, "open access". http://www.si2.org/openaccess/.

[3] University of michigan, "umich physical design tools". http://vlsicad.eecs.umich.edu/BK/PDtools/.

[4] G. Booch. *Object oriented analysis & design with application.* Pearson Education India, 2006.

[5] E. Gamma. *Design patterns: elements of reusable object-oriented software.* Pearson Education India, 1995.

[6] T.-W. Huang and M. D. Wong. Opentimer: A high-performance timing analysis tool. In *Proceedings of the IEEE/ACM International Conference on Computer-Aided Design*, pages 895–902. IEEE Press, 2015.

[7] J. Jung, I. H.-R. Jiang, G.-J. Nam, V. N. Kravets, L. Behjat, and Y.-L. Li. Opendesign flow database: the infrastructure for VLSI design and design automation research. In *Proceedings of the 35th International Conference on Computer-Aided Design*, page 42. ACM, 2016.

[8] A. B. Kahng, H. Lee, and J. Li. Horizontal benchmark extension for improved assessment of physical cad research. In *Proceedings of the 24th edition of the great lakes symposium on VLSI*, pages 27–32. ACM, 2014.

[9] M. Kim, J. Hu, J. Li, and N. Viswanathan. ICCAD-2015 CAD contest in incremental timing-driven placement and benchmark suite. In *ICCAD*, pages 921–926, 2015.

[10] R. Nystrom. *Game programming patterns.* Genever Benning, 2014.

[11] J. A. Sharp. Data oriented program design. *ACM SIGPLAN Notices*, 15(9):44–57, 1980.

Rsyn – An Extensible Physical Synthesis Framework

Guilherme Flach, Mateus Fogaça, Jucemar Monteiro,
Marcelo Johann and Ricardo Reis
Universidade Federal do Rio Grande do Sul (UFRGS) - Instituto de Informática - PGMicro/PPGC
{gaflach, mpfogaca, jucemar.monteiro, johann, reis}@inf.ufrgs.br

ABSTRACT

Due to the advanced stage of development on EDA science, it has been increasingly difficult to implement realistic software infrastructures in academia so that new problems and solutions are tested in a meaningful and consistent way. In this paper we present Rsyn, a free and open-source C++ framework for physical synthesis research and development comprising an elegant netlist data model, analysis tools (e.g. timing analysis, congestion), optimization methods (e.g. placement, sizing, buffering) and a graphical user interface. It is designed to be very modular and incrementally extensible. New components can be easily integrated making Rsyn increasingly valuable as a framework to leverage research in physical design. Standard and third party components can be mixed together via code or script language to create a comprehensive design flow, which can be used to better assess the quality of results of the research being conducted. The netlist data model uses the new features of C++11 providing a simple but efficient way to traverse and modify the netlist. Attributes can be seamlessly added to objects and a notification system alerts components about changes in the netlist. The flexibility of the netlist inspired the name Rsyn, which comes from the word resynthesis. Rsyn is created to allow researchers to focus on what is really important to their research spending less time on the infrastructure development. Allowing the sharing and reusability of common components is also one of the main contributions of the Rsyn framework. In this paper, the key concepts of Rsyn are presented. Examples of use are drawn, the important standard components (e.g. physical layer, timing) are detailed and some case studies based on recent Electronic Design Automation (EDA) contests are analyzed. Rsyn is available at **http://rsyn.design**.

Keywords

EDA, Physical Synthesis, Framework, Open Source

ISPD '17, March 19-22, 2017, Portland, OR, USA

ⓒ 2017 ACM. ISBN 978-1-4503-4696-2/17/03. . . $15.00

DOI: http://dx.doi.org/10.1145/3036669.3038249

1. INTRODUCTION

A common challenge faced by academia in physical synthesis research is the lack of an open, collaborative and standard framework in which the work can be conducted. This may be circumvented by narrowing the scope of the research, which may lead to oversimplification, making it hard to assess the real benefits of a technique when inserted in a full design flow.

Some public physical synthesis tools do exist as for timing analysis [14], placement [42], routing [22], but they usually are developed to solve one very specific problem, and are hard to integrate in a cohesive way into a design flow. The underlying data structures are typically tightly tied to the optimization problem and difficult to extend. Even when the tool offers an Application Program Interface (API), there may be memory and runtime overheads due to the maintenance of redundant information (e.g. netlist). Moreover, the code experience gained in one tool is not directly translated to another one making the learning process very timing consuming.

Those drawbacks often push researchers to implement their own infrastructure as the time required to integrate or learn third party tools may not compensate the familiarity and efficiency of an infrastructure developed specifically to solve the research problem of interest. Therefore, researchers end up devoting a lot of time to infrastructure development and less time in the core of the research project. Considering that many physical design problems share common infrastructure requirements, it is clear that a lack of a common and powerful infrastructure hinders the advancement of this field.

In the last decade, renowned conferences such as International Symposium on Physical Design (ISPD), Design Automation Conference (DAC), International Conference on Computer-Aided Design (ICCAD) and International Workshop on Timing Issues in the Specification and Synthesis of Digital Systems (TAU) have promoted research on emerging Electronic Design Automation (EDA) challenges [25, 39, 41, 30, 36, 18, 17] by organizing contests where teams compete to achieve the best results. The teams are composed by a small group of students who have few months to develop a tool [1] that solves the proposed problem. These contests usually boost research in the proposed field, which can be verified by the large number of related publications that follow the contests. Even though contests do a great job promoting research and creating standard ways to validate results,

---

[1] The tools are typically not required to be open-sourced.

there is still plenty room for more horizontal and vertical integration.

In this paper, an open-source, modular and extensible framework, called *Rsyn*, for physical synthesis research is presented. The elegant netlist data model and integrated tools allow fast prototyping of ideas. The modular design of the framework makes it possible to easily extend Rsyn for specific and general purposes. And the collaborative nature leverages it as an increasingly relevant and powerful framework for physical design research.

Rsyn provides support for common industrial file formats used in physical design, such as Library Exchange Format (LEF)/Design Exchange Format (DEF) [19], Liberty [28], Verilog [40] and the popular Bookshelf academic format [3]. Currently, Rsyn is already able to work on the benchmarks from the contests presented in Table 1.

Table 1: Current Contests Supported by Rsyn

Conference	Contest
ISPD 2005	Placement (Bookshelf)
ISPD 2006	Placement (Bookshelf)
ISPD 2012	Discrete Gate Sizing and Vt-Assignment
ISPD 2013	Discrete Gate Sizing and Vt-Assignment
ICCAD 2015	Incremental Timing-Driven Placement

The most relevant features currently provided by Rsyn infrastructure are summarized as follows:

- An elegant and dynamic netlist data model implemented using modern features of C++11.

- A notification system that alerts the modules in the framework when a change is made in the netlist;

- Extensibility of the netlist objects via user-specific attributes.

- Routing estimation and static timing analysis tools that can be configured to use different routing and timing models, including user-specific ones.

- An intuitive Graphical User Interface (GUI) with embedded features to help on analysing and debugging optimization techniques.

- Support for the widely-adopted industrial file formats, such as LEF/DEF [19].

The organization of the paper is as follows: Section 2 and Section 3 provide the description of the Rsyn architecture and the available standard components, respectively. In Section 4, we briefly summarize our recent research works using the Rsyn framework. In Section 5, the related works are shortly presented. Section 6 highlights the most relevant conclusions. The reader may refer to the official website [35] for more information, documentation and the source code.

2. ANATOMY OF RSYN FRAMEWORK

The core of Rsyn is composed of a netlist data model and three main components as shown in Figure 1: an engine, services, and processes.

The *netlist data model* stores structural and logical design data and can be extended via object attributes. It serves as a standard way to exchange and query design information

in the framework. The *engine* is the main hub in the Rsyn framework. It manages and provides access to the design, processes and services keeping session information. It is also responsible for command registrations and dispatch.

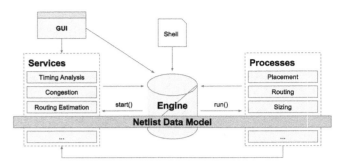

Figure 1: Rsyn Framework

2.1 Netlist Data Model

Rsyn implements a hierarchical [2] netlist data model which is managed by the object *design*. Figure 2 depicts the objects that compose the netlist data model. User-specific *attributes* can easily extend these objects and internally handle netlist modifications. A *notification system* is provided so that *observers* can be aware of changes in the netlist performed by third parties.

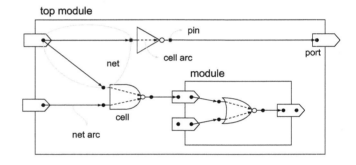

Figure 2: Netlist data model.

The netlist models a hierarchical directed graph where *pins* represent the nodes and *arcs* represent the edges. Arcs are classified into two types: cell and net arcs. Cell arcs represent the logical relation between the input and output pins of *cells*. Net arcs represent the logical relationship between the driver and sink of *nets*. Nets can only connect pins in the same hierarchy level [3]. The topological ordering of the nodes is incrementally updated whenever the netlist is changed allowing fast ordered traversal.

Hierarchies are represented by *modules* and connections between hierarchies by *ports*. *Instances* abstract modules, ports, and cells. The parent of an instance is the module where it is instantiated. The only instance with no parent is the top module.

All pins belong to one and only one instance and no instance has pins in different hierarchy levels. A port is associated to two pins: *inner pin* and *outer pin*. The inner pin

---

[2] Hierarchy support is still experimental.

[3] The concept of *supernets*, which will handle transparently sinks in different hierarchies, is yet to be implemented.

Listing 1: Rsyn Code Example

```
1 Rsyn::Attribute<Rsyn::Pin, int> data = design.
    createAttribute();
2 for (Rsyn::Net net : module.
    allNetsInTopologicalOrder()) {
3     for (Rsyn::Pin pin : net.allPins(Rsyn::SINK
        )) {
4         data[pin] = foo(net);
5     } // end for
6 } // end for
```

Listing 2: Rsyn Script Example

```
1 start "myService";
2 run "myOptimization1" {
3   "effort" : 1,
4   "debug" : "first_pass"
5 };
6 run "myOptimization2" {
7   "effort" : 10,
8   "debug" : "second_pass"
9 };
10 myReport "report.txt" -nets -cells;
```

belongs to the port itself and is inside the module where the port is instantiated. The outer pin belongs to the instance that represents the upper module in the hierarchy. Cells are associated with *library cells*. Similarly, cell pins and cell arcs are associated with the respective *library pins* and *library arcs* in the standard-cell library. This allows common data to be shared among cells, pins and arcs of the same type.

The snippet in Listing 1 shows the key concepts of the netlist data model. In the example, at line 1, an integer attribute for pins is created. At line 2 the nets are traversed in topological order. For each net, its sinks pins are swept at line 3. And at line 4 the attribute value is set.

2.2 Services and Processes

Services and *processes* provide the basic functionality required to implement a design flow. They are two related concepts that differentiate only by their lifespan. New services and processes created by users and collaborators will typically extend the Rsyn framework features. Services and processes are registered and managed via the *engine*.

A *service* usually is active during several flow steps implementing tasks that are recurrent and/or require a state to be kept. A typical usage of a service would be to create analysis tools (e.g. timing, power) and to implement the shared infrastructure among several flow steps (e.g. incremental legalization used by several optimization steps during detailed placement).

A *process* implements any task that does not require keeping its state after it is finished. They are normally used to implement a flow step. A typical usage of a process would be to create optimization steps (e.g. sizing, legalization, placement, routing). Even though these processes affect the state of the design, their internal data is not required anymore once they have finished. A typical process will rely on several services to perform its task.

2.3 Script

Currently, Rsyn implements its script language focused on simplicity. A script is a sequence of commands. Any command registered in the engine can be called via a Rsyn script. The command syntax mimics the GNU/Linux command line syntax. The parameters are divided into two types: positional and named. Positional parameters are assigned by their position and named parameters by their name. The command syntax is loosely defined as follows:

<command> [<value> ...] [-<param> <value> ...]

where <command> and <param> are any alfa-numeric identifier and <value> can be a number, string or JSON [23].

The JSON data type was chosen due to its flexibility and readability.

In Listing 2, a tiny Rsyn script is presented. Line 1 shows the call to start an Rsyn service while lines 2-5 and 6-9 show two calls to optimization flows and their user-defined parameters. Line 10 presents a call to a circuit report with some parameters.

2.4 Graphical User Interface (GUI)

A modular GUI is provided by the Rsyn framework to aid users to develop, improve, debug and better understand synthesis algorithms. It also has a great impact as an educational tool and in the engagement of students in EDA subjects. In Figure 3, a screen shot of the Rsyn's GUI is presented.

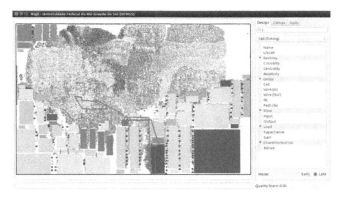

Figure 3: Graphical User Interface of the Rsyn framework showing Superblue18 circuit

The GUI is built using wxWidgets [45] and OpenGL [27] and can be compiled independently of the non-graphical functionalities. The GUI is extended via *overlays*, which can be loaded on demand to present visual data for a new feature (e.g. service).

The main overlay is the one responsible for presenting physical information of the design including standard-cells, macro-blocks, timing paths, and so forth. The circuit elements may be drawn and colorized by user-defined requirements and metrics, such as: criticality (e.g. slack), physical cell type (e.g. combinational, sequential), and so forth.

The property list on the right presents physical and timing information. These fields automatically show cell's data when it is selected. The command line shell location is at the bottom. There the user can issue any registered command in the engine.

2.5 Sandbox

Sandboxes allow creating a draft design that can be optimized independently of the main design. Once the optimization is finished, the changes can be committed. Sandboxes can be created from scratch or directly from a subset of elements of the design, as shown in Figure 4.

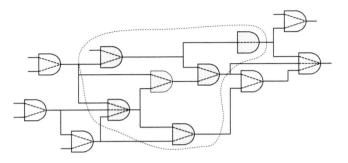

Figure 4: A sandbox extracted from the main design.

A sandbox provides similar API as a module from where instances can be created and connected via nets. However, it does not support hierarchy. Usually, sandbox represents a small design, and hence its implementation can take advantage of the reduced number of elements to improve efficiency.

3. STANDARD COMPONENTS

Section 2 highlighted the basic infrastructure to work and extend the Rsyn framework while this section presents several services, processes, and other standalone components already implemented. These are the parts that transform Rsyn from a simple netlist data model into a powerful framework to research physical synthesis and optimization methods.

3.1 Physical Design

The *physical design* comprises geometric information about the circuit layout and the technology, as illustrated in Figure 5. Physical design is responsible to aggregate and associate physical layout data to the attributes of the logic netlist. Moreover, the physical design also provides user-defined attributes mapped to the remaining layout elements (e.g. row, obstacle, die boundaries) and to the fabrication technology components. The notification system of the physical design alerts registered observers about third-party modification in the observed physical data. The hierarchical organization of physical design is inspired by the architecture of LEF and DEF formats.

3.2 Routing Estimation

The standard *routing estimation service* provides a way to estimate the physical interconnection among the pins of a net. Given a net, this service generates a Resistance–Capacitance (RC) tree as shown in Figure 6. Consequently, timing analysis, wire length estimation and congesting prediction may use the estimated tree.

Currently, the routing estimation service relies on a *routing estimation model* to generate the interconnection. This separation between the routing estimator and the routing model allows using different methodologies during a flow or

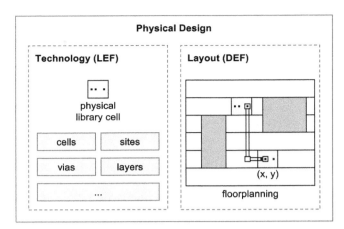

Figure 5: Schematic of the Physical Design Infrastructure. The physical design manages data of the circuit and the fabrication technology.

research project without requiring any additional changes to the service.

The default routing model integrated into Rsyn generates Steiner trees to estimate the interconnection. The Steiner tree is then translated to an RC tree using resistance and capacitance information from metal layers. The physical design service supplies the pin positions.

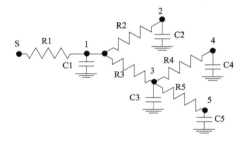

Figure 6: Routing Estimated RC tree.

3.3 Timing Analysis

Static Timing Analysis (STA) is essential to assert the performance of a design and to guide the optimization of a synthesis flow. It is extensively used in several steps and hence requires to be flexible and efficient.

The timer embedded in the Rsyn framework has the common functionality required by any STA tool, calculating the Total Negative Slack (TNS), Worst Negative Slack (WNS), arrival and required time at each pin and their slack, delay of the timing arcs and tracing the critical path. The timing propagation may be estimated for early, and late modes and the analysis is performed incrementally (i.e. only the elements that need the update are updated). Currently, the timer supports only one timing domain.

Similar to the routing estimation service, the timing analysis is independent of a *timing model*. Specific timing models can be used at different steps according to the availability of more accurate routing or sizing information for instance. Combined with the separation of routing and routing model estimation, it provides a flexible scheme for the algorithm development avoid code rewriting. The high-level organization of the timer is outlined in Figure 7.

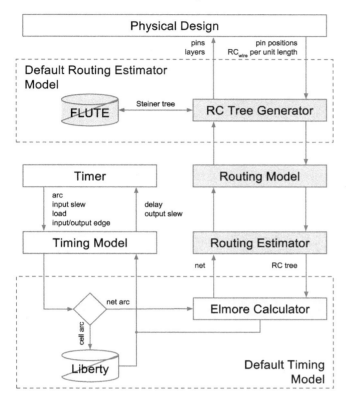

Figure 7: Timing analysis and routing estimator infrastructure.

Currently, the default timing model implemented in Rsyn is based on Elmore [6] delay following the guidelines presented in the ICCAD 15 contest. The default timing model uses the RC tree generated by the default routing estimator and cell characterization information obtained from a Liberty file.

3.4 Standard-Cell Library Characterization

Rsyn framework provides a simple *library characterization service* to compute the driver resistance and logical effort [38] of standard-cell timing arcs. Library characterization is performed by sampling the delay of the timing arc at different capacitance loads and estimating the delay via least squares regression as shown in Figure 8.

The drive resistance provides a linearized timing model, which is useful for analytical optimization algorithms. The drive resistance can also be used to sort cells by their drive strength and reduce the number of candidates for a gate-sizing algorithm, for instance.

3.5 Standard-Cell Legalization

Jezz legalizer [31] provides standard-cell legalization for minimum cell displacement based on Abacus [37]. It supports cell legality evaluation, to legalize cells in full and incremental modes, and cell legalization subject to maximum displacement. Jezz features are available in Rsyn framework via the service or process call systems.

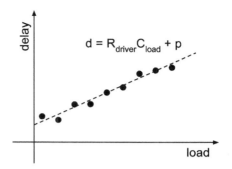

Figure 8: Driver Resistance Computation

3.6 Utilities

The utilities are features inside of Rsyn framework that provide shared resources to any element of the framework. The main idea of utilities is to abstract and encapsulate simple and very common required operations that are systematically performed inside of Rsyn components. A simple example is to compute the boundary area for the physical elements. There are several similar operations that are frequently used and are required in practically all the framework. The utilities may also be used to pass complex data, like boundaries definition, between independent Rsyn elements. The most relevant utilities already available in the framework are the following: colorize the design based on a user-defined metrics; customized step and stopwatches; command line parser; execution logger; float point comparator; definitions and operations for polygons and rectangles; and Cartesian point.

3.7 Third Party Software

Rsyn framework integrates a set of third party projects. They provide several features to the Rsyn framework. Below it is shortly described their main features. FLUTE [4] is an algorithm to build Steiner tree topologies that may be used to estimate routing. NCTUgr [22] is a global router tool. LEF and DEF [19] are parsers to recover data of the fabrication technology and circuit layout, respectively. Liberty [28] is a parser to recover timing and power information of the cell library from the Liberty files. JSON for Modern C++ [23] (Json) is a JavaScript Object Notation parser. Json scripts control the initialization of parameters and execution order for algorithms and flow. LEMON [20] is a graph library with a focus on combinatorial optimization mainly linked to graphs and networks. CPLEX [5] is a solver to mixed integer linear programming.

4. EXPERIMENTAL VALIDATION

Rsyn was created to fulfil the need to have a stable and versatile infrastructure upon which our research projects and contest tools could be developed. It was motivated to cope with our frustration of having to spend more time coding for infrastructure rather than optimization. Although our research group had been very successful in recent EDA contests, it was clear that the infrastructure developed for one contest was too tied to the contest problem and was not easily adapted to other contest or research projects.

So, after participating in the ICCAD 2014 Incremental Timing-Driven Placement Contest [18], we started to aggregate and refactor several years worth of coding into the Rsyn framework. The goals were to create a platform where all physical design related projects could be developed and that would grow incrementally to form a full academic design flow. The framework should be intuitive to improve code readability and allow fast prototyping of ideas, ultimately freeing researchers to focus on the core of the research project.

In this section, we explore some usages of Rsyn framework in our research projects, which already show the benefits of having such framework.

4.1 ICCAD 2015 Contest

The 2015's edition of the ICCAD contest [17] served as an opportunity to consolidate the new framework while developing the desired algorithms. The development and enhancement of the Rsyn framework overlapped with the development of our research on incremental timing-driven placement, which turned out to be a win-win relation. While using Rsyn as the platform for the optimization algorithms, several bugs were found and fixed, and new features were implemented. It became easier to enhance our research projects while consolidating the Rsyn framework.

We conceived a total of 9 analytical techniques to mitigate both early and late timing violations which will be released as default optimization methods of Rsyn. The techniques to mitigate early timing violation rely on useful clock skew, iterative cell spreading, register swaps and register-to-register path fix. In late timing violation, techniques go through clustered movements (based on [2]) and single cell movements aiming to reduce the load capacitance in the critical nets, and balance driver load capacitance based on the cells drive strength. Furthermore, moving non-critical cells away from over-utilized regions minimizes area utilization overflow. The large number of different techniques implemented was directly related to the flexibility to try new ideas provided by Rsyn.

The techniques were integrated into the flow depicted in Fig. 9. A diamond shape indicates that the steps run until the quality of the result stops improving while the circle shape means that the quality of the result may degrade a certain number of times before exiting. The flow produces the best-known results for the ICCAD 2015 contest infrastructure, reducing on average the late WNS slack by 11% and the late TNS by 33% w.r.t. the initial placement solution. This Timing-driven placement flow completely removes early timing violation on 62.5% of the benchmarks. For more details about the techniques, please refer to [7].

4.2 Routing-Aware Incremental Timing-Driven Placement

We have also extended our previous work [7] to avoid cell movement towards to routing bins that have routing overflow violation. Therefore, this flow mitigates early and late timing violations aware of routing congestion regions. Moreover, Rsyn infrastructure was extended to support routing data and a third party router. The 2016 IEEE Computer Society Annual Symposium on VLSI (ISVLSI) paper [24] addresses the proposed Routing-Aware Incremental Timing-Driven Placement flow.

This project shows how Rsyn can be enhanced incrementally. Although the congestion infrastructure still needed to

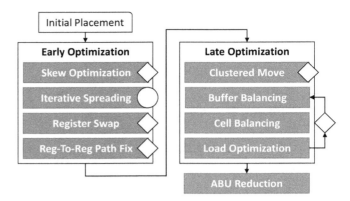

Figure 9: Our timing-driven flow

be developed, it is now part of the Rsyn framework being available to other projects.

4.3 Incremental Timing-Driven Quadratic Placement

One drawback of the proposed flow in [7] is the absence of global timing-driven placement techniques. The clustered cell movement is the only technique that moves more than one cell at the same time, and yet the limit of cells per cluster and the search area are small. To cope with that, we proposed an incremental quadratic formulation for timing-driven placement.

Quadratic formulations have been explored for global wirelength-driven placement [42, 21] and timing-driven placement [43, 34]. However, the existing techniques are purely constructive, i.e., do not consider previous solutions, a behavior which is not desired during incremental placement. In [8] a method is proposed to apply quadratic placement incrementally, which is called neutralization.

Figure 10 presents the key ideas of such technique. The original netlist (Fig. 10(a)) is transformed into a graph using the methodologies presented in [42] (Fig. 10(b)). Neutralization forces are added to avoid a major disturbance in the initial solution (Fig. 10(c)) and the critical paths are identified (Fig. 10(d)). Then extra edges are added between nodes of the critical path (Fig. 10) making the quadratic placement align the critical paths. The weights of these edges are set to address Elmore delay [6], which is another contribution of that work. Applying this formulation jointly with the flow presented in Section 4.1 improves the results, on average, by 9.4% and 7.6% regarding WNS and TNS, respectively.

In this project, we already could take advantage of the infrastructure implemented inside Rsyn, finally being able to fully focus on the optimization process. Many analysis and experimentation tasks were done exploring much of the infrastructure provided by Rsyn, such as critical path tracing, legalization and visualization.

5. RELATED WORKS

One of the most traditional open source projects among EDA community is ABC [1] from Berkley University. ABC is a logic synthesis and verification environment on which users may rely on user-friendly and flexible data structures. Just like Rsyn, ABC aims to support different applications. The project is consolidated, providing implementations of

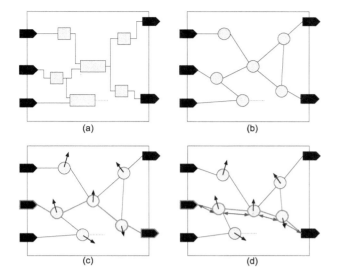

Figure 10: Incremental timing-driven quadratic placement strategy.The neutralization forces are drawn as the black single-edged arrows, the critical path as the bold red line and the additional forces as the double-edged blue arrows.

many state-of-art algorithms and support for many industrial and academic file formats [1].

Another open project on synthesis is Yosys [44], which translates Verilog code to an equivalent netlist, supporting both Application-Specific Integrated Circuit (ASIC) and Field-Programmable Gate Array (FPGA) flows. One of the Yosys goals is to make up for the lack of the extensibility of commercial synthesis tools. It features flexible data structures and tools for coarse grain synthesis. ABC is integrated into Yosys flow to perform logic minimization and technology mapping. Yosys is available on GitHub licensed under Internet Systems Consortium (ISC) license [16]. Once Rsyn and Yosys are both open sources and collaborative tools, a middleware could be build using both projects to provide logic and physical design.

OpenTimer [14] is an open-source tool for static timing analysis, winner of three awards in TAU contests [12, 11]. It implements a scheduler that aids to perform different tasks in parallel, achieving a runtime ten times smaller than other academic tools. Other features include Common Path Pessimism Removal (CPPR) and a fast incremental timing analysis. OpenTimer code is available on its website [13] under a General Public License (GPL) license [9]. Unfortunately, it is outside of any control version repository for the EDA community to share its contributions to the project. However, since OpenTimer is an accurate and fast academic tool, it may be integrated as part of Rsyn tools and repository and extended according to the community needs.

Parsing tools may compose the largest group of the available open projects. We highlight Icarus Verilog [15] for Hardware Description Language (HDL), Liberty Parser [28] for standard cell libraries and OpenAcess [26]. The OpenAccess is a C++ API that provides a solution for the wide range of complex file formats and syntax present today in the commercial design flow, such as LEF/DEF. Its source code is open, so the industry and academic community may

propose extensions. By adopting an open and verified API, the EDA engineers may avoid coding their parsers, leading to fewer errors in the design flow.

Until now, we addressed only individual tools. Qflow [32] proposes an entirely open source design flow, from Verilog description to physical layout. It takes advantage of other academic tools, like Yosys [44] for Verilog parsing, Graywolf [10] for placement and Qrouter [33] for detailed routing. The authors claim that small commercial circuits were already designed using Qflow and highlight that small startups which cannot afford commercial tools may take advantage of the design flow.

Ophidian [29] is an open source project focused on research and teaching to physical synthesis. However, the project has only support to parsing few types of circuit files, netlist, and placement.

We believe there is a wide space for projects like ABC and Yosys on the physical design domain. Since nowadays there is no open framework addressing physical design where EDA developers may share their implementations. Rsyn fits this task and it goes further providing tools to report results (e.g. graphics) and a user interface to aid in the debugging process.

6. CONCLUSION

This paper presented Rsyn, an open-source framework that provides a versatile and modular infrastructure for physical synthesis research. Rsyn is designed to be extended incrementally and already contains several components that allow researchers to focus on the core of the research project rather than on the infrastructure to support it. Rsyn provides a standard and collaborative platform to share implementations, optimization techniques and code reuse.

With Rsyn, we intend to build a comprehensive, but intuitive physical design environment where the EDA community can develop and analyze new techniques. Rsyn also aims at getting more students interested in EDA research by allowing a better interaction with optimization algorithms.

Our current experience with the framework, already shows its potential to increase productivity. Rsyn allowed us to enhance our current results and explore different research topics much faster than what would be possible without it.

Acknowledgments

This work is partially supported by Brazilian Coordination for the Improvement of Higher Education Personnel (CAPES) and by the National Council for Scientific and Technological Development (CNPq).

7. REFERENCES

[1] Berkeley Logic Synthesis and Verification Group, ABC: A System for Sequential Synthesis and Verification.
http://www.eecs.berkeley.edu/~alanmi/abc/.

[2] A. Bock, S. Held, N. Kammerling, and U. Schorr. Local search algorithms for timing-driven placement under arbitrary delay models. In *DAC*, pages 1–6, June 2015.

[3] Bookshelf. http://vlsicad.eecs.umich.edu/BK/ISPD06bench/BookshelfFormat.txt.

[4] C. Chu and Y. C. Wong. Flute: Fast lookup table based rectilinear steiner minimal tree algorithm for vlsi design. *TCAD*, 27(1):70–83, Jan 2008.

[5] Cplex. http://www-03.ibm.com/software/products/en/ibmilogcpleoptistud/.

[6] W. C. Elmore. The Transient Response of Damped Linear Networks with Particular Regard to Wideband Amplifiers. *Journal of Applied Physics*, 19(1):55–63, 1948.

[7] G. Flach, M. Fogaça, J. Monteiro, M. Johann, and R. Reis. Drive strength aware cell movement techniques for timing driven placement. In *ISPD*, 2016.

[8] M. Fogaça, G. Flach, J. Monteiro, M. Johann, and R. Reis. Quadratic timing objectives for incremental timing-driven placement optimization. In *ICECS*, 2016.

[9] Gnu general public license. https://www.gnu.org/licenses/gpl-3.0.en.html.

[10] Graywolf. https://github.com/rubund/graywolf.

[11] J. Hu, G. Schaeffer, and V. Garg. Tau 2015 contest on incremental timing analysis. In *ICCAD*, pages 882–889, Nov 2015.

[12] J. Hu, D. Sinha, and I. Keller. Tau 2014 contest on removing common path pessimism during timing analysis: Special session paper: Common path pessimism removal (cppr). In *ICCAD*, pages 591–591, Nov 2014.

[13] T.-W. Huang and M. D. F. Wong. Opentimer: An open-source high-performance timing analysis tool. https://web.engr.illinois.edu/~thuang19/software/timer/OpenTimer.html.

[14] T.-W. Huang and M. D. F. Wong. Opentimer: A high-performance timing analysis tool. In *ICCAD*, ICCAD '15, pages 895–902, Piscataway, NJ, USA, 2015. IEEE Press.

[15] Icarus verilog. http://iverilog.icarus.com/.

[16] Isc license (isc). https://opensource.org/licenses/ISC.

[17] M.-C. Kim, J. Hu, J. Li, and N. Viswanathan. Iccad-2015 cad contest in incremental timing-driven placement and benchmark suite. In *ICCAD*, ICCAD '15, pages 921–926, Piscataway, NJ, USA, 2015. IEEE Press.

[18] M.-C. Kim, J. Hu, and N. Viswanathan. Iccad-2014 cad contest in incremental timing-driven placement and benchmark suite. In *ICCAD*, ICCAD '14, pages 361–366, Piscataway, NJ, USA, 2014. IEEE Press.

[19] Lef/def. http://www.si2.org/. 2016-11-21.

[20] Library for efficient modeling and optimization in networks (lemon). https://lemon.cs.elte.hu/trac/lemon.

[21] T. Lin, C. Chu, J. R. Shinnerl, I. Bustany, and I. Nedelchev. POLAR: Placement based on novel rough legalization and refinement. In *ICCAD*, Nov 2013.

[22] W. H. Liu, W. C. Kao, Y. L. Li, and K. Y. Chao. Nctu-gr 2.0: Multithreaded collision-aware global routing with bounded-length maze routing. *TCAD*, 32(5):709–722, May 2013.

[23] N. Lohmann. Json. https://github.com/nlohmann/json. 2016-11-21.

[24] J. Monteiro, N. K. Darav, G. Flach, M. Fogaça, R. Reis, A. Kennings, M. Johann, and L. Behjat. Routing-aware incremental timing-driven placement. In *ISVLSI*, pages 290–295, July 2016.

[25] G.-J. Nam. Ispd 2006 placement contest: Benchmark suite and results. In *ISPD*, ISPD '06, pages 167–167, New York, NY, USA, 2006. ACM.

[26] Openaccess coalition. https://projects.si2.org/oac_index.php.

[27] Opengl. https://www.opengl.org/. 2016-11-21.

[28] Open source liberty. http://www.opensourceliberty.org/.

[29] Ophidian - open-source library for physical design research and teaching. https://github.com/eclufsc/ophidian.

[30] M. M. Ozdal, C. Amin, A. Ayupov, S. M. Burns, G. R. Wilke, and C. Zhuo. An improved benchmark suite for the ispd-2013 discrete cell sizing contest. In *ISPD*, ISPD '13, pages 168–170, New York, NY, USA, 2013. ACM.

[31] J. C. Puget, G. Flach, R. Reis, and M. Johann. Jezz: An effective legalization algorithm for minimum displacement. In *SBCCI*, pages 1–5, Aug 2015.

[32] Qflow. http://opencircuitdesign.com/qflow/.

[33] Qrouter. http://opencircuitdesign.com/qrouter/.

[34] B. M. Riess and G. G. Ettelt. SPEED: fast and efficient timing driven placement. In *ISCAS*, volume 1, 1995.

[35] Rsyn. http://rsyn.design.

[36] D. Sinha, L. Guerra e Silva, J. Wang, S. Raghunathan, D. Netrabile, and A. Shebaita. Tau 2013 variation aware timing analysis contest. In *ISPD*, ISPD '13, pages 171–178, New York, NY, USA, 2013. ACM.

[37] P. Spindler, U. Schlichtmann, and F. M. Johannes. Abacus: Fast legalization of standard cell circuits with minimal movement. In *ISPD*, ISPD '08, pages 47–53, New York, NY, USA, 2008. ACM.

[38] I. Sutherland, B. Sproull, and D. Harris. *Logical Effort: Designing Fast CMOS Circuits*. Morgan Kaufmann Publishers Inc., San Francisco, CA, USA, 1999.

[39] C. N. Sze, P. Restle, G.-J. Nam, and C. Alpert. Ispd2009 clock network synthesis contest. In *ISPD*, ISPD '09, pages 149–150, New York, NY, USA, 2009. ACM.

[40] Ieee standard verilog hardware description language. *IEEE Std 1364-2001*, pages 01–856, 2001.

[41] N. Viswanathan, C. Alpert, C. Sze, Z. Li, and Y. Wei. Iccad-2012 cad contest in design hierarchy aware routability-driven placement and benchmark suite. In *ICCAD*, pages 345–348, Nov 2012.

[42] N. Viswanathan and C. C. N. Chu. FastPlace: efficient analytical placement using cell shifting, iterative local refinement,and a hybrid net model. *TCAD*, 24, 2005.

[43] N. Viswanathan, G.-J. Nam, J. A. Roy, Z. Li, C. J. Alpert, S. Ramji, and C. Chu. ITOP: Integrating Timing Optimization Within Placement. In *ISPD*. ACM, 2010.

[44] C. Wolf. Yosys open synthesis suite. http://www.clifford.at/yosys/.

[45] wxwidgets. http://www.wxwidgets.org/. 2016-11-21.

Research Challenges in Security-aware Physical Design

Ramesh Karri
NYU Tandon School of Engineering
New York, New York
rkarri@nyu.edu

ABSTRACT

The presentation will discuss security techniques such as IC camouflaging and logic encryption.

Author Keywords: Hardware security

BIOGRAPHY

Ramesh Karri is a Professor of Electrical and Computer Engineering at New York University Polytechnic School of Engineering. He has a Ph.D. in Computer Science and Engineering from the University of California at San Diego. His research interests include trustworthy hardware (integrated circuits to processor architectures); High assurance nanoscale integrated circuits, architectures, and systems; VLSI Design and Test; Interaction between security and reliability.

He has over 190 journal and conference publications. He has written two invited articles in IEEE Computer on Trustworthy Hardware, an invited article on Digital Logic Design using Memristors in Proceedings of IEEE and an Invited article in IEEE Computer on Reliable Nanoscale Systems.

He is the recipient of the Humboldt Fellowship and the National Science Foundation CAREER Award. He is the area director for cyber security of the NY State Center for Advanced Telecommunications Technologies at NYU School of Engineering; Hardware security lead of the NYU Center for CyberSecurity - CCS, co-founder of the Trust-Hub and organizes the annual red team blue team event at NYU, the Embedded Systems Security Challenge.

He co-founded and served as the chair of the IEEE Computer Society Technical Committee on Nanoscale architectures. He co-founded and serves on the steering committee of the IEEE/ACM Symposium on Nanoscale Architectures (NANOARCH). He served as the Program Chair and General Chair of several conferences including IEEE Symposium on Hardware Oriented Security and Trust (HOST), IEEE Symposium on Defect and Fault Tolerant Nano VLSI Systems, IEEE/ACM NANOARCH. He serves on several program committees including DAC, VTS, ICCD, HOST, DFT, DTIS, and NANOARCH. He is the Associate Editor of IEEE Transactions on Information Forensics and Security, IEEE Transactions on CAD, and ACM Journal of Emerging Technologies in Computing. He is a IEEE Computer Society Distinguished Visitor 2013-2014.

He organized/delivered invited tutorials on Trustworthy Hardware (including 2012 IEEE VLSI Test Symposium 2012, IEEE International Conference on Computer Design 2012, IEEE North Atlantic Test Workshop 2013, Design Automation and Test in Europe 2013, IEEE International Test Conference 2013, IEEE Latin American Test Workshop 2014, IEEE/ACM Design Automation Conference 2014, and IEEE).

ISPD'17, March 19–22, 2017, Portland, OR, USA.
ACM. ISBN 978-1-4503-4696-2/17/03.
http://dx.doi.org/10.1145/3036669.3051456

Challenges and Opportunities: From Near-memory Computing to In-memory Computing

Soroosh Khoram, Yue Zha, Jialiang Zhang, Jing Li

Department of Electrical and Computer Engineering
University of Wisconsin-Madison

{khoram, yzha3}@wisc.edu, {jialiang.zhang,jli}@ece.wisc.edu

ABSTRACT

The confluence of the recent advances in technology and the ever-growing demand for large-scale data analytics created a renewed interest in a decades-old concept, processing-in-memory (PIM). PIM, in general, may cover a very wide spectrum of compute capabilities embedded *in close proximity to* or even *inside* the memory array. In this paper, we present an initial taxonomy for dividing PIM into two broad categories: 1) Near-memory processing and 2) In-memory processing. This paper highlights some interesting work in each category and provides insights into the challenges and possible future directions.

Keywords

In-memory processing; Near-memory processing; Nonvolatile Memory; 3D Integration

1. INTRODUCTION

The rapid explosion in data, while creating opportunities for new discoveries, is also posing unprecedented demand for computing capability to handle the ever-growing data volume, velocity, variety and veracity (also known as *"four V"*), from ubiquitous and networked devices to the warehouse-scale computers [1]. As the traditional benefits for expanding the processing capability of computers through technology scaling has diminished with the end of Dennard scaling, limitations in traditional compute system, also known as "Memory Wall" [2] and "Power Wall" [3] are being outpaced by the growth of Big Data to the point where a new paradigm is needed.

As such, processing in memory (PIM), a decades-old concept, has reignited interest among industry and academic communities, largely driven by the recent advances in technology (e.g., die stacking, emerging nonvolatile memory) and the ever-growing demand for large-scale data analytics. In this paper, we classify the existing PIM work into two broad categories: 1) near-memory processing (NMP) and 2) in-memory processing (IMP). In the following sections, we will present an overview of research progress on both types.

ISPD '17, March 19–22, 2017, Portland, OR, USA.

© 2017 ACM. ISBN 978-1-4503-4696-2/17/03. . . $15.00

DOI: http://dx.doi.org/3036669.3038242

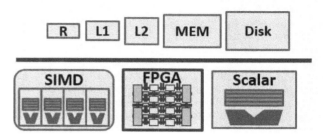

Figure 1: Conceptual diagram of Near-Memory Processing (NMP). Monolithic compute unit (multi-core, vector unit, GPU, FPGA, CGRA, ASIC etc.) are placed in close proximity to monolithic memory.

2. NEAR-MEMORY PROCESSING

The first category of PIM is near-memory processing (NMP). The underlying principle of NMP, as shown in Figure 1, is *processing in proximity of memory* – by physically placing monolithic compute units (multi-core, GPU, FPGA, ASIC, CGRA etc.) closer to monolithic memory – to minimize data transfer cost.

The original idea of implementing this type of PIM dates back to early 1990's. Since then, there has been great interest in the potential of integrating compute capabilities in large DRAM memories. Multiple research teams built NMP designs and prototypes, and confirmed speed-up in a range of applications [4, 5, 6, 7, 8, 9, 10]. Among them, EXECUBE [4], IRAM [5, 6], DIVA[7], FlexRAM[8] etc. are the representative early proposals. However, the implementation of NMP experienced great challenges in cost and manufacturability. Therefore, even with great potentials, the concept of NMP has never been embraced commercially in the early days.

Nevertheless, the practicality concerns and cost limitations of NMP are alleviated with recent advances in die-stacking technology [11, 12, 13]. Several specialized NMP systems were developed for important domains of applications [14, 15, 16, 17, 18, 19, 20]. In addition, advanced memory modules such as Hybrid Memory Cube (HMC)[21], High Bandwidth Memory (HBM) [22] and Bandwidth Engine (BE2)[23] have been developed by major memory vendors and made their commercial success. For instance, HMC that stacks multiple DRAM dies on top of a CMOS logic layer using through-silicon-via (TSV) technology effectively addressed the previous limitations of implementing NMP. HMC not only provides much better random access performance compared to traditional DDR DRAM due to its higher memory-level parallelism [2], but also supports near-memory operations, such as read-modify-write, locking, etc., on the base logic layer, making it possible for accelerating these operations near memory.

At UW-Madison, our research group was trying to understand what an NMP computer architecture might entail by combining the flexibility of modern FPGA with emerging memory module, i.e. HMC. Our initial efforts are on understanding the needs of the driving applications for HMC and developing collaborative software/ hardware techniques for efficient algorithmic mapping. In particular, we demonstrated the very first near-memory graph processing system on a real FPGA-HMC platform based on software/hardware co-design and co-optimization. The work aimed to tackle a challenging problem in processing large-scale sparse graphs, which have been broadly applied in a wide range of applications from machine learning to social science but are inherently difficult to process efficiently. It is not only due to their large memory footprint, but also that most graph algorithms entail memory access patterns with poor locality and a low compute-to-memory access ratio. To address these challenges, we leveraged the exceptional random access performance of HMC technology combined with the flexibility and efficiency of FPGA. A series of innovations were applied, including new data structure/algorithm and a platform-aware graph processing architecture. Our implementation achieved 166 million edges traversed per second (MTEPS) using GRAPH500 benchmark on a random graph with a scale of 25 and an edge factor of 16, which significantly outperforms CPU and other FPGA-based graph processors.

In another project, we tackled the challenge from a different angle. In particular, we demonstrated a high-performance near-memory OpenCL-based FPGA accelerator for deep learning. We applied a combination of theoretical and experimental approaches. Based on a comprehensive analysis, we identified that the key performance bottleneck is the on-chip memory bandwidth, largely due to the scarce memory resources in modern FPGA and the memory duplication policy in current OpenCL execution model. We proposed a new kernel design to effectively address such limitation and achieved substantially improved memory utilization, which further results in a balanced data-flow between computation, on-chip, and off-chip memory access. We implemented our design on an Altera Arria 10 GX1150 board and achieved 866 Gop/s floating point performance at 370MHz working frequency and 1.79 Top/s 16-bit fixed-point performance at 385MHz. To the best of our knowledge, our implementation achieves the best power efficiency and performance density compared to existing work.

3. IN-MEMORY PROCESSING

In-memory processing (IMP), as the second category of PIM, grew out of NMP from *processing in proximity of memory* to *processing inside memory* which seamlessly embeds computation in memory array, as depicted in Figure 2. As the compute units become more tightly coupled with memory, one can exploit more fine-grained parallelism for better performance and energy efficiency. In this section, we present the enabling technology for IMP and the exploratory IMP architectures.

Technology: The last decade has seen significant progress in emerging nonvolatile memory technologies (NVMs) in-

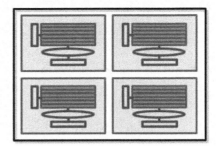

In Memory Processing (IMP)

Figure 2: Conceptual diagram of In-Memory Processing (IMP). Compute units are seamlessly embedded into memory array to better exploit the internal memory bandwidth.

cluding Spin Torque Transfer RAM (STT RAM)[24], phase change memory (PCM)[25] and resistive RAM (RRAM)[26]. Until now, the key industry players have all demonstrated Gb-scale capacity in advanced technology nodes, including 1Gb PCM at 45nm by Micron [27], 8Gb PCM at 20nm by Samsung [28], 32Gb RRAM at 24nm by Toshiba/Sandisk [29], 16Gb conductive bridge (CBRAM, a special type of RRAM) at 27nm by Micron/Sony [30], and most recently 128Gb 3D XPoint technology by Micron/Intel [31].

Even with successful commercialization, the insertion of these technologies to exiting computer systems as a direct drop-in replacement turns out not being effective. The fundamental reasons for that are 1) Technically, the inherent nature of these technologies does not align well with either main memory or persistent storage in terms of cost-per-bit, latency, power, endurance, and retention. 2) Economically, besides more investment to existing memory manufacturing facilities for producing these new technologies, it is difficult to convince end-users to switch to a new technology as long as they can still use DRAM or Flash for the same purpose, unless significant benefits are provided. Therefore, it is challenging for any of the emerging NVMs to take over the dominant mature market of DRAM or Flash. However, we envision that to enable a wide adoption of these NVM technologies, a potentially viable path is to explore non-traditional usage models or new paradigms beyond traditional memory applications, for instance, IMP. We believe that the emerging NVMs will become an enabling technology for IMP.

Architecture: The exploratory IMP architectures reported in literature can be further divided into the several types: **1)** One type is to utilize the inherent dot-product capability of the crossbar structure to accelerate matrix multiplication, which is a key computational kernel in a wide array of applications including deep learning, optimization, etc. Representative work includes PRIME [32], ISAAC [8], and memristive boltzmann machine [33]. By augmenting RRAM crossbar design with various digital or analog circuits in the periphery, these architectures can realize different accelerator functions that are built atop matrix multiplication. **2)** Another type is to implement a neuromorphic system, which exploits the analog nature of NVM array to implement synaptic network in order to mimic the fuzzy, fault-tolerant and stochastic computation of the human brain, without sacrificing its space or energy efficiency

[8, 32, 34, 35]. **3)** The third type is associative processor (AP), also known as nonvolatile Content addressable memory (nv-CAM) or Ternary content addressable memory (nv-TCAM), which supports associative search to locate data records by content rather than address. We demonstrated the very first large-scale PCM TCAM chip and prove the feasibility of implementing in-memory processing using emerging NVM in a cost-effective manner. Other representative work includes RRAM-based TCAM [36], AC-DIMM [37], and RRAM-based associative processor [38]. **4)** The fourth type is reconfigurable architecture (RA). Representative work includes nonvolatile field programmable gate array (nv-FPGA [39, 40]) and reconfigurable in-memory computing architecture that combines the best advantages of TCAM and FPGA [41].

Both AP (Type-3) and RA (Type-4) show great promise in implementing the concept of in-memory processing without necessarily incurring high cost. Specifically, they do not need expensive mixed-signal circuits (A/D, D/A) as Type-1 and Type-2 and thus, their adoption barrier is lower than Type-1 and Type-2. However, all of these types need to address a common challenge in operational robustness due to the limited ON/OFF resistance ratio of NVM technologies (except for CBRAM), which can be mitigated by advanced material engineering [42], cell design [43, 44, 45], and coding technique [46].

Among all the work, we would like to specifically highlight an interesting reconfigurable in-memory computing architecture (Type-4) developed by us. It shares some similarities to FPGA in morphable data-flow architecture but also radically differs from it by providing: 1) flexible on-chip storage, 2) flexible routing resources, and 3) enhanced hardware security. For the first time, it exploits a continuum of IMP capabilities across the whole spectrum, ranging from 0% (pure data storage) to 100% (pure compute engine), or intermediate states in between (partial storage and partial computation). Such superior programmability blurs the boundary between computation and storage. We believe it may open up rich research opportunities in driving new reconfigurable architecture, design tools, and developing new data-intensive applications, which were not generally considered to be suitable for FPGA-like accelerations.

4. OTHER CHALLENGES

PIM, including both NMP and IMP, offers a promising approach to overcome the challenges posed by emerging data-intensive applications. In our view, NMP has a relatively low adoption barrier than IMP, as there is no need to change the internal memory architecture, whereas IMP fully exploits the internal memory bandwidth to achieve more parallelism.

To make NMP or IMP practically viable, there are other challenges that need to be addressed, including virtual memory support to ensure a unified address space, memory/cache coherence, fault tolerance, security and privacy, thermal and power constraints, compatibility with modern programming models, etc.. All of them will require collaborative efforts between technologies, IC designers and system engineers.

5. REFERENCES

[1] Ling Liu. Computing infrastructure for big data processing. volume 7, pages 165–170, 2013.

[2] Wm. A. Wulf and Sally A. McKee. Hitting the memory wall: Implications of the obvious. *SIGARCH Comput. Archit. News*, 23(1):20–24, March 1995.

[3] T. Kuroda. Low-power, high-speed cmos vlsi design. pages 310–315, 2002.

[4] Peter M. Kogge. Execube-a new architecture for scaleable mpps. In *Proceedings of the 1994 International Conference on Parallel Processing - Volume 01*, ICPP '94, pages 77–84. IEEE Computer Society, 1994.

[5] David Patterson, Thomas Anderson, Neal Cardwell, et al. A case for intelligent ram. *IEEE Micro*, 17(2):34–44, March 1997.

[6] D. Patterson, T. Anderson, N. Cardwell, et al. Intelligent ram (iram): chips that remember and compute. In *1997 IEEE International Solids-State Circuits Conference. Digest of Technical Papers*, pages 224–225, Feb 1997.

[7] Mary Hall, Peter Kogge, Jeff Koller, et al. Mapping irregular applications to diva, a pim-based data-intensive architecture. In *Proceedings of the 1999 ACM/IEEE Conference on Supercomputing*, SC '99. ACM, 1999.

[8] J. Torrellas. Flexram: Toward an advanced intelligent memory system: A retrospective paper. In *2012 IEEE 30th International Conference on Computer Design (ICCD)*, pages 3–4, Sept 2012.

[9] D. G. Elliott, M. Stumm, W. M. Snelgrove, et al. Computational ram: implementing processors in memory. *IEEE Design Test of Computers*, 16(1):32–41, Jan 1999.

[10] K. Mai, T. Paaske, N. Jayasena, et al. Smart memories: a modular reconfigurable architecture. In *Proceedings of 27th International Symposium on Computer Architecture (IEEE Cat. No.RS00201)*, pages 161–171, June 2000.

[11] M. G. Farooq, T. L. Graves-Abe, W. F. Landers, et al. 3d copper tsv integration, testing and reliability. In *2011 International Electron Devices Meeting*, pages 7.1.1–7.1.4, Dec 2011.

[12] Y. Liu, W. Luk, and D. Friedman. A compact low-power 3d i/o in 45nm cmos. In *2012 IEEE International Solid-State Circuits Conference*, pages 142–144, Feb 2012.

[13] Antonis Papanikolaou, Dimitrios Soudris, and Riko Radojcic. *Three Dimensional System Integration: IC Stacking Process and Design*. Springer Publishing Company, Incorporated, 1st edition, 2010.

[14] R. Balasubramonian, J. Chang, T. Manning, et al. Near-data processing: Insights from a micro-46 workshop. *IEEE Micro*, 34(4):36–42, July 2014.

[15] Seth H Pugsley, Jeffrey Jestes, Huihui Zhang, et al. Ndc: Analyzing the impact of 3d-stacked memory+ logic devices on mapreduce workloads. In *Performance Analysis of Systems and Software (ISPASS), 2014 IEEE International Symposium on*, pages 190–200. IEEE, 2014.

[16] M. Wordeman, J. Silberman, G. Maier, et al. A 3d system prototype of an edram cache stacked over processor-like logic using through-silicon vias. In *2012 IEEE International Solid-State Circuits Conference*, pages 186–187, Feb 2012.

[17] Q. Zhu, B. Akin, H. E. Sumbul, et al. A 3d-stacked

logic-in-memory accelerator for application-specific data intensive computing. In *2013 IEEE International 3D Systems Integration Conference (3DIC)*, pages 1–7, Oct 2013.

[18] Q. Zhu, T. Graf, H. E. Sumbul, et al. Accelerating sparse matrix-matrix multiplication with 3d-stacked logic-in-memory hardware. In *2013 IEEE High Performance Extreme Computing Conference (HPEC)*, pages 1–6, Sept 2013.

[19] V. Seshadri, K. Hsieh, A. Boroum, et al. Fast bulk bitwise and and or in dram. *IEEE Computer Architecture Letters*, 14(2):127–131, July 2015.

[20] Vivek Seshadri, Yoongu Kim, Chris Fallin, et al. Rowclone: Fast and energy-efficient in-dram bulk data copy and initialization. In *Proceedings of the 46th Annual IEEE/ACM International Symposium on Microarchitecture*, MICRO-46, pages 185–197. ACM, 2013.

[21] J Thomas Pawlowski. Hybrid memory cube (hmc). In *IEEE Hot Chips*, 2011.

[22] D. U. Lee, K. W. Kim, K. W. Kim, et al. 25.2 a 1.2v 8gb 8-channel 128gb/s high-bandwidth memory (hbm) stacked dram with effective microbump i/o test methods using 29nm process and tsv. In *2014 IEEE International Solid-State Circuits Conference Digest of Technical Papers (ISSCC)*, pages 432–433, Feb 2014.

[23] M. J. Miller. Bandwidth engine 2; serial memory chip breaks 2 billion accesses/sec. In *2011 IEEE Hot Chips 23 Symposium (HCS)*, pages 1–23, Aug 2011.

[24] Weisheng Zhao et al. Spin transfer torque (stt)-mram–based runtime reconfiguration fpga circuit. *TECS*, 9(2):14, 2009.

[25] Benjamin C Lee et al. Architecting phase change memory as a scalable dram alternative. In *ACM SIGARCH Computer Architecture News*, volume 37, pages 2–13. ACM, 2009.

[26] H-S Philip Wong et al. Metal–oxide rram. *Proceedings of the IEEE*, 100(6):1951–1970, 2012.

[27] C. Villa, D. Mills, G. Barkley, et al. A 45nm 1gb 1.8v phase-change memory. In *2010 IEEE International Solid-State Circuits Conference - (ISSCC)*, pages 270–271, Feb 2010.

[28] Y. Choi, I. Song, M. H. Park, et al. A 20nm 1.8v 8gb pram with 40mb/s program bandwidth. In *2012 IEEE International Solid-State Circuits Conference*, pages 46–48, Feb 2012.

[29] T. Y. Liu, T. H. Yan, R. Scheuerlein, et al. A 130.7mm2 2-layer 32gb reram memory device in 24nm technology. In *2013 IEEE International Solid-State Circuits Conference Digest of Technical Papers*, pages 210–211, Feb 2013.

[30] M. Adams. 2015 winter analyst conference, 2 2015. Micron Technology, Inc.

[31] Micron Technology, Inc. Breakthrough Nonvolatile Memory Technology. http://www.micron.com/about/innovations/3d-xpoint-technology. Accessed: 2015-10-30.

[32] Natalie Enright Jerger, Li-Shiuan Peh, and Mikko Lipasti. Virtual circuit tree multicasting: A case for on-chip hardware multicast support. volume 36, pages 229–240. ACM, June 2008.

[33] G. Khodabandehloo, M. Mirhassani, and M. Ahmadi. Analog implementation of a novel resistive-type sigmoidal neuron. *IEEE Transactions on Very Large Scale Integration (VLSI) Systems*, 20(4):750–754, April 2012.

[34] Yu Wang, Tianqi Tang, Lixue Xia, et al. Energy efficient rram spiking neural network for real time classification. In *Proceedings of the 25th Edition on Great Lakes Symposium on VLSI*, GLSVLSI '15, pages 189–194. ACM, 2015.

[35] Chenchen Liu, Bonan Yan, Chaofei Yang, et al. A spiking neuromorphic design with resistive crossbar. In *Proceedings of the 52Nd Annual Design Automation Conference*, DAC '15, pages 14:1–14:6. ACM, 2015.

[36] Qing Guo, Xiaochen Guo, Yuxin Bai, et al. A resistive tcam accelerator for data-intensive computing. In *Proceedings of the 44th Annual IEEE/ACM International Symposium on Microarchitecture*, MICRO-44, pages 339–350. ACM, 2011.

[37] Qing Guo, Xiaochen Guo, Ravi Patel, et al. Ac-dimm: associative computing with stt-mram. In *ACM SIGARCH Computer Architecture News*, volume 41, pages 189–200. ACM, 2013.

[38] L. Yavits, S. Kvatinsky, A. Morad, et al. Resistive associative processor. *IEEE Computer Architecture Letters*, 14(2):148–151, July 2015.

[39] Y. Tsuji, X. Bai, A. Morioka, et al. A 2x logic density programmable logic array using atom switch fully implemented with logic transistors at 40nm-node and beyond. In *2016 IEEE Symposium on VLSI Circuits (VLSI-Circuits)*, pages 1–2, June 2016.

[40] Jason Cong and Bingjun Xiao. Fpga-rpi: A novel fpga architecture with rram-based programmable interconnects. *IEEE Trans. Very Large Scale Integr. Syst.*, 22(4):864–877, April 2014.

[41] Yue Zha and Jing Li. Reconfigurable in-memory computing with resistive memory crossbar. In *Proceedings of the 35th International Conference on Computer-Aided Design*, page 120. ACM, 2016.

[42] M. J. Lee, C. B. Lee, S. Kim, et al. Stack friendly all-oxide 3d rram using gainzno peripheral tft realized over glass substrates. In *2008 IEEE International Electron Devices Meeting*, pages 1–4, Dec 2008.

[43] S. H. Jo, T. Kumar, S. Narayanan, et al. Cross-point resistive ram based on field-assisted superlinear threshold selector. *IEEE Transactions on Electron Devices*, 62(11):3477–3481, Nov 2015.

[44] J. Zhou, K. H. Kim, and W. Lu. Crossbar rram arrays: Selector device requirements during read operation. *IEEE Transactions on Electron Devices*, 61(5):1369–1376, May 2014.

[45] S. H. Jo, T. Kumar, C. Zitlaw, et al. Self-limited rram with on/off resistance ratio amplification. In *2015 Symposium on VLSI Technology (VLSI Technology)*, pages T128–T129, June 2015.

[46] J. Li, R. K. Montoye, M. Ishii, et al. 1 mb 0.41 um2 2t-2r cell nonvolatile tcam with two-bit encoding and clocked self-referenced sensing. *IEEE Journal of Solid-State Circuits*, 49(4):896–907, April 2014.

Physical Design Considerations of One-level RRAM-based Routing Multiplexers

Xifan Tang[1], Edouard Giacomin[2], Giovanni De Micheli[1]
and Pierre-Emmanuel Gaillardon[2]
[1]École Polytechnique Fédérale de Lausanne (EPFL), Vaud, Switzerland
[2] University of Utah, Salt Lake City, Utah, USA
Email: xifan.tang@epfl.ch

ABSTRACT

Resistive Random Access Memory (RRAM) technology opens the opportunity for granting both high-performance and low-power features to routing multiplexers. In this paper, we study the physical design considerations related to RRAM-based routing multiplexers and particularly the integration of 4T(ransistor)1R(RAM) programming structures within their routing tree. We first analyze the limitations in the physical design of a naive one-level 4T1R-based multiplexer, such as co-integration of low-voltage nominal power supply and high voltage programming supply, as well as the use of long metal wires across different isolating wells. To address the limitations, we improve the one-level 4T1R-based multiplexer by re-arranging the nominal and programming voltage domains, and also study the optimal location of RRAMs in terms of performance. The improved design can effectively reduce the length of long metal wires by 50%. Electrical simulations show that using a 7nm FinFET transistor technology, the improved 4T1R-based multiplexers improve delay by 69% as compared to the basic design. At nominal working voltage, considering an input size ranging from 2 to 32, the improved 4T1R-based multiplexers outperform the best CMOS multiplexers in area by 1.4×, delay by 2× and power by 2× respectively. The improved 4T1R-based multiplexers operating at near-Vt regime can improve *Power-Delay Product* by up to 5.8× when compare to the best CMOS multiplexers working at nominal voltage.

1. INTRODUCTION

Resistive Random Access Memory (RRAM) technology [1, 2, 3] has attracted intensive research interests in granting both high-performance and low-power features to routing multiplexers [4, 5]. Similar to pass-transistors or transmission gates in *on/off* state, RRAMs exhibiting *High Resistance State* (HRS)/*Low Resistance State* (LRS) can propagate/block signals. The benefits of RRAM-based multiplexers come from two aspects: (1) RRAMs can reduce the resistances and capacitances of the critical path, leading to high performance; (2) Once programmed, RRAMs are not affected by a reduction of the operating voltage, unlike pass-transistors or transmission gates whose conductance degrades with a reduction of V_{DD}. Therefore, RRAM-based

multiplexers provide high-performance even when operating in the near-V_t regime [4, 5]. Previous works [4, 5, 6, 7, 8, 9] exploit RRAMs and 2T(ransistor)1R(RAM) programming structures to replace pass-transistors or transmission gates of CMOS multiplexers. Recently, 4T(ransistor)1R(RAM) programming structures [10] have been shown more efficient than 2T1R programming structures recently. The authors of [10] explain that both 2T1R and 4T1R programming structures have to employ a high programming voltage, different from nominal working voltage. This reveals a series of challenges at the physical design level, such as how to co-integration of low-voltage nominal power supply and high voltage programming supply, which have not been evaluated in previous works [4, 5, 6, 7, 8, 9, 10].

In this paper, we study the one-level 4T1R-based multiplexers by considering various physical design factors. We first investigate physical design implementation limitations of the naive design of a one-level 4T1R-based multiplexer and we propose an improved one-level 4T1R-based multiplexer, with an advanced physical design featuring: (1) a better granularity of the programming structures; (2) the protection of the datapath transistors from high programming voltage; (3) a 50% length reduction of the long metal wires across isolating wells. Electrical simulations show that, using a 7nm FinFET transistor technology, the modified 4T1R-based multiplexers improve delay by 69% as compared to the naive design. At nominal working voltage, considering an input size ranging from 2 to 32, the improved 4T1R-based multiplexers outperform the best CMOS multiplexers in area by 1.4×, delay by 2× and power by 2× respectively. Furthermore, the proposed 4T1R-based multiplexers operating at near-Vt regime can improve *Power-Delay Product* by up to 5.8× when compared to the best CMOS multiplexers working at nominal voltage.

The rest of this paper is organized as follows. Section 2 reviews on the background about RRAM technology and 4T1R-based programming structure. Section 3 introduces and analyzes a naive one-level 4T1R-based multiplexer at the physical design level. Section 4 proposes an improved one-level 4T1R-based multiplexer, overcoming difficulties in physical design. Section 5 presents the experimental results. Section 6 concludes this paper.

2. BACKGROUND AND MOTIVATION

In this part, we introduce the necessary background about RRAM technology, previous works on RRAM multiplexers and advancements in programming structures.

2.1 RRAM Technology

As one of the most promising emerging memory technology [11], *Resistive Random Access Memory* (RRAM) is envisaged to be integrated at low cost closely with conventional CMOS thanks to its *Back-End-of-the-Line* (BEoL) compatible fabrication process [3]. Indeed, RRAMs can be fabricated between

ISPD '17, March 19-22, 2017, Portland, OR, USA
© 2017 ACM. ISBN 978-1-4503-4696-2/17/03...$15.00
DOI: http://dx.doi.org/10.1145/3036669.3036675

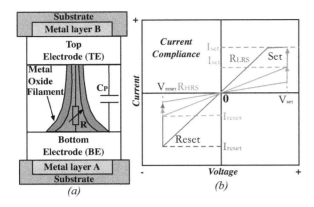

Figure 1: (a) RRAM structure and filamentary conduction; (b) I-V characteristics of set and reset processes.

the metal layers or even within the contact vias to the source or drain of a transistor, leading to a high co-integration density. The structure of a RRAM typically consists of three layers, where a transition metal oxide material stack is sandwiched between the top and bottom metal electrodes, as depicted in Fig. 1(a). Thanks to a filamentary switching mechanism, RRAMs can be switched between two stable resistance states: the *High Resistance State* (HRS) and the *Low Resistance State* (LRS). In addition to the resistive property, a RRAM also introduces a parasitic capacitance C_P. Depending on the employed materials, switching mechanisms of RRAMs are broadly classified to two categories: *Bipolar Resistive Switching* (BRS) and *Unipolar Resistive Switching* (URS). In this paper, we consider RRAM based on BRS only, which is a common choice in most literatures about RRAM-based circuits and systems [4, 5, 6, 7, 8, 9, 10].

Fig. 1(b) illustrates the I-V characteristics of a BRS RRAM. The switching between resistance states is triggered by applying a positive or negative programming voltage across the top and bottom electrodes. The minimum programming voltages required to trigger set and reset processes are defined as V_{set} and V_{reset}, respectively. The programming currents that are provided in set and reset processes are defined as I_{set} and I_{reset}, respectively. A current compliance on I_{set} is often enforced to avoid a permanent breakdown of the device, which is highlighted red in Fig. 1(b). Before being normally set/reset cycled, pristine RRAMs require a forming process to form their filament plug. Thanks to the filamentary conduction mechanism, the LRS resistance R_{LRS} can be dynamically adjusted by controlling the maximum I_{set}. For example, we show that a lower I_{set} leads to a smaller filament (highlighted green in Fig. 1(a)), resulting in a higher R_{LRS} (highlighted green in Fig. 1(b)) than the current compliance. Note that to reset a RRAM that is programmed with a I_{set} lower than current compliance, the required I_{reset} is also less than the maximum (see the green line in Fig. 1(b)). The tunable R_{LRS} is a unique feature of RRAM, which provides more flexibility in design space than other non-volatile memories, such as *Magnetic Random Access Memory* (MRAM) [12]. RRAMs can be scaled down effectively thanks to the filament mechanism. In advanced RRAM technology, an effective memory cell area can be as low as $4F^2$, where F is the feature size [13].

2.2 RRAM-based Multiplexer

RRAMs have attracted intensive research efforts on rout-

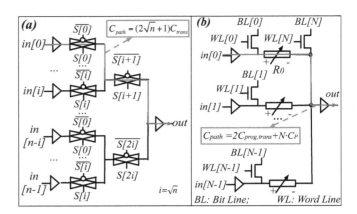

Figure 2: (a) Two-level CMOS multiplexer and (b) one-level 2T(ransistor)1R(RAM)-based multiplexer

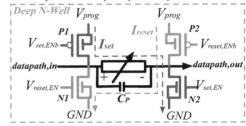

Figure 3: Schematic of a 4T(ransistor)1R(RAM)-based Programming Structure

ing multiplexer designs in recent years [4, 5, 6, 7, 8, 9]. Major research opportunities lie in that RRAMs can be exploited to replace the pass-transistors or transmission gates in the multiplexers with different structures. When a RRAM is programmed to LRS, it can propagate signals as a pass-transistor/transmission gate in *on* state would do. In contrast, a RRAM in HRS can block signals as a pass-transistor / transmission gate in *off* state. Fig. 2 compares a two-level CMOS multiplexer [14] with a one-level N-input RRAM-based multiplexer [6, 7, 8]. The capacitance of the output node of RRAM-based multiplexer has a more pronounced non-linearity as compared to CMOS multiplexers because the parasitic capacitance of a RRAM C_P is much smaller than a transistor. With the reduction of parasitic capacitances and a smaller equivalent resistance than transistors, RRAMs can significantly improve the delay and power of multiplexers. Previous works [4, 5, 6, 7, 8, 9] typically employ 2T(ransistor)1R(RAM) programming structures, and neglect parasitics of a RRAM C_P in their evaluation. Indeed, [4, 5, 6, 7, 8, 9] treat RRAMs as an ideal capacitive load, which has been proved unrealistic in [10]. Fig. 3 illustrates the 4T(ransistor)1R(RAM)-based programming structure, where set and reset process of the RRAM are enabled by two pairs of *p*-type and *n*-type transistors, respectively. In order to set a RRAM into LRS, transistors **P1** and **N2** are turned *on* and transistors **P2** and **N1** are turned *off*, allowing a programming current I_{set}, highlighted blue in Fig. 3, to flow through the RRAM. In order to drive the set and reset currents, the programming voltage V_{prog} should be high enough and is potentially larger than the datapath signals, which is also true for 2T1R programming structure. Therefore, in physical design, a deep N-well (highlighted red in Fig. 3) is required to provide a different voltage domain for the programming structure. However, deep N-wells typically require large

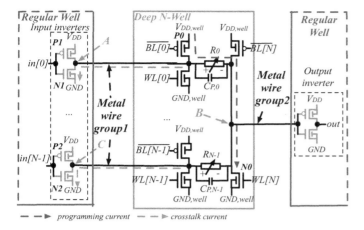

— — —▶ *programming current* — — —▶ *crosstalk current*

Figure 4: Circuit design and well arrangement of a naive $N:1$ one-level 4T1R-based multiplexer

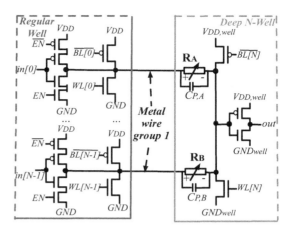

Figure 5: Circuit design and well arrangement of the improved one-level $N:1$ 4T1R-based multiplexer.

spacing between each other and also regular N-wells. This motivates us to take the parasitics into account and study the physical design aspects of integrating 4T1R programming structure into RRAM-based multiplexers, which has not been carefully studied yet to the best of our knowledge.

3. NAIVE 4T1R-BASED MULTIPLEXER

By adapting the circuit topology in Fig. 2, we illustrate in Fig. 4 a naive one-level $N:1$ multiplexer that can be programmed with 4T1R elements [10]. This naive one-level $N:1$ multiplexer consists of N pairs of 4T1R programming structures, which are controlled by $N+1$ Bit lines and $N+1$ Word lines. Note that all the RRAMs share a pair of programming transistors at the node B in Fig. 4, instead of using independent programming transistors. Sharing programming transistors can significantly reduce the parasitic capacitances at node B. All the RRAMs can be programmed in series. For instance, when a set process is required for RRAM R_0, control signals $\overline{BL[0]}$ and $WL[N]$ are enabled. Programming transistors **P0** and **N0** are turned *on* and drive a programming current (blue dash line in Fig. 4) flowing through RRAM R_0. Other programming transistors should be turned *off* during the programming period. However, such straightforward design in Fig. 4 encounters three limitations, as outlined next.

3.1 Limitation 1: Programming Currents Contribution from Datapath Transistors

Whether a RRAM can be programmed into a reasonable R_{LRS} highly depends on the amount of programming current that can be driven through the RRAM. In order to accurately control the programming current of a RRAM, only a pair of p-type and n-type transistors is turned *on* during programming. However, during programming, some datapath transistors in *on* state could inject or distribute the programming currents, leading to the achieved R_{LRS} to be out of the specification range. Take the example in Fig. 4, assume that RRAM R_0 is being programmed by enabling transistors **P0** and **N0**. Pull-down transistors of the input inverters, such as transistors **N1** and **N2**, could potentially be in *on* state, creating additional leakage paths, as highlighted by red dashed lines. This would disturb the V_{DS} of programming transistors and cause the programming current (blue dashed lines) to be smaller than expected, leading to a higher R_{LRS}. Note that not only pull-down transistors, but pull-up transistors of input inverters,

such as **P1** and **P2**, can interfere with the programming current.

3.2 Limitation 2: Breakdown Threats of Datapath Transistors

To achieve a reasonable R_{LRS}, programming voltage $V_{DD,well}$ should be large enough to drive a high enough programming current. For instance, a programming voltage can be as high as $V_{DD,well} = 3.0V$ while the nominal voltage of the datapath transistors is only $VDD = 0.9V$ [10]. Such large gap between $V_{DD,well}$ and V_{DD} could cause the datapath transistors to breakdown during RRAMs' programming phases. Take the example in Fig. 4, the voltage of node A, V_A, can reach $V_{DD,well}$ while programming RRAM R_0, leading to the source-to-drain voltage of transistor **P1** being $V_{DD,well}-V_{DD}$. Assume that $V_{DD,well} = 3.0V$ and $V_{DD} = 0.9V$, both the gate-to-source voltage V_{GS} and source-to-drain voltage V_{DS} of transistor **P1** are $2.1V$, possibly leading transistor **P1** to breakdown. Note that not only transistor **P1** but also all the transistors belonging to the input and output inverters in Fig. 4 can be in a breakdown condition. While exposed to these conditions, even if datapath transistors do not break down, their reliability, i.e., lifetime, would significantly degrade.

3.3 Limitation 3: Long Interconnecting Wires between Wells

Since RRAMs require a programming voltage which is higher than the nominal one, a deep N-well isolation (highlighted red in Fig. 4) is required for the programming structures, resulting in three N-wells as shown in Fig. 4. In physical designs, a large spacing is required between a deep N-well and a regular N-well, which introduces long interconnecting wires. As illustrated in Fig. 4, two groups of long interconnecting wires have to be employed: one is between input inverters and programming structures while the other is between programming structures and output inverters. The long metal wires introduce parasitic resistances and capacitances to 4T1R-based multiplexers, potentially causing delay and power degradation.

4. IMPROVED 4T1R-BASED MULTIPLEXER

In this section, in order to address the limitations of the presented naive 4T1R-based multiplexer, we propose a robust one-level 4T1R-based multiplexer by employing tri-state

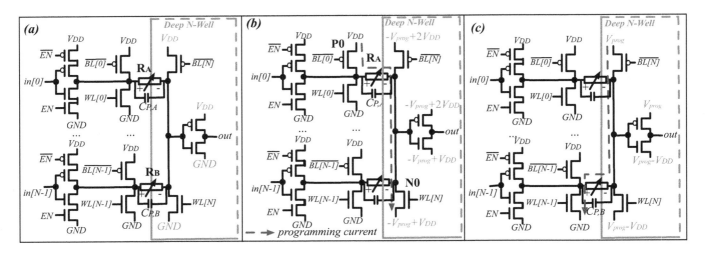

Figure 6: Improved one-level $N:1$ 4T1R-based multiplexer: (a) operating mode ($V_{DD,well} = V_{DD}$, $GND_{well} = GND$); (b) set process ($V_{DD,well} = -V_{prog} + 2V_{DD}$, $GND_{well} = -V_{prog} + V_{DD}$); (c) reset process ($V_{DD,well} = V_{prog}$, $GND_{well} = V_{prog} - V_{DD}$;

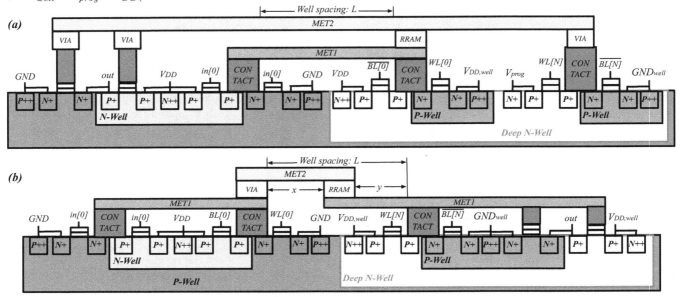

Figure 7: Cross-section of the layout of 4T1R multiplexers: (a) naive design; (b) improved design.

input and output inverters, and also rearranging the voltage domains and deep N-wells. We first introduce the improved design, and then discuss its advantages in physical design aspects.

4.1 Multiplexer Structure and Programming Strategy

Fig. 5 depicts the improved circuit designs, which are different from the naive circuit design (Fig. 4) in two aspects: (a) the datapath input inverters are power-gated in order to eliminate the contribution of the datapath transistors in the programming phase;
(b) the two power domains (and the isolation deep N-well) are organized differently to Fig. 4.
Indeed, the input inverters and part of 4T1R programming structures are driven by a constant voltage domain V_{DD} and GND while the output inverter and the rest of 4T1R programming structures are driven by switchable voltage sup-

plies $V_{DD,well}$ and GND_{well}. During operation, $V_{DD,well}$ and GND_{well} are configured to be equal to V_{DD} and GND respectively, as shown in Fig. 6(a). Note that the RRAM programming voltages are typically selected to be larger than V_{DD}, ensuring that RRAMs are not parasitically programmed during operation. When a set operation is triggered, input inverters are disabled and $V_{DD,well}$ and GND_{well} are switched to be $-V_{prog} + 2V_{DD}$ and $-V_{prog} + V_{DD}$ respectively, as highlighted red in Fig. 6(b). During reset operations, input inverters are disabled and $V_{DD,well}$ and GND_{well} are switched to be V_{prog} and $V_{prog} - V_{DD}$ respectively, as highlighted red in Fig. 6(c). As such, the voltage difference across the RRAM during set or reset is $\pm V_{prog}$ and the working principle of the 4T1R programming structure can still be applied. Indeed, to enable the programming current path highlighted blue in Fig. 6(b), bit line $\overline{BL[0]}$ is configured to be GND and word line $WL[N]$ is configured to be $-V_{prog} + 2V_{DD}$ while other programming transistors should be turned off by configuring $\overline{BL}[i] = VDD, WL[j] = GND, 1 \leq i \leq N-1, 0 \leq j \leq N-1$ and $\overline{BL}[N] = -V_{prog} + 2V_{DD}$.

4.2 Physical Design Advantages

The improved 4T1R-based multiplexer layout has two major advantages over the initial design in Fig. 4:

(1) the voltage drop across each datapath transistor can be limited to V_{DD}, allowing the use of logic transistors instead of I/O transistors (thicker oxides and higher breakdown voltage). Logic transistors occupy less area and introduce less capacitances than I/O transistors, potentially improving the footprint and delay of RRAM multiplexers. During the set and reset processes, the voltage drop of each transistor can be boosted from V_{DD} to $V_{DD,max}$, approaching the maximum reliable voltage without breakdown limitation. Boosted $V_{DD,max}$ leads to higher current density driven by transistors, further contributing to a lower R_{LRS} [10]. Note that the set and reset processes typically require short amount of time, i.e., typically $200ns$ for each RRAM [10]. Since programming does not occur many times (non-volatility), very low stress is applied on the transistors, further contributing to a robust operation.

(2) Only one connection between regular and deep N-Wells is necessary. As a result, only one group of long interconnecting wires is employed, potentially reducing the parasitics from metal wires. To be more illustrative, we depict in Fig. 7 and compare the cross-sections of the naive and improved designs at layout level. In each illustrative cross-section, we consider an input inverter $in0$, an output inverter, and a 4T1R programming structure. We assume that, in the naive design, input and output inverters can be accommodated with a regular N-well, so as to be more area efficient. However, even when the regular N-well is shared, long metal wires are still required because interconnections between datapath logics and programming structures have to include a large space between regular N-well and deep N-well. The length of metal wires $MET1$ and $MET2$ in Fig. 7(a) are dominated by the large well spacing L. Fig. 7(b) depicts the cross-section of the improved circuit in Fig. 5. Since RRAMs can be fabricated between metal lines, they can be located in any position between the two wells. Whatever location the RRAM is, there is only one long metal wire ($MET2$ and part of $MET1$) across two wells, while the other metal wires $MET1$ connect transistors inside the same well. Note that the length of interconnecting wires inside the same well is much smaller than those across two wells L. As a result, the length of metal wires in the naive design is dominated by $2 \cdot L$, while the improved design is dominated by L. Therefore, the improved design can reduce 50% the length of interconnecting wire than the naive design, contributing to smaller parasitic resistances and capacitances.

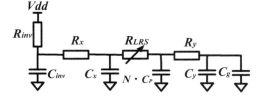

Figure 8: RC equivalent of a critical path of 4T1R-based multiplexer corresponding to the cross-section in Fig. 7(b).

4.3 Physical Position of RRAMs

As illustrated in Fig. 7(b), RRAMs are flexible in their location between the two wells. However, the choice of the location of RRAMs lead to different distribution of parasitics inside the 4T1R-based multiplexer, and further resulting in difference in performance. In this part, we study the impact of location of RRAMs on the performance, by using the Elmore Delay model [15]. We represent the distance between the RRAM and the regular N-well as $x \in [0, L]$, as shown in Fig. 7(b). We extract the critical path of the improved 4T1R-based multiplexer by considering the parasitics in Fig. 7(b) and depicts its equivalent RC model in Fig. 8. R_{inv} and C_{inv} represent the equivalent resistance and capacitance of an input inverter. (R_x, C_x) and (R_y, C_y) are the parasitic resistances and capacitances of the long metal wires, corresponding to (x, y) in Fig. 7(b) respectively. R_{LRS} denotes the resistance of a RRAM in LRS, and $N \cdot C_P$ is the total parasitic capacitances of RRAMs in a one-level 4T1R-based multiplexer. C_g is the gate capacitance of the output inverter. The Elmore Delay of the critical path is:

$$
\begin{aligned}
\tau = & R_{inv} \cdot C_{inv} + (R_{inv} + R_x)C_x \\
& + (R_{inv} + R_x + R_{LRS}) \cdot N \cdot C_P \\
& + (R_y + R_{inv} + R_x + R_{LRS})(C_y + C_g)
\end{aligned} \quad (1)
$$

Note that $R_x + R_y = x \cdot R_\square + y \cdot R_\square = L \cdot R_\square$ and $C_x + C_y = x \cdot C_\square + y \cdot C_\square = L \cdot C_\square$, where $R_\square$ and $C_\square$ are the square resistance and capacitance of a unit metal wire respectively. Equation 1 can be simplified:

$$
\begin{aligned}
\tau = & R_{inv} \cdot C_{inv} + L \cdot R_\square(C_g + L \cdot C_\square) \\
& + (R_{inv} + R_{LRS})(\cdot N \cdot C_P + C_g + L \cdot C_\square) \\
& + (R_\square C_\square)x^2 + [R_\square(\cdot N \cdot C_P - L \cdot C_\square) - C_\square \cdot (R_{inv} + R_{LRS})]x
\end{aligned} \quad (2)
$$

The minimum delay τ_{min} is achieved when:

$$
x_{opt} = \frac{L}{2} + \frac{R_{inv} + R_{LRS}}{2R_\square} - \frac{N \cdot C_P}{2C_\square} \quad (3)
$$

Among parameters $L, N, R_{inv}, R_{LRS}, R_\square, C_P$ and $C_\square$, only N is the design parameter, while the others are all determined by a process technology. Equation 3 shows that x_{opt} decreases when N is increased. In other word, in large 4T1R-based multiplexer, RRAMs should be located close to the N-well.

4.4 Sharing deep N-Well between multiplexers

Deep N-wells can be efficiently shared between two cascaded 4T1R-based multiplexers, as illustrated in Fig. 9. The input inverters and part of programming structures of $MUX1$ in Fig. 9 can share a deep N-well with the output inverter and part of programming structures of $MUX0$. Note that the polarities of RRAMs of $MUX1$ are opposite to the RRAMs of $MUX0$, allowing simple programming strategies. As such, when set processes are required, $V_{DD,well}$ and GND_{well} are switched to $-V_{prog} + 2V_{DD}$ and $-V_{prog} + V_{DD}$ respectively; while during reset processes, $V_{DD,well}$ and GND_{well} are switched to V_{prog} and $V_{prog} - V_{DD}$ respectively; Otherwise, if all the RRAMs have had the same polarity, switching $V_{DD,well}$ and GND_{well} depends not only on the programming operation (either set or reset) but also on the location of multiplexers, requiring additional circuitry.

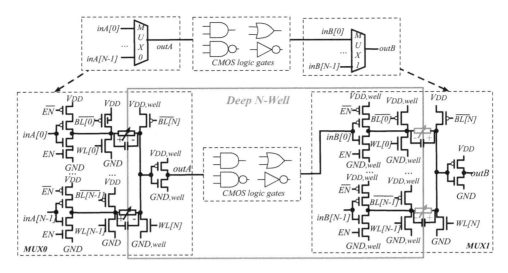

Figure 9: Cascading two improved one-level 4T1R-based multiplexers: share Deep N-Wells efficiently.

5. EXPERIMENTAL RESULTS

In this section, we first introduce our experimental methodology and then report area, delay and power results.

5.1 Experimental Methodology

In this paper, we consider a RRAM technology [5] with programming voltages $V_{set} = |V_{reset}| = 0.9V$ and a maximum current compliance of $I_{set} = |I_{reset}| = 500\mu A$. The lowest achievable on-resistance R_{LRS} of a RRAM is $1.6k\Omega$ while the off-resistance R_{HRS} is $23M\Omega$. The parasitic capacitance of a RRAM, C_P, is estimated to be $4.5aF$ by considering that the RRAMs are embedded in the *MET1* and *MET2* vias of our considered technology. The pulse width of a programming voltage in both set and reset processes is set to be $200ns$. The Stanford RRAM compact model [16] is used to model the considered RRAM technology. The ASAP 7nm FinFET design kit from ASU [17] is used in the circuit designs of datapath logics and 4T1R programming structures. Datapath circuits are built with standard logic transistors (regular-V_t), while the 4T1R programming structures employ I/O transistors for the naive design [10], and low-V_t transistors for the improved designs. The standard logic transistors have a nominal working voltage $V_{DD} = 0.7V$, and the I/O transistors can be overdriven to $1.8V$ while staying in their reliability limits. We compare area, delay and power of the naive and the improved 4T1R-based multiplexers to the CMOS multiplexers, by sweeping input size from 2 to 32. The baseline CMOS multiplexers are implemented with transmission gates. When input size $N \le 12$, a one-level structure is considered, while when input size $N > 12$, a two-level structure is considered to guarantee the best performance. Input and output inverters, transmission gates are implemented with a pair of n-type and p-type FinFETs. Each of FinFET contains three fins. Area evaluations consider the layout area, while delay and power results are extracted from HSPICE [18] simulations.

5.2 Programming Transistor Sizing

As explained in [4], the sizing of programming transistors can significantly impact the delay of RRAM-based multiplexers. In this paper, we extend this study to the naive and improved 4T1R-based multiplexers in the specific context of FinFETs, by sweeping the number of fins from 1 to 3 in each

FinFET. We selected a maximum of three fins, because, in the considered design kit, three fins allow the 4T1R structure to match the standard cell height, simplifying the layout considerations. Fig. 10 shows both delay and power difference of the improved 4T1R-based multiplexers ($x = L$) under various V_{DD}. A proper number of fins indeed can reduce the delay of 4T1R-based multiplexers by 14%-21% and also the power by 25% respectively. In terms of delay, the best number of fins is three for all the cases, which can be explained as follows: Three fins lead to lower achievable RRAM resistances than one or two fins, which, in turn, performs better in driving the large parasitic capacitances of long metal wires. Similar conclusions can be found for other 4T1R-based multiplexers in this paper. In the rest of this paper, we consider three fins for each FinFET in 4T1R-based multiplexers to achieve best delay metric.

5.3 Optimal RRAM Location

As shown in Equation 3, the location of RRAMs can influence the delay of 4T1R-based multiplexers. From the consider design kit, we extract process parameters $L = 0.8\mu m$, $R_{inv} = 4.5k\Omega$, $R_\square = 67.5\Omega/\mu m$ and $C_\square = 67.5aF/\mu m$. According to Equation 3, the best location of the RRAMs is $x_{opt} = L$ unless $N > 2080$. Therefore, in this part, we study only two locations for RRAMs : $x = 0$ and $x = L$. Fig. 11 compares the delay of naive and improved 4T1R-based multiplexers with different locations of RRAMs $x = 0$ and $x = L$. The improved design significantly reduces the delay by 35%-69% as compared to the naive design. Such large delay reduction comes from two aspects: (a) The input tri-state inverters guarantee a high programming current through RRAMs, resulting in a low R_{LRS}; (b) As the length of long metal wires is reduced by 50%, the parasitic resistances and capacitances of the improved design are smaller. Note that, in the naive design, the input inverters cause serious interference on the programming current when input size increases. Consequently, when input size is larger than 16, RRAM-based multiplexers cannot be programmed successfully. The best location of RRAMs is $x = L$, leading to a 5% delay improvement over $x = L$, which satisfies Equation 3. In the rest of this paper, we consider the improved design with $x = L$ in the comparison with CMOS multiplexers.

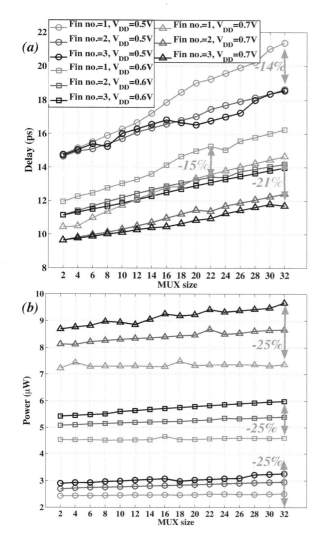

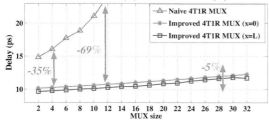

Figure 10: Best number of fins in each FinFET of improved 4T1R-based multiplexer ($x = L$) under different V_{DD} in terms of (a) Delay and (b) Power.

Figure 11: Delay comparison between naive and improved 4T1R-based multiplexers ($x = 0$ and $x = L$).

5.4 Area Results

In order to properly study the area of the 4T1R-based considering routing, well organization etc., and compare with the CMOS counterpart, we realized the layout of a 16-input two level CMOS multiplexer and a 4T1R-based one-level multiplexer. The CMOS multiplexer is built with two levels and must use SRAMs to store the configuration bits. As explained in the previous subsection, we can efficiently share the wells between different 4T1R-based multiplexers

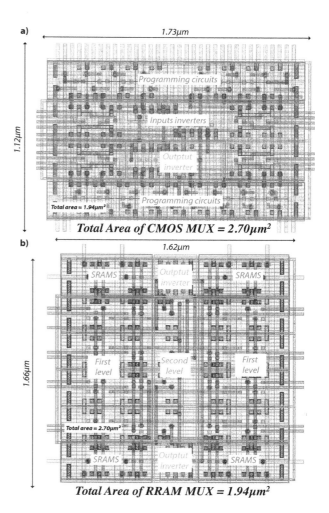

Figure 12: Layout of 16-input a 4T1R-based one-level multiplexer

leading to less area overhead. Therefore, the layout of the 16-input 4T1R-based one-level multiplexer only consists of the programming structures and input inverters of a first multiplexer and the output inverter of another multiplexer in a regular well. The output inverter and the associated programming structures will be located in a *deep N-well*, as well as the input inverters and associated programming structures of the other multiplexer. The space required by the topological design rule between the regular well and the *deep N-well* can be efficiently used to accommodate standard n-type transistors and route the multiplexers input signals. Fig. 12 depicts the layout organisation of the 16-input 4T1R-based one-level multiplexer. The input inverters are placed together in two stages so we can access to the multiplexer inputs from both sides through the horizontal lines (8 inputs in each side). The programming structures are placed above and under the input inverters and each associated $\overline{BL[N]}$ and WL[N] are accessible through the vertical metal lines. As a result, the 4T1R-based multiplexer area ($1.94um^2$) is $1.4\times$ more efficient than its CMOS counterpart ($2.70um^2$).

5.5 Delay and Power Results

Fig. 13 compares the delay and power of the improved 4T1R-based multiplexers ($x = L$) and CMOS multiplexers under different V_{DD} respectively. Thanks to the significant

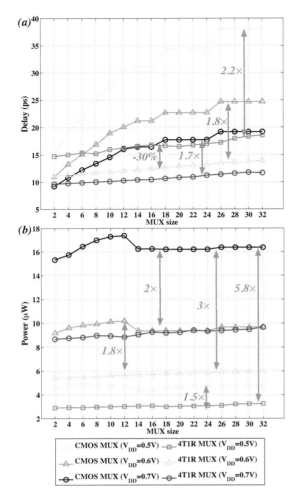

Figure 13: (**Comparison between the improved 4T1R-based multiplexers** ($x = L$) **and CMOS multiplexer under different** V_{DD}**: (a) delay; (b) power.**

reduction on the capacitances in critical paths, at nominal voltage, the 4T1R-based multiplexers improves delay significantly by $1.7\times$ as compared to their CMOS counterparts. Since the resistances of RRAMs are independent from working voltages, at near-V_t regime, the delay improvements of the 4T1R-based multiplexers increase to $1.7\times$ and $2.2\times$ respectively. Note that the 4T1R-based multiplexers operating at $V_{DD} = 0.6V$ is still 30% more delay efficient than the CMOS multiplexers at $V_{DD} = 0.7V$. The reduction on the capacitances in critical paths also contributes to a significant improvement in power consumption. Compared to CMOS multiplexer, the 4T1R-based multiplexers improve the power by $1.5 - 2\times$ under various V_{DD}. More importantly, such power improvements are achieved without delay loss. Take the example of the 4T1R-based multiplexers operating at $V_{DD} = 0.5V$, their delays are similar to the CMOS multiplexers at $V_{DD} = 0.7V$, while the power consumption is reduced by $5.8\times$.

6. CONCLUSIONS

In this paper, we first investigate the naive design of a one-level 4T1R-based multiplexer and addresses its limitations from a physical design standpoint. We propose an improved one-level 4T1R-based multiplexer with advanced

physical design considerations: (1) a better granularity of the programming structures; (2) the protection of the datapath transistors from high programming voltage; (3) a 50% length reduction of the long metal wires across isolating wells. Electrical simulations show that, using a 7nm FinFET transistor technology, the modified 4T1R-based multiplexers improve delay by 69% as compared to the naive design. At nominal working voltage, considering an input size ranging from 2 to 32, the improved 4T1R-based multiplexers outperform the best CMOS multiplexers in area by $1.4\times$, delay by $2\times$ and power by $2\times$ respectively. Furthermore, the proposed 4T1R-based multiplexers operating at near-Vt regime can improve *Power-Delay Product* by up to $5.8\times$ when compared to the best CMOS multiplexers working at nominal voltage.

7. ACKNOWLEDGMENTS

This work was supported by the Swiss National Science Foundation under the project number 200021-146600.

8. REFERENCES

[1] R. Waser *et al.*, *Nanoionics-based Resistive Switching Memories*, Nature Materials, Vol. 6, 2007, pp. 833-840.

[2] H. Akinaga *et al.*, *Resistive Random Access Memory (ReRAM) Based on Metal Oxides*, Proceedings of the IEEE, Vol. 98, No. 12, 2010, pp. 2237 - 2251.

[3] H.-S. P. Wong *et al.*, *Metal-Oxide RRAM*, Proceedings of the IEEE, Vol. 100, No. 6, 2012, pp. 1951-1970.

[4] X. Tang *et al.*, *A High-performance Low-power Near-Vt RRAM-based FPGA*, IEEE ICFPT, 2014, pp. 207-215.

[5] X. Tang *et al*, *Accurate Power Analysis for Near-V_t RRAM-based FPGA*, IEEE FPL, 2015, pp. 174-177.

[6] S. Tanachutiwat *et al.*, *FPGA Based on Integration of CMOS and RRAM*, IEEE TVLSI, Vol. 19, No. 11, 2010, pp. 2023-2032.

[7] P.-E. Gaillardon *et al.*, *Emerging Memory Technologies for Reconfigurable Routing in FPGA Architecture*, IEEE ICECS, 2010, pp. 62 - 65.

[8] J. Cong and B. Xiao, *FPGA-RPI: A Novel FPGA Architecture With RRAM-Based Programmable Interconnects*, IEEE TVLSI, Vol. 22, No. 4, 2014, pp. 864-877.

[9] P.-E. Gaillardon *et al.*, *GMS: Generic Memristive Structure for Non-Volatile FPGAs*, IEEE/IFIP VLSI-SoC, 2012, pp. 94-98.

[10] X. Tang *et al.*, *A Study on the Programming Structures for RRAM-Based FPGA Architectures*, IEEE Transaction on Circuits And Systems I (TCAS-I): Regular Papers, Vol. 63, No. 4, pp. 503-516.

[11] G.W. Burr *et al.*, *Overview of Candidate Device Technologies for Storage-Class-Memory*, IBM J. R&D, Vol. 52, No. 4/5, July/Sept. 2008.

[12] J. Zhu, *Magnetoresistive Random Access Memory: The Path to Competitiveness and Scalability*, Proceedings of the IEEE, Vol. 96, No. 11, pp. 1786 - 1798, 2008.

[13] Y. S. Chen *et al.*, *Highly Scalable Hafnium Oxide Memory with Improvements of Resistive Distribution and Read Disturb Immunity*, IEEE IEDM, 2009, pp.1-4.

[14] E. Lee *et al.*, *Interconnect Driver Design for Long Wires in Field-Programmable Gate Arrays*, Journal of Signal Processing Systems, Springer, Vol. 51, No. 1, April 2008.

[15] W.C. Elmore, *The Transient Response of Damped Linear Networks with Particular Regard to Wideband Amplifiers*, Journal of Applied Physics, Vol. 19, No. 1, 1948, pp. 55-63.

[16] J. Jiang *et al.*, *Verilog-A Compact Model for Oxide-based Resistive Random Access Memory*, IEEE SISPAD, 2014, pp. 41-44.

[17] L.T. Clark *et al.*, *ASAP7: A 7-nm FinFET Predictive Process Design Kit*, Microelectronics Journal, vol. 53, pp. 105-115, July 2016.

[18] Synopsys, *HSPICE User Guide: Simulation and Analysis*, Version I-2013.12, December 2013.

Hierarchical and Analytical Placement Techniques for High-Performance Analog Circuits

Biying Xu, Shaolan Li, Xiaoqing Xu, Nan Sun, and David Z. Pan
ECE Department, University of Texas at Austin, Austin, TX, USA
{biying,slliandy,xiaoqingxu.austin}@utexas.edu,
nansun@mail.utexas.edu, dpan@ece.utexas.edu

ABSTRACT

High-performance analog integrated circuits usually require minimizing critical parasitic loading, which can be modeled by the critical net wire length in the layout stage. In order to reduce post-layout circuit performance degradation, critical net wire length minimization should be considered during placement, in addition to the conventional optimization objectives of total area and half perimeter wire length (HPWL). In this paper, we develop effective hierarchical and analytical techniques for high-performance analog circuits placement, which is a complex problem given its multi-objectives and constraints (e.g. hierarchical symmetric groups). The entire circuit is first partitioned hierarchically in a top-down, critical parasitics aware, hierarchical symmetric constraints and proximity constraints feasible manner, where the placement subproblem for each partition at each level can be solved in reasonable run-time. Then, different placement variants are generated for each partition from bottom up, taking advantage of the computation power of modern multi-core systems with parallelization. To assemble the placement variants of different subpartitions, a Mixed Integer Linear Programming (MILP) formulation is proposed which can simultaneously minimize critical parasitic loading, total area and HPWL, and handle hierarchical symmetric constraints, module variants selection and orientation. Experimental results demonstrate the effectiveness of the proposed techniques.

1. INTRODUCTION

With the expanding market share of emerging applications, including consumer electronics, automotive, and Internet of Things (IoT), the demands in analog and mixed-signal (AMS) integrated circuits (ICs) are becoming higher and higher. The complexity explosion of the design rules and circuit performance requirements in nano-meter IC era also dramatically increases the complexity of their layouts. Hence, it is necessary to have design automation tools for AMS ICs [1].

ISPD '17, March 19-22, 2017, Portland, OR, USA
© 2017 ACM. ISBN 978-1-4503-4696-2/17/03. . . $15.00
DOI: http://dx.doi.org/10.1145/3036669.3036678

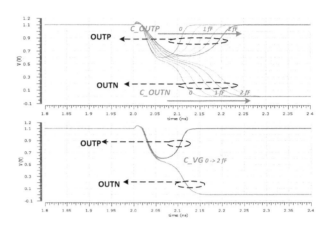

Figure 1: Transient simulations of a comparator. Top: critical parasitics effects; Down: effects of non-critical ones.

1.1 Critical Parasitics in Analog Layout

One key goal and challenge in high-performance analog layout circuits is the minimization of critical parasitics effects on the post-layout circuit performance. Critical parasitics in analog design are the parasitics that would trigger major impacts on key analog performance metrics when they vary. The critical parasitics and their effects on performance are usually identified by the analog circuit designers before starting layout, in order to efficiently minimize the degradation of post-layout performance.

W.l.o.g., we can demonstrate the significance of critical parasitics management through a dynamic latch comparator, as shown in Fig. 2. The parasitic capacitances that are of our interest are drawn, where C_* (e.g. C_OUTP) indicates a net's self-capacitance to substrate, and CC_* (e.g. CC_OUT) indicates the coupling capacitance between two nets. The speed of a comparator cannot be optimized simply through the minimization of total wire length, which may be over-emphasized by conventional analog placement methodologies. In fact, it is only strongly related to certain capacitances which are called critical parasitic capacitances, while other parasitic capacitances have much weaker or marginal effects on the speed. The critical parasitics identified by the circuit designers are highlighted by the red boxes. We perform simulations to show the difference in the effects caused by the critical parasitics and non-critical ones. Simulation results of the comparator transition waveform are shown in Fig. 1. In the simulation setting, the capacitors are swept

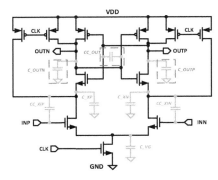

Figure 2: Example comparator circuit.

Table 1: Notations

WL, CL	the total HPWL and critical net HPWL.
W, H	the total width and height of the placement.
M	the set of all devices/subpartitions.
$w_i^{(k)}, h_i^{(k)}$	the width and height of the k-th variant of the i-th device/subpartition $M_i^{(k)}$.
x_i, y_i	the horizontal and vertical coordinates of the location of the i-th device/subpartition.
N, N_c	the set of all nets and critical nets.
wl_i	the HPWL of net i.
S	the set of all hierarchical symmetric groups, $S = \{S_1, S_2, \cdots, S_m\}$.
L	the placement solution.
A	the summation of the average area over all variants of the devices/subpartitions, i.e. $A = \sum_i ((\sum_{k_i} w_i^{(k_i)} \cdot h_i^{(k_i)})/k_i)$.

from 0 to 2 fF, which are typical values of parasitic capacitance in modern processes. It can be clearly seen that the capacitance loading of the outputs (C_OUTP and C_OUTN) presents major impact (2x increase in delay). On the other hand, other parasitic capacitances (e.g. C_VG) have much less impact on the comparator speed. Therefore, in terms of speed, the parasitics on nodes OUTP and OUTN are the critical ones, while others can be loosely managed. The wire lengths of OUTP and OUTN should be minimized to reduce the self-parasitic capacitances.

From the above discussion, it can be seen that constraints in analog design are net-specific. Conventional optimization techniques without considering net-specific requirements become suboptimal in optimizing high-performance analog circuits. High-performance analog layout synthesis requires a critical net aware algorithm.

1.2 Related Works

[2] used a branch-and-bound technique in the building block layout problem to consider critical nets with maximum length constraints. Their work considered maximum critical net length constraints for digital circuits rather than minimizing the critical parasitics for analog circuits. [3] proposed to first perform circuit analysis to determine the sensitivity of circuit performance to each parasitic loading, and then optimize performance degradation, among other metrics. However, exhaustive circuit analysis without taking advantage of the designer's knowledge was time-consuming and could potentially lead to inaccuracy. Proximity constraints have been used to restrict some modules to be placed in close proximity [4–7]. However, they did not impose net-specific requirements, and thus were not enough to minimize critical parasitics. Boundary constraints were applied in [8] for analog placement to reduce wiring parasitics, which were also insufficient because the devices may still be far away even if they are placed on the boundary of a group. [9] considered monotonic current paths constraints to reduce the routing-induced parasitics. Recently, [10] fully separated analog and digital signal paths for noise reduction of AMS circuits. Nevertheless, these heuristics did not minimize critical parasitic loading explicitly, either.

Analog circuit hierarchy has been taken into account during placement previously by [10,11] which demonstrated the effectiveness of the hierarchical approach. However, neither of them considered critical parasitics explicitly. Meanwhile, topological approaches have been widely used to solve the analog placement problem, including B* tree [4, 5], Corner Block List (CBL) [7], Sequence Pair [12, 13], Slicing

Tree [14], etc. Nonetheless, they require a packing step before wire length can be estimated, while absolute coordinates approaches [11,15] could provide a more accurate estimation of wire length by construction.

1.3 Our Contributions

Our main contributions are summarized as follows.

- We formulate the high-performance analog circuits placement problem which minimizes the total area, HPWL and critical parasitics simultaneously while accommodating analog placement constraints.

- Since AMS circuits typically have the hierarchical structure, we propose a hierarchical scheme for analog placement which can comprehend the designer's intent and obtain good circuit performance.

- The proposed hierarchical analog placement algorithm is parallelizable and scalability is demonstrated.

- Experimental results show that circuit performance degradation is reduced by minimizing the critical parasitics while keeping other objectives satisfactory.

- To the best of our knowledge, this is the first work that explicitly minimizes critical parasitics for analog placement.

The rest of this paper is organized as follows: Section 2 gives the problem formulation of the high-performance analog circuits placement problem. Section 3 proposes the hierarchical analog placement framework. Section 4 shows the experimental results. Section 5 concludes the paper.

2. PROBLEM FORMULATION

This section shows the formulation for the high-performance analog IC placement problem. The notations we use are listed in Table 1.

Firstly, we give the optimization objectives of the placement problem for high-performance analog ICs. As discussed in Subsection 1.1, the performance of an analog circuit is strongly affected by the critical parasitics. Several factors could affect parasitic capacitance of a net, e.g. net length, metal overlap with other nets, spacing with other nets running in parallel with it, etc. While the metal overlap and parallel spacing are often hard to control in the placement stage, the critical net wire length can be effectively modeled by its HPWL during placement. Therefore, the total critical net HPWL can be expressed as $CL = \sum_{net_i \in N_c} wl_i$, and total HPWL can be written as $WL = \sum_{net_i \in N} wl_i$. The high-performance analog placement problem tries to minimize CL in addition to the conventional optimization objectives of WL and the total area A.

Secondly, we discuss how analog placement constraints are considered. Practical analog layout designs typically contain hierarchical structure and symmetric constraints. In a multi-level hierarchical structure, symmetric constraints may apply to subpartitions at each level, thus generating hierarchical symmetric constraints, which we define as follows:

Definition 1 (Hierarchical Symmetric Constraint). *A hierarchical symmetric constraint is a placement constraint requiring at least one symmetric group to be symmetric to at least one other symmetric group or component, which forms a new hierarchical symmetric group.*

An example hierarchical symmetric constraint is illustrated in Fig. 3. The blue boxes indicate symmetric constraints with horizontal axes (H symmetric), the red boxes indicate those with vertical axes (V symmetric), and the magenta boxes indicate those requiring both horizontal and vertical symmetry (H and V symmetric). For instance, rectangles {1, 2, 3} form an H symmetric group, where 1 and 2 form a symmetric pair and rectangle 3 is self-symmetric with respect to the same axis as the symmetric pair {1, 2}. The V symmetric constraint in this example is a hierarchical symmetric constraint, because it contains the H symmetric groups of {1, 2, 3} and {6, 7, 8} as a hierarchical symmetric pair, and requires the H and V symmetric group of {5, 9, 10} and rectangle 4 to be self-symmetric in the mean time.

[5] mentioned the concept of hierarchical symmetric constraints and discussed how they could be handled using hierarchical symmetric feasible B* trees. However, no experiment has been done to demonstrate the effectiveness of this technique for practical analog placement. In this paper, we consider hierarchical symmetric constraints in a hierarchical and analytical placement engine. Suppose M_l and M_r are any 2 devices/subpartitions which form a symmetric pair in a vertical hierarchical symmetric group S_j, and M_m is any self-symmetric device/subpartition in the same S_j. We have $x_l + x_r + w_r = 2 \cdot a_j$, and $2 \cdot x_m + w_m = 2 \cdot a_j$, where a_j is the vertical symmetric axis of S_j. The horizontal hierarchical symmetric constraints can be written similarly. Furthermore, proximity constraints require some devices/subpartitions to be in close proximity, which will be satisfied by construction of the circuit hierarchy in our placement engine. A legal placement also needs to satisfy the non-overlapping constraints which forbid overlap between any devices. Besides, orientation and variants selection will be addressed by our analog placement engine.

Finally, the high-performance analog circuit placement problem can be stated as follows:

Problem 1 (High-Performance Analog Placement). *The high-performance analog placement problem is to find legal device placement/s given the circuit netlist and device variants in different sizes, which simultaneously minimizes critical net wire length, the total wire length and area, while accommodating hierarchical symmetric constraints, proximity constraints, and non-overlapping constraints.*

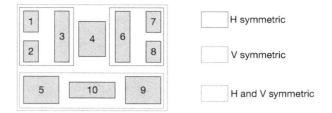

Figure 3: Example hierarchical symmetric constraints.

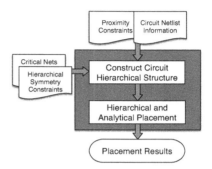

Figure 4: Hierarchical Analytical analog placement flow.

3. HIERARCHICAL PLACEMENT FRAMEWORK

The overall flow of our hierarchical analytical placement algorithm for high-performance analog circuits is shown in Fig. 4. If the circuit hierarchy is provided by the designer, our algorithm takes it as input directly. Otherwise, we apply a critical parasitics aware, symmetric and proximity constraints feasible hierarchical circuit partitioning technique. After the circuit hierarchy is obtained, hierarchical and analytical placement is performed from bottom up. Different placement subproblems at the same level in the circuit hierarchy are solved in parallel. MILP formulation is used to solve the placement subproblems for all subpartitions.

3.1 Hierarchical Circuit Partitioning

Analog circuits are typically organized in a hierarchical manner. The circuit hierarchy input by circuit designers often reflects their expertise and insights, such as which components should be placed in close proximity to avoid process variation induced circuit performance degradation, etc. Also, placing the modules in the way designers partition the circuit would increase the readability of the placement results by the designers. Therefore, our analog placement engine will respect the circuit hierarchy if it is provided, as in [4, 12, 16]. Nevertheless, while the circuit designers have more insights in electrical performance optimization, they may have difficulty optimizing geometrical metrics (e.g. area) and electrical performance simultaneously. Therefore, in addition to being able to take the circuit hierarchy as an input, our analog placement engine will also be able to perform circuit partitioning specific to analog circuits for geometrical and electrical metrics co-optimization.

Although there are many existing well-established circuit partitioning techniques [17–20], they are not directly applicable to analog circuits because of the analog placement constraints. However, we can adapt these algorithms to fol-

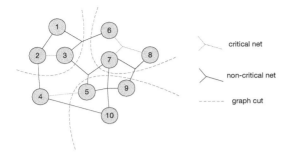

Figure 5: Example hypergraph partitioning.

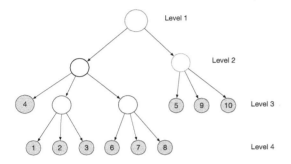

Figure 6: Example circuit hierarchy.

low the following guidelines to make it aware of the parasitic loading and analog placement constraints:

- Modules in a hierarchical symmetric group should be in the same hierarchical partition.

- Modules belonging to a proximity group should be in the same partition (the proximity constraint is satisfied by construction).

- Different criticality of different parasitic capacitances could be reflected by different net weights.

In this work, we adapted the hMetis [21] hypergraph partitioning algorithm by specifying fixed module partitions and setting proper weights for critical nets, with the implementation details clarified in Section 4. The entire netlist is modeled by a hypergraph, which we call the top-level hypergraph, where the placement devices (e.g. transistors) are its vertices and the nets are its hyperedges. It is first partitioned following the high-performance analog circuit partitioning guidelines above, and results in several subpartitions, each of which is a sub-hypergraph of the top-level hypergraph. The *internal hyperedges/nets* of a sub-hypergraph are derived from the hyperedges of the top-level hypergraph that connect only vertices within the sub-hypergraph. The *external hyperedges/nets* are the those connecting different vertices in different sub-hypergraphs. Similarly, each sub-hypergraph of the top-level hypergraph is partitioned following the same guidelines, but now only the internal hyperedges will be considered. The partitioning continues hierarchically until the desired number of placement devices are left in each leaf-level subpartition.

An example hierarchical partitioning of the circuit with hierarchical symmetric constraints and critical nets is shown in

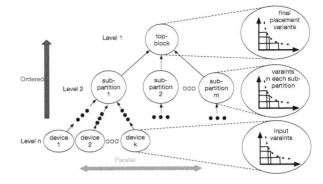

Figure 7: Hierarchical analog placement illustration.

Fig. 5, and the constructed circuit hierarchy from this partitioning is as in Fig. 6. Critical nets of the circuit netlist are colored in red, and the others in black are non-critical nets. This example circuit has hierarchical symmetric constraints as in Fig. 3. While the partitioning algorithm tries to avoid cutting critical nets, it may still do so if much better area balance could be achieved or if other ways of partitioning cannot satisfy the hierarchical symmetric constraints or proximity constraints for the desired number of partitions and desired number of levels in the circuit hierarchy specified by the designers. An example of the resulting circuit hierarchy for the example circuit is shown in Fig. 6. In this case, the partitioning algorithm first separates the H and V symmetric group (in magenta) of {5, 9 10} and others into 2 subpartitions at the second level. The other devices are further partitioned into 3 subpartitions of the H symmetric groups of {1, 2, 3} and {6, 7, 8} and device 4 at the third level. A subpartition may contain a single placement device as a special case.

3.2 Hierarchical and Analytical Placement

Given the circuit hierarchy constructed from the user input hierarchical circuit netlist or from the proposed analog circuit partitioning, our placement algorithm is illustrated in Fig. 7.

The leaf nodes of the circuit hierarchy represent primitive placement devices such as transistors or subcircuits that have been pre-laid out by the designers, and the internal nodes (non-leaf nodes) indicates hierarchical partitions. Each node in the hierarchy contains several *variants*, and exactly one of them will be selected by the placement algorithm. For a leaf node, the variants are inputs from the designers. For example, the variants of a transistor leaf node are different layouts that can be considered electrically equivalent (with the same transistor width and length) but have a different number of fingers and thus different geometrical shapes (with different geometrical width and height). For an internal node, the variants are the placement results for that hierarchical partition, which have different bounding box shapes (with different total widths and heights), different aspect ratios, and different locations, orientations, or selected input variants for the devices. The different variants of an internal node are generated by solving a *placement subproblem* (defined in Subsection 3.2.1) of a subpartition, which then propagate and become inputs to the placement subproblem of its parent node. Different placement subproblems at different levels in the circuit hierarchy are solved orderly from bottom-up, while those at the same level can be solved in parallel (see Subsection 3.2.2). Finally, the different variants contained in the root node are the set of placement results for the top-block.

3.2.1 Solving Placement Subproblems

Since the proximity constraints are satisfied during our construction of the circuit hierarchy, the placement subproblem of a subpartition does not need to handle these constraints. It is formulated as below:

Problem 2 (Placement Subproblem). *Given a set of subpartitions each containing different variants and the external nets (as defined in 3.1) connecting them, the high-performance analog placement subproblem is to find legal placement/s of these subpartitions which simultaneously minimizes the critical net wire length and total wire length within these subpartitions and total area of them, while accommodating hierarchical symmetric constraints and non-overlapping constraints among these subpartitions.*

This is a multiple objectives optimization (MOO) problem, and generally, the optimal values of different objectives are usually not achieved at the same solution. We say that a solution s of a MOO problem dominates another solution $\widetilde{s}$ if s has better values for one or more objectives than $\widetilde{s}$ and the same values for all other objectives as $\widetilde{s}$. The aim of the high-performance analog IC placement subproblem is to try to obtain the placement solutions that are non-dominated by any other solution in terms of the objectives of critical net wire length, the total HPWL, total width and total height.

To solve each placement subproblem, first, a list of initial widths $\{W_0^{(1)}, W_0^{(2)}, \cdots, W_0^{(r)}\}$ are calculated based on the desired initial aspect ratios and total area by GetInitialWidths (Alg. 1), where $AR_0^{(i)} = (W_0^{(i)})/(H_0^{(i)}), i = 1, \cdots, r$ are the input initial aspect ratios by the designers. The normalization factors can be obtained in different ways, e.g. by $H_0^{(i)} = (W_0^{(i)})/(AR_0^{(i)})$, and $WL_0^{(i)} = (H_0^{(i)} + W_0^{(i)})/2 \cdot n$, where n is the number of nets.

Then, three approaches with different optimization flavors towards different objectives are explored which are shown in DifferentMOOFlavors (Alg. 2), each variating the general MILP problem as shown below, where total width/height boundary constraints specify the placement boundaries:

$$\min_L \alpha \cdot \frac{H}{H_0} + \beta \cdot \frac{W}{W_0} + \theta \cdot \frac{WL + \gamma \cdot CL}{WL_0}$$

$$\text{s.t. hierarchical symmetric constraints}$$

$$\text{non-overlapping constraints}$$

$$\text{total width/height boundary constraints}$$

- SequentialMin finds a solution on the Pareto Front by sequentially minimizing H, W and the weighted sum of WL and CL. First, it minimizes H given a specific W_0 with MinHeightMILP by setting β and θ to 0 in the general MILP, and the width boundary to W_0. $\widetilde{H}$ indicates the resulting optimal height, and $\widetilde{L_1}$ represents the placement result of this step. Then, it minimizes W given the obtained optimal height $\widetilde{H}$ with MinWidthMILP by setting α and θ to 0, and the width and height boundaries to W_0 and $\widetilde{H}$. $\widetilde{W}$ indicates the resulting optimal width, and $\widetilde{L_2}$ represents

---

Algorithm 1 GetInitialWidths

1: **procedure** GetInitialWidths($A, AR_0^{(1)}, \cdots, AR_0^{(r)}$)
2: $\quad \widetilde{W_0} \leftarrow sqrt(A)$
3: $\quad$ **for all** i **do**
4: $\quad\quad W_0^{(i)} \leftarrow sqrt(AR_0^{(i)}) \cdot \widetilde{W_0}$
5: $\quad$ **end for**
6: $\quad$ **return** $\{W_0^{(1)}, W_0^{(2)}, \cdots, W_0^{(r)}\}$
7: **end procedure**

Algorithm 2 DifferentMOOFlavors

1: **procedure** SequentialMin(W_0, M, S)
2: $\quad \widetilde{H}, \widetilde{L_1} \leftarrow$ MinHeightMILP(W_0, M, S).
3: $\quad \widetilde{W}, \widetilde{L_2} \leftarrow$ MinWidthMILP($\widetilde{H}, M, S$).
4: $\quad \widetilde{L} \leftarrow$ MinWLCLMILP($\widetilde{W}, \widetilde{H}, M, S$).
5: $\quad$ **return** $\widetilde{L}$
6: **end procedure**
7: **procedure** FixedAreaMin(W_0, H_0, A_m, M, S)
8: $\quad W_m \leftarrow sqrt(\frac{A_m}{A}) \cdot W_0$
9: $\quad H_m \leftarrow sqrt(\frac{A_m}{A}) \cdot H_0$
10: $\quad \widetilde{L} \leftarrow$ MinWLCLMILP(W_m, H_m, M, S).
11: $\quad$ **return** $\widetilde{L}$
12: **end procedure**
13: **procedure** WeightedSumMin(W_0, H_0, WL_0, M, S)
14: $\quad \widetilde{L} \leftarrow$ MinWSMILP(W_0, H_0, WL_0, M, S).
15: $\quad$ **return** $\widetilde{L}$
16: **end procedure**

---

the placement result of this step. Finally, it tries to minimize the weighted sum of WL and CL with MinWLCLMILP by setting α and β to 0, and the height and width boundaries to the optimal height and width $\widetilde{H}$ and $\widetilde{W}$ obtained from the previous 2 steps, respectively.

- FixedAreaMin tries to minimize the weighted sum of WL and CL given maximum area A_m, by setting α and β to 0, and the width and height boundaries to W_m and H_m which are calculated as the maximum total width and height if the initial aspect ratio is maintained, respectively.

- WeightedSumMin uses MinWSMILP which is identical to the general MILP. In this approach, the placement boundaries can be tuned in order to get the desirable placement results.

3.2.2 Parallelization

In our algorithm, when solving the placement subproblem of a subpartition, the locations of the other components outside of the subpartition have not been determined. Therefore, we will ignore the interconnections between the components inside and outside of the subpartition of concern, and the placement subproblems of different subpartitions at the same level in the circuit hierarchy can be regarded as "independent" by our algorithm. Moreover, the placement subproblems to generate different variants with different aspect ratios for the same subpartition do not depend on the results of each other. Hence, the proposed algorithm is well-suitable for parallelization, which can take advantage of the computation power of modern multi-core systems. In the ideal case, the fully parallelized version of our algorithm finishes in wall time proportional to the number of levels in the circuit hierarchy, assuming the circuit is partitioned such that each subproblem at each level can be solved in reasonable amount of time. In reality, the available computation resource may not allow for full parallelism, thus perfect run-time scaling may not be achieved.

4. EXPERIMENTAL RESULTS

Table 2: Benchmark circuits

Circuit	#Mod.	#Sym. Mod.	Mod. Area	#Nets	#Crit. Nets
comparator	15	14	-	14	2
ring sampler slice	102	32	-	57	4
xerox	10	0	19.35	203	16
apte	9	8	46.56	97	-
hp	11	8	8.83	83	-
ami33	33	6	1.16	123	-
ami49	49	4	35.45	408	-

We implemented the hierarchical analytical placement algorithms for high-performance analog ICs in C++ and all experiments were performed on a Linux machine with 2 8-core CPUs (2.9GHz Intel(R) E5-2690) and 192GB memory. Gurobi [22] is adopted as our MILP solver. When circuit partitioning is performed, the same parameters in hMetis are used except the number of levels in the circuit hierarchy, the number of partitions, hyperedge weights, and fixed components. The number of levels and partitions are tuned to balance run-time and placement quality. The hyperedge weight reflects the net criticality, and the components in the same hierarchical symmetric group or proximity group are fixed in the same hierarchical partition accordingly.

Table 2 lists the benchmark circuits information used in our experiments, which include real analog circuits and MCNC benchmark circuits. If not otherwise specified, the units for the real analog circuits is in μm and μm^2, and those of the MCNC benchmark circuits are in mm and mm^2. The columns in the table indicate the total number of modules, the number of modules that belong to any symmetric group, the sum of the area of all modules, the total number of nets, and the number of critical nets, respectively. The comparator circuit is of small size and a slice of a ring sampler circuit is of medium to large size. Since in real analog circuits the transistors can have multiple input variants with different numbers of fingers and different area, we do not calculate the total area of all the placement devices for those circuits. Both of the real analog designs are intended to achieve high performance, so the parasitic capacitances of the critical nets need to be minimized to reduce post-layout circuit performance degradation. For completeness, we also run experiments on the MCNC benchmark circuits used by other previous works on analog placement to compare results.

4.1 Critical Parasitics Minimization

4.1.1 Comparator Circuit

Table 3 includes the experimental results for the comparator circuit with and without critical parasitics minimization. Different rows represent different variants generated from different initial aspect ratios. It can be seen that the proposed techniques consistently reduce the critical net wire length CL for all variants with different aspect ratios. While the resulting WL slightly increases, this metric is not crucial for the high-performance analog IC placement problem, as the simulation results in Subsection 1.1 show that the parasitics of non-critical nets have a marginal impact on the circuit performance. Hence, CL has a much more significant effect than WL when shooting for high circuit performance. Two example placement results which have the same area and the same aspect ratio but different critical net wire lengths are shown in Fig. 8. In this figure, the rectangular regions filled with pink represents different placement devices. The bounding boxes for critical nets are highlighted in red, while those for non-critical nets are indicated in blue. We can see clearly that the placement considering critical parasitics minimization yields smaller bounding boxes for the critical nets than the other one. This shows that even with the same area and aspect ratio, we can get better critical parasitics results using the proposed placement techniques. Meanwhile, symmetry is also observed in the resulting layouts.

4.1.2 Ring Sampler Slice Circuit

We extracted the HSPICE format hierarchical netlist of the slice of ring sampler circuit from the analog schematic design environment, and takes the file as input and constructs the circuit hierarchical structure. We ran the parallelized hierarchical placement algorithm for it. Two example placement results are shown in Fig. 9, with the symmetric groups highlighted in yellow and the critical net bounding boxes in red. Hierarchical symmetric groups can also be observed in the results, i.e. some symmetric groups are symmetric to other symmetric groups. The first variant has a smaller area and slightly longer CL than the second one, while the latter achieves better CL but is less compact in terms of total area. Our algorithm generates several nondominated placements so that designers can choose from them according to their trade-offs.

After obtaining the critical net lengths and the metal to substrate capacitance parameters from the target process technology files, we are able to estimate the critical parasitic loading of each critical net, and do the schematic-level circuit performance simulation with these estimated parasitic capacitances injected to the corresponding critical nets. Non-critical net parasitics are not injected since their effects are marginal and can be ignored for estimation purpose. We compare our placement results with the manual layout by experienced designers using the same performance simulation method, except that the critical net half perimeter wire lengths are measured from the manual layout. Unit capacitance per μm for minimum wire width we used to do simulation is 0.111fF/μm. Table 4 shows the comparisons of the simulation results for our second variant and the manual layout. Note that since the manual layout is post-routing, it is natural that it will have longer CL than our placement result. In the table, K_{vco} is the voltage-controlled oscillator (VCO) gain, which determines the loop gain, and has a direct impact on the signal to noise ratio (SNR). Smaller critical parasitics can reduce the degradation of K_{vco}, maintaining a good SNR. I_{bias} is the VCO bias current sampled at VCO frequency of 110MHz. As the critical parasitics loading increases, power increases in order to maintain the same center frequency. Overall, the simulation results show that it is compelling to minimize critical parasitics in the layout synthesis of high-performance analog circuits, and demonstrate the merits of this work.

Table 3: Comparisons with and without minimizing critical parasitics of comparator circuit

Size			w/o considering critical parasitics		Considering critical parasitics	
W	H	Area	WL	CL	WL	CL
4.44	11.04	49.02	465.4	53.8	466.8	52.4
5.7	7.52	42.86	500.6	113.2	505.8	97.2
6.38	7.38	47.08	514.6	130.2	515.8	129.6
6.8	6.58	44.74	541.5	110.4	551.1	105.6
7.48	6	44.88	427.6	84.2	472.2	52.4

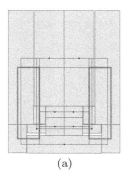 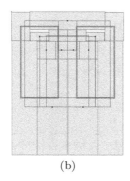

(a)   (b)

Figure 8: Placement results of comparator circuit: (a) considers critical nets (b) does not consider critical nets.

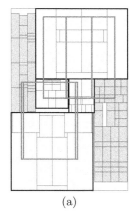 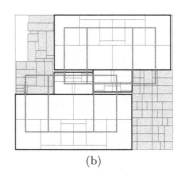

(a)   (b)

Figure 9: Placement results of a slice of ring sampler circuit: (a) variant 1 (b) variant 2.

4.2 Comparisons on Different MOO Flavors

This set of experiments was run using the xerox circuit, both without and with critical parasitics consideration, whose results are shown in Table 5 and Table 6. Different input aspect ratios are used, and placements are run using the 3 MOO flavors for the same amount of time (e.g. 100s) for each initial aspect ratio. For SEQUENTIALMIN, the run-time

Table 4: Simulation results of our placement and the manual layout of ring sampler circuit

Layout	CL (μm)	K_{vco} (THz/A)	I_{bias} (μA)	SNR (dB)	Finish time
ours	19.88	2.418	38.7	72.6	1243s
manual	43.44	2.35	40	72	1 month

* Our CL was based on placement results, and that of the manual layout were extracted from post-routing layout.

is accumulated from its first to the last step. When considering critical parasitics, the critical net weight γ is set to a high weight (e.g. 20x higher than non-critical ones). For FIXEDAREAMIN, the fixed area is set such that the maximum white space is 0.3.

Table 5 lists the placement results of 2 example initial aspect ratios without considering critical parasitics. Since critical nets are not assigned higher weights than the non-critical ones, comparing CL is not meaningful in this case. Therefore we only compare area and total wire length WL as highlighted. The results indicate that from SEQUENTIALMIN, WEIGHTEDSUMMIN to FIXEDAREAMIN approach we get placements with increasing area but decreasing WL.

On the other hand, when we consider critical parasitics and the critical net weight is high enough, it means CL is our primary focus and WL has less importance. Therefore, in this circumstance we only compare the total area and critical net wire length CL as highlighted in Table 6. SEQUENTIALMIN results in the most compact placements in terms of area, FIXEDAREAMIN leads to better CL at the expense of area, while WEIGHTEDSUMMIN realizes the trade-off between them.

Table 5: Comparisons of different MOO flavors w/o considering critical parasitics (run-time of each flavor: 100s).

Initialized with: MOO Flavor	Aspect ratio 1			Aspect ratio 2		
	Area (mm^2)	WL (mm)	CL (mm)	Area (mm^2)	WL (mm)	CL (mm)
Sequential	19.8	646.5	52.6	20	760.1	61.1
Weighted Sum	21.9	626.7	45.9	21.8	748	72.2
Fixed Area	24.3	600.2	49.9	25.4	634.2	51.1

Table 6: Comparisons of different MOO flavors considering critical parasitics (run-time of each flavor: 100s).

Initialized with: MOO Flavor	Aspect ratio 1			Aspect ratio 2		
	Area (mm^2)	WL (mm)	CL (mm)	Area (mm^2)	WL (mm)	CL (mm)
Sequential	19.8	648.5	53	20.2	586.4	41.3
Weighted Sum	21.9	690.1	49.5	23.5	579.4	32
Fix Area	26.5	769	45	24.2	517.3	30

4.3 Comparisons with Previous Work

In this subsection, we compare the placement results of our proposed techniques with the state-of-the-art analog placement work [5]. For larger benchmarks (ami33 and ami49), we run our hierarchical circuit partitioning algorithm on them. Parameters including the number of levels in the circuit hierarchy, the number of partitions in different levels, and the number of variants kept in each subpartition are determined according to the trade-off between optimization quality and efficiency. W.l.o.g., this set of experiments is run using the SEQUENTIALMIN approach to solve the placement subproblems. Comparisons are shown in Table 7. We do not compare HPWL results for apte and hp circuits, because there might be some difference in the way they calculated HPWL for these 2 benchmarks per our discussion with the authors of [5] which makes the two numbers incomparable, and their detailed results and the executable of their program were not obtainable. The results demonstrate that our algorithm achieves better total area and HPWL results with tolerable run-time overhead.

Table 7: Comparisons with state-of-the-art analog placement work.

Bench-marks	[5]			This work				
	Area	HPWL	Time (s)	Area	change	HPWL	change	Time (s)
apte	47.9	*	3	47.08	-1.72%	297.12	-	6
hp	10.1	*	16	9.57	-5.25%	74.38	-	32
ami33	1.29	47.23	39	1.26	-2.36%	45.05	-4.62%	348
ami49	41.32	769.99	96	39.52	-4.35%	763.93	-0.79%	559

5. CONCLUSION

In the paper, we propose hierarchical and analytical placement techniques for high-performance analog ICs. The circuit hierarchical structure is either obtained from the designers' input or with the proposed critical parasitic loading aware, hierarchical symmetric constraints and proximity constraints feasible hierarchical circuit partitioning, followed by a hierarchical and parallelized placement algorithm for high-performance analog circuits. An MILP formulation is proposed to solve the placement subproblem for each subpartition, which minimizes critical parasitic loading, the total area and HPWL simultaneously, and handles hierarchical symmetric constraints, orientations and variants selection at the same time. Experimental results demonstrate that our proposed techniques are able to obtain analog placement results with high circuit performance in reasonable run-time.

Acknowledgment

This work is supported by the National Science Foundation under Grant No. 1527320.

6. REFERENCES

[1] Mark Po-Hung Lin, Yao-Wen Chang, and Chih-Ming Hung. Recent research development and new challenges in analog layout synthesis. In *IEEE/ACM Asia and South Pacific Design Automation Conference (ASPDAC)*, pages 617–622, 2016.

[2] Hidetoshi Onodera, Yo Taniguchi, and Keikichi Tamaru. Branch-and-bound placement for building block layout. In *ACM/IEEE Design Automation Conference (DAC)*, pages 433–439, 1991.

[3] Koen Lampaert, Georges Gielen, and Willy M Sansen. A performance-driven placement tool for analog integrated circuits. *IEEE J. Solid-State Circuits*, 30(7):773–780, 1995.

[4] Martin Strasser, Michael Eick, Helmut Gräb, Ulf Schlichtmann, and Frank M Johannes. Deterministic analog circuit placement using hierarchically bounded enumeration and enhanced shape functions. In *IEEE/ACM International Conference on Computer-Aided Design (ICCAD)*, pages 306–313, 2008.

[5] Po-Hung Lin, Yao-Wen Chang, and Shyh-Chang Lin. Analog placement based on symmetry-island formulation. *IEEE Transactions on Computer-Aided Design of Integrated Circuits and Systems (TCAD)*, 28(6):791–804, 2009.

[6] Hui-Fang Tsao, Pang-Yen Chou, Shih-Lun Huang, Yao-Wen Chang, Mark Po-Hung Lin, Duan-Ping Chen, and Dick Liu. A corner stitching compliant b*-tree representation and its applications to analog placement. In *IEEE/ACM International Conference on Computer-Aided Design (ICCAD)*, pages 507–511, 2011.

[7] Qiang Ma, Linfu Xiao, Yiu-Cheong Tam, and Evangeline FY Young. Simultaneous handling of symmetry, common centroid, and general placement constraints. *IEEE Transactions on Computer-Aided Design of Integrated Circuits and Systems (TCAD)*, 30(1):85–95, 2011.

[8] Cheng-Wu Lin, Jai-Ming Lin, Chun-Po Huang, and Soon-Jyh Chang. Performance-driven analog placement considering boundary constraint. In *ACM/IEEE Design Automation Conference (DAC)*, pages 292–297, 2010.

[9] Po-Hsun Wu, Mark Po-Hung Lin, Yang-Ru Chen, Bing-Shiun Chou, Tung-Chieh Chen, Tsung-Yi Ho, and Bin-Da Liu. Performance-driven analog placement considering monotonic current paths. In *IEEE/ACM International Conference on Computer-Aided Design (ICCAD)*, pages 613–619, 2012.

[10] Mark Po-Hung Lin, Po-Hsun Chang, Shuenn-Yuh Lee, and Helmut E Graeb. Demixgen: Deterministic mixed-signal layout generation with separated analog and digital signal paths. *IEEE Transactions on Computer-Aided Design of Integrated Circuits and Systems (TCAD)*, 35(8):1229–1242, 2016.

[11] Ricardo Martins, Nuno Lourenço, and Nuno Horta. Multi-objective optimization of analog integrated circuit placement hierarchy in absolute coordinates. *Expert Systems with Applications*, 42(23):9137–9151, 2015.

[12] Po-Hung Lin and Shyh-Chang Lin. Analog placement based on hierarchical module clustering. In *ACM/IEEE Design Automation Conference (DAC)*, pages 50–55, 2008.

[13] Mark Po-Hung Lin, Hongbo Zhang, Martin DF Wong, and Yao-Wen Chang. Thermal-driven analog placement considering device matching. pages 593–598, 2009.

[14] Po-Hsun Wu, Mark Po-Hung Lin, Tung-Chieh Chen, Ching-Feng Yeh, Tsung-Yi Ho, and Bin-Da Liu. Exploring feasibilities of symmetry islands and monotonic current paths in slicing trees for analog placement. *IEEE Transactions on Computer-Aided Design of Integrated Circuits and Systems (TCAD)*, 33(6):879–892, 2014.

[15] Hung-Chih Ou, Kai-Han Tseng, Jhao-Yan Liu, I-Peng Wu, and Yao-Wen Chang. Layout-dependent effects-aware analytical analog placement. *IEEE Transactions on Computer-Aided Design of Integrated Circuits and Systems (TCAD)*, 35(8):1243–1254, 2016.

[16] Takashi Nojima, Xiaoke Zhu, Yasuhiro Takashima, Shigetoshi Nakatake, and Yoji Kajitani. Multi-level placement with circuit schema based clustering in analog ic layouts. In *IEEE/ACM Asia and South Pacific Design Automation Conference (ASPDAC)*, pages 406–411, 2004.

[17] C. M. Fiduccia and R. M. Mattheyses. A linear-time heuristic for improving network partitions. In *ACM/IEEE Design Automation Conference (DAC)*, pages 175–181, 1982.

[18] L. A. Sanchis. Multiple-way network partitioning. *IEEE Trans. Comput.*, 38:62–81, January 1989.

[19] Jianhua Li, Laleh Behjat, and Jie Huang. An effective clustering algorithm for mixed-size placement. In *International Symposium on Physical Design (ISPD)*, pages 111–118, 2007.

[20] Jackey Z. Yan, Chris Chu, and Wai-Kei Mak. Safechoice: a novel clustering algorithm for wirelength-driven placement. In *International Symposium on Physical Design (ISPD)*, pages 185–192, 2010.

[21] George Karypis and Vipin Kumar. Multilevel k-way hypergraph partitioning. In *ACM/IEEE Design Automation Conference (DAC)*, pages 343–348, 1999.

[22] Gurobi. GUROBI. http://www.gurobi.com/html/academic.html, 2014.

Physical Design Challenges and Innovations to Meet Power, Speed, and Area Scaling Trend

Lee-Chung Lu
TSMC, Ltd.
lclu@tsmc.com

ABSTRACT

In the advanced process technologies of 7nm and beyond, the semiconductor industry faces several new challenges: (1) aggressive chip area scaling with economically feasible process technology development, (2) sufficient performance enhancement of advanced small-scale technology with significantly increased wire and via resistances, (3) power density sustainability with ever shrinking chip area, and (4) advanced chip packaging integration solutions for complex SOC systems. In this presentation, novel physical design solutions of robust IP and design methodologies will be explored to solve these challenges. These innovations are made possible by the co-optimization of process technology, IP design and design flow automation.

Density scaling is the most important indicator in the continuation of Moore's law. Before 10nm, chip area reduction is mainly achieved by fundamentally shrinking transistor and metal dimensions. Starting from 7nm, maintaining sufficient and economical scaling is hard to achieve through dimension decrease alone. We present two cost-effective enablers, FIN depopulation and EUV, along with their associated innovative standard cell structures and physical design flows, to realize additional area reduction beyond process dimension scaling.

Achieving high performance is always a key index for CPU designs. However, the resistance of interconnects has grown significantly as the dimensions of wires and vias are scaled aggressively. We present novel physical design solutions of the via pillar approach using metal layer promotion and multiple-width configurable wires. This fully automated via pillar design flow mitigates the high resistance impact and becomes indispensable in high performance designs for advanced process technologies.

Maintaining power densities while aggressively shrinking chip areas is also a critical requirement, especially for mobile and IoT applications. Lowering supply voltages is one of the most effective means to reducing power consumption, especially for FinFET devices with much lower threshold voltages than planar devices. However, process and timing variation is high even for FinFET devices operating at very low voltages. We present robust ultra-low voltage IP design solutions and the current status and issues of non-Gaussian and asymmetric variation modeling for ultra-low voltage timing signoffs.

Finally, advanced chip packaging is presented as a viable solution for integration and system level scaling for complex SOC systems. Specific packaging solutions can meet different requirements of system die and package size, form factor, bandwidth, power and homogeneous or heterogeneous integration. For a silicon-proven system, quantitative advantages of advanced packaging over traditional packaging in silicon thickness, thermal dissipation and voltage drop are presented. Chip packaging integration flow and requirements will also be discussed.

Keywords: Moore's law, Process and Design Co-optimization.

ISPD '17, March 19–22, 2017, Portland, OR, USA.
ACM. ISBN 978-1-4503-4696-2/17/03.
DOI: http://dx.doi.org/10.1145/3036669.3038255

Modern Challenges in Constructing Clocks

Charles J. Alpert
Cadence Design Systems

Historically, the clock tree synthesis algorithms seek to build zero-skew trees, and today skew remains an important design consideration. However, in today's the era of concurrent clock and datapath optimization, the challenges are more nuanced in several ways.

- Clock construction must optimize for useful skew so that high performance designs can achieve their frequency targets.
- While power as always been part of the objective function, low power is critical enough where other constraints can be relaxed if it makes sense for the global design objectives.

- Advanced nodes have heterogeneous layers and highly-resistive vias, making routing estimation algorithms increasingly critical.
- Correlation between these estimates and the DRC-clean detailed routing results is also a key factor for clock tree quality.
- Utilizing thick metal most effectively to drive the global clock distribution
- Clock gating, enable timing, and clock logic can restrict an algorithms ability to find good solution.

This talk discusses these challenges (and others) in automating clock tree synthesis to solve today's complex design problems. The field remains fruitful for innovation.

ISPD'17, March 19–22, 2017, Portland, OR, USA.
ACM. ISBN 978-1-4503-4696-2/17/03.
DOI: http://dx.doi.org/10.1145/3036669.3045793

Clock Tree Construction based on Arrival Time Constraints

Rickard Ewetz[†] and Cheng-Kok Koh[‡]

[†]Department of Electrical and Computer Engineering, University of Central Florida, Orlando, US[*]
[‡]School of Electrical and Computer Engineering, Purdue University, West Lafayette, US
rickard.ewetz@ucf.edu,chengkok@purdue.edu

ABSTRACT

There are striking differences between constructing clock trees based on dynamic implied skew constraints and based on static arrival time constraints. Dynamic implied skew constraints allow the full timing margins to be utilized, but the constraints are required to be updated (with high time complexity). In contrast, static arrival time constraints are decoupled and are not required to be updated. Therefore, the constraints can be obtained in constant time, which facilitates the exploration of various tree topologies. On the other hand, arrival time constraints do not allow the full timing margins to be utilized. Consequently, there is a trade-off between topology exploration and timing margin utilization. In this paper, the advantages of static arrival time constraints are leveraged to construct clock trees with useful skew while exploring various tree topologies. Moreover, the constraints are specified and respecified throughout the synthesis process reduce the cost of the constructed clock trees. It is experimentally demonstrated that the proposed approach results in clock trees with 16% lower average capacitive cost compared with clock trees constructed based on dynamic implied skew constraints.

1. INTRODUCTION

Limited routing resources and tight power budgets require clock trees to be constructed with short wire length and small buffer area. Moreover, useful skew is required to meet irregular timing constraints and to improve robustness. Sequential circuits are synchronized by a clock signal, which is delivered using a clock tree, from a clock source to a set of sequential elements (or clock sinks). Clock skew is the difference in the arrival time of the clock signal between a pair of clock sinks. There is an explicit skew constraint between each pair of sinks that are only separated by combinational logic. These explicit skew constraints can be captured in a

[*]Rickard Ewetz performed part of this research at Purdue University. This research was partially supported by NSF awards CFF-1065318 and CFF-1527562.

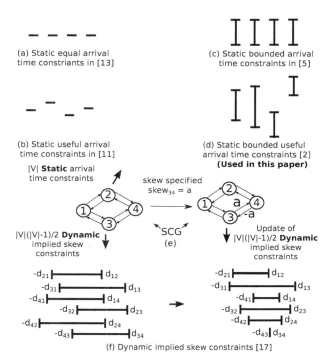

Figure 1: The tree construction in this paper is based on the bounded useful arrival time constraints in (d), which dominates the arrival time constraints in (a), (b), and (c). The static constraints are decoupled from the SCG in (e), in contrast with the dynamic implied skew constraints in (f). $|V|$ is the number of clock sinks and d_{ij} denotes the length of the shortest path from vertex i to vertex j in the SCG.

skew constraint graph (SCG) [17], as shown in Figure 1(e). In an SCG, each vertex represents a sink and each edge represents an explicit skew constraint between the corresponding two sinks.

Based on the explicit skew constraints, there is a dynamic implied skew constraint between every pair of sinks, as shown in Figure 1(f). The bounds of each constraint are defined by the length of two shortest paths in the SCG. Clock trees meeting the explicit skew constraints can be constructed based on iteratively merging subtrees (or sinks) while considering the *dynamic implied skew constraints* [17, 6, 8]. When a pair of sinks are merged, the skew between the sinks is specified and edge weights are required to be updated in the SCG, which in turn requires every implied skew constraint to be updated (with high run-time complexity).

For example, the implied skew constraint between sink 1 and sink 4 may change when the skew between sink 3 and sink 4 is specified, as illustrated in Figure 1(e) and (f). In [17], the Greedy-UST/DME algorithm was proposed to construct useful skew trees based on implied skew constraints. However, only a limited number of topologies were explored, as it is costly in run-time to update the constraints [17, 6, 8].

An alternative to implied skew constraints is *static arrival time constraints* [13, 11, 5, 2], which consist of a range (or in special cases a point) as the arrival time constraints for each sink, as shown in Figure 1(a)–(d). The constraints are satisfied if the clock signal is delivered within the ranges. The advantage of static arrival time constraints is that the constraints are not required to be updated because they are defined with respect to an arbitrary reference point. Using the reference point, the constraints can be obtained in constant time. However, static constraints are inherently more restrictive than implied skew constraints.

Zero skew trees (ZSTs) and useful skew trees (USTs) can be constructed using static equal [13] and static useful [11] arrival time constraints, both of which are point constraints, as shown in Figure 1(a) and (b), respectively. A ZST is constructed using zero-skew merging by storing the delay of each subtree [13]. The useful arrival time constraints in Figure 1(b) can be obtained using a linear programming (LP) formulation that optimizes clock period or robustness [11]. Next, using virtual delay offsets to account for the non-alignment of the point constraints, a clock tree can be constructed using zero-skew merging [13].

In [5], bounded skew trees (BSTs) were constructed based on static bounded arrival time constraints, which are range constraints, as illustrated in Figure 1(c). The expansion of a point constraint to a range constraint resulted in clock trees with shorter wire lengths. As the skew bound can be obtained in constant time and that the minimum and the maximum delay of each subtree can be stored, subtrees pairs can be merged in constant time [5], which facilitates the exploration of various tree topologies. In [5], the exploration was guided by a rerooting feature that transforms a subtree into subtrees with different tree topologies (further details in Section 2.1 and Figure 2). However, static bounded arrival time constraints do not allow useful skews.

In [12], USTs were constructed based on the static bounded useful arrival time constraints [2], as shown in Figure 1(d). The constraints allow both range constraints and useful skew to be utilized. Given the explicit skew constraints, alternative sets of range constraints can be specified [2]. In [12], the range constraints were specified to maximize the length of the range constraints, to potentially reduce the cost of the constructed clock trees. The limitation of this approach is that by maximizing the length of the range constraints, the range constraints may become unaligned, which constrains the tree construction. Moreover, while merging subtrees, no routing tree topologies were maintained and no interconnect delays were computed (in contrast with in [13, 11, 5]).

In this paper, we propose a tree construction algorithm based on static bounded useful arrival time constraints. The algorithm allows clock trees with useful skew to be constructed while both exploring various tree topologies and accounting for interconnect delays. Moreover, the range constraints are specified using a LP formulation that aims to reduce the capacitive cost of the constructed clock trees.

The BST construction (in [5]) is extended such that an UST can be constructed given a set of static bounded useful arrival time constraints. The extension is based on introducing a virtual minimum delay offset and a virtual maximum delay offset for each sink, i.e., combining the construction techniques for the constraints in Figure 1(b) and (c). The values of the offsets are defined by the arrival time constraints. The extension maintains that pairs of subtrees can be merged in constant time, facilitating the exploration of various tree topologies. In contrast with the tree construction in [12], the proposed approach allows routing topologies to be maintained and interconnect delays to be computed while merging subtrees.

Given a set of explicit skew constraints, many alternative sets of static bounded useful arrival time constraints can be specified [2]. Each set of constraints results in a clock tree with a different capacitive cost. We attempt to minimize the capacitive cost by specifying the arrival time constraints while considering both the length and the alignment of the constraints using an LP formulation. In [2, 12], only the length of the range constraints was considered.

Although the static bounded useful arrival time constraints do not allow for full utilization of timing margins, the ability to explore various topologies translates into cost reduction, as a larger solution space is explored. Experimental results show that the proposed approach is capable of constructing clock trees with similar robustness and 16% lower cost.

The remainder of the paper is organized as follows: the constraints and the problem formulation are introduced in Section 2 and in Section 3, respectively. The tree construction is outlined in Section 4. In Section 5, the static constraints are specified using an LP formulation. The synthesis flow and experimental results are presented in Section 6 and Section 7. We conclude in Section 8.

2. STATIC AND DYNAMIC CONSTRAINTS

Setup and hold time constraints are imposed between each pair sequential elements, or flip flips (FFs), that are separated by only combinational logic. The setup and hold time constraints between a launching flip flop FF_i and a capturing flip flop FF_j are formulated as follows:

$$t_i + t_i^{CQ} + t_{ij}^{max} + t_j^S \leq t_j + T, \quad (1)$$

$$t_i + t_i^{CQ} + t_{ij}^{min} \geq t_j + t_j^H, \quad (2)$$

where t_i and t_j are the arrival times of the clock signal to FF_i and FF_j, respectively. t_{ij}^{min} and t_{ij}^{max} are the minimum and maximum propagation delay through the combinational logic; t_i^{CQ} is the clock to output delay of FF_i; T is the clock period; t_j^S and t_j^H are the setup and hold time of FF_j, respectively. The setup and hold time constrains in Eq (1) and Eq (2) can be reformulated into **explicit skew constraints** as follows:

$$t_h - t_k \leq c_{hk}, \quad (3)$$

where t_h, t_k, and c_{hk} are respectively equal to t_i, t_j, and $T - t_i^{CQ} - t_{ij}^{max} - t_j^S - M_{user}$, for each setup constraint in Eq (1). In addition, t_h, t_k, and c_{hk} are respectively equal to t_j, t_i, and $t_{ij}^{min} + t_i^{CQ} - t_j^H - M_{user}$, for each hold time constraint in Eq (2). M_{user} is a user specified non-negative safety margin that is introduced to account for on-chip variations.

The explicit skew constraints in Eq (3) can be captured in a skew constraint graph (SCG). In an SCG $G = (V, E)$, V is the set of sequential elements and E is the set of skew

Table 1: Comparisons of tree construction techniques. A '*' implies that rerooting was not performed but it would be easy to apply. 'n/a' denotes that no tree topology is maintained while merging subtrees.

Tree construction proposed in	Constraints	Update required?	Ease of exploring tree topologies based on rerooting	Useful skews allowed	Degree of utilization of timing margins	Considers interconnect delays during merging
[13]	Static equal arrival time [13]	No	easy*	No	low	Yes
[13]	Static useful arrival time [11]	No	easy*	Yes	low	Yes
[5]	Static bounded arrival time [5]	No	easy	No	medium	Yes
[12]	Static bounded useful arrival time [2]	No	'n/a'	Yes	high	No
[17]	Dynamic implied skew [17]	Yes	difficult	Yes	full	Yes
This paper	Static bounded useful arrival time [2]	No	easy	Yes	high	Yes

constraints. For each skew constraint in Eq (3), an edge e_{hk} from vertex h to vertex k is added with a weight $w_{hk} = c_{hk}$. Throughout the synthesis process, skews are specified between pairs of sequential elements. If a skew $skew_{ij} = t_i - t_j = a$ is specified between sink i and sink j, the weight of the edges e_{ij} and e_{ji} are updated to $w_{ij} = a$ and $w_{ji} = -a$, respectively, as shown in Figure 1(e).

Dynamic implied skew constraints are imposed between each pair of sinks by the explicit skew constraints. In [17], it was shown that the implied skew constraints between a pair of sinks is defined as follows:

$$-d_{ji} \leq t_i - t_j \leq d_{ij}, \tag{4}$$

where d_{ij} and d_{ji} denotes the shortest path from vertex i to vertex j and from vertex j to vertex i, respectively, in the SCG. As the implied skew constrains are defined based on the SCG, they are required to be updated when any skew is specified in the SCG. The time complexity to compute or update an implied skew constraint is $O(V \log V + E)$ [6].

A **static arrival time constraint** is a range of arrival time constraints, denoted r_i, for each sink i, with respect to an arbitrary reference point. The arrival time constraints are satisfied if the clock signal is delivered to the sinks within the range constraints [2]. A set of arrival time constraints are defined to be *valid* if they guarantee that the explicit skew constraints in the SCG are satisfied, which can be ensured as follows:

$$x_i^{lb} \leq x_i^{ub}, \quad \forall i \in V \tag{5}$$
$$x_i^{ub} - x_j^{lb} \leq w_{ij}, \quad \forall (i,j) \in E \tag{6}$$

where x_i^{lb} and x_i^{lb} respectively denote the lower and the upper bound of the range r_i. V and E are the vertices and the edges in an SCG, respectively. (The x_i^{lb} and x_i^{ub} notation is illustrated in Figure 3 in Section 4.2.)

As the arrival time constraints are specified with respect to an arbitrary reference point, they are not required to be updated when skews are specified in the SCG. Moreover, the reference point is not required to be specified.

2.1 Arrival time vs. implied skew constraints

In Table 1, it can be observed that the proposed tree construction is advantageous to the earlier tree construction approaches based on **static arrival time constraints** [2].

The proposed tree construction dominates the tree construction approaches in [13, 5] because the tree construction is based on the static useful bounded arrival time constraints illustrated in Figure 1(d), which is a dominating generalization of the constraints used in [13, 11, 5], shown in Figure 1(a), (b), and (c), respectively.

Both the proposed tree construction and the tree construction in [12] are based on the static bounded useful arrival time constraints. Consequently, both approaches allow useful skew and have a high degree of timing margins utilization, as unaligned range constraints are used. The difference is that the proposed approach (in similar to in [13, 5]) maintains the routing tree topology of each subtree, which is not performed in [12]. Without a tree topology, interconnect delays cannot be computed, as indicated in Table 1. However, it should be noted that after sufficiently large subtrees have been formed in [12], a tree topology is generated for each subtree and interconnect delays are computed. Nevertheless, these generated tree topologies may violate the skew constraints as the interconnect delays were not considered during the tree generation.

In tree construction based on static bounded useful arrival time constraints, a set of range constraints are required to be specified based on the explicit skew constraints. The specification is coupled with the tree construction problem, as alternative sets of range constraints translate into clock trees with different capacitive cost. In [2], it was observed that the longer range constraints correspond to less constrained tree construction. Therefore, the lengths of the range constraints were lexicographically maximized, i.e., the minimum length range constraint was iteratively maximized up to a threshold. However, for two sinks that are located physically close to be able to be merged meeting the timing constraints, the range constraints have to intersect. (Minor misalignments can be compensated by the interconnect delays in the routing tree topology.) The formation of intersecting range constraints is not directly captured in [2]. Therefore, we propose to specify the range constraints while considering both alignment and length using an LP formulation, which is further discussed in Section 5.

Compared with using **dynamic implied skew constraints** [17], the advantage of performing tree construction based on static arrival time constraints is that the constraints are not required to be updated, they are decoupled from the SCG. Consequently, a pair of subtrees can be merged in constant time. Therefore, it is run-time feasible to evaluate merging two subtrees while exploring various tree topologies. In [5], the topology exploration is performed using a rerooting feature. A subtree with $n \geq 2$ leaf nodes can be rerooted into $2n - 3$ subtrees with different tree topologies, which is illustrated in Figure 2. Consequently, two subtrees with $n \geq 2$ and $m \geq 2$ respective leaf nodes can be merged to a subtree with $(n+m)$ leaf nodes while considering $(2n-3) \cdot (2m-3)$ tree topologies. The two drawbacks of tree construction based on static arrival time constraints are: (i) Arrival time constraints are inherently more restrictive than the explicit skew constraints stored in the SCG. This can be understood because the explicit skew constraints between a pair of sinks have to be satisfied for any pair of arrival times within the respective ranges, see Eq (6); (ii) The static approach does not leverage that the SCG is updated with skew information throughout the tree construction process, which may expose additional timing margins.

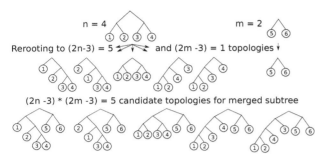

Figure 2: For a subtree with n leaf nodes, $2n-3$ tree topologies are explored by rerooting [5].

The advantage of tree construction based on using dynamic implied skew constraints is that the full timing margins can be utilized. However, it is costly in terms of runtime to explore various topologies, as the implied skew constraints have to be updated after each skew in a topology is specified. The update of each implied skew constraints is $O(V \log V + E)$ [6].

In Table 1, it can be observed that there exists a trade-off between using static arrival time constraints and dynamic implied skew constraints, i.e., ease of topology exploration versus degree of utilization of timing margins. To allow the static approach to expose additional timing margins, we propose to re-specify the static bounded useful arrival time constraints periodically throughout the tree construction process, i.e., mitigating the shortcomings of static arrival time constraints. Further details are provided in Section 6.1.

3. PROBLEM FORMULATION

This paper considers a useful skew clock tree synthesis problem. The problem consists of constructing a clock tree that delivers a clock signal from a clock source to a set of sequential elements while meeting the skew constraints in Eq (3) and transition time constraints. The source to sink connections are realized using wires and buffers from a wire and buffer library, respectively. The objective is to construct clock trees using the least amount of wire and buffer resources. The resource utilization is measured in capacitive cost, which is known to correlate closely with power consumption.

We approach the problem by extending the BST construction such that an UST can be constructed given a set of static bounded useful arrival time constraints (see Section 4). Given an SCG, many alternative sets of static arrival time constraints can be specified, each resulting in a clock tree with a different capacitive cost. In Section 5, we specify the static bounded useful arrival time constraints with the goal of minimizing the capacitive cost of a clock tree constructed using the constraints.

4. BST AND UST TREE CONSTRUCTION

In Section 4.1, we review the BST construction in [5]. In Section 4.2, the BST construction is extended such that USTs can be constructed based on static bounded useful arrival time constraints while considering interconnect delays.

4.1 BST tree construction in [5]

In [5], the BST construction is based on the observation that if the maximum skew between any pair of sinks is less than B, the clock signal will be delivered within the range constraints, illustrated in Figure 1(c). Here, B is equal to the range, i.e., the difference of upper and lower bounds, of each arrival time constraints.

To facilitate the construction of such a BST, the minimum and maximum delay of each subtree i are stored and denoted min_t_i and max_t_i, respectively. Initially, min_t and max_t are set to 0 for a subtree (or sink). Next, a clock tree is constructed by iteratively merging subtrees while ensuring that $max\_t_k - min\_t_k \leq B$ of each formed subtree k.

A pair of subtrees i and j are merged into a larger subtree k with $max\_t_k - min\_t_k \leq B$ as follows: the subtrees i and j are connected with a wire and the length of the wire is equal to the Manhattan distance between the subtrees. (For certain pairs of delay imbalanced subtrees, detour wiring is required [13].) Next, the alternative locations for the root of subtree k are determined on the wire. This can be performed in constant time, as the skew bound B can be obtained in constant time and min_t_k and max_t_k can be computed incrementally as follows:

$$min\_t_k = \min\{min\_t_i + w(k,i), min\_t_j + w(k,j)\}, \quad (7)$$

$$max\_t_k = \max\{max\_t_i + w(k,i), max\_t_j + w(k,j)\}, \quad (8)$$

where $w(k,i)$ and $w(k,j)$ denotes the interconnect delay of the wire between the root of the subtree k and the root of the subtrees i and j, respectively.

Before merging a pair of subtrees, each subtree can be rerooted into multiple subtrees with different topologies, as illustrated in Figure 2. During rerooting, it is utilized that min_t_p and max_t_p are computed and stored for each partial subtree p of a larger subtree. Moreover, each rerooted subtree can be obtained by pairwise merging three partial subtrees of the initial subtree (or a previously rerooted subtree). Therefore, each rerooted subtree can be formed in constant time. The run-time is linear with respect to the number of rerooted topologies that are explored.

As no routing tree topologies are generated in [12], no interconnect delays can be computed, which is equivalent to setting $w(k,i) = 0$ and $w(k,j) = 0$ in both Eq (7) and Eq (8).

It can be understood that the reference point to which the range constraints are defined is arbitrary, because only the relative delay between pairs of sinks is required to meet a skew bound. With a non-arbitrary reference point, the skew bound $B = 50$ could for example mean that the clock signal must be delivered to each sink with a delay in $[200, 250]$ ps.

In the next section, we extend the BST construction such that an UST can be constructed based on static bounded useful arrival time constraints, as shown in Figure 3.

4.2 Proposed UST construction

The extension is based on using a maximum skew bound B^v (in similar to B in [5]) and virtual minimum and virtual maximum delay offsets to account for the non-alignment and the range of the arrival time constraints, similar to using single delay offsets to handle the constraints in Figure 1(b) based on ZST construction [13].

Based on the arrival time constraints, B^v is set to an arbitrary value that satisfies $\frac{B^v}{2} \geq x_i^{ub}$ and $\frac{B^v}{2} \geq -x_i^{lb}$ for all $i \in V$, which is illustrated in Figure 3. The virtual minimum delay offset off_i^{min} and virtual maximum delay offset off_i^{max} for a sink i are specified by the arrival time constraints and B^v as follows:

$$off_i^{min} = -\frac{B^v}{2} - x_i^{lb}, \tag{9}$$

$$off_i^{max} = \frac{B^v}{2} - x_i^{ub}, \tag{10}$$

Finally, an UST can be constructed in a similar fashion as an BST in [5], by setting $B = B^v$ and $min\_t_i = off_i^{min}$ and $max\_t_i = off_i^{max}$ for each sink i, respectively.

The skew bound B^v can be obtained in constant time and min_t and max_t can still be incrementally computed for each subtree. Therefore, it is possible to merge subtrees in constant time and explore various topologies. Note that the reference point is arbitrary and not specified and that B^v can in fact be defined to an arbitrary value by the offsets.

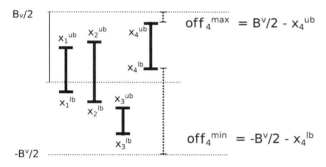

Figure 3: Tree construction based on static bounded useful skew constraints.

Now that we have explained how a UST can be constructed given a set of static bounded useful arrival time constraints, we focus on specifying the constraints with the goal of minimizing the capacitive cost of a clock tree constructed using the constraints.

5. PROPOSED SPECIFICATION OF ARRIVAL TIME CONSTRAINTS

In this section, valid static bounded useful arrival time constraints are specified based on the explicit skew constraints. It is not difficult to specify a set of valid arrival time constraints. Every feasible solution of an LP formulated with the constraints in Eq 6 and Eq 5 forms a set of valid arrival time constraints. The challenge is how to define a suitable objective function, such that the solution to the LP formulation results in arrival time constraints that help to minimize the capacitive cost of the clock tree constructed.

We approach this challenge by observing the following property of arrival time constraints: let r^I be the intersection of the arrival time constraints of all sinks and let $|r^I|$ be the range of r^I (if the intersection is non-empty). *All subtree(s) constructed from the sinks satisfying a skew bound $B = |r^I|$ will satisfy the arrival time constraints.*

It can be easily understood that the larger the $|r^I|$ is, the less constrained the tree construction is and therefore, the more likely the clock tree will have lower capacitive cost. Suppose we construct the bottom k stages of a clock tree without considering any skew constraints, where a stage consists of subtrees, each driven by a buffer. Let $skew^{(k)}$ denote the maximum skew between any pair of sinks in the subtrees of these bottom k stages constructed in such a fashion. We attempt to specify the arrival time constraints with $|r^I| \geq skew^{(k)}$. This would imply that the k bottom-most stages could be constructed in an unconstrained fashion, which probably would result in clock trees with small capacitive cost, as it is well known that a majority of the capacitive cost of a clock tree is located in the bottom most stages [7, 3].

The limitation of the proposed approach is that if any explicit skew constraints require useful skew to be satisfied, i.e., $t_i - t_j \leq -b$, where $b > 0$. No common intersection r^I exists, which is the main limitation of the bounded arrival time constraints in [5].

It can also be understood that by lexicographically maximizing the length of the range constraints as in [2], intersecting range constraints may be formed. However, it may be more effective to both consider length and alignment in the specification process, as in the approach proposed in the next section. The capacitive cost of the clock trees constructed based on the two approaches are compared in Section 6.

5.1 Proposed LP formulation

We propose to specify the arrival time constraints with the following goals: (1) The range constraints have to be valid, i.e., the constraints in Eq. (6) and Eq. (5) have to be satisfied. (2) The lower and upper bounds of each range constraint should be minimized and maximized, respectively. (3) The arrival time constraints should be aligned although they are allowed to be unaligned (to allow insertion of useful skews). (4) Arrival time constraints of similar range are preferred. The motivation for this preference is that a subtree is always more constrained timing wise than the subtrees from which it was constructed. Tree construction is constrained by the arrival time constraints with the smallest range.

With these goals, we propose the following LP formulation:

$$\min \sum_{i \in V} f(x_i^{lb})^{lb} + f(x_i^{ub})^{ub} \tag{11}$$

$$x_i^{lb} \leq x_i^{ub}, \quad \forall i \in V \tag{12}$$

$$x_i^{ub} - x_j^{lb} \leq w_{ij}, \quad \forall (i,j) \in E \tag{13}$$

where, $f(x)^{lb}$ and $f(x)^{ub}$ are convex p-part piecewise linear functions shown in Figure 4. In Figure 4, $c_1, \cdots, c_p$ are user specified weights and $\frac{skew^{(1)}}{2}, \cdots, \frac{skew^{(p-1)}}{2}$ are stage skews.

It is evident that the formulation achieves the goals (1) and (2) by the constraints in Eq (12) and Eq (13) and the objective function. The formulation achieves the goals (3) and (4) by setting the slope of the piecewise linear functions $f(x)^{lb}$ and $f(x)^{ub}$ as illustrated in Figure 4(a) and (b). In the figure, it can be observed that there is a heavy penalty if the lower bound (the upper bound) of a range is not set to be lesser (greater) than $-\frac{skew^{(1)}}{2}$ ($\frac{skew^{(1)}}{2}$). Moreover, the slopes of $f(x)^{lb}$ and $f(x)^{ub}$ are changed at certain multiples of $-\frac{skew^{(1)}}{2}$ and $\frac{skew^{(1)}}{2}$, to encourage similar ranges and arrival constraints that are aligned and centered in $[-\frac{skew^{(1)}}{2}, \frac{skew^{(1)}}{2}]$ to be formed. Empirically, we find that it is important to set the slope, of the different parts to be drastically different, to avoid having constraints with disproportionately small ranges. In our implementation, $c_i = 200^i/20000$.

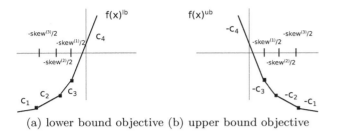

(a) lower bound objective (b) upper bound objective

Figure 4: Convex piecewise linear functions $f(x)^{lb}$ and $f(x)^{ub}$.

6. CTS AND ITS EVALUATION

6.1 Flow for tree construction

Clock trees with buffers are constructed by integrating the proposed constraints into a classical bottom-up tree construction framework, which is based on algorithms in [17, 5, 4, 8, 10]. An overview of the framework is shown in Figure 5.

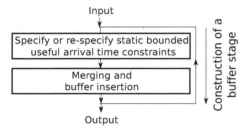

Figure 5: Flow for tree construction.

A clock tree is constructed buffer stage by buffer stage. A buffer stage consists of a set of subtrees, each driven by a buffer. The input to the construction of the bottom most stage is the clock sinks, and the input to the construction of the consecutive stages are the input pins of the driving buffers of the previous buffer stage. Each buffer stage is constructed by specifying (or re-specifying) the static arrival time constraints (see Section 5). Next, subtrees are iteratively pairwise merged to form larger subtrees while satisfying the arrival time constraints (see Section 4.2). Lastly, buffers are inserted to drive the constructed subtrees such that the transition time constraints are satisfied [4, 8, 10]. The iterative buffer stage construction process continues until only a tree remains.

Specify or re-specify static arrival time constraints: In the construction of the bottom buffered stage, the arrival time constraints are specified with respect to the sinks, as described in Section 5. In the construction of a higher-level buffer stage, each subtree can be viewed as a sink and the arrival time constraints are re-specified, i.e., a single range constraint is specified for each subtree. The re-specification exposes additional timing margins by including the skew information in the SCG obtained from the construction of lower-level buffer stages.

6.2 Experimental evaluation

In the remainder of this section, we present experimental results to demonstrate the effectiveness of the proposed constraints and algorithms in reducing capacitive cost of clock trees. (We demonstrate that the proposed techniques can be used to construct clock trees that are robust to OCV in Section 7.) The algorithms are implemented in C++ and the experiments are performed on a 10 core 5.0 GHz Linux machine with 64 GB of memory.

Using the proposed tree construction framework, various different tree structures are constructed. (1) The D-UST structure is a tree structure that is constructed using dynamic implied skew constraints, i.e., the Greedy-UST/DME algorithm in [17]. (2) The PS-UST structure is a tree structure constructed using static useful arrival time constraints where the arrival time constraints for each sink are in the form of a point. (3) The LS-UST structure is a tree structure that is constructed based on static bounded useful arrival time constraints. The range constraints are are specified to maximize the lengths lexicographically as in [2, 12]. (4) The S-UST structure is a tree structure that is constructed based on static bounded useful arrival time constraints. The range constraints are specified using the LP formulation in Section 5. (5) The TS-UST structure is the S-UST structure with the additional feature of using rerooting to explore topologies. (6) The RTS-UST structure is equal to the TS-UST structure with the additional feature that the arrival time constraints are re-specified after the synthesis of each buffer stage, as described in Section 6.1.

6.3 Evaluation of various trees structures

In Table 2, we present the results of the various tree structures constructed on the twelve circuits in Table 3, which are available online [7]. The top seven circuits have been used in earlier studies. We compare the performance in terms of the capacitive cost in the column labeled "Cap cost" and the run-time in the column labeled "Run-time".

No direct comparison is provided with [12]. However, using the LS-UST structure, a direct comparison is provided with the method of specifying the constraints in [2, 12].

The S-UST structures have 5% lower average capacitive cost when compared with the D-UST structures. The lower capacitive costs may stem from that the S-UST structures have relatively aligned arrival time constraints (specified before the tree construction). In the D-UST structure, the arrival times to the sinks may be significantly skewed, as skews are incrementally specified within implied skew constraints.

Compared with the S-UST structures, the PS-UST structures have 48% higher cost on the average, as the arrival time constraints in PS-UST are in the form of points. The LS-UST structures have 37% higher average cost compared with the S-UST structures. This is because the range constraints are specified to maximize the lengths lexicographically [2, 12], instead of considering both length and alignment. The TS-UST structures have 8% lower average capacitive cost when compared with the S-UST structures. This can be understood because the TS-UST structures allows subtrees to be rerooted, facilitating the exploration of various tree topologies. As a greater solution space is explored, clock trees with lower capacitive costs are obtained. Even though the TS-UST structures have a lower utilization of timing margins compared with the D-UST structures, the average capacitive cost is lower because of the topology exploration.

Table 2: Comparisons of various tree structures.

Circuits	Cap cost (pF)						Run-time (min)					
(name)	D-UST	PS-UST	LS-UST	**S-UST**	**TS-UST**	**RTS-UST**	D-UST	PS-UST	LS-UST	**S-UST**	**TS-UST**	**RTS-UST**
scaled_s1423	3.3	4.4	9.9	3.9	**3.2**	3.2	1	1	1	1	1	1
scaled_s5378	**5.7**	10.7	9.6	6.3	6.2	5.8	1	3	2	2	20	2
scaled_s15850	18.3	20.5	28.3	20.0	20.0	**17.5**	16	18	11	20	20	9
msp	1.7	2.5	1.8	1.8	**1.5**	1.5	1	2	5	1	4	4
fpu	2.1	2.9	2.0	2.0	**1.9**	1.9	1	1	1	1	4	4
ecg	34.5	50.3	76.4	30.4	28.3	**26.9**	26	30	64	23	53	63
aes	207.5	372.0	204.4	202.4	207.5	**200.7**	186	324	114	127	214	155
usbf	8.0	9.9	8.0	5.2	**4.5**	4.5	4	9	5	3	9	10
dma	7.3	11.9	6.4	5.8	**5.3**	5.3	4	11	5	3	14	14
pci_bridge32	15.1	15.5	11.2	8.9	7.8	**7.7**	10	8	10	5	24	24
des_peft	19.2	29.8	44.1	22.7	19.7	**18.9**	8	14	20	16	36	32
eht	23.6	44.7	23.7	23.3	**21.2**	21.2	16	25	16	15	72	78
Norm.	1.00	1.48	1.30	0.95	0.87	**0.84**						

Table 3: Properties of synthesized circuits.

Circuit	Used in	Sinks	Skew constraints
(name)		(num)	(num)
scaled_s1423	[8]	74	78
scaled_s5378	[8]	179	175
scaled_s15850	[8, 10]	597	318
msp	[8]	683	44990
fpu	[8]	715	16263
ecg	[8, 10]	7674	63440
aes	[10]	13216	53382
usbf		1765	33438
dma		2092	132834
pci_bridge32		3578	141074
des_peft		8808	17152
eht		10544	450762

The RTS-UST structures have 3% lower average capacitive cost when compared with the TS-UST structures, as the arrival time constraints are re-specified during the synthesis process to expose additional timing margins after each buffer stage. However, capacitive reductions are only obtained on six out of the twelve circuits. The explanation for this is that the skew constraints have to be relatively stringent for the exposed timing margins to translate into reduction in capacitive cost.

As the arrival time constraints do not have to be updated, the S-UST structures are expected to have shorter run-times when compared with the D-UST structures, the construction of which requires updates of the dynamic implied skew constraints. This is particularly true for larger circuits. Compared with the S-UST structures, the TS-UST structures are expected to have a longer run-times because rerooting is applied to explore various tree topologies. The RTS-UST structures are expected to have shorter run-times compared with the TS-UST structures, as the re-specification of the arrival time constraints may make the tree construction less constrained. Ideally, we would like to control the run-time of the topology exploration more closely. Nevertheless, there are many second order effects that influences the run-time. In particular, a big component of the run-times is related to NGSPICE circuit simulations for guiding the synthesis process.

7. EVALUATION OF ROBUSTNESS TO OCV

In this section, the trees structures constructed by our framework are compared with the clock trees in [8, 10], in terms of timing yield and capacitive cost. The comparison is performed using the Monte Carlo framework proposed in [8], which is an extension of the ISPD 2010 clock contest formulation in [16].

In [10], the clock trees were constructed using a CTS phase and a clock tree optimization (CTO) phase. After an initial

clock tree has been constructed in the CTS phase, some timing violations may still exist. The CTO phase is employed to remove these violations. The optimization is performed by realizing delay adjustments in the tree by inserting buffers and detour wires. The delay adjustments are specified using an LP formulation [14, 15, 9]. For further technical details of the CTO phase, please refer to [14, 15, 9]. To facilitate a fair comparison with [8, 10], we apply CTO [14, 15, 9] to the RTS-UST structures constructed by our framework. Before we present the experimental results, we first describe the evaluation framework.

7.1 Monte Carlo evaluation framework

Each clock tree is evaluated in terms of timing yield and capacitive cost. The timing yield of a clock tree is determined by simulating the clock tree with 500 Monte Carlo simulations. In each simulation, the clock tree is subject to wire width variations ($\pm 5.0\%$), supply voltage variations ($\pm 7.5\%$), temperature variations ($\pm 15.0\%$), and channel length variations ($\pm 5.0\%$) around the nominal values.

Each simulation represents the testing of a chip, if all the skew and transition times are satisfied, the chip is classified as good. If any timing constraint is violated, the chip is classified as defective. The timing yield is defined to be the number of good chips divided by the number of tested chips.

7.2 Evaluation of timing yield and cost

In Table 4, we compare the RTS-UST structures constructed in this work with the D-UST structures constructed in [8], which reported results on six of the twelve benchmark circuits. We also compare against the D-UST structures and LD-UST structures in [10], which reported results on three circuits. The LD-UST structure in [10] is an extension of the D-UST structure in that the structure can meet both skew constraints and a user-specified latency bound at the expense of increased capacitive cost. The normalized capacitive results (labeled "Norm." in Table 4) are obtained with respect to the capacitive cost of the RTS-UST structures after CTO.

First, we compare the results after CTS (and before CTO). Compared with the RTS-UST structures, the D-UST structures in [8], the D-UST structures in [10], and the LD-UST structures in [10] have 35%, 15%, 16% higher capacitive cost, respectively, which is similar to the results reported for the D-UST structures in Table 2.

After CTO, we observe that the capacitive cost of the RTS-UST structures have only increased by 0.4% on the average (by comparing RTS-UST structures obtained after CTS and after CTO). Therefore, it can be understood that the RTS-UST structures have 43%, 13%, and 16% lower

Table 4: Evaluation of clock trees in timing yield and capacitive cost. A '-' in the CTO run-time column means that CTO is not required to achieve 100% yield.

Circuit	Work	Structure	M_{user}	After CTS				After CTO			
				Cap	Latency	Yield	Run-time	Cap	Latency	Yield	Run-time
(name)		(name)	(ps)	(pF)	(ps)	(%)	(min)	(pF)	(ps)	(%)	(min)
scaled_s1423	[8]	D-UST	0	3.4	140	100.0	1	3.4	140	100.0	-
	this work	RTS-UST	0	3.2	128	100.0	1	3.2	128	100.0	-
scaled_s5378	[8]	D-UST	0	5.7	130	100.0	1	5.7	130	100.0	-
	this work	RTS-UST	0	5.8	205	57.8	2	5.8	205	100.0	1
scaled_s15850	[8]	D-UST	27	20.2	405	96.6	5	20.7	425	99.4	13
	[10]	D-UST	25	17.3	328	81.4	4	17.9	424	81.4	14
	[10]	LD-UST	25	17.7	291	99.2	5	18.1	313	100.0	11
	this work	RTS-UST	25	17.5	244	99.8	9	17.7	256	100.0	14
msp	[8]	D-UST	0	1.9	98	100.0	4	1.9	98	100.0	-
	this work	RTS-UST	0	1.5	89	100.0	4	1.5	89	100.0	-
fpu	[8]	D-UST	0	2.3	87	100.0	2	2.3	87	100.0	-
	this work	RTS-UST	0	1.9	109	93.2	4	1.9	109	100.0	1
ecg	[8]	D-UST	30	66.8	417	98.8	39	75.7	474	91.6	341
	[10]	D-UST	30	35.8	382	99.4	20	36.3	401	99.4	33
	[10]	LD-UST	30	35.0	318	94.6	29	35.2	345	100.0	51
	this work	RTS-UST	30	26.9	234	99.6	63	27.0	247	100.0	32
aes	[10]	D-UST	50	207.5	2207	82.8	245	208.3	2320	97.6	180
	[10]	LD-UST	50	233.9	1863	100.0	133	234.7	1933	99.0	152
	this work	RTS-UST	50	200.7	1172	86.8	155	202.0	1242	96.6	103
usbf	this work	RTS-UST	30	4.5	135	100.0	10	4.5	135	100.0	-
dma	this work	RTS-UST	30	5.3	118	100.0	14	5.3	118	100.0	-
pci_bridge32	this work	RTS-UST	30	7.7	150	100.0	24	7.7	150	100.0	-
des_peft	this work	RTS-UST	30	18.9	148	100.0	32	18.9	148	100.0	-
eht	this work	RTS-UST	30	21.2	144	100.0	78	21.2	144	100.0	-
Norm.	[8]	D-UST		1.36				1.43			
	[10]	D-UST		1.15				1.13			
	[10]	LD-UST		1.16				1.16			
	this work	RTS-UST		0.996				1.00			

capacitive costs compared with the D-UST structures in [8], the D-UST structures in [10], and the LD-UST structures in [10], respectively, after CTO. In addition, even though we do not apply any form of latency optimization, the latencies of the RTS-UST structures are 28% lower compared with the LD-UST structures. We believe that this stems from smaller RTS-UST structures being constructed.

The RTS-UST structures have slightly worse results in yield after CTS (and before CTO). However, in terms of timing yield after CTO, the RTS-UST obtains a 100% yield on all circuits except aes, where a yield of 96.6% is obtained. As mentioned earlier, this improvement is achieved with a 0.4% overhead. Compared with the D-UST structures in [8], the RTS-UST structures obtain better or equal timing yield on all six considered circuits. Compared with the D-UST structures in [10], the RTS-UST structures obtain better timing yield on scaled_s15850 and ecg but slightly worse timing yield on aes. Compared with the LD-UST in [10], the RTS-UST obtains slightly worse timing yield on aes.

Clearly, the RTS-UST structures demonstrate better quality in terms of both capacitive cost and timing yield when compared to the D-UST and LD-UST structures on all circuits except for aes and scaled_s5378. On these two circuits, the RTS-UST structures are only marginally worse.

8. SUMMARY AND FUTURE WORK

In this paper, it is demonstrated that static bounded useful arrival time constraints can be used to construct clock trees meeting useful skew constraints while exploring various topologies. In the future, we plan to extend our framework to consider latency minimization techniques as in [10, 12].

9. REFERENCES

[1] A. Agarwal, D. Blaauw, and V. Zolotov. Statistical timing analysis for intra-die process variations with spatial correlations. ICCAD'03, pages 900–907, 2003.

[2] C. Albrecht, B. Korte, J. Schietke, and J. Vygen. Maximum mean weight cycle in a digraph and minimizing cycle time of a logic chip. *Discrete Applied Math.*, 123(1-3):103–127, 2002.

[3] Y.-C. Chang, C.-K. Wang, and H.-M. Chen. On construction low power and robust clock tree via slew budgeting. ISPD '12, pages 129–136, 2012.

[4] Y. P. Chen and D. F. Wong. An algorithm for zero-skew clock tree routing with buffer insertion. EDTC'96, pages 230–237, 1996.

[5] J. Cong, A. B. Kahng, C.-K. Koh, and C.-W. A. Tsao. Bounded-skew clock and steiner routing. *ACM Trans. Des. Autom. Electron. Syst.*, 3(3):341–388, July 1998.

[6] R. Ewetz, S. Janarthanan, and C.-K. Koh. Fast clock skew scheduling based on sparse-graph algorithms. ASP-DAC '14, pages 472–477, 2014.

[7] R. Ewetz, S. Janarthanan, and C.-K. Koh. Benchmark circuits for clock scheduling and synthesis. https://purr.purdue.edu/publications/1759, 2015.

[8] R. Ewetz and C.-K. Koh. A useful skew tree framework for inserting large safety margins. ISPD '15, pages 85–92, 2015.

[9] R. Ewetz and C.-K. Koh. MCMM clock tree optimization based on slack redistribution using a reduced slack graph. ASP-DAC '16, pages 366 – 371, 2016.

[10] R. Ewetz, C. Tan, and C.-K. Koh. Construction of latency-bounded clock trees. ISPD '16, 2016.

[11] J. Fishburn. Clock skew optimization. *IEEE Transactions on Computers*, pages 945–951, 1990.

[12] S. Held, B. Korte, J. Massberg, M. Ringe, and J. Vygen. Clock scheduling and clocktree construction for high performance asics. ICCAD'03, pages 232–239, 2003.

[13] R.-S. Tsay. Exact zero skew. In *ICCAD'91*, 1991.

[14] V. Ramachandran. Construction of minimal functional skew clock trees. ISPD'12, pages 119–120, 2012.

[15] S. Roy, P. M. Mattheakis, L. Masse-Navette, and D. Z. Pan. Clock tree resynthesis for multi-corner multi-mode timing closure. ISPD'14, pages 69–76, 2014.

[16] C. N. Sze. ISPD 2010 high performance clock synthesis contest: Benchmark suite and results. ISPD'10, pages 143–143, 2010.

[17] C.-W. A. Tsao and C.-K. Koh. UST/DME: a clock tree router for general skew constraints. *TODAES*, pages 359–379, 2002.

A Fast Incremental Cycle Ratio Algorithm*

Gang Wu and Chris Chu
Department of Electrical and Computer Engineering, Iowa State University, IA
{gangwu, cnchu}@iastate.edu

ABSTRACT

In this paper, we propose an algorithm to quickly find the maximum cycle ratio (MCR) on an incrementally changing directed cyclic graph. Compared with traditional MCR algorithms which have to recalculate everything from scratch at each incremental change, our algorithm efficiently finds the MCR by just leveraging the previous MCR and the corresponding largest cycle before the change. In particular, the previous MCR allows us to safely break the graph at the changed node. Then, we can detect the changing direction of the MCR by solving a single source longest path problem on a graph without positive cycle. A distance bucket approach is proposed to speed up the process of finding the longest paths. Our algorithm continues to search upward or downward based on whether the MCR is detected as increased or decreased. The downward search is quickly performed by a modified Karp-Orlin algorithm reusing the longest paths found during the cycle detection. In addition, a cost shifting idea is proposed to avoid calculating MCR on certain type of incremental changes. We evaluated our algorithm on both random graphs and circuit benchmarks. A timing-driven detailed placement approach which applies our algorithm is also proposed. Compared with Howard's and Karp-Orlin MCR algorithm, our algorithm shows much more efficiency on finding the MCR in both random graphs and circuit benchmarks.

1. INTRODUCTION

Given a directed cyclic graph and each edge in the graph is associated with two numbers: *cost* and *transition time*. Let the cost (respectively, transition time) of a cycle in the graph be the sum of the costs (respectively, transition times) of all the edges within this cycle. Assuming the transition time of a cycle is non-zero, the ratio of this cycle is defined as its cost divided by its transition time. The maximum cycle ratio (MCR) problem finds the cycle whose ratio is the maximum in a given graph [1]. The MCR problem is closely related to the optimization of VLSI circuits. In particular, for synchronous circuits, MCR reflects the optimization potential of the retiming or clock skew scheduling techniques being applied to the circuits [2]. For asynchronous circuits, MCR directly corresponds to the circuit performance [3].

There are also applications in other areas, e.g., time separation analysis of concurrent systems, graph theory [4].

In practice, most of the optimization processes which apply MCR algorithms are actually performed incrementally. For example, during the detailed placement stage of VLSI circuits, one step of the algorithm adjusts the coordinates of only a few cells. Then, evaluation is performed for this modified circuit before the next move [5] [6]. Similarly, in the gate sizing process of circuits, the algorithm might adjust the size of one gate at a time, instead of changing the sizes of all the gates at once [7]. Considering the above type of applications which only few changes are made at each step, the MCR algorithm might also be able to do the calculation "incrementally" by leveraging the information calculated at the previous step, and therefore be able to find the MCR much faster. In this paper, we focus on the MCR problem considering such incremental changes, which we referred to as the incremental MCR problem. By leveraging the previously calculated information, we expect the incremental MCR algorithm to be faster than traditional MCR algorithms, which have to recalculate everything from scratch at each step.

The MCR problem without considering the incremental changes has been well studied [1] [4] [8]. One way to solve the MCR problem is by linear programming [9]. In addition, various MCR algorithms are proposed to solve the problem more efficiently. Experimental study of existing MCR algorithms shows the Karp and Orlin's algorithm (KO) [10] and an efficient implementation of KO [11] is the fastest among them [4]. When the graph size is small, the Howard's algorithm (HOW) [12] is also able to generate comparable results [1]. For the incremental MCR problem, only very few researches have been done. In [13], the authors developed an adaptive negative cycle detection algorithm and incorporated it into the Lawler's MCR algorithm [14]. However, the experiments in [13] are performed only on very small graphs, and thus the efficiency of the algorithm cannot be confirmed. In addition, Lawler's algorithm finds MCR based on the binary search idea, which is much slower compared with KO and HOW [4].

In this paper, we propose an efficient incremental MCR algorithm. The only information we need to leverage is the previous MCR and the corresponding largest cycle in the graph before the incremental change is made. Our algorithm contains three parts: cycle detection, local upward search and global downward search. After an incremental change is made on the given graph, the cycle detection is performed first. During the cycle detection, we use our cost shifting idea to filter out the cases which the incremental change will not affect the MCR. For the remaining cases which affect the MCR, the algorithm continues to detect whether the MCR is increased or decreased. If the MCR is detected to be increased, we perform the local upward search to identify the

*This work is supported in part by NSF award CCF-1219100.

ISPD '17, March 19-22, 2017, Portland, OR, USA

© 2017 ACM. ISBN 978-1-4503-4696-2/17/03. . . $15.00

DOI: http://dx.doi.org/10.1145/3036669.3036670

new MCR in the changed graph. Otherwise, we perform the global downward search to identify the new MCR. To speed up the cycle detection and the local upward search, we propose a bucket distance idea which can quickly build a longest path tree in a graph without positive cycle. Also, we propose a modified KO algorithm to speed up the global downward search by reusing the longest paths found in the cycle detection step. We evaluate our algorithm on both random graphs and the ISPD 2005 placement benchmarks [15]. To evaluate our algorithm on circuit benchmarks, we propose a timing-driven detailed placement approach which applies our incremental MCR algorithm. The experimental results show our algorithm is very efficient on calculating MCR compared with the fastest traditional MCR algorithms.

The rest of this paper is organized as follows. In Section II, we briefly review the Howard's algorithm and the Karp-Orlin algorithm. In Section III, we present our incremental MCR algorithm. In Section IV, we present our timing-driven detailed placement approach. Finally, the experimental results are shown in Section V.

2. PRELIMINARIES

2.1 Maximum cycle ratio problem

We formally define the MCR problem in this section. Let $G = (V, E)$ be a directed cyclic graph. Each edge $e \in E$ is associated with a cost denoted as $w(e)$ and a transition time denoted as $t(e)$. Let c denotes a cycle in G. Let $\tau(c)$ denotes the cycle ratio of c. With the assumption that $\sum_{\forall e \in c} t(e) > 0$, the MCR problem finds the maximum $\tau(c)$ $\forall c \in G$ as:

$$\tau^*(G) = \max_{c \subset G} \left\{ \frac{\sum_{\forall e \in c} w(e)}{\sum_{\forall e \in c} t(e)} \right\}$$

Here, we use $\tau^*(G)$ to denote the MCR of G. As an example, Fig. 1 shows a graph with two cycles (a, b, c) and (a, b, d, c). The two numbers associated with each edge denote its cost and transition time respectively. By calculating the ratio of both cycles, we can identify the largest cycle shown as the dotted lines in Fig. 1. However, for larger graphs, it is difficult for us to enumerate all the cycles to find out which one is the largest, as the total number of cycles can be exponential to the graph size.

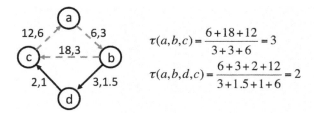

Figure 1: Finding the maximum cycle ratio in a graph.

One way to solve the maximum cycle ratio problem is to formulate it as a linear program [9]:

Minimize $\quad \tau$

Subject to $\quad d(i) + w(i, j) - t(i, j) * \tau \leq d(j) \quad \forall (i, j) \in E$

Here, (i, j) denotes the edge connecting node i to node j. $d(i)$ and $d(j)$ are free variables for each node $v \in V$ denoting its *distance*.

In addition to the linear program solution, various algorithms have been proposed and are able to solve the problem more efficiently. We discuss these algorithms below.

2.2 Traditional maximum cycle ratio algorithms

Given a cycle ratio τ, we can construct another graph $G_\tau = (V, E_\tau)$ based on G. G_τ is identical to G, except now each edge in E_τ is associated with only one number *length*, instead of having two numbers (i.e. cost and transition time). Each $e \in E_\tau$ will have a corresponding edge $e' \in E$, and the *length* of e is defined as $l(e) = w(e') - \tau * t(e')$. Correspondingly, the *length* of a cycle $c \in G_\tau$ is defined as $l(c) = \sum_{\forall e \in c} l(e)$.

G_τ has many interesting features which can help us identify the largest cycle in G. In particular, if G_τ contains positive length cycles, it means the given cycle ratio τ is less than $\tau^*(G)$. If G_τ contains zero length cycles and does not contain positive length cycles, the given τ will be equal to $\tau^*(G)$, and the zero length cycle in G_τ will correspond to the most critical cycle in G. If G_τ only contains negative cycles, it means the given cycle ratio τ is larger than $\tau^*(G)$. In this case, single source longest path trees rooted at any node $v \in V$ exist in G_τ. Detailed proofs of these facts can be found in [4].

Most of the MCR algorithms use the above facts to transfer the MCR problem into the problem of either detecting positive cycles in G_τ or maintaining a longest path tree in G_τ. Howard's algorithm and Karp-Orlin algorithm are two of the fastest algorithms among them, and they tackle the MCR problem in exactly opposite directions. In particular, Howard's algorithm starts with a very small τ and gradually increases τ until it cannot detect a positive length cycle in G_τ. Karp and Orlin's algorithm starts with a very large τ and gradually decreases τ while maintaining a longest path tree in G_τ.

2.2.1 Howard's algorithm (HOW)

HOW can be separated into two phases: the discovery phase and the verification phase. If the starting cycle ratio τ is small enough, all the cycles in G_τ will have a positive length. In the discovery phase, an arbitrary positive length cycle $c \in G_\tau$ is located, and we increase τ to τ' such that $l(c) = 0$ in $G_{\tau'}$. Next, in the verification phase, a positive cycle detection algorithm (e.g., the Bellman–Ford algorithm) can be used to check if there are still positive cycles in $G_{\tau'}$. If so, we repeat the discovery phase. If not, we are safe to exit the algorithm and output τ' as $\tau^*(G)$. More details and pseudo code for HOW can be found in [1] [4].

2.2.2 Karp and Orlin's algorithm (KO)

KO starts with a large enough τ such that all cycles in G_τ is negative and thus longest paths are well defined in G_τ. Here, we use a simple example to illustrate the basic idea of KO. For more details, please refer to [1] [4] [11].

In the beginning, KO modifies G by adding a node s and a set of edges E_s connecting s to all nodes $v \in V$, with $w(e) = 0$ and $t(e) = 1$ for all $e \in E_s$. Let a path from s to node v in G be denoted by $p(s, v)$, which corresponds to the path from root s to v in the longest path tree T_s in G_τ. For each node $v \in V$, we have $w(v) = \sum_{\forall e \in p(s, v)} w(e)$ and $t(v) = \sum_{\forall e \in p(s, v)} t(e)$, shown as $(w(v), t(v))$ in Fig. 2. For each edge $(i, j) \in E$, let $\Delta w(i, j) = w(i) + w(i, j) - w(j)$ and $\Delta t(i, j) = t(i) + t(i, j) - t(j)$. Then, a max heap containing all the edges in G is maintained using the key value calculated as follows:

$$key(i,j) = \begin{cases} \Delta w(i,j)/\Delta t(i,j), & \text{if } \Delta t(i,j) > 0. \\ -\infty, & \text{otherwise.} \end{cases}$$

Fig. 2 shows the process of calculating $\tau^*(G)$ using KO for the graph G shown in Fig. 1. Fig. 2(a) shows the initial longest path tree T_s in G_{τ_0} and the corresponding max heap. Next, edge (b, c) which has the maximum key value is retrieved from the heap, and T_s is updated by replacing edge (s, c) with (b, c) as shown in Fig. 2(b). This tree update makes T_s to be the longest path tree in G_{τ_1}. We will continue the max heap update and tree update until a cycle is found which gives us $\tau^*(G)$, as shown in Fig. 2(d).

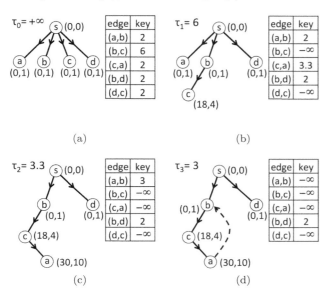

(a)

(b)

(c)

(d)

Figure 2: An example of Karp and Orlin's algorithm

3. PROPOSED ALGORITHM

We define an incremental change on an edge as a cost change on this edge, and an incremental change on a node as the cost changes on all input and output edges directly connected to the node. The transition times remain to be the same for both the edge change and the node change. In Section III-A, we first look into details about how MCR is affected by an edge change. In Section III-B, we consider the incremental changes happened on a node, which is the assumption made by our algorithm.

3.1 Considering incremental changes on an edge

Let e denotes the changed edge. We use C_e to denote the set of cycles passing through e, and when $w(e)$ changes, only the cycles in C_e will be affected. In addition, we use G to denote the graph before the change and G' to denote the graph after the change, with corresponding largest cycle to be c^* and $c^{*\prime}$ respectively. Based on whether $w(e)$ is decreased or increased and whether $e \in c^*$ or not, we can separate the incremental changes into the following four cases:

3.1.1 $e \notin c^*$ and $w(e)$ is decreased

This is the easiest case, as it can be guaranteed that $c^{*\prime} = c^*$ after the incremental change. Before the change happens, we know $\tau(c) \le \tau(c^*) \ \forall c \in C_e$. Since decreasing the cost of e will only decrease $\tau(c) \ \forall c \in C_e$, none of these cycles will get a chance to become larger than c^*. Thus, c^* will remain to be the largest cycle in G'.

3.1.2 $e \notin c^*$ and $w(e)$ is increased

Increasing $w(e)$ will increase $\tau(c) \ \forall c \in C_e$. It is possible that $\tau(c)$ of a cycle $c \in C_e$ becomes larger than $\tau(c^*)$ and thus dominates all other cycles and becomes the largest cycle in G'. If this happens, we have $c^{*\prime} = c$, and thus it can be guaranteed that $c^{*\prime}$ is passing through e.

3.1.3 $e \in c^*$ and $w(e)$ is decreased

Decreasing $w(e)$ will decrease $\tau(c^*)$. Thus, another cycle in G can replace c^* and becomes dominating in G'. If this happens, there is no clue for us to know where this new largest cycle is located.

3.1.4 $e \in c^*$ and $w(e)$ is increased

Increasing $w(e)$ will increase $\tau(c^*)$ and also increase $\tau(c) \ \forall c \in C_e$. Thus, it is guaranteed that $c^{*\prime}$ is passing through e. However, there is no guaranteed that $c^{*\prime} = c^*$. As an example, let the graph in Fig. 1 to be G and the graph in Fig. 3 to be G'. It can be seen that after increase $w(c, a)$ from 12 to 400, the largest cycle also get changed.

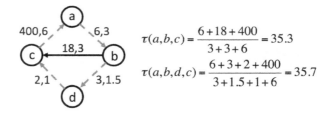

Figure 3: $e \in c^*$ and $w(e)$ is increased.

3.2 Considering incremental changes on a node

Only considering changes on a single edge is certainly not enough, as applications typically involve multiple edge changes. We can transform the multiple edge changes into single edge change by only processing one edge at a time, but this can slow down the incremental MCR algorithm. Therefore, instead of only considering a single edge change, our algorithm handles the case of a single node change, which makes it more suitable for real applications. A single node change can create more complicated situations compared with an edge change, as cycle ratio of some cycles can decrease while others can increase at the same time. However, similar to the edge change, only the cycles passing through the changed node will be affected. If the change is happened on more than one node, our algorithm will just transform it to the single node change by processing one node change at a time.

3.3 Considering HOW and KO incrementally

HOW and KO are not suitable to perform the MCR calculation incrementally. One reason is that most of the middle information (i.e. node distances, the longest path tree) is calculated based on G_τ whose edge lengths depend on the parameter τ. Once τ is changed, all edge lengths in G_τ will be updated and the middle information calculated in the previous iteration will become useless. It is also not realistic to keep these middle information for each possible τ value, as the possible τ values correspond to all cycles in the graph whose total number is exponential to the graph size. Another reason is that, the cycle ratio can change in both directions when an incremental change is made, while HOW or KO can only search from one direction. In particular, if MCR is decreased, it will be difficult for HOW to go backward and locate the new largest cycle. Similarly for KO when MCR is increased. This suggests the incremental MCR algorithm needs to be able to search from both directions. When MCR is increased, the algorithm can search upward starting from the previous MCR, similar to HOW. When MCR is decreased, the algorithm can search downward similar to KO. This is just the basic idea of our algorithm, which we will discuss below.

3.4 An overview of our proposed algorithm

An overview of our incremental MCR algorithm is shown in Fig. 4. Give an initial graph G with its MCR to be $\tau^*(G)$ and the corresponding largest cycle to be c^*. Assuming a node v in G is updated and the set of cycles passing through v is C_v, our algorithm first detects the changing direction of MCR. If the MCR is detected as increased, we perform a local upward search to identify the new MCR. If the MCR is detected as decreased, we perform a global downward search to identify the new MCR. The output of our algorithm is $\tau^*(G')$ and $c^{*'}$ for G' which denotes the graph after the change.

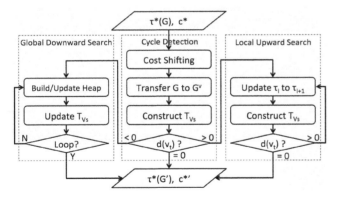

Figure 4: Overview of our incremental MCR algorithm.

3.5 Cycle detection

In the beginning, at our cost shifting step, we filter out the incremental change which will not affect MCR. If this is the case, we can directly exit the MCR algorithm and output $\tau^*(G)$ as $\tau^*(G')$. If the change has a potential to affect MCR, we continue to detect whether the MCR is increased or decreased. To do this, we first transform G into G^v by replacing node $v \in V$ with two new node v_s, v_t. Next, we build the longest path tree T_{v_s} rooted at v_s. Finally, based

on the longest distance from v_s to v_t, we will be able to detect the changing direction of MCR.

3.5.1 Cost shifting

As we discussed in Section III-A case 1), if the changed edge is not on c^* and the edge cost is decreased, we can guarantee that the MCR will not be affected. The idea of cost shifting is to transform all edge changes into this particular case, by shifting edge costs from the input (or output) edges of v to the output (or input) edges of v. As an example, Fig. 5(a) shows the current edge cost changes of v with 4 decreased edges and 1 increased edge. By shifting 9 units of cost from the output edges of v to the input edges of v, we get the new cost changes shown in Fig. 5(b). Assuming $v \notin c^*$, since only decreased edges exist after cost shifting, this change of v can be identified as not affecting MCR.

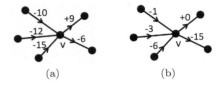

Figure 5: (a) Before the cost shifting. (b) After the cost shifting.

In general, by applying the cost shifting idea, we can exit the MCR algorithm if $v \notin c^*$ and the increment change belongs to one of the following two cases: (1) all edge costs are decreased. (2) all edge costs on one side (input or output) of v are decreased, and the smallest amount of decreasing at the decreased side is larger than largest amount of increasing on the other side.

3.5.2 Transform G into G^v

If the incremental change has a potential to affect MCR, we continue to this step and transform G into G^v as follows. We remove v from G and add two new nodes v_s, v_t to G, with v_s connecting to all v's output edges and v_t connecting to all v's input edges as shown in Fig. 6.

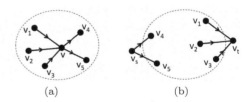

Figure 6: (a) Before breaking at v. (b) After breaking at v.

Let $\tau_0 = \tau^*(G)$, we can get the corresponding $G^v_{\tau_0}$ for G^v. Let T_{v_s} denotes the longest path tree rooted at v_s. Then we can have the following Theorem:

Theorem 1. T_{v_s} is well defined in $G^v_{\tau_0}$.

Proof: Before the incremental change, we have $l(c) \leq 0 \ \forall c \in G_{\tau_0}$. After the incremental change, only the cycles passing through v can be positive in G_{τ_0}. Since all $c \in C_v$ is broken at v in $G^v_{\tau_0}$, they will not form a positive cycle in $G^v_{\tau_0}$. Therefore, we have $l(c) \leq 0 \ \forall c \in G^v_{\tau_0}$, and thus the longest paths in $G^v_{\tau_0}$ are well defined. $\square$

3.5.3 Constructing T_{v_s} on $G_{\tau_0}^v$

Constructing T_{v_s} on $G_{\tau_0}^v$ is equivalent to the problem of finding a single source longest path tree in a graph without positive cycle. Since $G_{\tau_0}^v$ contains both negative and positive length edges, Dijkstra's algorithm is not applicable here. One way to construct T_{v_s} is to use the Bellman–Ford algorithm and update the node distances in a breath first search manner, as suggested in [16]. However, the breath first search has a very limited control on the updating order of the nodes, and thus each node can be repeatedly updated for many times [17]. Therefore, the runtime of this approach is not good.

We propose a distance bucket approach to help us update the nodes in an appropriate order, which can effectively reduce the total number of updates on each node and therefore speed up the process of constructing T_{v_s}. The basic idea of the distance bucket approach is similar to the Dijkstra's algorithm: we always pick the node which has the largest distance to update. Different from Dijkstra's algorithm, this cannot guarantee that the updated node will not be updated again, but the chance that this node get updated again will be much smaller compared with a random updating order. Instead of maintaining a priority queue to exactly find the node with largest distance, we only differentiate the nodes by putting them into certain buckets based on the range of their distance. One reason we do this is that it is not necessary to differentiate the node distances exactly, as repeated update of the nodes cannot be avoided anyway. Another reason is that maintaining a priority queue is expensive, especially considering the total number of edge update operations is huge.

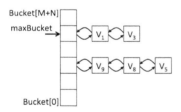

Figure 7: The distance bucket data structure.

Assuming we have $M + N$ buckets denoted from $bucket[0]$ to $bucket[M + N - 1]$ with M buckets for negative distances and N buckets for positive distances, as shown in Fig. 7. Let d_u be a unit range of distance covered by a bucket. Then, for a particular node v, its corresponding bucket index can be calculated as $M + d(v)/d_u$. Instead of storing a copy of all the contained nodes, the distance bucket only pointing to one of the contained node as shown in Fig. 7. The rest of the contained nodes will simply be connected to the this node in a doubly linked list manner. The details of our distance bucket approach is shown in Algorithm 1.

3.5.4 Detecting the changing direction of MCR

After constructing T_{v_s}, we can get $d(v_t)$ which is the longest distance from v_s to v_t in $G_{\tau_0}^v$. If $d(v_t) > 0$, it means a positive cycle passing through v exists in G_{τ_0}, and $\tau^*(G) < \tau^*(G')$. Therefore, we search upwards to find the new MCR. If $d(v_t) = 0$, it means $\tau^*(G) = \tau^*(G')$ and c^* remains to be the largest cycle in G'. So we can exit the

---

Algorithm 1 The distance bucket approach

Ensure: Constructing T_{v_s} on $G_{\tau_0}^v$.
1: Insert s to $bucket[0]$ and set $max := 0$;
2: **while** $max > 0$ **do**
3:     Pick and delete node u from the $bucket[max]$.
4:     **for each** $(u, v) \in E_{\tau_0}$ **do**
5:         **if** $d(v) < d(u) + l(u, v)$ **then**
6:             $d(v) := d(u) + l(u, v)$;
7:             Find the bucket index i based on $d(v)$;
8:             **if** v is not in any buckets **then**
9:                 Insert v to $bucket[i]$;
10:             **else**
11:                 Delete v from its current bucket;
12:                 Insert v to $bucket[i]$;
13:             **end if**
14:             **if** $i > max$ **then**
15:                 $max := i$;
16:             **end if**
17:         **end if**
18:     **end for**
19:     **while** $bucket[max]$ is empty **do**
20:         $max := max - 1$
21:     **end while**
22: **end while**

MCR algorithm. If $d(v_t) < 0$, it means the largest cycle passing through v in G_{τ_0} is negative. If $v \notin c^*$, we can exit the MCR algorithm as the MCR will not be affected in this case. Otherwise, it means $\tau^*(G) > \tau^*(G')$ and we search downwards to find the new MCR.

3.6 Local upward search

In this step, we search upwards until $\tau^*(G')$ is identified. It is safe for us to only perform a local search among all the cycles in C_v based on the following theorem:

Theorem 2. If $\tau^*(G') > \tau^*(G)$, $c^{*\prime} \in C_v$.

Proof: In Section III-A, the only cases which the incremental change can increase the MCR are case 2) and case 4). As we have discussed, we can guarantee $c^{*\prime}$ is passing through the changed edge e in both these two cases. Since e is connected to v, this means $c^{*\prime}$ must also pass through v. □

The strategy we used to perform the local upward search is similar to HOW. Assuming the current cycle ratio is τ_i, we first increase τ_i to τ_{i+1}, which makes $d(v_t) = 0$ in current T_{v_s}. Next, we construct the new T_{v_s} in $G_{\tau_{i+1}}^v$ using Algorithm I and get the corresponding new $d(v_t)$. If $d(v_t) > 0$, it means there are still positive cycles existing in $G_{\tau_{i+1}}$ whose cycle ratio is larger than τ_{i+1}. So we repeat the first step and keep updating the cycle ratio. Otherwise, we can exit the MCR algorithm and output τ_{i+1} as $\tau^*(G')$.

3.7 Global downward search

Our algorithm enters this step only when the cycle ratio of the previous largest cycle is decreased, i.e., $\tau(c^*) < \tau^*(G)$ in G'. In one case, c^* might remain to be the largest cycle in G' and we need to perform a global search to verify that $\tau(c) \leq \tau(c^*)\ \forall c \in G'$. In the other case, another cycle can replace c^* and becomes the new largest cycle in G'. Since we have no clue where this largest cycle is located, a global search for all cycles in G' is also required.

We leverage KO to perform this downward global search. In particular, the T_{v_s} we calculated during the cycle detection can be reused here. Thus, instead of running KO starting from a very large τ with the initial longest path tree as shown in Fig. 2(a), we can start KO from $\tau^*(G)$ with T_{v_s}. However, T_{v_s} is a longest path tree in $G^v_{\tau_0}$ rooted at node v, while the original KO requires the longest path tree rooted at an artificial node s, as shown in Fig. 2. Simply starting KO from $\tau^*(G)$ with T_{v_s} will make all cycles $c \in C_v$ cannot be examined, and the algorithm will be incorrect if $c^{*\prime} \in C_v$. Therefore, we modify KO like this: we add a pseudo edge (v_t, v_s) which is connecting node v_t to node v_s, and insert (v_t, v_s) into the max heap with $key(v_t, v_s) = d(v_t)/t(v_t)$. If (v_t, v_s) is picked during the execution of KO, it means $c^{*\prime} \in C_v$. Since $d(v_t)$ represents the largest cycle in C_v, it is safe for us to exit the MCR algorithm and output $\tau^*(G') = d(v_t)/t(v_t)$.

4. TIMING-DRIVEN DETAILED PLACEMENT

We propose a timing-driven detailed placement approach which applies our incremental MCR algorithm. Considering the type of circuits, i.e. asynchronous circuits [3] or synchronous circuits using retiming or clock scheduling techniques [2], whose performance is bounded by the MCR of the most critical cycle (c^*) in the circuit. For asynchronous circuits, c^* is defined as the timing loop which has the largest cycle delay divided by the number of tokens along the cycle. For synchronous circuits, c^* is defined as the timing loop which has the largest cycle delay divided by the number of flip-flops along the cycle. Here, we assume delay is proportional to the wirelength. Given an initial legalized placement, our goal is to reduce the MCR of the circuit by sequentially swapping a cell on c^* with one which is not on c^*.

The basic idea of our approach is illustrated in Fig. 8. First, we randomly pick a cell on c^*, i.e. cell v in Fig. 8. Next, we find the two neighboring cells of v on c^*, i.e. cell v_1 and v_2. The coordinates of v_1 and v_2 can define an optimal region $(x(v_1), x(v_2), y(v_1), y(v_2))$ for v, shown as the blue rectangle in Fig. 7. Assuming v' is a cell within this optimal region, by swapping v with v', we can minimize the total Manhattan distance of (v_1, v) and (v, v_2). Thus, $\tau(c^*)$ is reduced. However, it is possible that some cycle passing through v' becomes worse than c^* after the swap. Hence, we need to perform timing analysis using the incremental MCR algorithm to see whether the swap is beneficial before actually swapping the two cells. The details of our approach is shown in Algorithm 2.

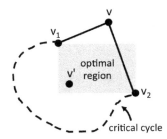

Figure 8: Timing-driven detailed placement.

5. EXPERIMENTS

The proposed incremental mean cycle algorithm is implemented in C++ and runs on a Linux PC with 94 GB of memory and 2.67 GHz Intel Xeon CPU.

Algorithm 2 A timing-driven detailed placement approach
Ensure: Reduce MCR of the circuit
1: $n = 1$; /* loop counter */
2: $best\_MCR = +\infty$;
3: **while** $n < limit$ **do**
4:      Randomly pick a cell v on c^* with neighboring cells v_1, v_2;
5:      Set $optimal\_region := (x(v_1), x(v_2), y(v_1), y(v_2))$;
6:      Set $x_{opt} := 0.5 * (x(v_1) + x(v_2))$;
7:      Set $y_{opt} := 0.5 * (y(v_1) + y(v_2))$;
8:      Move v to (x_{opt}, y_{opt}).
9:      Incrementally calculate MCR;
10:      **for each** v' in $optimal\_region$ **do**
11:          Move v' to (x_v, y_v);
12:          Incrementally calculate MCR as $current\_MCR$;
13:          **if** $current\_MCR < best\_MCR$ **then**
14:              $best\_MCR = current\_MCR$;
15:              $best\_node = v'$;
16:          **end if**
17:      **end for**
18:      Move v to $(x_{best\_node}, y_{best\_node})$;
19:      Incrementally calculate MCR;
20:      Move $best\_node$ to (x_v, y_v);
21:      Incrementally calculate MCR as $best\_MCR$;
22:      $n = n + 1$;
23: **end while**

We generate a set of random graphs following the same graph size and method used in [4]. Given an input total number of nodes and total number of edges, we first generate the desired number of nodes in the graph. Next, we randomly pick two nodes in the graph and connect them. This step is repeated until the desired number of edges is reached. The self loops (an edge connecting a node to itself) and duplicated edges (two edges connecting the same pair of nodes) are disallowed. In addition, we connect all the nodes using a circle to make the graph strongly connected. Both the cost and transition of each edge is randomly generated between 1 and 300.

In the beginning (i.e., before any incremental changes is made), our algorithm uses KO to find the initial MCR and the corresponding largest cycle as a starting point. For all the random graphs and circuit benchmarks, our algorithm sets both the total number of negative and positive buckets to be 10^6. In addition, we set d_u to be 10. Thus, a distance range $[-10^7, +10^7]$ is covered, which is more than enough. In case any node has a distance below or above this range, we will assign it to the first or last bucket. We implement three other MCR algorithms for comparison: the linear programming (LP) approach, HOW and KO. The LP is formulated as we discussed in Section II-A, and solved using the API of Gurobi optimizer [18]. Both HOW and KO are implemented following the description in [1] [4]. In particular, we implement a binary heap as the max heap used in KO.

For each random graph, we sequentially perform 100 node changes and calculate the MCR after each change. For each changing node, we randomly change the costs of all its input and output edges. Two different methods are used to pick the changing node. In one method, which we referred as "M1", we randomly pick a node among all the nodes in the graph. Our algorithm is able to run faster in this case, as only the upward search might be performed if we are not changing c^*, which is quite often in M1. In another method, which we referred as "M2", we always pick a node on c^* to

Table I. Comparison on random graphs

Graph	# of nodes	# of edges	MCR			M1 Runtime (s)				M2 Runtime (s)			
			Init	M1	M2	LP	HOW	KO	Ours	LP	HOW	KO	Ours
r01	12752	36681	4.03	4.03	3.76	566.43	4.07	1.92	0.44	720.50	3.97	2.58	1.15
r02	19601	61829	4.39	4.39	4.06	2238.94	4.69	3.12	0.74	2885.36	9.92	4.79	2.06
r03	23136	66429	5.04	5.04	3.81	2380.95	3.20	2.72	0.92	3130.45	8.26	5.07	2.32
r04	27507	74138	4.50	4.50	3.61	2963.66	3.65	3.20	0.94	3866.92	12.48	5.16	2.77
r05	29347	98793	4.39	4.49	4.18	5090.83	18.03	8.07	1.42	4644.15	20.34	10.28	4.12
r06	32498	93493	3.87	3.87	3.56	6829.63	14.60	7.50	1.42	9060.00	24.86	9.35	4.02
r07	45926	127774	4.18	4.18	3.58	12377.20	9.95	6.93	1.80	15743.50	33.72	13.38	5.57
r08	51309	154644	4.84	4.84	4.11	–	10.01	7.52	2.11	–	27.24	11.40	6.31
r09	53395	161430	4.70	4.70	4.18	–	9.19	8.28	2.12	–	41.73	15.24	6.42
					Norm.	–	6.496	4.136	1.000	–	5.253	2.223	1.000
r10	69429	223090	4.45	4.50	4.36	–	70.51	24.41	4.09	–	66.74	23.96	9.78
r11	70558	199694	3.84	3.84	3.57	–	95.00	24.77	4.20	–	95.62	24.42	9.53
r12	71076	241135	4.83	4.83	4.47	–	109.14	24.35	4.77	–	91.43	24.91	10.57
r13	84199	257788	4.79	4.79	4.07	–	29.65	17.12	4.25	–	100.52	23.84	10.80
r14	154605	394497	5.08	5.08	3.48	–	32.52	18.99	5.43	–	103.43	30.80	17.90
r15	161570	529562	6.30	6.30	4.45	–	22.46	22.59	7.21	–	268.69	52.77	26.33
r16	183484	589253	4.76	4.76	4.36	–	187.87	42.79	8.44	–	315.99	66.09	28.64
r17	185495	671174	5.24	5.24	4.94	–	488.10	74.59	12.75	–	620.42	98.54	42.62
r18	210613	618020	4.34	4.34	4.17	–	390.57	64.55	11.27	–	442.07	82.08	36.02
					Norm.	–	22.848	5.034	1.000	–	10.952	2.224	1.000
r19	262144	851968	5.14	5.14	4.38	–	90.15	63.92	13.36	–	481.11	115.48	46.68
r20	311744	1013166	6.03	6.03	4.48	–	65.41	62.41	16.18	–	705.11	134.60	55.87
r21	370728	1204865	4.65	4.65	4.41	–	341.74	125.63	25.92	–	1023.05	169.74	65.69
r22	440879	1432834	5.06	5.06	4.65	–	399.31	154.68	36.86	–	1329.38	178.20	76.65
r23	524288	1703936	6.04	6.04	4.50	–	268.13	149.38	48.55	–	1112.68	240.61	97.21
r24	623487	2026333	4.59	4.59	4.44	–	1868.32	327.39	49.96	–	1679.11	305.82	116.13
r25	741455	2409729	29.75	29.75	43.13	–	71.00	47.10	38.21	–	75.93	53.94	91.21
r26	881744	2865667	5.52	5.52	4.66	–	294.65	189.08	44.39	–	1222.89	297.44	141.97
r27	1048576	3407872	4.78	4.78	4.57	–	1217.15	332.73	54.74	–	3355.29	450.52	180.88
					Norm.	–	14.066	4.426	1.000	–	12.593	2.231	1.000

Table II. Analysis on medium and large size random graphs

Graph	Updates per node		M2 Runtime (s)		DB Runtime Breakdown (s)			
	BFS	DB	BFS	DB	CD	LUS	GDS	Others
r10	9.00	1.23	27.03	9.78	3.53	1.84	4.03	0.37
r11	9.58	1.32	22.17	9.53	3.65	1.00	4.53	0.35
r12	9.21	1.35	24.96	10.57	4.27	1.36	4.59	0.35
r13	9.27	1.21	28.89	10.80	3.84	1.30	5.31	0.35
r14	6.27	1.09	40.13	17.90	6.05	2.27	9.00	0.58
r15	9.75	1.19	72.70	26.33	8.39	3.78	13.48	0.66
r16	9.68	1.16	77.73	28.64	9.98	3.87	13.80	0.99
r17	10.14	1.16	89.75	42.62	13.09	5.65	22.49	1.39
r18	9.74	1.16	90.33	36.02	12.17	6.15	15.96	1.74
Norm.	7.614	1.000	2.465	1.000	0.338	0.142	0.485	0.035
r19	9.98	1.24	132.18	46.68	15.89	6.19	23.17	1.43
r20	10.71	1.21	175.30	55.87	19.02	8.25	27.04	1.56
r21	11.18	1.27	199.96	65.69	23.51	8.58	31.33	2.27
r22	11.22	1.15	232.59	76.65	24.71	8.71	40.64	2.58
r23	10.32	1.19	268.26	97.21	34.86	11.28	48.30	2.77
r24	10.99	1.29	381.76	116.13	42.58	15.95	52.21	5.40
r25	3.17	1.00	205.87	91.21	37.04	20.43	30.83	2.91
r26	8.85	1.05	439.19	141.97	44.63	21.62	70.85	4.87
r27	11.07	1.20	779.65	180.88	62.75	23.76	87.36	7.01
Norm.	8.257	1.000	3.227	1.000	0.350	0.143	0.472	0.035

Table III. Comparison on ISPD 2005 benchmarks

Design	# of nodes	# of nets	c* moves	Skip moves	Total moves	HPWL x 10^6 (nm)		MCR		Runtime (s)		
						Init	Final	Init	Final	HOW	KO	Ours
adaptec1	210861	644176	39	2	514	77.78	77.89	2582.00	1390.60	248.42	409.98	48.19
adaptec2	254425	731135	23	4	398	87.68	87.73	4301.60	3456.80	80.10	49.43	34.40
adaptec3	450642	1289483	18	7	280	203.33	203.35	8084.50	2523.00	139.44	130.75	35.13
adaptec4	494590	1246535	24	1	482	183.59	183.72	2729.00	2115.00	327.05	171.16	95.88
bigblue1	277022	794445	24	2	225	97.21	97.30	3125.67	2973.00	40.99	30.59	32.13
bigblue2	528704	1267929	35	2	422	147.80	147.81	3494.91	3491.91	305.14	104.46	98.49
bigblue3	1094904	2511616	26	6	413	324.91	325.05	6020.33	3692.25	305.37	261.76	178.60
bigblue4	2168351	5691264	29	4	448	790.65	790.85	6085.50	3885.25	1128.32	704.68	403.59
		Norm.	0.069	0.009	1.000	1.000	1.000	1.000	0.646	2.779	2.011	1.000

change. This is the most difficult case for our algorithm, as both the downward and upward search might be performed.

Table I shows the experimental results for random graphs, which are divided into three sets to simulate the applications with different scale. Columns "Init", "M1" and "M2" reports the initial MCR, the final MCR after 100 node changes using M1, and the final MCR after 100 node changes using M2 respectively. In general, LP is much slower than other algorithms. We denote the runtime of LP as "–", if it exceeds our runtime limit. Compared with HOW, our algorithm is about 5X~23X faster among all the experiments. The performance of HOW is not good especially on large size graphs. Compared with KO, our algorithm is about 2X~5X faster among all the experiments. In addition, as expected, the runtime of our algorithm in M1 is better than the runtime in M2.

Table II shows analysis of our algorithm in M2 on medium and large size graphs. We compare our MCR algorithm using the distance bucket approach (DB) with our MCR algorithm using the BFS approach described in [16]. The column "Updates per node" shows the average number of distance updates per node, and is calculated as (total # of node distance updates)/(# of T_{v_s} × # of nodes in the graph). It shows the DB approach is effectively reducing the updates per node and thus can achieve faster runtime. In addition, we show a runtime break down of our algorithm using DB. The columns "CD", "LUS" and "GDS" denote the cycle detection, local upward search and global downward search process respectively.

We use ISPD 2005 benchmarks [15] as the circuit benchmarks. Assuming a hypernet is connecting one output pin and p input pins of some gates, we represent this hypernet with p two-pin nets, by connecting the output pin with each input pin. Since there is no cell library type information in [15], we cannot calculate the wire delay. Instead, we set the cost of each two-pin net to be its HPWL, and the transition time of each two-pin net to 1. In addition, we ignore the fixed cells (i.e. terminals, macro blocks) and the nets connecting to them.

We stop the detailed placement if the improvement of MCR is less than 0.1% when we do the swap. Since our algorithm needs to incrementally calculate MCR at each move, a swap operation will need two calculations, while it only needs one calculation for HOW and KO. Thus, line 9 and line 19 in Algorithm 2 is required for our algorithm, but it is not needed for HOW and KO. Therefore, the total # of MCR calculations for our algorithm is larger than HOW and KO in this application. Table III shows the experimental results on circuit benchmarks. Columns "c^* moves", "Skip moves" and "Total moves" denote the # of moves on c^*, the # of moves skipped using our cost shifting idea and the total # of moves respectively. The runtime of the proposed detailed placement approach using three different MCR algorithms for timing analysis is compared. In particular, the placer based on our MCR algorithm is about 2X faster than the KO version and 2.8X faster than the HOW version.

6. CONCLUSIONS

In this paper, we have proposed an incremental MCR algorithm. The previous MCR allows us to break the graph at the changed node, and therefore detecting the changing directions of the MCR by solving a longest path problem in a graph without positive cycle. Based on the detected direc-

tion, our algorithm will either search upward or downward until the new MCR is found. We preform experiments on both random graphs and circuit benchmarks. The results show our algorithm is more efficient compared with HOW and KO.

7. REFERENCES

[1] A. Dasdan, S. Irani, and R. K. Gupta, "An Experimental Study of Minimum Mean Cycle Algorithms," *Tech. rep. 98-32, UC Irvine*, 1998.

[2] A. P. Hurst, P. Chong, and A. Kuehlmann, "Physical Placement Driven by Sequential Timing Analysis," in *ICCAD 2004*, pp. 379–386.

[3] P. A. Beerel, R. O. Ozdag, and M. Ferretti, *A Designer's Guide to Asynchronous VLSI*. Cambridge University Press, 2010.

[4] A. Dasdan, "Experimental Analysis of The Fastest Optimum Cycle Ratio and Mean Algorithms," *TODAES*, vol. 9, no. 4, pp. 385–418, 2004.

[5] P. Min, N. Viswanathan, and C. Chu, "An Efficient and Effective Detailed Placement Algorithm," in *ICCAD 2005*, pp. 48–55, Nov 2005.

[6] G. Wu and C. Chu, "Detailed Placement Algorithm for VLSI Design with Double-Row Height Standard Cells," *TCAD*, no. 99, pp. 1–1, 2015.

[7] G. Wu, A. Sharma, and C. Chu, "Gate Sizing and Vth Assignment for Asynchronous Circuits Using Lagrangian Relaxation," in *ASYNC*, pp. 53–60, 2015.

[8] L. Georgiadis, A. V. Goldberg, R. E. Tarjan, and R. F. Werneck, "An Experimental Study of Minimum Mean Cycle Algorithms," in *Proceedings of the Meeting on Algorithm Engineering & Expermiments*, pp. 1–13, Society for Industrial and Applied Mathematics, 2009.

[9] J. Magott, "Performance Evaluation of Concurrent Systems using Petri Nets," *Information Processing Letters*, vol. 18, no. 1, pp. 7–13, 1984.

[10] R. M. Karp and J. B. Orlin, "Parametric Shortest Path Algorithms with An Application to Cyclic Staffing," *Discrete Applied Mathematics*, vol. 3, no. 1, pp. 37–45, 1981.

[11] N. E. Young, R. E. Tarjant, and J. B. Orlin, "Faster Parametric Shortest Path and Minimum-balance Algorithms," *Networks*, vol. 21, no. 2, pp. 205–221, 1991.

[12] R. A. Howard, "Dynamic Programming And Markov Process," *The M.I.T Press, Cambridge, Mass*, 1960.

[13] N. Chandrachoodan, S. S. Bhattacharyya, and K. Liu, "Adaptive Negative Cycle Detection in Dynamic Graphs," in *ISCAS 2001*.

[14] E. L. Lawler, "Combinatorial Optimization: Networks and Matroids ," *Holt, Rinehart and Winston, New York*, 1976.

[15] G.-J. Nam, C. J. Alpert, P. Villarrubia, B. Winter, and M. Yildiz, "The ISPD2005 Placement Contest and Benchmark Suite," in *ISPD 2005*.

[16] R. E. Tarjan, "Shortest Paths," *Tech reports*, 1981.

[17] B. V. Cherkassky, A. V. Goldberg, and T. Radzik, "Shortest Paths Algorithms: Theory and Experimental Evaluation," *Mathematical programming*, vol. 73, no. 2, pp. 129–174, 1996.

[18] Gurobi Optimizer: http://www.gurobi.com.

iTimerM: Compact and Accurate Timing Macro Modeling for Efficient Hierarchical Timing Analysis

Pei-Yu Lee
Institute of Electronics
National Chiao Tung University
Hsinchu 30010, Taiwan
palacedeforsaken@gmail.com

Iris Hui-Ru Jiang
Department of Electronics Engineering
National Chiao Tung University
Hsinchu 30010, Taiwan
huiru.jiang@gmail.com

Ting-You Yang
Institute of Electronics
National Chiao Tung University
Hsinchu 30010, Taiwan
anitpr825@hotmail.com

ABSTRACT

As designs continue to grow in size and complexity, EDA paradigm shifts from flat to hierarchical timing analysis. In this paper, we propose compact and accurate timing macro modeling, which is the key to achieve efficient and accurate hierarchical timing analysis. Our macro model tries to contain only a minimal amount of interface logic. For timing graph reduction, we propose anchor pin insertion and deletion by generalizing existing reduction techniques. Furthermore, we devise a lookup table index selection technique to achieve high model accuracy over the possible operating condition range. Compared with two common models used in industry, extracted timing model and interface logic model, our model has high model accuracy and small model size. Based on the TAU 2016 timing contest on macro modeling benchmark suite, our results show that our algorithm delivers superior efficiency and accuracy: Hierarchical timing analysis using our model can significantly reduce runtime and memory compared with flat timing analysis on the original design. Moreover, our algorithm outperforms TAU 2016 contest winner in model accuracy, model size, model usage runtime and memory.

Keywords

Static timing analysis; hierarchical timing analysis; timing macro modeling; extracted timing model; interface logic model.

1. INTRODUCTION

As design evolution continues, designs rapidly grow in size and complexity. IP reuse and hierarchical design are the key to bridge the design productivity gap. A large-scale integration design can be hierarchically partitioned into manageable blocks that can be implemented in parallel (many of them are duplicate IPs), thus saving design time.

During chip design, static timing analysis (STA) is recognized as an essential task that directly influences design cycle time. To handle a billion gate design, traditional full-chip flat timing analysis may take days and consume much memory. Therefore, along with the hierarchical design trend, EDA paradigm shifts from flat to hierarchical timing analysis to ease the time-to-market pressure [1][2][3].

ISPD '17, March 19–22, 2017, Portland, OR, USA.
© 2017 ACM. ISBN 978-1-4503-4696-2/17/03...$15.00.
DOI: http://dx.doi.org/10.1145/3036669.3036674

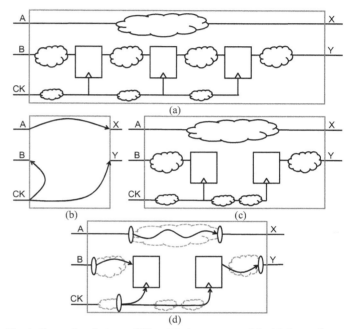

Fig. 1. Comparison between different timing macro models. (a) A sample block design. (b) Extracted timing model (ETM). (c) Interface logic model (ILM). (d) Our model.

Hierarchical timing analysis is enabled by analyzing a block once, generating the corresponding simplified timing macro model, and reusing the macro model for all duplicate blocks at the parent or top level of hierarchy to alleviate detailed analysis. Efficient and accurate hierarchical timing analysis relies on compact and accurate macro modeling. Nevertheless, there is a tradeoff among model size, model accuracy, and model generation time.

In addition to the tradeoff, the main challenge of timing macro modeling is context independency [4]. Context means the conditions under which a block is analyzed. To avoid accuracy loss, the context range considered during model generation ideally should cover the whole scope within which the block will be operated at upper-level STA. One example of reflecting the difficulty of context independency is the clock common path pessimism removal (CPPR) effect. It is difficult to model the CPPR credits of the top-level common source at the block-level analysis.

Two most commonly used timing macro models in physical design are the extracted timing model (ETM) and the interface logic model (ILM) [5]. ETM contains timing arcs for only block interfaces and frequently takes the form of a Liberty model [6] (see Fig. 1(b)). ETM is an abstract model hiding implementation details; it is suitable for IP providers, but incurs some accuracy loss and cannot handle the CPPR effect. ILM is a partial gate-level netlist containing only interface logic (see Fig. 1(c)). ILM is more accurate than ETM, but larger. On the other hand, to reduce the timing graph size, several graph reduction techniques have been investigated in literature. For example, serial and parallel merging is developed in [7]; biclique-star replacement is proposed in [8]; tree merging is devised in [9].

In this paper, we propose a novel algorithm to generate a compact and accurate timing macro model. For achieving context independency, efficiency, and accuracy, our key idea is to retain only a small amount of necessary interface logic (removing all unnecessary and unobservable logic, while preserving every pin that may affect accuracy). In our algorithm flow, we first convert a design into an initial timing graph. Second, we capture interface logic and remove internal logic. Third, we mark necessary pins, including pins on gates in the first few stages within the fanout cone of each input port, on gates directly connected to output ports, or on gates with multiple fanouts in the clock network. Fourth, we iteratively reduce the timing graph without touching the marked pins. We devise anchor pin insertion and deletion by generalizing existing graph reduction techniques. Combining with parallel merging and clock network merging, our reduction technique leads to a small model size and guarantees to recover CPPR credits. Fifth, if a restricted Liberty model is used (e.g., [10]), we additionally insert pseudo pins. Finally, to achieve high accuracy over the possible operating condition range, we determine proper lookup table indices for timing arcs and output a timing macro model. Compared with ETM and ILM, our model has high accuracy and small model size. (see Fig. 1 (d).)

Our experiments are conducted on the TAU 2016 timing contest on macro modeling benchmark suite [10]. Experimental results show that our algorithm delivers superior efficiency and accuracy: Hierarchical timing analysis using our model can significantly reduce runtime and memory compared with flat timing analysis on the original design. Moreover, our algorithm outperforms TAU 2016 contest winner in model accuracy, model size, model usage runtime and memory.

The remainder of this paper is organized as follows. Section 2 briefly introduces ETM, ILM, and problem formulation. Section 3 presents our timing macro model generation algorithm. Section 4 describes our lookup table index selection. Section 5 shows experimental results. Finally, Section 6 concludes this work and indicates future directions.

2. PRELIMINARIES AND PROBLEM FORMULATION

In this section, we briefly introduce two common timing macro models and give the problem formulation.

2.1 Extracted Timing Model (ETM)

An ETM abstracts the interface behavior of a block and replaces the original netlist with a library cell (frequently in Liberty format) (see Fig. 1(b)). The cell contains only pin-to-pin timing arcs, and each arc corresponds to a timing path in the original design from an input port to a register, from an input port to an output port, and from a register to an output port. Generally, an ETM has long model generation time but very short runtime when it is used at top-level timing analysis. Because this model provides a

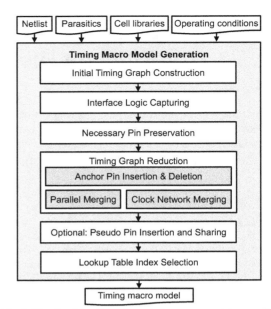

Fig. 2. The algorithm flow of our timing macro model generation.

reasonable accuracy and hides detailed design implementation information, it is ideal for IP providers.

2.2 Interface Logic Model (ILM)

An ILM is a partial gate-level netlist that contains only the interface logic of a block and eliminates the internal register-to-register logic (see Fig. 1(c)). An ILM includes the combinational logic from each input port to the first stage of registers of the block, the combinational logic from the last stage of registers to each output port of the block, the clock paths to these registers, and combinational paths from the input ports that do not encounter a register and pass directly to output ports. Generally, an ILM maintains a good balance among model size, model accuracy, and model generation time.

2.3 Problem Formulation

As mentioned earlier, compact and accurate timing macro modeling is the key to achieve efficient and accurate hierarchical timing analysis. In this paper, we adopt the timing macro modeling problem formulation used in the TAU 2016 timing contest on macro modeling, which can be described as follows.

The timing macro modeling problem: Given the gate-level netlist and the net parasitics of a block, the early and late cell libraries (describing cell functionality, early and late timing information), and timing assertions (operating conditions), the goal is to create a timing macro model that encapsulates the timing behavior of the block such that the model size is minimized and accuracy satisfies a given error bound.

To satisfy the accuracy requirement, the generated macro model shall include sufficient timing arcs and internal pins. The accuracy is measured by comparing hierarchical timing analysis using the generated model with post-CPPR flat timing analysis on the original design.

The inputs and output files follow industrial standard formats, including gate-level netlist in Verilog (.v), net parasitics (in terms of RC network) in Standard Parasitic Exchange Format (.spef), cell libraries (including cell functionality and early/late timing information) and macro model in (restricted) Liberty (.lib).

The timing macro modeling problem is challenging because there is a tradeoff among 1) model accuracy, 2) model size (in terms of the number of internal arcs and pins), 3) model generation performance (runtime and memory), and 4) model usage performance (runtime and memory). When targeting sign-off timing, the model generation algorithm should place the highest emphasis on accuracy; subsequently, our results show a very small error bound can be achieved.

3. TIMING MACRO MODELING
In this section, we detail our timing macro model generation algorithm.

3.1 Algorithm Flow
The overall algorithm flow of our timing macro model generation is shown in Fig. 2. For achieving context independency, efficiency, and accuracy, our key idea is to retain only a small amount of necessary interface logic.

First, a design is converted into an initial timing graph (see Section 3.2). Second, interface logic is captured, whereas internal logic is removed (see Section 3.3). Third, necessary pins are marked, including pins on gates in the first few stages within the fanout cone of an input port, on gates directly connected to output ports, or on gates with multiple fanouts in the clock network (see Section 3.4). Fourth, the timing graph is iteratively reduced without touching the marked pins (see Section 3.5). Fifth, pseudo pins are inserted if a restricted Liberty model is used (see Section 3.6). Finally, for achieving high accuracy over the possible operating condition range, appropriate lookup table indices for each timing arc are determined (see Section 4), and a timing macro model is generated accordingly. Fig. 3 demonstrate key steps in our algorithm. We devise anchor pin insertion and deletion by generalizing existing graph reduction techniques. Combining with parallel merging and clock network simplification, our reduction technique effectively simplify the timing graph, and CPPR credits are well maintained.

3.2 Initial Timing Graph Construction
An initial timing graph is a directed graph constructed based on the given netlist and early/late cell libraries. For facilitating graph manipulation and timing computation, we create two nodes (one rise pin and one fall pin) for each cell pin, primary input (input port), primary output (output port), and clock source. An edge represents a timing arc between two pins, describing a timing type and a timing sense (positive, negative or non-unate [11]). Each node (rise/fall pin) is associated with its early/late timing, e.g., arrival time, required arrival time. Setup and hold times are also attached to sequential element nodes. Each edge (timing arc) is associated with early/late output slew and early/late delay lookup tables indexed by input slew and output loading.

3.3 Interface Logic Capturing
Because interface logic is sensitive to the changes on boundary conditions and our goal is to generate a compact and accurate macro model, we try to retain only a small amount of necessary interface logic. To achieve this goal, we start from interface logic capturing.

First, we perform a forward traversal starting from primary inputs except clock source pins until endpoints (primary outputs or data pins of sequential elements) are reached. The reached endpoints, the clock pins of reached sequential elements are collected. Second, we perform a backward traversal from primary outputs and from the collected points. During the backward traversal,

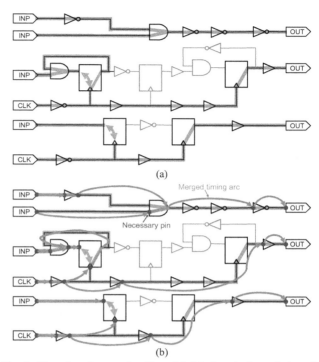

Fig. 3. Key steps in our algorithm: (a) Interface logic capturing. (b) Necessary pin preservation and timing graph reduction.

passing pins and timing arcs are saved, unvisited part is discarded; thus, interface logic is captured (the highlighted paths in Fig. 3(a)).

3.4 Necessary Pin Preservation
During interface logic capturing, we also mark necessary pins, and these marked pins do not participate subsequent timing graph reduction to maintain accuracy.

Several facts influence necessary pin preservation: 1) Lookup tables in cell libraries are indexed by input slew and output loading. 2) The shielding effect of slew propagation: The impact of variant input slews is degraded and stabilized after several stages. 3) The output loading is variant only for gates directly connected to primary outputs, while constant for other gates (obtained from the given net parasitics).

First, we mark primary inputs, primary outputs, clock source, and the data pins and clock pins of the reached sequential elements collected by forward traversal during interface logic capturing.

Second, we mark other necessary pins as follows. During traversing the interface logic, we propagate minimum and maximum slew values of operating condition from primary inputs. With the shielding effect, the minimum/maximum slew values converge after several stages. Convergence means the difference between minimum and maximum slew values is less than a user defined tolerance. During the traversal, when slews on the incoming arcs of a pin have not converged yet, this pin is marked. Typically, only pins on gates at the first few stages are preserved by this process. The input pins of a gate connected to some primary output are marked, whereas its output pin is allowed to be merged with its output net (thus handling the effect of variant loading at primary outputs). Considering the CPPR effect, the output pins of multiple fanout gates in captured clock network are marked. (It can be shown that the common points for launching and capturing clock paths occur only at multiple fanout gates in

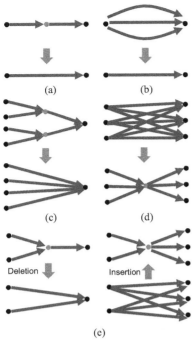

Fig. 4. Timing graph reduction. (a) Serial merging. (b) Parallel merging. (c) Tree merging. (d) Biclique-star replacement. (e) Generalization: anchor pin insertion and deletion.

clock network [9].) For example, the highlighted dots in Fig. 3(b) are preserved necessary pins of the captured interface logic in Fig. 3(a). By preserving necessary pins, we can avoid accuracy loss at subsequent graph reduction.

3.5 Timing Graph Reduction
After interface logic capturing and necessary pin preservation, we iteratively reduce the timing graph without touching the marked pins. In the following, we first briefly review existing reduction techniques and then present the generalization.

3.5.1 Existing Reduction Techniques
As shown in Fig. 4, existing reduction techniques include: Serial merging combines two consecutive timing arcs into one and eliminates the intermediate pin (Fig. 4(a)). Parallel merging combines multiple timing arcs between two pins into one (Fig. 4(b)). Tree merging replaces a tree-structured subgraph by direct arcs from leaves to the root (Fig. 4(c)). Biclique-star replacement replaces a complete bipartite graph with a star structure (Fig. 4(d)).

3.5.2 Anchor Pin Insertion and Deletion
Herein, we introduce the generalization of serial merging, tree merging, and biclique-star replacement. Fig. 4(e) illustrates the concept of anchor pin insertion and deletion.

First, we discuss anchor pin deletion. The deletion gain of pin p_i can be computed as

$$\text{delgain}(p_i) = \text{indegree}(p_i) + \text{outdegree}(p_i) - \text{indegree}(p_i) \cdot \text{outdegree}(p_i), \qquad (1)$$

where indegree means the number of incoming timing arcs of p_i, whereas outdegree means the number of outgoing timing arcs of p_i. When a deletion gain is negative, anchor pin deletion increases the number of timing arcs, this is undesired. Interestingly, in most cases, we observe that the accuracy is slightly improved for zero

deletion gain in our experiments. Hence, we perform anchor pin deletion when a pin has a nonnegative deletion gain (delgain $\geq$ 0). Anchor pin insertion is the reverse form of anchor pin deletion; the insertion gain can be defined similarly.

It can be seen that serial merging is a special case of anchor pin deletion; tree merging can be obtained by iteratively performing anchor pin deletion on a tree-structured subgraph; biclique-star replacement is a special case of anchor pin insertion.

3.5.3 Clock Network Simplification
We simplify the clock network by necessary pin preservation plus iterative anchor pin deletion. According to the way we preserve necessary pins in the clock network, the CPPR effect can be captured well.

3.6 Optional: Pseudo Pin Insertion & Sharing
There is an assumption for the used Liberty format in TAU 2016 timing contest [10]: Only one timing arc is allowed between two pins, i.e., one-to-one correspondence between a timing arc and its corresponding pins. The reduced timing graph obtained in Section 3.5 may not be compatible with this assumption. Therefore, we present pseudo pin insertion and sharing.

In the reduced graph, the connections between two pins can be classified into fifteen types (Fig. 5), where each pin corresponds to one rise pin and one fall pin. With a special encoding, types 1, 2, 4, 8 are primitive types. Any of the remainder is composed of two or more primitive types, e.g., type 12 is composed of types 4 and 8.

Seven types listed in Fig. 5(b) are incompatible with the restricted Liberty format. Therefore, we create a pseudo pin to break a timing arc in each incompatible type. Because an inserted pseudo pin corresponds to one rise pin and one fall pin, either only the

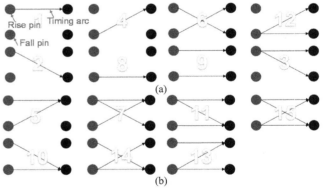

Fig. 5. Pin connection types. (a) Compatible types. (b) Incompatible types.

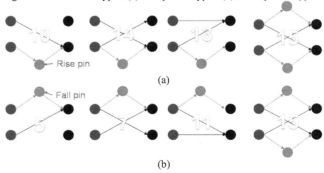

Fig. 6. Pseudo pin insertion and sharing. (a) The rise pin of an added pseudo pin is used. (b) The fall pin of an added pseudo pin is used.

rise pin (Fig. 6(a)) or only the fall pin (Fig. 6(b)) of an added pin is used. We further share pseudo pins between these two groups to reduce the total number of inserted pseudo pins, i.e., types 10 and 5 are shared, types 14 and 7 are shared, types 13 and 11 are shared, and type 15 is shared itself.

4. LOOKUP TABLE INDEX SELECTION

In this section, we determine our lookup table indices to minimize the interpolation error when the generated model is used.

As mentioned in Section 3.4, the shielding effect of slew propagation makes slews converge into a user defined tolerance range after few stages; the output loading for gates unconnected to primary outputs is constant (obtained from the given net parasitics). The lookup table of a mergeable timing arc (converged slew and constant loading) can be easily computed.

In the following, we focus on the part of interface logic affected by variant operating conditions—timing arcs connecting to preserved pins (unconverged slews or variant loadings).

4.1 Wire Timing Arc Indexing

A wire timing arc is associated with delay and output slew. The delay is directly computed based on its parasitic RC tree, and the delay value is independent of slews. Herein, we discuss selecting proper input slew indices for output slew lookup tables on a slew-unconverged wire timing arc.

According to [12], the output slew can be approximated by a function f as follows:

$$f(x) = \sqrt{x^2 + c^2}, \quad (2)$$

where x means input slew, c is contributed by the second moment of the slew. A more sophisticated approximation can also be used. Our goal is to select n most significant points from the input slew range $[x_0, x_{n+1}]$ such that the difference between the area under curve f and the area under piece-wise linear function via these selected points is minimized. The line segment connecting x_i and x_{i+1} can be written as:

$$L_i(x) = \frac{f(x_{i+1}) - f(x_i)}{x_{i+1} - x_i}(x - x_i) + f(x_i), x \in [x_i, x_{i+1}]. \quad (3)$$

The area difference between approximated lines and f is:

$$\sum_{i=0}^{n} \int_{x_i}^{x_{i+1}} (L_i - f(x)) dx. \quad (4)$$

By taking gradient on Equation (4),

$$\nabla \sum_{i=0}^{n} \int_{x_i}^{x_{i+1}} (L_i - f(x)) dx = 0. \quad (5)$$

Consider initially sampled points $x_0 < x_1, x_2, \dots, x_n < x_{n+1}$. The minimum area difference occurs when x_i moves to x_i',

$$x_i' = c \sqrt{\frac{m^2}{1 - m^2}}, \quad (6)$$

where m is the slope of a straight line connecting $(x_{i-1}, f(x_{i-1}))$ and $(x_{i+1}, f(x_{i+1}))$, $m < 1$.

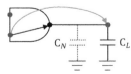

Fig. 7. An output cell and its output net are lumped together. C_L is the output loading, and C_N is the net lumped capacitance.

We can start with a set of uniformly sampled indices and then obtain final indices by iteratively applying the calculation of Equation (6) until each index value stabilizes within a small enough region. If the stable value is outside $[x_0, x_{n+1}]$, x_0 and x_{n+1} are used instead.

4.2 Cell Timing Indexing

Cell timing contains delay, output slew, and timing constraints. Delay and output slew depend on only the input slew of a related pin because output loading is fixed (directly obtained from output net parasitics). Given the minimum and maximum propagated slews of a related pin, cell timing indices can be defined as the minimum and maximum propagated slews and the original indices covering the interval of minimum and maximum propagated slews. For example, if a cell has original slew indices as {1, 3, 5, 10, 20, 30, 100}, the respective minimum and maximum propagated slews of this cell are 6 and 15, then the selected indices for this cell timing arc are {5, 6, 10, 15, 20}. On the other hand, timing constraints depend on the slews on both constrained pin and related pin. Thus, we adjust both indices similarly.

4.3 Output Cell Arc Indexing

A wire connected to an output port has a linear response to output loading variation. The exact loading at an output port is unknown during model generation. We merge the cell timing arc and wire connection together in our model (Fig. 7), and query the output cell timing according to the output loading context.

$$cell_{ex}(C_L) = cell_{ori}(C_L + C_N) + wire_{ori}(C_L + C_N), \quad (7)$$

where $cell_{ex}$ is cell timing after merged, $cell_{ori}$ is the original cell timing, $wire_{ori}$ means wire RC timing, C_L is the output loading, and C_N is the net lumped capacitance. The net lumped capacitance is viewed as an internal capacitance which is invisible in the generated model; thus, we shift down the original cell indices by an offset (equal to C_N) as our indices for output loading. Notably, output cell timing still depends on input slew and output loading, and thus cell timing indexing described in Section 4.2 is applied here to reduce slew indices.

5. EXPERIMENTAL RESULTS

We implemented our algorithm in the C++ programming language and compiled it with g++ 4.8.2. We executed the program on a platform with two Intel Xeon 3.5 GHz CPUs and with 64 GB memory.

Experiments were conducted on the TAU 2016 timing contest on macro modeling benchmark suite released by [10] as listed in Table I. '#PIs' denotes the number of primary inputs, '#POs' the

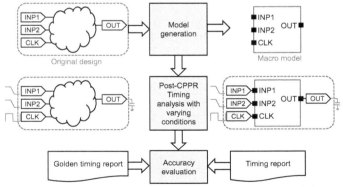

Fig. 8. Experimental framework: The baseline is post-CPPR flat timing analysis on the original design by a reference timer.

TABLE I. STATISTICS OF THE TAU 2016 TIMING CONTEST ON MACRO MODELING BENCHMARK SUITE.

Design	#PIs	#POs	#Gates	#Nets	Total (#Gates+#Nets)	Runtime (s)	Memory (MB)
mgc_edit_dist_iccad_eval	2.6K	12	222.1K	224.1K	446.2K	9.00	1229.81
vga_lcd_iccad_eval	85	99	286.4K	286.5K	572.9K	10.19	1572.60
leon3mp_iccad_eval	254	79	1.5M	1.5M	3.0M	69.23	8810.25
netcard_iccad_eval	1.8K	10	1.6M	1.6M	3.2M	74.03	9263.12
leon2_iccad_eval	615	85	1.9M	1.9M	3.8M	91.38	11004.60

* 'Runtime' and 'Memory': runtime and memory of the baseline (post-CPPR flat timing analysis by a reference timer).

TABLE II. COMPARISON WITH TAU 2016 TIMING CONTEST WINNER.

Design		Max Error (ps)	Model File Size (MB)	Generation Runtime (s)	Generation Memory (MB)	Usage Runtime (s)	Usage Memory (MB)
mgc_edit_dist_iccad_eval	Ours	0.04	90	14.12	709.78	10.01	1014.89
	LibAbs	0.49	249	20.39	2189.00	20.83	1991.64
	Ratio	0.08	0.36	0.69	0.32	0.48	0.51
vga_lcd_iccad_eval	Ours	0.03	84	14.67	845.13	9.44	986.35
	LibAbs	0.42	295	23.72	2740.62	25.50	2357.25
	Ratio	0.07	0.28	0.62	0.31	0.37	0.42
leon3mp_iccad_eval	Ours	0.04	96	54.65	4050.87	11.31	1094.64
	LibAbs	0.42	1700	144.76	15428.40	152.12	13760.36
	Ratio	0.10	0.06	0.38	0.26	0.07	0.08
netcard_iccad_eval	Ours	0.06	435	78.76	4550.45	47.42	5115.72
	LibAbs	0.19	1800	187.86	16114.60	148.28	13961.41
	Ratio	0.32	0.24	0.42	0.28	0.32	0.37
leon2_iccad_eval	Ours	0.06	713	113.32	5595.22	74.94	8167.34
	LibAbs	0.24	2100	201.42	19241.30	193.42	17317.70
	Ratio	0.25	0.34	0.56	0.29	0.39	0.47
Average Ratio 1	**Ours/LibAbs**	**0.16**	**0.26**	**0.53**	**0.29**	**0.33**	**0.37**
Average Ratio 2	**Ours/Baseline**	-	-	-	-	**0.73**	**0.57**

* 'Max Error': accuracy measured by max error (difference) compared with post-CPPR flat timing anlysis using the original design.
** 'Ratio' and 'Average Ratio 1': measured by Ours/LibAbs.
*** 'Average Ratio 2': measured by Ours/Baseline, where baseline performance is listed as 'Runtime' and 'Memory' in Table I.

number of primary outputs, '#Gates' the number of gates, '#Nets' the number of nets, and 'Total' the sum of #Gates and #Nets.

Fig. 8 shows the experimental framework. The operating conditions for model generation are that any input slew ranges from 5 ps to 250 ps, any output loading ranges from 5 fF to 250 fF, and input delay ranges from 0 ps to 2000 ps (for evaluating the correctness of the CPPR effect handling). Two macro models are generated, one for early timing and one for late timing. The baseline is post-CPPR flat timing analysis on the original design reported by a reference timer, with varying operating conditions (e.g., input slews, output loadings, input arrival times). The runtime and memory of baseline for each benchmark design is listed as 'Runtime' and 'Memory' in Table I.

We compared our algorithm with TAU 2016 contest winner, LibAbs, to demonstrate our effectiveness and efficiency. The program of LibAbs was provided by the winning team and executed on the same platform as described above. LibAbs and our algorithm are both evaluated by 1) model accuracy, 2) model file size, 3) model generation performance (runtime and memory), and 4) model usage performance (runtime and memory). Table II lists the detailed comparison. 'Max Error' reflects model accuracy, which is measured by the maximum difference between the baseline timing report and the timing report conducted by hierarchical timing analysis using the generated macro model. 'Model File Size' reflects model size, which is measured by the file size of a generated macro model. 'Generation Runtime' represents model generation time, while 'Generation Memory' means model generation memory requirement. 'Usage Runtime' and 'Usage Memory' are similarly defined for hierarchical timing analysis. 'Ratio' means the ratio of our result to LibAbs for each

design. Overall, our algorithm outperforms LibAbs in model accuracy, model size, model generation performance (runtime and memory), and model usage performance (runtime and memory). On average, compared with LibAbs, our algorithm can improve model accuracy, model file size, model generation runtime, model generation memory, model usage runtime, and model usage memory by 84%, 74%, 47%, 71% 67%, 63% reduction, respectively (see 'Average Ratio 1'). First, our model is extremely accurate: The maximum error is much less than 0.1 ps, implying that our algorithm maintains context independency and handles the CPPR effect very well. Second, considering our algorithm is single-threaded, whereas LibAbs is multi-threaded, our model generation performance (runtime and memory) is superior (only 53% and 29% of LibAbs). Usually, there are many duplicate blocks on a chip, and hierarchical timing analysis is rerun many times; thus, the model generation effort can be amortized, and the overall performance is promising—the incentive of hierarchical timing analysis.

It can be seen that our macro model is compact and accurate, thus facilitating efficient and accurate hierarchical timing analysis. In

TABLE III. EFFECTIVENESS OF GRAPH REDUCTION ON MODEL SIZE.

Design	Model File Size (MB)		Ratio
	Ours: Interface Logic	Ours: Final	
mgc_edit_dist_iccad_eval	411	90	21.90%
vga_lcd_iccad_eval	390	84	21.54%
leon3mp_iccad_eval	434	96	22.12%
netcard_iccad_eval	1900	435	22.89%
leon2_iccad_eval	3000	713	23.77%
Average	-	-	**22.44%**

* 'Ratio': model file size ratio (%), measured by 'Final' / 'Interface Logic'.

fact, when accuracy is a major concern, there is no imperative need to generate macro models for relatively small blocks (e.g., mgc and vga_lcd in our experiments). Compared with the baseline performance, our model usage performance leads to average 27% and 43% reduction on runtime and memory, respectively (see 'Average Ratio 2'). Generally, hierarchical timing analysis using our model can significantly reduce runtime and memory compared with flat timing analysis on the original design.

Table III shows the effectiveness of our graph reduction technique on model size. 'Ours: Interface Logic' means our algorithm without performing graph reduction (i.e., keeping the whole interface logic), while 'Ours: Final' means the complete version of our algorithm. Our graph reduction technique contributes over 77% reduction on model file size; we retain only a very small amount of interface logic in our model. It can be seen that our macro model is very compact and accurate.

6. CONCLUSION

To achieve efficient and accurate hierarchical timing analysis, in this paper, we propose compact and accurate timing macro modeling. Our key idea is to make our macro model contain only a small amount of interface logic and maintain high accuracy. To generate a compact model, we generalize existing graph reduction techniques to anchor pin insertion and deletion. To generate an accurate model, we preserve necessary pins and wisely select proper index values of lookup tables to describe timing arcs. Our experiments are conducted on the TAU 2016 timing contest on macro modeling benchmark suite. Experimental results show that our algorithm delivers superior efficiency and accuracy: Hierarchical timing analysis using our model can significantly reduce runtime and memory compared with post-CPPR flat timing analysis on the original design. Moreover, our algorithm outperforms TAU 2016 contest winner in model size, model accuracy, and model usage performance (in terms of runtime and memory). Future work includes expediting our model generation by distributed computing, developing a new format to facilitate model generation and usage, and considering coupling effects in hierarchical timing analysis.

7. REFERENCES

[1]   F. Dartu and Q. Wu. To do or not to do hierarchical timing? In *Proc. ACM International Symposium on Physical Design (ISPD)*, p. 180, Mar. 2013.

[2]   B. Anunay. Hierarchical timing concepts. *EDN Network*, Oct. 2013.

[3]   S. Walia. Reducing turnaround time with hierarchical timing analysis. *EE Times*, Oct. 2011.

[4]   C. Visweswariah, O. Levitsky, Q. Wu, A. Shaligram, A. Rubin, G. Wolski, A. Skourikhin, L. Brown, I. Keller. EDA court: Hierarchical construction and timing sign-off of SoCs. *ACM International Workshop on Timing Issues in the Specification and Synthesis of Digital Systems (TAU)*, Mar. 2013.

[5]   A. J. Daga, L. Mize, S. Sripada, C. Wolff, and Q. Wu. Automated timing model generation. In *Proc. ACM/IEEE Design Automation Conference (DAC)*, pp. 146-151, June 2002.

[6]   Liberty: The semiconductor industry's most widely used library modeling standard. Available at: https://www.opensourceliberty.org/

[7]   C. W. Moon, H. Kriplani, and K. P. Belkhale. Timing model extraction of hierarchical blocks by graph reduction. In *Proc. ACM/IEEE Design Automation Conference (DAC)*, pp. 152-157, June 2002.

[8]   S. Zhou, Y. Zhu, Y. Hu, R. Graham, M. Hutton, and C.-K. Cheng. Timing model reduction for hierarchical timing analysis. In *Proc. IEEE/ACM International Conference on Computer-Aided Design (ICCAD)*, pp. 415-422, Nov. 2006.

[9]   Y. M. Yang, Y. W. Chang and I. H. R. Jiang. iTimerC: Common path pessimism removal using effective reduction methods. In *Proc. IEEE/ACM International Conference on Computer-Aided Design (ICCAD)*, pp. 600-605, Nov. 2014.

[10] TAU 2016 Timing Contest on Macro Modeling. Available at: https://sites.google.com/site/taucontest2016/

[11] J. Bhasker and R. Chadha. *Static Timing Analysis for Nanometer Designs: A Practical Approach*, Springer, 2009.

[12] C. V. Kashyap, C. J. Alpert, F. Liu and A. Devgan. Closed-form expressions for extending step delay and slew metrics to ramp inputs for RC trees", *IEEE Transactions on Computer-aided Design of Integrated Circuits and Systems (TCAD)*, vol. 23 no. 4, 2004, pp. 509-516.

DSAR: DSA aware Routing with Simultaneous DSA Guiding Pattern and Double Patterning Assignment *

Jiaojiao Ou†, Bei Yu‡, Xiaoqing Xu†, Joydeep Mitra♯, Yibo Lin†, David Z. Pan†

†ECE Department, The University of Texas at Austin
‡CSE Department, The Chinese University of Hong Kong
♯Mentor Graphics Corporation

ABSTRACT

Directed self-assembly (DSA) is a promising solution for fabrication of contacts and vias for advanced technology nodes. In this paper, we study a DSA aware detailed routing problem, where DSA guiding pattern assignment and guiding pattern double patterning (DP) compliance are resolved simultaneously. We propose a net planning technique, which pre-routes some nets based on their bounding box positions, to improve both metal layer and via layer qualities. We also introduce a new routing graph model with DSA and DP design rule considerations. The DSA and DP aware detailed routing is then performed based on the net planning result, followed by a post-routing optimization on DSA guiding pattern assignment and decomposition. The experimental result demonstrates that our proposed approach can achieve promising DSA and DP friendly layout, i.e., conflict free on DSA guiding pattern with double patterning assignment for via layer. In addition, our proposed detailed router is able to effectively reduce 20% via number and 15% total wirelength than one recent DSA aware detailed router.

1. INTRODUCTION

With the delay of extreme ultraviolet lithography (EUV), industry is heavily looking for other lithography alternatives, such as multiple patterning lithography (MPL) for $7nm$ technology node and beyond [16, 25, 33]. Besides, they are also looking for other options such as multiple e-beam or directed self-assembly (DSA) lithography, to serve as the next generation lithography techniques to extend $193nm$ immersion (193i) lithography further or combine with EUV to reduce manufacturing cost [12, 21]. Recently, one dimensional (1D) design has been used to simplify the design rule explosion in advanced technology nodes. Litho-friendly 1D standard cell design method, place and route algorithm have been developed to improve chip yield and performance [2, 10, 21].

With the scaling of technology nodes, the via density has increased dramatically on routing layers, leading to triple and even quadruple patterning for via layer printing with conventional 193i

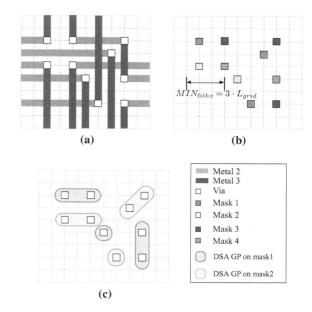

Figure 1: (a) Original layout; (b) Print via layer with quadruple patterning; (c) Print via layer with DSA and double patterning.

lithography [13, 21]. The situation becomes even worse for the 1D design where more vias may be introduced due to extreme regular routing patterns. As a result, the cost grows tremendously for the mask manufacturing. On the other hand, the number of masks for contacts/vias layer can be reduced by DSA because of its pitch multiply ability to group several contacts/vias in a single DSA guiding pattern [5, 6, 13, 15, 19, 20, 26, 28, 29, 32]. For example, in order to print the via layer in Figure 1(a), at least four masks with 193i lithography should be used, as shown in Figure 1(b). If DSA is applied on via layer, since the dense distributed vias can be grouped in the same DSA pattern, then only two masks are required for printing of DSA guiding patterns (GP), as shown in Figure 1(c). In this way, both the cost and number of masks can be greatly reduced.

As an emerging lithography technique, DSA can formulate ultra regular cylinders inside the guiding patterns. The pitch of cylinders is multiplied when several cylinders are formulated inside the same guiding pattern. The self-assemble process is enabled by micro-phase separation of Block Copolymer (BCP) material, and it is directed by different guiding pattern shapes to generate different contacts/vias patterns. DSA is considered as a potential complementary hole shrinking technique to EUV lithography [5, 19]. Nevertheless, DSA also suffers from placement error caused by the

*This work is supported in part by NSF, SRC, and CUHK Direct Grant for Research.

mismatch between final and target patterns. For instance, it is discovered that the placement error may be quite large for complex DSA group patterns [19], thus some regular DSA group patterns are preferred due to yield consideration. However, due to the limited patterns of DSA, it is difficult to cover the randomly distributed contacts and vias in conventional design by a single guiding pattern mask. Therefore, multiple patterning for DSA guiding patterns is a straightforward and natural extension.

There are several works on DSA guiding pattern assignment and decomposition problem. [17, 22, 23, 30] studied the DSA guiding pattern assignment and redistribution of cut masks in 1D design; [20] first addressed the challenges of applying DSA to contacts and vias, and proposed the initial ideas of multiple patterning in DSA; [3, 4, 14, 31] investigated the DSA guiding pattern assignment, and proposed different methods to decompose these patterns in order to reduce variations. It should be noted that decomposition conflicts may not be completely removed if vias in the design is fixed, so considering DSA patterns during design stage becomes necessary. [7] proposed an SAT algorithm to optimize the contact topology of 1D standard cell library in order to reduce complexity of DSA guiding patterns. [8] proposed a detailed routing method to assign DSA guiding patterns to vias during the detailed routing stage. [9] considered the DSA pattern during the redundant via insertion stage, and solved this problem by using integer linear program (ILP) and maximum independent set method; [24] extended the DSA aware redundant via insertion problem, and solved the guiding pattern assignment and redundant via insertion simultaneously. [27] proposed a method to remove the grouping conflicts between the standard cell boundaries in the post-placement stage.

However, none of the previous research consider DSA and multiple patterning constraints simultaneously during detailed routing stage. In this paper, we investigate detailed routing algorithms considering DSA and double patterning (DSA+DP) on guiding patterns. The purpose of this study is to obtain a detailed routing layout with DSA and double patterning friendly via distribution, while the impact on conventional metrics such as wirelength and via number are minimized as well. Our major contributions of this paper can be summarized as follows:

- This is the first work considering DSA with double patterning for DSA guiding patterns on via layer in detailed routing stage to the best of our knowledge.

- A pre-route net planning algorithm is proposed to improve routing quality in terms of total via number and wirelength.

- A routing graph model with DSA+DP considerations is developed for detailed routing.

- The DSA guiding pattern assignment and decomposition for via layer can be performed simultaneously in the routing stage.

- A post-route DSA guiding pattern assignment and decomposition method is adopted to further improve the result.

The rest of the paper is organized as follows: Section 2 introduces the DSA pattern constraints and problem formulation. Section 3 presents the details of our proposed method. Section 4 demonstrates the experimental results. Then Section 5 concludes the paper.

2. PRELIMINARIES

In this section, we introduce the DSA related design rules and present our problem formulation. The design is assumed as gridded design.

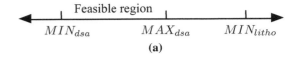

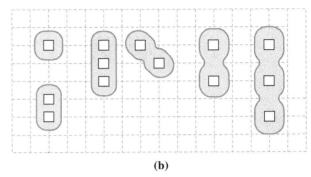

Figure 2: (a) DSA design rules: Vias whose distance is within $[MIN_{dsa}, MAX_{dsa}]$ can be grouped in the same guiding template; otherwise they can not be grouped. (b) Feasible regular DSA patterns. As the last three patterns have larger pitch than the natural pitch of DSA material, their guiding templates will have complex shapes in order to obtain higher confinement on the final patterns. Without loss of generality, all the guiding templates are illustrated as rectangles in the following sections.

2.1 DSA Design Rules

The minimum and maximum pitches that DSA material can obtain are defined as MIN_{dsa} and MAX_{dsa}. The MIN_{dsa} is almost the same to the natural pitch L_O of DSA material. Only when two vias are within the region between MIN_{dsa} and MAX_{dsa}, can they be grouped in the same DSA group. Otherwise, they have to be decomposed into different masks when the distance is smaller than the conventional minimum lithography distance MIN_{litho}. In this paper, in order not to lose any generality, we assume the size of the grids is L_{grid}, and the minimum lithography distance $MIN_{litho} \geq 3 \times L_{grid}$. And $MIN_{dsa} \leq L_{grid}$, $2 \times L_{grid} \leq MAX_{dsa} \leq 3 \times L_{grid}$. The above assumptions are illustrated in Figure 2(a). Moreover, as the non-collinear and non-manhattan aligned DSA patterns are not reliable with 193i lithography, and fork or cycle shaped patterns are difficult to synthesis, thus these kind of patterns are forbidden. In addition, the number of contacts/vias in a single DSA guiding pattern are also restricted. Therefore, the regular and simple DSA patterns are adopted in this work to improve the robustness and yield of DSA lithography, as shown in Figure 2(b). When the distance between adjacent holes is different from the natural pitch of DSA material, more confinement is required on the guiding template. Thus, the shapes of masks for the last three guiding templates are more complex than the first three.

2.2 Forbidden Via Distribution

For unidirectional design, cut masks are often used to cut off the metal lines to formulate logic connections. But it should be noted that there are minimum area constraints for the cut masks. As illustrated in Figure 3(a), the tip-to-tip design with two adjacent vias on different nets might violate the design rules. Therefore, this kind of adjacent via distributions on different nets are forbidden. However, the minimum area violation can be avoided for adjacent vias on the same nets, as shown in Figure 3(b).

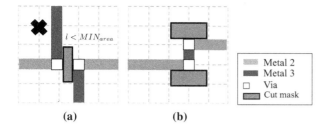

(a)   **(b)**

| Metal 2 |
| Metal 3 |
| Via |
| Cut mask |

Figure 3: (a) The cut mask violates the minimum area design rule for adjacent vias on different nets. (b) If the adjacent vias are on the same net, the cut mask will not violate the rule.

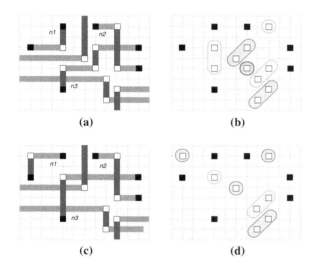

(a)   **(b)**

(c)   **(d)**

Figure 4: (a) Initial detailed routing without DSA consideration. (b) Three masks are required for via layer. (c) Redistribute the via by rerouting net 1 and net 3 to make the via layer DSA friendly. (d) Only two masks are used with DSA consideration.

2.3 Problem Formulation

Figure 4 gives an example of DSA incompatible routing and DSA friendly routing. Without DSA consideration on the via layer, the via distribution in Figure 4(a) requires three DSA masks to print the vias as in Figure 4(b). By rerouting net 1 and net 3 with DSA consideration, we can pattern the vias with only two DSA masks, as illustrated in Figure 4(d). The problem formulation of our DSA and double patterning aware routing (DSAR) is as follows:

Problem 1 (DSAR). *Given a placed netlist with source/target pins, a set of feasible DSA patterns and corresponding design rules, we will perform detailed routing and DSA+DP guiding pattern assignment simultaneously, and minimize the number of unroutable nets and total wire length at the same time.*

3. DSAR: DSA+DP AWARE ROUTING

This section introduces a pre-route net planning algorithm and a new routing graph model. It also provides the details of algorithms that have been used.

3.1 Pre-route Net Planning

Net planning is one of the important problems in the detailed routing stage, which has been studied in many different ways. In

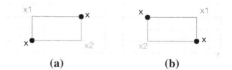

(a)   **(b)**

Figure 5: (a)(b) Corners for net x.

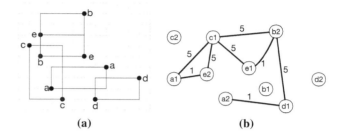

(a)   **(b)**

Figure 6: (a) Bounding boxes of nets. (b) Conflict graph for the two corners of all nets.

the following, we present a new algorithm to estimate the via distribution with DSA+DP considerations and net routability before performing the A* path search in detailed routing. The proposed algorithm generates a pre-route net path assignment based on the bounding box locations of all the nets. By determining the routing path for nets that do not have too much interference or impact on other nets with DSA+DP constraints in advance, the pre-route net planning could be able to reduce the via number, the total wire-length and conflict number.

3.1.1 Conflict Graph Construction for Nets

We first construct a conflict graph for the possible vias based on the bounding box locations of each net. As for unidirectional routing, different metal layers have certain routing direction, running either horizontally or vertically. Therefore, it is reasonable to take the jogs of the bounding box as a via between different metal layers. So besides the source and target pins, each bounding box has two corners, denoted as x_1 and x_2. The first one indicates the upper corner, and the latter one indicates the lower corner, as shown in Figure 5. The two corners are used as the vertices in the conflict graph. One corner may contain one to three vias depending on the pin locations. To make it simple, we assume that no via is inserted on the pins in the example. A conflict edge will be added between vertices when their distance is less than the minimum lithography distance. For edge whose vertices can not be grouped in the same DSA guiding pattern, a larger weight is assigned to it. Similarly, a smaller weight is assigned to edge whose vertices can be grouped in the same DSA guiding pattern.

Figure 6 shows an example of conflict graph construction, where there are fives nets and ten vertices for each corner of all the nets. As the two possible vias in the lower corner a_2 of net a and upper corner d_1 of net d can be grouped in the same DSA pattern, a smaller weight is assigned to the edge between a_2 and d_1. The above rules can be applied to other vertices and edges in the same way.

3.1.2 Conflict Graph Bipartization

In our net planning algorithm, we want to determine the routing path for as many nets as possible. With the conflict graph, the target is to find the maximized number of vertices which are 2-colorable, by grouping vias in the same DSA group. Therefore, this problem

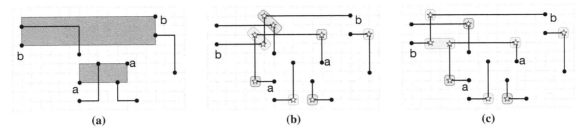

Figure 8: (a) Bipartization result, net a and b are undetermined. (b) Route b first results in longer wire length. (c) Route a first results less wire length.

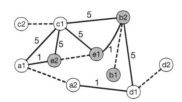

Figure 7: Conflict graph constraints.

Table 1: Pre-route Net Planning Notations

c_v	vertices deletion coverage for vertex v
s_v	color assignment for vertex v
α_v	cost of vertex v
N	total number of vertices
E_s	solid edge set
E_d	dashed edge set
V_f	forbidden vertex set

can be formulated as a constrained DSA+DP vertex bipartization algorithm, which converts the conflict graph to a bipartite graph by deleting minimized number of vertices.

It should be noted that at most one corner can be selected for each net. A net corner is strictly forbidden if it goes through the source/-target pins of another net. Other constraints for conflict graph are demonstrated in Figure 7. The dashed line means that the two corners belong to the same net, and at most one corner can exist at the same time. The dashed lines will not be counted as the conflict edge during the graph bipartization. The shadowed vertices indicate that the corresponding corner goes through the source/target pins of another net, so these vertices have to be deleted in advance. The ideal case is that there exists a set of valid corners for each net that are 2-colorable for the original conflict graph. ILP formula (1) is proposed to solve the problem. Some notations are explained in Table 1.

$$\textbf{min} \quad \sum_{i=1}^{N}(\alpha_i \times c_i) \tag{1a}$$

$$\textbf{s.t.} \quad s_v + s_u + (c_v + c_u) \geq 1, \quad \forall\{v, u\} \in E_s, \tag{1b}$$

$$s_v + s_u - (c_v + c_u) \leq 1, \quad \forall\{v, u\} \in E_s, \tag{1c}$$

$$c_v + c_u \geq 1, \quad \forall\{v, u\} \in E_d, \tag{1d}$$

$$c_v = 1, \quad \forall v \in V_f. \tag{1e}$$

c_v is a binary variable indicating the vertices deletion coverage for v. $c_v = 1$ means vertex v is deleted. The cost of c_v is denoted as

α_v, which is calculated as $\alpha_v = \dfrac{1}{\sum_{e \in V} Cost_e}$. It is calculated as the reciprocal of the sum of connected edge cost. With the cost, we prefer to delete the most congested and DSA unfriendly vertices to avoid decomposition conflicts during the bipartization process. s_v is also a binary variable indicating the color assignment for vertex v. $s_v = 0$ means that v is assigned with color 0, and vice versa for $s_v = 1$. And N is the total number of vertices. The objective is to delete as few vertices as possible with minimized cost. The first two constraints forbid both endpoints of a conflict edge to have the same color while none of them is deleted. The third constraint forbids the two corners of the same net to exist at the same time. The forth constraint forbids the vertices if corresponding corner of its bounding box occupies the source/target pin locations of other nets.

3.1.3 DSA+DP Net Ordering

Due to the congested bounding box distribution, the routing path of some nets can not be decided with ILP. Therefore, these nets will be routed in the detailed routing stage. Before that, a net ordering method is proposed based on previous ILP result. Generally, the net order of the undetermined nets are determined in the ascending order based on the size of bounding box of each net. However, if the bounding box size is the same, the net with more overlaps with other nets will be routed first. Figure 8 shows that routing paths of nets a and b are not determined, net a is routed first since it has smaller bounding box.

3.2 Detailed Routing

3.2.1 Routing graph model

Since we only consider the DSA guiding pattern decomposition on via layer where the metal layers are all unidirectional, previous routing graph model for multiple patternings [18] may no longer be suitable for the DSA+DP aware detailed routing. To avoid the generations of DSA guiding pattern conflicts, we propose the following DSA+DP aware routing graph model to perform DSA guiding pattern assignment and decomposition simultaneously.

Without loss of any generality, we assume that the vertical wire indicates metal 2, and the horizontal wire indicates metal 3. A via is inserted when the routing direction changes. A routing box for each routing grid is used to indicate the inserted via and its color assignment, as illustrated in Figure 9(a). There are four outlets on the sides of the routing box to denote the routing direction of the net. Inside the routing box, several lines are used to indicate the routing paths to the next grid. The horizontal and vertical lines are used for routing metals on different layers. The diagonal lines indicate the direction change of the routing path, and the direction change means a via is inserted between different metal layers. There are

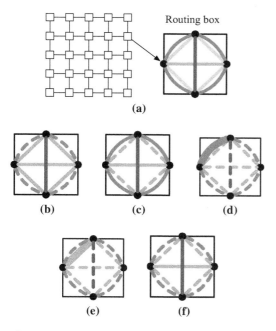

(a)

(b)   **(c)**   **(d)**

(e)   **(f)**

Figure 9: (a) Routing graph model. The inner path inside the routing box will be marked as dashed lines when it is forbidden. (b) Red via is forbidden. (c) Green via is forbidden. (d) Red via is inserted. (e) Green via is inserted. (f) All vias are forbidden.

four routing direction changes in each routing box. In order to show the DSA guiding pattern assignment to the inserted via, and the decomposition of these templates, we use color green and red to indicate each direction change. If the line is dashed, then this color is not allowed in this routing box. Figures 9(b)–9(f) demonstrate different routing box states, where Figures 9(b) and 9(c) forbid a certain via color assignment inside the routing box, Figures 9(d) and 9(e) show that if a via is inserted, the metal lines and any other vias are forbidden in the routing box. Figure 9(f) shows that vias are forbidden but metal lines are allowed in the routing box.

With the definition of the routing box, the cost from current grid to next grid (c_i^{next}) can be calculated based on the relative locations of both grids.

$$c_i^{next} = \begin{cases} c_{via} + L_{grid}, & d_i \neq d_{next}, \\ c_m + L_{grid}, & d_i = d_{next}. \end{cases} \quad (2)$$

Besides the basic wire length cost L_{grid}, we have the metal cost c_m and via cost c_{via} to be added to the cost based on the direction of current grid d_i and next grid d_{next}. A larger weight M should be assigned to the cost if the routing direction is forbidden.

Once a net is routed, we need to update the status for corresponding routing boxes. It is observed that once a via has been inserted in the routing box, all the other routing paths should be forbidden. And if a vertical metal line goes through a routing box, the horizontal metal line is still valid to go through the routing box, but all via paths are forbidden. As shown in Figure 10(a), when a green via is inserted, the neighboring routing boxes of the inserted via are marked as via-forbidden. For other routing boxes whose distance is less than the minimum lithography distance, but they can not be grouped with current via in the same DSA pattern, then these routing boxes can only be assigned to the opposite colors. If the grid distance to the inserted via is larger than minimum lithography distance, no coloring constraints is required. Figure 10(b) gives an example for the updated routing boxes. When both via colors are

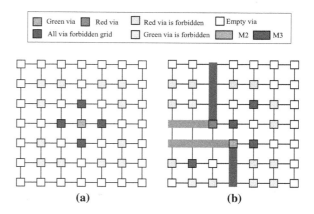

Figure 10: (a) Nearby routing box state update. (b) Example layout shows the updated routing box state.

forbidden in a routing box, then it is marked as infeasible routing box for all vias.

3.2.2 General Cost Function

Assume current grid is i, and next grid is $next$. Let $cost_s^i$ denote the cost from source to i. Let $dist_{next}^t$ denote the estimated distance from $next$ to target. Let $usage(i)$ denote the number of nets in the grid. Besides, we also need to consider the grid conflicts cost and related history cost for the A* search. Thus, let $h(i)$ be the current history cost of grid i, $h(i)'$ be the previous history cost of grid i. And $h_{dsa}(i)$ is the DSA violation history.

$$h(i) = h(i)' + A \times usage(i) + B \times h_{dsa}(i). \quad (3)$$

Therefore, according to the routing box cost explained in Section 3.2.1, the current grid cost $c(i)$ and estimated net cost $p_i(s,t)$ so far can be calculated as follows:

$$c(i) = cost_s^i + c_i^{next} + h(i), \quad (4)$$

$$p_i(s,t) = c(i) + \sigma \times dist_{next}^t. \quad (5)$$

We assign a higher value to σ if the HPWL of current net is less than the estimated cost to help the A* search.

$$\sigma = \begin{cases} 1, & c(i) \leq l_{HPWL}, \\ 1 + \dfrac{c(i)}{HPWL}, & c(i) > l_{HPWL}. \end{cases} \quad (6)$$

For A* search, we need to search the neighbors of current grid, and create a priority queue to store the neighbors with estimated net cost. If the nearby grid does not exist in the priority queue, or the new estimated path cost is smaller than the previous one, we update the priority with the new estimated path cost. The search continues until we reach the target pin of current net.

3.2.3 DSA+DP aware Detailed Routing

The detailed routing algorithm is illustrated in Algorithm 1. A* search scheme is adopted in this work. We update the corresponding grid cost after a net is routed, and use a queue to store all the violated grids and all the nets information in these grids. If a net path generates a violation, the net path will be rip-up, and its nearby grid status should be updated. The net will be rerouted to remove the violation. If a new violation is generated after the rip-up and reroute, the new conflict should be pushed into the queue. This rip-up and reroute iteration continues until the violation queue is empty or the runtime exceeds the maximum time requirement.

Algorithm 1 DSA+DP aware detailed routing

Input: Netlists from net planning algorithm.
Output: Routed nets with DSA friendly via layer.
1: Route determined nets;
2: Update grids cost;
3: Initial routing iteration;
4: Q ← nets in violated grids;
5: **while** !Q.empty() **do**
6:     $g(i)$ ← Q.pop(); $Nets \in g(i)$;
7:     **for** each net $k \in Nets$ **do**
8:         Pre-route with cost evaluation;
9:     **end for**
10:    Rip-up net k that has maximum cost improvement;
11:    Route net k;
12:    **for** each grid $g(j)$ of net k **do**
13:       Update grid cost;
14:       **if** $g(j)$ is violated **then**
15:          Q ← nets in this $g(j)$;
16:       **end if**
17:    **end for**
18:    **if** $g(i)$ is still violated **then**
19:       Q ← $g(i)$;
20:    **end if**
21: **end while**

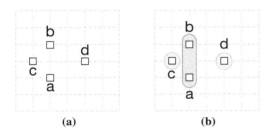

Figure 11: (a) Example layout for post routing optimization. (b) Optimal guiding pattern assignment and decomposition for the example layout.

3.3 Post Routing Optimization

In the post-routing stage, we propose a method to further minimize the DSA pattern cost and conflicts by re-assigning DSA guiding patterns to the via layer. For example, the original via pattern is shown in Figure 11(a), the optimized DSA guiding pattern assignment and decomposition is shown Figure 11(b). To find the optimized solution, we will first construct a new conflict graph for the via layer, as illustrated in Figure 12(a). The vertices represent the vias. An edge is added between any two vias when their distance is less than the minimum lithography distance. In addition, the edge is marked with black color if its vias can be grouped in the same DSA group, and the edge is marked with red color if its vias can not be grouped in the same DSA group. Because larger DSA groups can increase mask complexity and placement error between the target via and final via, thus minimizing large DSA groups and the number of conflicts at the same time are the primary goals for the post-routing optimization.

This problem can be formulated as the edge bipartization problem: convert the conflict graph to a bipartite graph by deleting minimized numbers of edges. This formulation is slightly different from the pre-route net planning formulation, as shown in Formula (7).

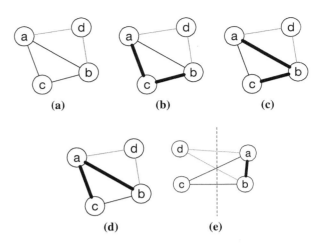

Figure 12: (a) Conflict graph for post routing optimization of the example layout. Because vias a, b and c cannot be grouped in the same DSA guiding template, therefore: (b) Edge ac and bc can not be deleted at the same time. (c) Edge ab and bc can not be deleted at the same time. (d) Edge ab and ac can not be deleted at the same time. (e) The conflict graph can be converted to a bipartite graph by deleting edge ab with minimum cost.

$$\min \quad \sum e_{v_i v_j} + M \cdot \sum e_{v_k v_h} \tag{7a}$$

$$\text{s.t.} \quad t_{v_i} + t_{v_j} + e_{v_i v_j} \geq 1, \qquad \forall \{e_{v_i v_j}\} \in E, \tag{7b}$$

$$t_{v_i} + t_{v_j} - e_{v_i v_j} \leq 1, \qquad \forall \{e_{v_i v_j}\} \in E, \tag{7c}$$

$$e_{v_i v_j} + e_{v_i v_k} \leq 1, \qquad \forall (i,j,k) \text{ infeasible}, \tag{7d}$$

$$e_{v_i v_j} + e_{v_j v_k} + e_{v_k v_h} \leq 2, \quad \forall (i,j,k),(j,k,h) \text{ groupable}, \tag{7e}$$

$$e_{v_i v_j}, t_{v_i} \in \{0,1\}. \tag{7f}$$

The first item in the objective function is the sum of edges with groupable vias, while the second item is the sum of edges with un-groupable vias. v_i represents via i, while $e_{v_i v_j}$ is a binary variable to indicate the edge between v_i and v_j. $e_{v_i v_j} = 1$ means that the edge is deleted. But if v_i and v_j can not be grouped in the same DSA pattern, a conflict is generated. Therefore, in order to discourage deleting the un-groupable edge, a large coefficient M is assigned to these edges in the objective function. t_{v_i} indicates which masks that v_i has been assigned to. The first two constraints will try to divide the vias on the same edge into two masks. The third constraint will avoid the forbidden DSA patterns, such as forks and circles. And the forth constraint restricts the sizes of feasible DSA patterns. As illustrated in Figures 12(b)–12(c), the bold edges can not be deleted at the same time to avoid infeasible DSA patterns. And the optimal solution can be achieved by deleting the edge between a and b to make the conflict graph a bipartite graph, as shown in Figure 12(e).

3.4 Overall Flow

Figure 13 shows the overall flow of our DSA+DP aware detailed routing algorithm. First, the algorithm input consists of blockages, net list with source and target pins, a set of DSA pattern constraints and corresponding design rules. Next, we perform the pre-route net planning to determine the routing paths for some nets. For nets whose routing paths can not be decided during the pre-route stage,

Table 2: Benchmark Statistics

bench	#net	#pin	Grid size
ecc	1671	3342	436×446
efc	2219	4438	406×421
ctl	2706	5412	496×503
alu	3108	6216	406×408
div	5813	11626	636×646
top	22201	44402	1176×1179

the rip-up and reroute based A* search algorithm is performed on our DSA+DP aware routing graph model to find the routing paths for them. After that, the post routing optimization algorithm is applied on the via layer to further reduce template cost.

4. EXPERIMENTAL RESULTS

We implemented the proposed algorithms in C++. All the experiments are performed on a 3.4 GHz Intel workstation with 32GB memory. The state of art optimization tool GUROBI 6.5 [11] is used as the ILP solver. The benchmarks are the synthesized OpenSparc T1 design [1]. It is assumed that only Metal 2 (M2) and Metal 3 (M3) layers are available for routing, where M2 and M3 run horizontally and vertically. The benchmarks are grid-based, and statistics of the benchmarks are shown in Table 2.

In order to demonstrate the effectiveness of our approach, we implemented the conventional 1D detailed router without DSA considerations, and also the DSA-aware detailed router proposed in [8], in which DP is not considered. Although the DSA patterns and design rules are different in [8], we adjusted the method with our own design rules and feasible DSA patterns. The parameters A and B in Equation (3) are set as 1 and 10 respectively.

Table 3 compares experimental results of conventional 1D detailed router, DSA-aware detailed router in [8], and our proposed DP+DSA aware detailed router (DSAR). In the table, "#Via" is the total via number; "WL" is the total wire length; "#CFLT" is number of the DP+DSA conflicts; while "CPU" is the runtime in seconds.

As shown in the table, our DSAR can effectively reduce via number by around 1% and 20% compared to conventional 1D detailed router and DSA aware detailed router without double patterning considerations [8]. In addition, DSAR outperforms [8] in terms of total wire length "WL" by reducing it by 15%. The wirelength of DSAR increases less than 1% compared to conventional 1D routing. These demonstrate that our proposed detailed routing algorithm is quite effective to reduce the wire length and via num-

ber than DSA aware detailed router without DP consideration, and with little impact compared to conventional 1D router. Moreover, compared to conventional 1D router, our DSAR can reduce 269 more DP+DSA conflicts between DSA guiding patterns, and reduce 8 conflicts than DSA router without double patterning considerations, which demonstrates the effectiveness of our proposed algorithms on DSA+DP considerations. The runtime is a little longer because of more iterations to resolve double patterning conflicts and more search spaces during A* search process. Besides, as all the algorithms can achieve 100% routability, thus routability is not shown in the comparison table.

The impact of our proposed net planning method is also analyzed in terms of total via number, total wirelength and runtime. The comparisons are illustrated in Figure 14. We can observe from Figures 14(a) and 14(b) that, with our proposed pre-route net planning, the via number and the wire length can be effectively reduced by 19% and 8%, respectively. Note that with more pre-routed nets the A* search based maze routing takes more time to search for the neighboring grids, thus the runtime has been slightly increased by around 7%, as shown in Figure 14(c). It indicates that with pre-route net planning, the solution quality can be improved at a cost of small runtime increase. Overall, we can still claim that the proposed net planning method is effective to reduce the total number of inserted vias and wirelength.

5. CONCLUSION

With the pitch multiplication ability, DSA can be applied on the printing of contacts/vias layer to reduce the number of masks. In this paper, we have proposed an effective DSA aware detailed routing algorithm with double patterning consideration on guiding patterns. We have also proposed a pre-route net planning algorithm to improve the routing quality in terms of via number and total wirelength. The detailed routing was performed on a new routing model with DSA+DP consideration, followed by a post routing optimization algorithm to further improve the DSA guiding pattern assignment and decomposition. The experimental results show that our proposed algorithm effectively reduces coloring conflicts on via layer with DSA and double patterning considerations.

6. REFERENCES

[1] OpenSPARC T1.
http://www.oracle.com/technetwork/systems/opensparc/index.html.

[2] V. Axelrad, K. Mikami, M. Smayling, K. Tsujita, and H. Yaegashi. Characterization of 1D layout technology at advanced nodes and low k1. In *Proceedings of SPIE*, volume 905213–905213, 2014.

[3] Y. Badr, A. Torres, and P. Gupta. Mask assignment and synthesis of DSA-MP hybrid lithography for sub-7nm contacts/vias. In *ACM/IEEE Design Automation Conference (DAC)*, pages 70:1–70:6, 2015.

[4] Y. Badr, J. A. Torres, Y. Ma, J. Mitra, and P. Gupta. Incorporating DSA in multipatterning semiconductor manufacturing technologies. In *Proceedings of SPIE*, volume 9427, 2015.

[5] I. Bita, J. K. W. Yang, Y. S. Jung, C. A. Ross, E. L. Thomas, and K. K. Berggren. Graphoepitaxy of self-assembled block copolymers on two-dimensional periodic patterned templates. *Science*, 321(5891):939–943, 2008.

[6] L.-W. Chang, X. Bao, B. Chris, and H.-S. P. Wong. Experimental demonstration of aperiodic patterns of directed self-assembly by block copolymer lithography for random logic circuit layout. In *IEEE International Electron Devices Meeting (IEDM)*, pages 33.2.1–33.2.4, 2010.

[7] Y. Du, D. Guo, M. D. F. Wong, H. Yi, H.-S. P. Wong, H. Zhang, and Q. Ma. Block copolymer directed self-assembly (DSA) aware contact layer optimization for 10 nm 1D standard cell library. In *IEEE/ACM International Conference on Computer-Aided Design (ICCAD)*, pages 186–193, 2013.

[8] Y. Du, Z. Xiao, M. D. F. Wong, H. Yi, and H.-S. P. Wong. DSA-aware detailed routing for via layer optimization. In *Proceedings of SPIE*, volume 9049, 2014.

[9] S.-Y. Fang, Y.-X. Hong, and Y.-Z. Lu. Simultaneous guiding template optimization and redundant via insertion for directed self-assembly. In *IEEE/ACM International Conference on Computer-Aided Design (ICCAD)*, pages 410–417, 2015.

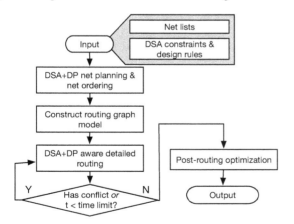

Figure 13: Overall flow of detailed routing with DSA+DP consideration.

Table 3: Routing Result Comparison

bench	Conventional 1D router				SPIE-14 [8]				DSAR			
	#Via	WL	#CFLT	CPU(s)	#Via	WL	#CFLT	CPU(s)	#Via	WL	#CFLT	CPU(s)
ecc	3243	37452	1	4.26	4068	44193	0	10.56	3269	37801	0	13.66
efc	5059	48712	2	19.9	6162	57024	1	27.5	5102	49686	0	26.69
ctl	5782	60059	1	22.02	6989	69397	0	57.9	5782	60574	0	56.94
alu	7303	65139	9	20.19	8999	77322	2	56.12	7489	67140	0	45.87
div	12897	124108	11	97.03	15689	144316	1	246.09	12974	125734	0	278.47
top	49347	424869	245	1558.32	57744	491182	4	4382.50	48044	423194	0	4133.30
Sum.	83631	760339	269	1721.72	99651	883434	8	4780.67	82660	764129	0	4554.93
Norm.	1.01	0.99	–	0.38	1.20	1.15	–	1.05	1.00	1.00	–	1.00

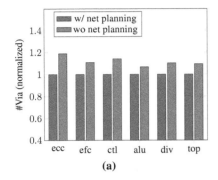 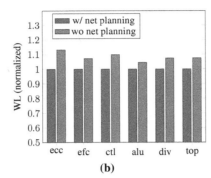 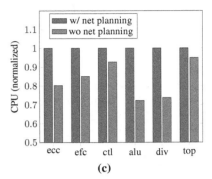

      (a)   (b)   (c)

Figure 14: Results comparison between algorithm with net planning and without net planning for (a) total via number, (b) total wirelength, (c) runtime. The data has been normalized for comparison.

[10] W. Gillijns, S. Sherazi, D. Trivkovic, B. Chava, B. Vandewalle, V. Gerousis, P. Raghavan, J. Ryckaert, K. Mercha, D. Verkest, et al. Impact of a SADP flow on the design and process for N10/N7 metal layers. In *Proceedings of SPIE*, volume 9427, 2015.

[11] Gurobi Optimization Inc. Gurobi optimizer reference manual. http://www.gurobi.com, 2014.

[12] R. Ikeno, T. Maruyama, S. Komatsu, T. Iizuka, M. Ikeda, and K. Asada. A structured routing architecture and its design methodology suitable for high-throughput electron beam direct writing with character projection. In *ACM International Symposium on Physical Design (ISPD)*, pages 69–76, 2013.

[13] I. Karageorgos, J. Ryckaert, M. C. Tung, H. S. P. Wong, R. Gronheid, J. Bekaert, E. Karageorgos, K. Croes, G. Vandenberghe, M. Stucchi, and W. Dehaene. Design strategy for integrating DSA via patterning in sub-7nm interconnects. In *Proceedings of SPIE*, volume 9781, 2016.

[14] J. Kuang, J. Ye, and E. F. Y. Young. Simultaneous template optimization and mask assignment for DSA with multiple patterning. In *IEEE/ACM Asia and South Pacific Design Automation Conference (ASPDAC)*, pages 75–82, 2016.

[15] A. Latypov, T. H. Coskun, G. Garner, M. Preil, G. Schmid, J. Xu, and Y. Zou. Simulations of spatial DSA morphology, DSA-aware assist features and block copolymer-homopolymer blends. In *Proceedings of SPIE*, volume 9049, 2014.

[16] L. Liebmann, A. Chu, and P. Gutwin. The daunting complexity of scaling to 7nm without EUV: Pushing DTCO to the extreme. In *Proceedings of SPIE*, volume 9427, 2015.

[17] Z.-W. Lin and Y.-W. Chang. Cut redistribution with directed self-assembly templates for advanced 1-D gridded layouts. In *IEEE/ACM Asia and South Pacific Design Automation Conference (ASPDAC)*, pages 89–94, 2016.

[18] Q. Ma, H. Zhang, and M. D. F. Wong. Triple patterning aware routing and its comparison with double patterning aware routing in 14nm technology. In *ACM/IEEE Design Automation Conference (DAC)*, pages 591–596, 2012.

[19] Y. Ma, J. Lei, J. A. Torres, L. Hong, J. Word, G. Fenger, A. Tritchkov, G. Lippincott, R. Gupta, N. Lafferty, Y. He, J. Bekaert, and G. Vanderberghe. Directed self-assembly (DSA) grapho-epitaxy template generation with immersion lithography. In *Proceedings of SPIE*, volume 9423, 2015.

[20] Y. Ma, J. A. Torres, G. Fenger, Y. Granik, J. Ryckaert, G. Vanderberghe, J. Bekaert, and J. Word. Challenges and opportunities in applying grapho-epitaxy DSA lithography to metal cut and contact/via applications. In *Proceedings of SPIE*, volume 9231, 2014.

[21] A. Mallik, J. Ryckaert, A. Mercha, D. Verkest, K. Ronse, and A. Thean. Maintaining Moore's law - enabling cost-friendly dimensional scaling. In *Proceedings of SPIE*, volume 9422, 2015.

[22] J. Ou, B. Yu, J.-R. Gao, and D. Z. Pan. Directed self-assembly cut mask assignment for unidirectional design. *Journal of Micro/Nanolithography, MEMS, and MOEMS (JM3)*, 14(3), 2015.

[23] J. Ou, B. Yu, J.-R. Gao, D. Z. Pan, M. Preil, and A. Latypov. Directed self-assembly based cut mask optimization for unidirectional design. In *ACM Great Lakes Symposium on VLSI (GLSVLSI)*, pages 83–86, 2015.

[24] J. Ou, B. Yu, and D. Z. Pan. Concurrent guiding template assignment and redundant via insertion for DSA-MP hybrid lithography. In *ACM International Symposium on Physical Design (ISPD)*, pages 39–46, 2016.

[25] J. Ryckaert, P. Raghavan, P. Schuddinck, H. B. Trong, A. Mallik, S. S. Sakhare, B. Chava, Y. Sherazi, P. Leray, A. Mercha, et al. DTCO at N7 and beyond: patterning and electrical compromises and opportunities. In *Proceedings of SPIE*, volume 9427, 2015.

[26] Y. Seino, H. Yonemitsu, H. Sato, M. Kanno, H. Kato, K. Kobayashi, A. Kawanishi, T. Azuma, M. Muramatsu, S. Nagahara, et al. Contact hole shrink process using directed self-assembly. In *Proceedings of SPIE*, volume 8323, 2012.

[27] S. Shim, W. Chung, and Y. Shin. Defect probability of directed self-assembly lithography: Fast identification and post-placement optimization. In *IEEE/ACM International Conference on Computer-Aided Design (ICCAD)*, pages 404–409, 2015.

[28] H.-S. P. Wong, C. Bencher, H. Yi, X.-Y. Bao, and L.-W. Chang. Block copolymer directed self-assembly enables sublithographic patterning for device fabrication. In *Proceedings of SPIE*, volume 8323, 2012.

[29] S. Wuister, T. Druzhinina, D. Ambesi, B. Laenens, L. H. Yi, and J. Finders. Influence of litho patterning on DSA placement errors. In *Proceedings of SPIE*, volume 9049, 2014.

[30] Z. Xiao, Y. Du, M. D. F. Wong, and H. Zhang. DSA template mask determination and cut redistribution for advanced 1D gridded design. In *Proceedings of SPIE*, volume 8880, 2013.

[31] Z. Xiao, C.-X. Lin, M. D. F. Wong, and H. Zhang. Contact layer decomposition to enable DSA with multi-patterning technique for standard cell based layout. In *IEEE/ACM Asia and South Pacific Design Automation Conference (ASPDAC)*, pages 95–102, 2016.

[32] H. Yi, X.-Y. Bao, J. Zhang, R. Tiberio, J. Conway, L.-W. Chang, S. Mitra, and H.-S. P. Wong. Contact-hole patterning for random logic circuit using block copolymer directed self-assembly. In *Proceedings of SPIE*, volume 8323, 2012.

[33] B. Yu, X. Xu, S. Roy, Y. Lin, J. Ou, and D. Z. Pan. Design for manufacturability and reliability in extreme scaling vlsi. *SCIENCE CHINA Information Science*, 2016.

Automatic Cell Layout in the 7nm Era

Pascal Cremer   Stefan Hougardy   Jan Schneider   Jannik Silvanus
Research Institute for Discrete Mathematics, University of Bonn, Germany
{cremer, hougardy, silvanus}@or.uni-bonn.de, schneider.jan@gmail.com

ABSTRACT

Multi patterning technology used in 7nm technology and beyond imposes more and more complex design rules on the layout of cells. The often non local nature of these new design rules is a great challenge not only for human designers but also for existing algorithms. We present a new flow for the automatic cell layout that is able to deal with these challenges by globally optimizing several design objectives simultaneously. Our transistor placement algorithm not only minimizes the total cell area but simultaneously optimizes the routability of the cell and finds a best folding of the transistors. Our routing engine computes a detailed routing of all nets simultaneously. In a first step it computes an electrically correct routing using a mixed integer programming formulation. To improve yield and optimize DFM, additional constraints are added to this model.

We present experimental results on current 7nm designs. Our approach allows to compute optimized layouts within a few minutes, even for large complex cells. Our algorithms are currently used for the design of 7nm cells at a leading chip manufacturer where they improved manufacturability and led to reduced turnaround times.

1. INTRODUCTION

So far an experienced designer is able to craft cell layouts which are of higher quality than automatically generated layouts. However, with each new technology the need for high quality automatic cell layout generators increases. This is due to the fact that design rules and DFM (design for manufacturability) requirements become more and more complex and the number of different cells used in modern designs is growing steadily. Moreover, the manual layout of a complex cell can take several days making this process a severe bottleneck in turnaround time.

In this paper, we present a new flow for the automatic generation of cell layouts, both for placement and routing. Our approach provides solutions that are optimal in terms of area consumption and routability. In practice it also reduces

ISPD '17, March 19-22, 2017, Portland, OR, USA

© 2017 ACM. ISBN 978-1-4503-4696-2/17/03... $15.00

DOI: http://dx.doi.org/10.1145/3036669.3036672

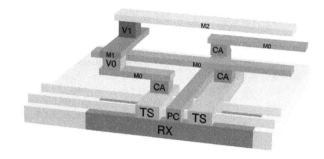

Figure 1: Schematic view of a 7nm layout showing a single finFET and some wiring. Fins (yellow), M0, and M2 are horizontal while PC, TS, and M1 are vertical layers. The diffusion area is denoted by RX. The via layers are CA, V0, and V1.

the need for manual interaction significantly. We consider many complex design rules and DFM requirements already during the placement and the routing phase. This is a crucial requirement for the current 7nm technology and beyond as design rule cleanness and DFM requirements can no longer be achieved by local post-processing operations alone.

In 7nm all layers are uni-directional (see Figure 1). PC and TS are used to contact gates and source/drain contacts of the finFETs. A finFET can have more than one gate. We refer to the number of gates as the number of *fingers* of the transistor. A transistor is called *folded* if it has more than one finger. Three additional wiring layers M0, M1, and M2 are available that alternately have horizontal and vertical orientation. As M2 is also used for inter cell connections, it should be used for internal cell wiring only if necessary. The wiring layers are connected by via layers CA, V0, and V1, where CA connects both PC and TS with M0, V0 connects M0 with M1, and V1 connects M1 with M2. Different multiple patterning techniques are applied for these layers. SAQP (self aligned quadruple patterning) is used for the fins, SADP (self aligned double patterning) for the metal layers, and up to LELELELE (four times litho-edge) for the via layers [19].

The *cell layout problem* can be described as follows. As input an image of the cell is given, i.e. an area with predefined horizontal power tracks at the top and bottom of the cell, equidistant vertical tracks for PC, TS, and M1, fin positions, and (not necessarily equidistant) horizontal tracks for M0 and M2. The finFETs, partitioned into p-FETs and

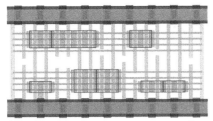
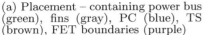

(a) Placement – containing power bus (green), fins (gray), PC (blue), TS (brown), FET boundaries (purple)

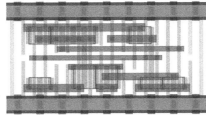
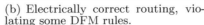

(b) Electrically correct routing, violating some DFM rules.

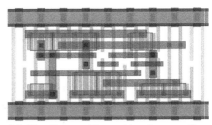

(c) Routing with optimal manufacturability and wire length.

Figure 2: Example results after placement and both routing phases. The green shapes on the top and bottom represent the power tracks of a circuit row.

n-FETs, have to be placed in two rows in between the power tracks (see Figure 2(a)). The electrical connectivity of the FETs and their size is described in a netlist. The task is to decide how many fingers a FET should use and to assign a location to each FET. Both choices are subject to the design rules and DFM constraints. Here, the width of the image is the most important optimization criterion as this determines the area of the cell on the chip. Given a placement of FETs, the goal in routing is to find an embedding of rectilinear Steiner trees which realizes the given netlist. This has to be done meeting the design rules and DFM constraints, as well. As overall goal in routing, we minimize weighted net length, with the topmost available layer M2 being more expensive than other layers. Other objectives (e.g. pin access [18], number of vias, or electromigration reliability [19, 12]) can easily be included as well.

A crucial point to obtain high quality cell layouts is for the placement algorithm to have a very good estimate of where and how much free area is needed in the routing step. If the placement is too pessimistic this will result in a waste of space, whereas a too optimistic placement is not routable. We have designed an objective function for the placement step that very accurately estimates the quality of a placement with respect to later routability (see Section 2.1). In many cases we can prove that our placement solution is *optimal* with respect to our objective function.

Simple sequential rip-up and reroute approaches turned out to fail for most of our placements. Instead we use an approach that allows to route all nets *simultaneously* and consider many design rules and DFM constraints already while building up the nets. The latter is required because only few design rule violations can be fixed after routing due to the limited space of our compact placements. We also have successfully extended our approach to *multi-bit* cells (see Section 2.5).

In Section 2, we discuss the placement algorithm, followed by the routing solution in Section 3. Section 4 reports the results of our implementation on cells at the 7nm technology node.

1.1 Related Work

Most previous work on cell layout only focuses on subproblems or restricted versions of the general cell layout problem and is not directly applicable to 7nm layouts. Moreover, design rules and DFM requirements are more restrictive in 7nm

than in previous 14nm/15nm [9] and 10nm finFET technology nodes.

Many different approaches have been suggested for the transistor placement problem. In [2, 8] combinatorial algorithms are presented that optimize the cell area, but assume a given transistor folding. [4] use an integer programming approach that optimizes cell area and includes transistor folding but assumes the possibility to pair n-FETs and p-FETs. In [14] a branch-and-bound approach is used for transistor placement that allows to optimize additional objectives, but transistor folding is not considered.

The placement algorithm has to consider the complicated dependencies between positions of n-FETs and p-FETs that arise due to the design rules of the SADP cut mask for the PC layer. Several approaches to handle SADP in automated design have been suggested [17, 19]. Our approach differs in that we allow variable gate widths during cut mask generation and guarantee to find valid solutions (if existent) in polynomial runtime. To the best of our knowledge, our placement algorithm is the first to guarantee a legal SADP layer decomposition without wasting cell area (see Section 2.6).

For intra cell routing many different approaches are known. Traditional channel routing [15] and simple rip-up and reroute strategies [10] fail in recent technologies. More successful are SAT-based [13] and the closely related integer-programming based [18] approaches. In these approaches a set of candidate solutions is generated for each net. A SAT-formulation or an integer linear program is used to select one realization for each net so that all design rules are met.

Our routing approach is also based on an integer programming formulation. However, we do not need to pre-compute candidate solutions for each net but instead generate all possible routings for all nets simultaneously while packing them. Using this approach we do not have to restrict the candidate solutions in advance (e.g. by restricting them to lie within some bounding box around the terminals) but are able to consider all possible routings. While this makes the search space much larger, our well chosen integer programming formulation turns out to be quickly solvable by standard MIP solvers. Typically, cells with up to 15 FETs are solved within a few minutes.

2. PLACEMENT

The input of the cell placement problem is a set $\mathcal{F}$ of FETs, a set $\mathcal{N}$ of nets and a large number of technology-

100

specific constraints. A *FET* is characterized by a tuple $(W, N_g, N_s, N_d, n_s, t)$, where

- $W \in \mathbb{N}$ is the total width of the gate measured in the number of fins it intersects,

- $N_g, N_s,$ and N_d are the nets connected to gate, source, and drain, respectively,

- $t \in \{\text{n-FET}, \text{p-FET}\}$ is the FET's type.

We allow FETs to be folded, i.e. realized with different numbers of *fingers*. Therefore, solving the placement problem does not only include the assignment of locations to each transistor but also deciding how many fingers should be used. The total width W of a FET can be distributed to a number of fingers. Using only one finger, the FET is realized with one gate, intersecting W fins. Using a larger number of fingers, the FET is realized with several gates, located next to each other, which in total intersect W fins. If, for example, the width of a FET is 6 (measured in fins) it can be realized with 1, 2, 3, and 6 fingers, each covering 6, 3, 2, and 1 fin respectively. Additionally, the user can allow rounding, which means that the same FET can also be realized with 4 and 5 fingers, covering 2 and 1 fins respectively. Note that in this case the width of the implemented FET is only approximately the specified width. Depending on the used cell image, some fin configurations can be forbidden, e.g. most images do not allow fingers covering a single fin only. A FET realized with f fingers has f gates and $f + 1$ source and drain contacts. A FET with several fingers connects source and drain nets alternately. The placement algorithm is also allowed to swap FETs. In this case, the source and drain contacts of the FET exchange their places. Figure 3 shows the same FET realized in three different ways.

All gates are manufactured with self-aligned double patterning (SADP). In the first step, a regular pattern of unidirectional poly (PC) shapes is generated. In the second step, these shapes are cut off by the cut (CT) mask, leaving the desired gates. Not all placements admit a legal layer decomposition. Situations for which no legal cut mask exists are detected by our placement algorithm and excluded from the search tree as soon as possible.

The output of the placement algorithm consists of

- FET locations $(x, y) : \mathcal{F} \to \mathbb{R}^2$,

- finger numbers $\phi : \mathcal{F} \to \mathbb{N}_{>0}$, and

- swap status $s : \mathcal{F} \to \{\text{yes}, \text{no}\}$.

This information is then passed to the routing algorithm (see Section 3). The transistors are arranged in two *stacks*, one next to each power rail. One stack consists of the cell's n-FETs and is placed directly next to the lower power rail, whereas the other stack contains the p-FETs and is placed directly next to the upper power rail. Our program is also capable to realize multi-bit cells. These cells occupy multiple circuit rows and have several pairs of stacks placed upon each other. For the moment, we focus on single-bit instances with two stacks, more details on our multi-bit implementation will be given in Section 2.5.

The main design rules that have to be obeyed during placement are horizontal and vertical distance rules.

1. A function d specifies the minimum size of gaps between FETs in the following way: If F_2 is the right neighbor of F_1

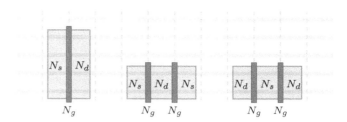

Figure 3: A FET of width 4 realized with 1 finger, 2 fingers, and 2 fingers swapped. Gates are shown in blue, Source and drain contacts in gray.

on one of the stacks, then the gates must have a distance of at least $d := d(F_1, \phi(F_1), s(F_1), F_2, \phi(F_2), s(F_2)) \in \{1, 3\}$ tracks. For $d = 1$, the rightmost contact of F_1 may overlap the leftmost contact of F_2 and for $d = 3$ the FETs are separated by two empty PC tracks. In the first case the diffusion regions overlap and the contact is used simultaneously by both FETs.

2. The SADP manufacturing process for the gates uses a cut mask (CT). The design rules for CT require that there is enough vertical space between FETs with different gate nets (see Section 2.6). Additionally, gates cannot be connected on the diffusion region but only in between both stacks. Therefore, enough vertical space between the FETs must be reserved for their connection as well.

2.1 Objective Function

We want to find placements which are small and as "routable" as possible. To do so, we use an efficiently computable model to measure the quality of a placement P involving the following two values:

- $W(P)$, defined as the *width* of the placement, i.e. the number of required PC tracks,

- The *gate-gate net length*, $\text{ggnl}(P) := \sum_{N \in \mathcal{N}} \text{ggnl}(N)$, where $\text{ggnl}(N)$ is the width of the bounding box of all gate contacts in N.

The algorithm returns a placement which respects all design rules (including vertical constraints) and additionally globally minimizes the placement width $W(P)$. If there are several such placements the algorithm chooses a placement among them with the minimum gate-gate net length. This does not guarantee routability but turns out to be a very good indicator for real-world 7nm cells. A very similar objective function was already used in [1]. In [17] the number of required M2 tracks is used as secondary objective.

2.2 Placement Algorithm

Our placement algorithm, as outlined in algorithms 1–3, implements at its core a recursive enumeration of all possible placements that backtracks as soon as the current (partial) solution cannot be part of a placement that is better than the best placement that has been found so far. We search for legal solutions with increasing cell width. The minimum width of a single stack, ignoring the constraints imposed by the other stack, can be calculated very efficiently. The minimum width of both stacks are lower bounds for the minimum width of the entire cell. Therefore, we take the maximum $W_{\max}$ of both lower bounds and start by looking for solutions

Algorithm 1 TWOSTACKPLACEMENT

1: **for all** $S \in \{N, P\}$ **do**
2:      $W_{\max}^S \leftarrow 0$
3:      **while** ENUMERATESTACK$(\mathcal{F}_S, W_{\max}^S) = \emptyset$ **do**
4:          $W_{\max} \leftarrow W_{\max} + 1$
5:      **end while**
6: **end for**
7: $W_{\max}^{\mathrm{init}} \leftarrow \max(W_{\max}^P, W_{\max}^N)$
8: **for** $W_{\max} = W_{\max}^{\mathrm{init}}, W_{\max}^{\mathrm{init}} + 1, \ldots$ **do**
9:      Enumerate placements on both stacks with width at
        most $W_{\max}$.
10:      **if** found optimal placement P **then**
11:          **return** P
12:      **end if**
13: **end for**

Algorithm 2 ENUMERATESTACK$(\mathcal{F}, W_{\max})$

1: $\kappa \leftarrow 0$
2: $\mathcal{P} \leftarrow \emptyset$
3: **while** LOWERBOUNDADDFINGERS$(\kappa) \leq W_{\max}$ **do**
4:      **for all** possibilities to add κ fingers to $\mathcal{F}$ **do**
5:          STACKRECURSION$(\mathcal{F})$
6:      **end for**
7:      $\kappa \leftarrow \kappa + 1$
8: **end while**
9: **return** $\mathcal{P}$

---

whose width is at most $W_{\max}$. This describes lines 1–7 of Algorithm 1. If no solution can be found with this restriction, the cell width is increased and we repeat this procedure until a placement is found. This means that parts of the search tree are visited multiple times. However, this does not cause a significant performance penalty, since the running time of the last iteration usually dominates the running time of all previous iterations.

2.3 Placing a Single Stack

An important subroutine of our placement method is ENUMERATESTACK (Algorithm 2). Its input is a set $\mathcal{F}$ of unplaced FETs and a width restriction $W_{\max}$. It outputs a list of all legal placements with width at most $W_{\max}$, or that no such placement exists.

ENUMERATESTACK is implemented by distributing fingers to the FETs. Initially, all FETs start with the minimum number of fingers they can have. Afterwards, an increasing number of fingers is distributed to all FETs, trying every distribution. Before assigning an additional finger to the FETs, we use a fast routine to calculate a lower bound for the width of placements with κ additional fingers. We can exit the loop as soon as this lower bound exceeds the width bound $W_{\max}$. Once all fingers are distributed, STACKRECURSION (Algorithm 3) is called.

Algorithm 3 is called recursively. In the beginning some of the FETs have already been placed. We keep the positions of these FETs fixed and compute a lower bound for the total cell width where all FETs are placed. The minimum width needed by a set of FETs with fixed number of fingers equals the total number of fingers plus 2 additional tracks for each gap that has to be inserted between two FETs. For our lower bound calculation we use that a gap has to be inserted if the nets of the rightmost contact of the left FET

Algorithm 3 STACKRECURSION$(\mathcal{F}_u)$

1: **if** LOWERBOUND$(\mathcal{F}_u) > W_{\max}$ **then**
2:      return
3: **else if** $\mathcal{F}_u = \emptyset$ **then**
4:      $\mathcal{P} \leftarrow \mathcal{P} \cup \{\text{current placement}\}$
5: **else**
6:      **for all** $F \in \mathcal{F}_u$ **do**
7:          Place F on the leftmost possible track
8:          STACKRECURSION$(\mathcal{F}_u \setminus \{F\})$
9:          Unplace F
10:          Swap F and repeat lines 7 − 9
11:      **end for**
12: **end if**

---

and the leftmost contact of the right FET are not the same. We count the number of times a net connects a leftmost or rightmost FET contact and denote it by C^N. If C^N is odd, it is not possible to place all contacts of this net next to each other, avoiding gaps. However, the additional gap can be avoided by placing one contact of the net at the cell boundary. This can at most be done for two nets, one on the left and the other on the right cell boundary. This gives the following lower bound for the cell width.

$$W_{\mathrm{lb}}(\mathcal{F}_u) = W(\mathcal{F} \setminus \mathcal{F}_u) + \sum_{F \in \mathcal{F}_u} \phi(F) + 2 \cdot \max\{0, n_{\mathrm{odd}} - 2\},$$

where $W(\mathcal{F} \setminus \mathcal{F}_u)$ is the width of the already placed FETs, $\sum_{F \in \mathcal{F}_u} \phi(F)$ the number of fingers yet to place, and n_{odd} the number of nets with C^N odd.

If this bound does not exceed the width limit $W_{\max}$, we recursively place FETs in the stack from left to right, trying every permutation of FETs. Given a partial solution, it takes every yet unplaced FET and places it at the smallest legal horizontal coordinate on top of the partial solution − once unswapped and once swapped.

If only a single width-minimal placement (not necessarily optimal w.r.t. the entire objective function) is required, as in line 3 of Algorithm 1, a faster version of ENUMERATESTACK is used that considers only partial solutions with a specific block structure.

2.4 Placing Both Stacks

The placement algorithm on an entire cell is done by placing one stack after the other. In contrast to single stack placement where only horizontal constraints have to be obeyed, vertical constraints are important for two stack placement as well.

We fix a cell width and enumerate placements for both stacks (Line 9 of Algorithm 1). This is done by enumerating all placements with width at most $W_{\max}$ on the first stack, and for each of these placements enumerating placements with width at most $W_{\max}$ on the second stack. For the second stack, an extended version of Algorithm 2 is used. This extended version checks the vertical constraints between the two stacks. Additionally, it is checked whether the space between the transistor rows is large enough to allow gate wiring and a legal PC cut mask. Quickly deciding whether a legal PC cut mask exists is a non-trivial problem and will later be discussed in some detail (see Section 2.6). To speed up the algorithm, this is already checked for a partial placement of

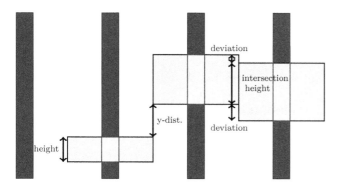

Figure 4: Cut mask rules. PC in blue, cut mask in gray. Height of each cut shape has to be at least d. y-distance between cut shapes on neighboring tracks has to be at least v or cut shapes have to touch. In the second case their deviation has to be at most s and their intersection height at least d.

the second stack, allowing to prune entire branches of the search tree.

Additional pruning can be accomplished since we are only interested in a single optimum solution. We calculate lower bounds for ggnl(.) and wnl(.) given a partial placement. If these values exceed the upper bound given by an already found placement we can prune all placements containing these partial placements.

2.5 Multi-Bit Cells

Very large cells are typically not implemented on one but several neighboring circuit rows. Such *multi-bit* cells can also be placed with our program. To place a cell with k bits, we first compute candidates for assignments of FETs to the bits. We then evaluate the quality of these assignments (by their number of bit-crossing connections, etc.) and solve the most promising candidates with a variation of Algorithm 1. The bits are placed one after the other with each new placement respecting constraints due to already placed bits.

2.6 Cut Shapes

Gates, i.e. poly conductors (PC) manufactured by a single exposure lithographic process suffer from major drawbacks in modern technology nodes [7]. One issue is that the spacing of printed line-ends becomes too large to allow dense packing of transistors. To overcome this effect, self-aligned double patterning (SADP) is used to produce lines and line-ends separately. This reduces line end roughness (LER), creates straighter PC lines [7] and doubles the density of PC stripes, allowing a smaller PC pitch.

Using this double patterning technique means that design rules have to be obeyed for a cut (CT) mask which removes extraneous features. We assume that all gates are placed on a regular pattern, where all PC lines are parallel to each other and have equal distance. We call the possible positions of gates *tracks*. The CT mask is then used to remove undesired features, i.e. to remove a connection between two transistors. It is composed of several rectilinear cut shapes which have to obey certain rules. These rules are depicted in Figure 4.

Given some (partial) non-overlapping transistor placement and gate routing we need to decide if a legal CT mask ex-

ists. If two transistors on different stacks using the same gate track need to be disconnected, we need a cut shape in between them. The exact position of the cut shape is not important to obtain an LVS clean solution but matters regarding cut shape design rules. This leads to the following formal definition of the CUT SHAPES problem.

CUT SHAPES

Instance: Boundary intervals $[l_1, u_1], \ldots, [l_n, u_n] \subseteq \mathbb{N}$, minimum height $d \in \mathbb{N}$, maximum deviation $s \in \mathbb{N}$, minimum y-distance $v \in \mathbb{N}$.

Task: Find cut shape intervals $[x_1, y_1], \ldots, [x_n, y_n] \subseteq \mathbb{N}$, s.t. $[x_i, y_i] \subseteq [l_i, u_i], y_i - x_i \geq d$, for $i = 1, \ldots, n$ and either

1. $\begin{aligned} |x_i - x_{i-1}| \leq s, |y_i - y_{i-1}| \leq s, \\ |x_i - y_{i-1}| \geq d, |y_i - x_{i-1}| \geq d \end{aligned}$, or

2. $x_i \geq y_{i-1} + v$, or

3. $y_i \leq x_{i-1} - v$

for $i = 2, \ldots n$.

It can be proven that it is enough to deal with the special case that no y-distance has to be left between neighboring cut shapes i.e. $v = 0$:

LEMMA 1. *An algorithm A which solves CUT SHAPES instances for $v = 0$ in time T can be used to solve arbitrary CUT SHAPES instances with runtime $T + \mathcal{O}(n)$.*

A fast algorithm for CUT SHAPES is important as it is called many times during the placement algorithm and dominates its total running time. In the following, we present a polynomial time algorithm. The idea is to use a dynamic programming approach, going through the instance track by track. Since the number of coordinates inside an interval $[l_i, u_i]$ is in general exponential in the input size, we have an exponential number of states resulting in an exponential runtime. To reduce the number of states, we show that a polynomially sized subset of coordinates always contains a solution. We formally state this result after introducing some notation.

DEFINITION 1. *The coordinate sum of a feasible solution $[x_i, y_i]_{i=1,\ldots,n}$ is defined as $\sum_{i=1}^n (x_i + y_i)$. A solution is called uppermost optimal if no other solution with larger coordinate sum exists.*

THEOREM 1. *For a given instance of the cut shape problem, let $B := \{l_1, \ldots, l_n, u_1, \ldots, u_n\}$ be the set of boundary coordinates and $[x_i, y_i]_{i=1,\ldots,n}$ an uppermost optimal solution. Furthermore, using the Minkowski sum and product, let $B^\star := B + \{0, -d, d, -s, s\}^{2n}$. Then $x_i, y_i \in B^\star$ for $i = 1, \ldots, n$.*

We will not give a formal proof here, but intuitively any legal solution can be "shifted upwards" until it becomes uppermost optimal. One can then show that the coordinates used by this new solution are a subset of $B^\star$.

REMARK 1. *The size of $B^\star$ is polynomially bounded in the number of tracks n. We have $B^\star := B + \{0, -d, d, -s, s\}^{2n}$, $|B| = \mathcal{O}(n)$, and $|\{0, -d, d, -s, s\}^{2n}| = \mathcal{O}(n)$. Therefore, $|B^\star| = \mathcal{O}(n^2)$.*

Algorithm 4 CUT SHAPES

1: **for** $x_1, y_1 \in B^\star \cap [l_1, u_1]$ with $y_1 - x_1 \geq d$ **do**
2:     Set $[x_1, y_1]$ as solution of $P_1(x_1, y_1)$
3: **end for**
4: **for** $i = 2, \ldots, n$ **do**
5:     **for** $x_i, y_i \in B^\star \cap [l_i, u_i]$ with $y_i - x_i \geq d$ **do**
6:         **for** $[x_{i-1}, y_{i-1}]$ s.t. $P_{i-1}(x_{i-1}, y_{i-1})$ has a solution and $[x_{i-1}, y_{i-1}], [x_i, y_i]$ are legal neighbors **do**
7:             Set $[x_{i-1}, y_{i-1}], [x_i, y_i]$ as solution of $P_i(x_i, y_i)$
8:         **end for**
9:     **end for**
10: **end for**
11: Pick legal cut shape on track n and use backtracking to obtain entire solution.

DEFINITION 2. *Let $P_i(\bar{x}, \bar{y})$ be the problem instance restricted to tracks $1, \ldots, i$, with the additional constraints $x_i = \bar{x}$, $y_i = \bar{y}$.*

As shown by Theorem 1, it suffices to search for optimal solutions on the coordinate set $B^\star$. This motivates Algorithm 4.

THEOREM 2. *Algorithm 4 solves* CUT SHAPES *optimally and can be implemented with runtime $\mathcal{O}(nk^4)$, where $k := |B^\star|$. Using Remark 1, this gives a runtime of $\mathcal{O}(n^9)$.*

REMARK 2. *By iterating over $x_i, y_i, x_{i-1}, y_{i-1}$ in lines 5 to 9 more cleverly, the runtime of these lines can be improved to $\mathcal{O}(k^2)$. This gives a total runtime of $\mathcal{O}(nk^2) = \mathcal{O}(n^5)$.*

In practice the number of y-coordinates on which cut shapes can start or end is limited. In our application there are about 500 possible coordinates which gives a constant upper bound on k. Therefore, Algorithm 4 has a runtime of $\mathcal{O}(n)$ in practice.

3. ROUTING

In order to solve the routing problem on a placed cell, we use a mixed integer programming (MIP) approach.

Next to the input already given for the placement problem (Section 2), the cell routing problem expects the location of each FET from the placement. Furthermore, external connections may be present for a net, together with a desired location for this external input and output. During routing, our goal is to minimize the wire length and number of vias in order to optimize the power, timing, and yield properties of the cell.

3.1 Grid Graph Construction

Since each wiring layer only allows either vertical or horizontal wires, we represent the cell routing space by a three-dimensional grid graph $G = (V, E)$ with edge costs. For each layer, we are given a set of routing tracks specifying feasible positions for wires which are not necessarily equidistant.

By intersecting routing tracks on adjacent layers, we obtain the vertex set V. The edge set E consists both of line segments connecting adjacent intersections on the same layer as well as vias between stacked vertices on adjacent layers.

Edge costs are given by multiplying their geometric length by a layer-specific constant. This allows to e.g. increase costs on M2 in order to leave more space for inter-cell routing, and to trade off wire length against the number of vias.

On this graph, we are seeking a minimum-cost Steiner tree packing that contains for each net a tree connecting its terminals, which are given by the gate, source, and drain contacts as well as its external pins. Furthermore, the packing is subject to additional constraints.

3.2 Design Rules and Coloring

For the wiring within a cell, design rules fall into two basic categories: *Diff-net rules* require a certain minimum distance between wires that belong to different nets. *Same-net rules* are in place to avoid geometric configurations with features below the lithographic capabilities and resolution, and to reserve space for optical proximity correction (OPC). While diff-net rules are most important, same-net rules have become more and more important with each new technology. Especially in routing, it is particularly important to obey all these rules already during the routing algorithm because it is not possible to fix errors in post-processing due to a lack of space.

All features are manufactured using multiple masks in order to increase packing density: Shapes on different masks are allowed to have a smaller distance than shapes on the same mask. Hence, a valid routing does not only consist of a disjoint Steiner tree packing, but also requires features on such layers to be assigned to masks such that certain design rules are met. We call this assignment *coloring*. However, in 7nm technology this only affects vias, since all wires are colored using an alternating track-based coloring scheme.

3.3 Mixed Integer Programming Formulation

First, we describe the core MIP we use to model the Steiner tree packing problem in graphs. Then, in Section 3.4, we explain how design rules are incorporated into the model.

We ensure connectivity by adding for each net a relaxation of the Steiner tree problem in graphs to the model. In [3], the undirected cut relaxation is used for that purpose: For each cut $X \subseteq V$ separating the terminal set, the undirected cut relaxation requires at least one edge in $E(X, V \setminus X)$ to be contained in the Steiner tree. However, the undirected cut relaxation has an integrality gap of 2, which is already asymptotically attained in the special case that G is a circuit, even if all vertices are terminals. One can strengthen the relaxation by using a bidirected auxiliary graph $G' = (V, A)$ with $A = \{(i, j) : \{i, j\} \in E\}$ which contains two opposing edges (i, j) and (j, i) for each original edge $\{i, j\} \in E(G)$. Let r be an arbitrary root terminal and add variables for all edges $e \in A$. Then, for each cut $r \in X \subseteq V$ that does not contain all terminals, require that at least one edge leaving the cut is used. Finally, lower bound the usage of each original edge $\{i, j\} \in E$ by the *sum* of the usages of both directed edges (i, j) and (j, i). This relaxation is called bidirected cut relaxation. The integrality gap of the bidirected cut relaxation is unknown, the worst known example due to Skutella (reported in [6]) has an integrality gap of $\frac{8}{7}$.

By introducing additional flow variables, one can eliminate the exponential number of cut constraints, resulting in the multicommodity flow relaxation, first introduced in [16]. This relaxation is equivalent to the bidirected cut relaxation [11] and was already used in [5] to solve Steiner tree packing problems. We will also use the multicommodity flow relaxation:

For each net $k \in \mathcal{N}$, we denote by $T_k \subseteq V$ the set of its terminals. A decision variable x_e^k is introduced for each net $k \in \mathcal{N}$ specifying whether k is using an edge $e \in E$ of the graph G. For each net k, we choose an arbitrary root terminal $r_k \in T_k$ and denote the set of sink terminals $T_k \setminus \{r_k\}$ by S_k. Then, the multicommodity flow relaxation introduces a commodity for each sink $t \in S_k$ and requires a flow of one unit of the commodity from r_k to t to be supported by x^k. More precisely, for each net $k \in \mathcal{N}$, terminal $t \in S_k$ and directed edge $(i, j) \in A$, a flow variable f_{ij}^t is introduced representing the flow of the commodity t along the directed edge (i, j). Then, we add flow conservation constraints at vertices in $V \setminus \{t, r_k\}$ and enforce that r_k sends one unit of flow and that t receives one unit of flow of commodity t. Furthermore, for each net k and each edge $(i, j) \in A$, we add directed edge usage variables $\vec{x}_{ij}^k$ that upper bound the directed flow variables f_{ij}^t and require $\vec{x}_{ij}^k + \vec{x}_{ji}^k \leq x_{\{i,j\}}^k$. For ease of notation, we combine the usage of each edge $e \in E(G)$ also to a single variable x_e. Also, we denote by $f^t(v) := f^t(\delta^+(v)) - f^t(\delta^-(v))$ the flow balance of sink t at a vertex $v \in V(G)$. The complete model is as follows:

$$
\begin{aligned}
\min \quad & \sum_{e \in E} c_e x_e \\
\text{s.t.} \quad & x_e = \sum_{k \in \mathcal{N}} x_e^k && \forall\, e \in E \\
& x_e \in \{0, 1\} && \forall\, e \in E \\
& x_e^k \in \{0, 1\} && \forall\, e \in E, k \in \mathcal{N} \\
& f^t(v) = \begin{cases} 1 & \text{if } i = r_k \\ -1 & \text{if } i = t \\ 0 & \text{else} \end{cases} \\
& && \forall\, v \in V, k \in \mathcal{N}, t \in S_k \\
& 0 \leq f_{ij}^t \leq \vec{x}_{ij}^k && \forall\, (i, j) \in A, k \in \mathcal{N}, t \in S_k \\
& \vec{x}_{ij}^k + \vec{x}_{ji}^k \leq x_{\{i,j\}}^k && \forall\, \{i, j\} \in E, k \in \mathcal{N}
\end{aligned}
$$

In this basic formulation, no additional constraints, especially with respect to distances between wires resulting from the Steiner tree, are taken into consideration. Furthermore, two nets may actually share the same vertex, but not the same edge. Further constraints ensuring correctness in this sense, but also modeling coloring and the additional DRC constraints, are presented next.

3.4 Mapping DRC Constraints

To ensure vertex disjointness, for each $k \in \mathcal{N}$ and vertex $v \in V(G)$, we add a vertex usage variable $x_v^k \in \{0, 1\}$. Then, for each net $k \in \mathcal{N}$ and $v \in e \in E(G)$, we add the constraint $x_e^k \leq x_v^k$, and add $\sum_{k \in \mathcal{N}} x_v^k \leq 1$ for all $v \in V(G)$.

On via layers, we need to assign colors to used edges. To that end, for each such edge $e \in E$, net $k \in \mathcal{N}$ and color $m \in M$, we add a binary variable $^m x_e^k$ and enforce

$$
x_e^k = \sum_{m \in M} {}^m x_e^k.
$$

Moreover, for each such edge e and color m, we add a binary variable $^m x_e = \sum_{k \in \mathcal{N}} {}^m x_e^k$, representing whether edge e is used with color m by any net.

The transistor placement already induces forbidden edges which are immediately mapped to the respective variables.

The basic distance rules are then mapped as follows. Suppose that if an edge $e \in E$ is used by the wiring of net $k \in \mathcal{N}$, then a nearby edge $e' \in E$ cannot be used by another net.

The inequality

$$
x_e^k + \sum_{i \in \mathcal{N} \setminus \{k\}} x_{e'}^i \leq 1
$$

prohibits this situation. All basic diff-net distance rules can be modeled this way, including via distances and the inter-layer via rules that prescribe minimum distances between vias in adjacent via layers. Simple same-color and diff-color spacing constraints can be modeled as well, using the corresponding $^m x_e^k$ variables. We also add some of these distance constraints for segments of the same net, as there are also same-net rules for spacing between non-adjacent segments of the same net.

An important same-net rule requires that each wire must have a certain minimum length, depending on its layer. Let e, e' be adjacent edges and assume that e is used and e' is not used. In order to fulfill the required minimum length, a set F of edges must also be used, c.f. Figure 5. We model this implication by the constraint

$$
\sum_{f \in F} x_f \geq |F| \cdot (x_e - x_{e'}).
$$

Clearly, in the situation depicted above, this constraint requires $x_f = 1$ for all $f \in F$, and is non-binding otherwise.

Figure 5: Minimum length rule implementation: If e is used and e' is not used, then f_1, f_2 and f_3 must also be used.

Other rules like minimum via overhangs are modeled in a similar way.

To route a cell, we first solve the model described in Section 3.3 together with vertex-disjointness constraints to obtain an electrically correct routing. Then, we add the additional variables and constraints described in Section 3.4 and re-solve, which yields an optimum routing obeying the design rules and DFM constraints.

4. EXPERIMENTAL RESULTS

The described algorithms are implemented and tested on real-world 7nm instances. Table 1 reports on runtime and quality of our results, split into placement and routing part, for several characteristic current 7nm cells. All experiments were done single-threaded on a 2.20GHz Intel Xeon E5-2699 v4 machine using CPLEX 12.6 as MIP-solver.

For the first 9 instances shown in Table 1 a placement with provably smallest possible area was found in a few seconds. Placements with optimal routability were found after at most 2 min and their optimality was proven after a maximum of 5 min. Cells 10 and 11 were placed with provably minimal area after less than 2 min. Here placements with improved routability were found after up to 7 min. While it could not be proven within a time limit of 60 min, it is still possible that the found placements were already globally optimal w.r.t. routability.

All cells were routed in two phases. First, an electrically correct routing was computed which took up to 30 s on the first 9 instances and 2 min and 11 min on cells 10 and 11, respectively. This solution can already be used for tasks

Table 1: Results on 7nm testbed: $|\mathcal{F}|$ number of fets, $|\mathcal{N}|$ number of nets, w cell width in tracks, t_1 time until an area optimal placement has been found, t_2 time until a placement with optimal routability has been found, t_3 time until optimal routability has been proven, t_4 time until electrically correct routing has been found, t_5 time until routing with optimal manufacturability and wire length has been found. M_2 number of used M2 tracks. All times in [mm:ss].

	Cell			Placement			Routing		
#	$|\mathcal{F}|$	$|\mathcal{N}|$	w	t_1	t_2	t_3	t_4	t_5	M_2
1	8	11	6	0:00	0:00	0:00	0:03	0:06	0
2	8	10	6	0:00	0:00	0:00	0:05	0:08	0
3	8	11	12	0:00	0:00	0:13	0:08	0:16	0
4	8	11	12	0:00	0:00	0:26	0:11	0:26	0
5	14	16	12	0:00	1:27	4:28	0:09	0:39	1
6	8	11	16	0:01	1:38	2:37	0:24	2:42	0
7	17	22	12	0:00	1:00	2:33	0:09	0:17	0
8	11	15	12	0:03	0:19	0:36	0:09	0:20	0
9	8	11	16	0:08	1:03	1:04	0:28	2:08	0
10	14	18	30	0:38	6:47	–	1:48	18:36	1
11	8	11	44	1:09	1:13	–	11:04	33:28	0

that do not require optimal manufacturability, for example timing analysis. This allows a fast prototyping flow where changes in the input and their consequences on the layout can be tested quickly.

In the second phase additional rules were incorporated into the model to improve DFM. From the set of all routings fulfilling these additional constraints our router then found the solution with minimal net length. For the first 9 instances this took up to 3 min, cell 10 and 11 needed 19 min and 33 min, respectively. The final generated layout of cell 10 can be seen in Figure 6.

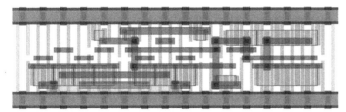

Figure 6: Generated layout of cell 10 with 30 tracks width. Only a single M2 wire (bottom left, green) has been used.

5. CONCLUSION

We have presented a new flow for the automatic cell layout that is able to deal with the challenges arising in 7nm technology. The main features are the global optimization of several design objectives, full integration of cut shape computation into the placement algorithm, and an efficiently solvable two stage MIP formulation in routing.

Acknowledgment

The authors would like to thank our cooperation partners at IBM, in particular Gerhard Hellner, Iris Leefken, and Tobias Werner.

6. REFERENCES

[1] R. Bar-Yehuda, J. A. Feldman, R. Y. Pinter, and S. Wimer. Depth-first-search and dynamic programming algorithms for efficient CMOS cell generation. *IEEE Trans. CAD*, 8:737–743, 1989.

[2] B. Basaran and R. A. Rutenbar. An $O(n)$ algorithm for transistor stacking with performance constraints. In *Proc. DAC'96*, pages 221–226, 1996.

[3] M. Grötschel, A. Martin, and R. Weismantel. The Steiner tree packing problem in VLSI design. *Mathematical Programming*, 78:265–281, 1997.

[4] A. Gupta and J. P. Hayes. Optimal 2-D cell layout with integrated transistor folding. In *ICCAD'98*, pages 128–135. IEEE, 1998.

[5] N.-D. Hoàng and T. Koch. Steiner tree packing revisited. *Math Meth Oper Res*, 76(1):95–123, 2012.

[6] J. Könemann, D. Pritchard, and K. Tan. A partition-based relaxation for Steiner trees. *Mathematical Programming*, 127(2):345–370, 2011.

[7] K. Lai et al. 32 nm logic patterning options with immersion lithography. In *Proc. SPIE 6924, Optical Microlithography XXI, 69243C*, 2008.

[8] C. Lazzari, C. Santos, and R. Reis. A new transistor-level layout generation strategy for static CMOS circuits. In *ICECS'06*, pages 660–663, 2006.

[9] M. Martins et al. Open cell library in 15nm freePDK technology. In *ISPD'15*, pages 171–178. ACM, 2015.

[10] C. J. Poirier. Excellerator: Custom CMOS leaf cell layout generator. *IEEE Trans. CAD*, 8(7):744–755, 1989.

[11] T. Polzin. *Algorithms for the Steiner problem in networks*. PhD thesis, MPII Saarbrücken, 2003.

[12] G. Posser, V. Mishra, P. Jain, R. Reis, and S. S. Sapatnekar. Cell-internal electromigration: Analysis and pin placement based optimization. *IEEE Trans. CAD*, 35(2):220–231, 2016.

[13] N. Ryzhenko and S. Burns. Standard cell routing via boolean satisfiability. In *DAC'12*, pages 603–612, 2012.

[14] B. Taylor and L. Pileggi. Exact combinatorial optimization methods for physical design of regular logic bricks. In *DAC'07*, pages 344–349. ACM, 2007.

[15] S. Wimer, R. Y. Pinter, and J. A. Feldman. Optimal chaining of CMOS transistors in a functional cell. *IEEE Trans. CAD*, 6(5):795–801, 1987.

[16] R. T. Wong. A dual ascent approach for Steiner tree problems on a directed graph. *Mathematical Programming*, 28(3):271–287, 1984.

[17] P.-H. Wu, M. P.-H. Lin, T.-C. Chen, T.-Y. Ho, Y.-C. Chen, S.-R. Siao, and S.-H. Lin. 1-D cell generation with printability enhancement. *IEEE Transactions on Computer-Aided Design of Integrated Circuits and Systems*, 32(3):419–432, 2013.

[18] W. Ye, B. Yu, Y.-C. Ban, L. Liebmann, and D. Z. Pan. Standard cell layout regularity and pin access optimization considering middle-of-line. In *GLSVLSI'15*, pages 289–294. ACM, 2015.

[19] B. Yu, X. Xu, S. Roy, Y. Lin, J. Ou, and D. Z. Pan. Design for manufacturability and reliability in extreme-scaling VLSI. *Science China Information Sciences*, 59(6):1–23, 2016.

Improving Detailed Routability and Pin Access with 3D Monolithic Standard Cells

Daohang Shi, and Azadeh Davoodi
University of Wisconsin - Madison
{dshi7,adavoodi}@wisc.edu

ABSTRACT

We study the impact of using 3D monolithic (3DM) standard cells on improving detailed routability and pin access. We propose a design flow which transforms standard rows of single-tier '2D' cells into rows of standard 3DM cells folded into two tiers. The transformation preserves layout characteristics such as overall area and number of metal layers for signal routing (i.e., M2 and above). It also creates redundant pins and free routing tracks in the two tiers used by the 3DM cells. We then propose an Integer Linear Program which routes as many nets as possible on the free 3DM routing tracks, leaving the rest of the nets to be routed via a standard global and detailed router on the metal layers dedicated for signal routing. Our experiments show significant improvement in detailed routability metrics using 3DM cells compared to using 2D standard cells.

1. INTRODUCTION

With the dusk of Moore's law, feature scaling in Integrated Circuits has resulted in significant challenges for the CAD tools in order to obtain a violation-free design. From a place and route view, a main challenge is to facilitate detailed routability by reducing the related design rule violations observed at the detailed routing stage; indeed there are recent calls by industry highlighting the need to develop detailed routability-driven placement techniques as well as techniques to bridge the gap between global and detailed routing [5, 15] which have ignited research in both placement and routing areas [6, 7, 12, 13, 14].

A main issue complicating the detailed routability effort is the pin access challenge which at a fundamental level occurs in dense layouts with devices implemented with a very fine pitch size. An effort from academia showed tha-t a new device structure called VeSFET can significantly improve pin access by allowing two-sided routing [11]. Recently, industry is exploring a new technology, namely 3D monolithic (or 3D VLSI) [2, 3, 4, 10] which among its various features allows creation of '3D' logic cells. These cells can be implemented on two separate tiers which can then be accessed separately.

ISPD '17, March 19-22, 2017, Portland, OR, USA
© 2017 ACM. ISBN 978-1-4503-4696-2/17/03...$15.00
DOI: http://dx.doi.org/10.1145/3036669.3036676

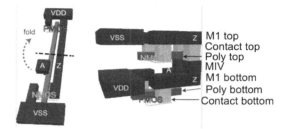

Figure 1: Two layouts of an inverter from [9] (a) a single-tier standard cell, and (b) its folded two-tier 3D monolithic one.

To implement a 3D cell, one way is to fold a '2D' cell by placing the NMOS portion on the top tier and PMOS portion on the bottom tier [3, 4, 9]. Here by a '2D' cell we mean a standard logic cell that is implemented on a single tier. Figure 1 from [9] shows an example of how the folding is done for an inverter. The left side shows the 2D cell. The right side shows its 3D monolithic counter-part which we denote by a '3DM' cell in this work. The figure shows how pin Z can be made accessible in both the top and bottom tiers by creating separate pins on each tier and internally connecting them using monolithic inter-*tier* vias (MIVs).

In this work we utilize the above model of transforming 2D cells into 3DM cells to highlight the substantial benefits to improve detailed routability and pin access. We note while the above folding technique for a 2D cell was shown before, its usage to improve routability has not been studied so far.

Specifically, first we propose a design flow to translate a placed design with 2D cells into one which has 3DM cells with redundant pins. The translation creates an extra tier to implement the 3DM cells but it ensures the layout area and number of layers for signal routing (i.e., M2 and above) remain the same, while creating new opportunities to improve routability and pin access.

Figure 2 shows overview of our design flow. Compared to a traditional flow, we first apply a transformation to translate a pair of back-to-back 2D standard *rows* (with shared VDD or VSS in the middle) into a pair of 3DM standard *rows* with free routing tracks in the middle, moving the VDD/VSS lines to the sides and individual tiers. This transformation is explained in Section 2.1.

Next, we try to route as many nets as possible on the top tier of metal 1 (denoted by M1T) and the bottom tier (denoted by M1B). We do this in two steps: First, we apply cell-to-cell track routing to directly connect adjacent cells on the same tier, by also taking advantage of redundant pins. This step is explained in Section 2.2.

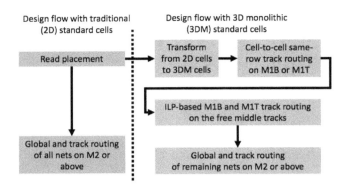

Figure 2: Design flow with traditional (2D) standard cells versus 3D monolithic (3DM) standard cell

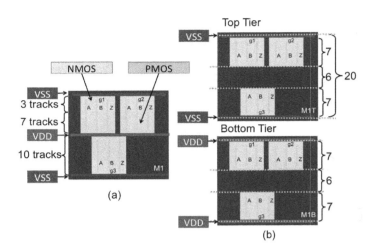

Figure 3: Example transforming 2D to 3DM standard rows

Next, we discuss an Integer Linear Program which routes as many remaining nets as possible on the free tracks running between a pair of 3DM rows on M1T or M1B. We discuss this process in Section 2.3. Finally, all remaining unrouted nets are global and detailed routed on M2 and above layers using a commercial global and detailed router.

Our experiments show that the number of segment violations and DRC errors are reduced on-average by 29.8% and 20.7%, respectively. This work is the first to highlight the promise of 3D monolithic cells to improve detailed routability via better pin access.

2. OUR FRAMEWORK

2.1 Transforming 2D to 3DM Standard Rows

Figure 3 shows the transformation from 2D to 3DM standard rows using an example. In Figure 3(a) two standard rows are shown with a height of 10 M1 pitches per row which is the case for the ISPD'2015 benchmark suite [5]. The rows are placed back-to-back so a pair of rows either share VDD (as shown in Figure 3(a)) or share VSS. For each 2D cell, the area occupied by NMOS and PMOS transistors are shown. For a standard CMOS layout, the PMOS transistors will be placed closer to VDD and NMOS transistors are placed closer to VSS. Due to the difference in carrier mobility, the PMOS to NMOS channel lengths have a ratio >1 and for example a ratio of 7:3 in Figure 3(a). Therefore if we assume a standard cell height of 10 pitches, the PMOS and NMOS take 7 and 3 tracks respectively as shown in Figure 3(a).

We use the same folding technique described in [3, 9] with the feature of having redundant pins inside the 3DM cells.

As shown in Figure 3(b), the '2D' standard rows will be transformed into 3D monolithic (3DM) standard cells folded over two tiers, i.e., NMOS on the top tier and PMOS on the bottom tier. Here two rows of NMOS are enclosed by VSS lines running in parallel, and similarly two rows of PMOS are enclosed by VDD lines after the transformation. To ensure creating standard 3DM rows, i.e., with the same height, we keep the height of the PMOS and NMOS portions on the two tiers equal to each other which are 7 tracks in this example, as shown in Figure 3(b). This results in unused area in the NMOS portion. Note the width of each 3DM cell remains the same as its 2D counterpart.

From a routing perspective, instead of metal layer M1 in 2D, two layers of M1T (top) and M1B (bottom) are added.

The two M1T and M1B layers connect with monolithic inter-*tier* vias (denoted by MIVs), which are placed only inside each 3DM cell. Specifically, for each pin on M1 in the 2D case, we create two pins in the 3DM cell, one located on M1T and the other located on M1B which connect to each other by MIVs as also shown in Figure 1. These *redundant* pins allow improving pin access because they are connected to each other within the standard cell and a route can connect to either one of them on either tier. For example in Figure 3(b), notice for cell g1 that each of pins A, B, and Z are paired with a redundant one on the other tier. In the figure the pins are drawn to have equal height for simplicity.

Moreover, we assume the transformation preserves the placement of each cell. Given the same width for each cell but shorter height, the transformation results in additional tracks running between the two 3DM rows (per tier) which is 6 ($= 20 - 7 - 7$) free tracks in the example shown in Figure 3(b). This assumes the shared VDD line in the center is ignored but it should be added as an additional track otherwise so in that case there will be 7 free tracks in the center. Overall, the above transformation results in the same layout area. However, *it is also possible to trade off (reduce) the number of these free tracks for smaller layout area as we show in our experiments.*

2.2 Cell-to-Cell Intra-Row Track Routing

After the 2D to 3DM standrd row transformation, we try to route as many nets which connect adjacent cells within the same 3DM row on either M1B or M1T. Note this is intra-row routing and does not use the free tracks in the middle of two standard rows. Figure 4 shows an example of two 2-pin nets. One net connects g1.Z to g2.A, and the other one connects g3.Z to g4.A. In the case when the two pins of a net that need to connect are in adjacent standard cells, we can connect them directly in either M1B or M1T (because of redundant pins), assuming there exists a common and free track which connects the two pins to each other.

Specifically, in our framework, after the 3DM cell transformation, we visit all the nets. For each visited 2-pin net, we then check if it can be routed on the same row between two neighboring cells. *As we show in our experiments, in practice only a very small fraction of nets can be routed using this technique so next we apply inter-row track routing.*

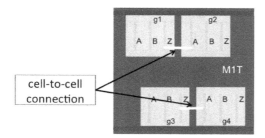

Figure 4: Cell-to-cell intra-row track routing on M1T

2.3 ILP-Based Inter-Row Track Routing

In this section we present an ILP-based track routing technique which maximizes the number of nets that *may* be routed on the free tracks running between a pair of standard 3DM rows on either M1T or M1B. It also takes advantage of the redundant pins in 3DM cells.

The ILP is written for a double-row 'panels' with each panel containing two standard rows with free tracks in between, as shown in Figure 3(b). One panel is located in the top tier and its corresponding panel is located in the bottom pier. The ILP considers routing all the nets with pins completely inside the double-row panels (which were *not* routed using the intra-row cell-to-cell technique.)

Recall during the transformation stage, each pin of a 2D cell translates into a pair of redundant pins located on M1B and M1T which are internally connected by MIVs. In order to simplify the discussions in this section, we only refer to the pins inside one of the double-row panels but the discussions hold for the corresponding pins in the other panel as well.

If a net has all its pins within a double-row panel, each pin belongs to either the higher or the lower standard row. We denote all the pins of net i belonging to the higher row as its north pins and all the pins of net i belonging to the lower row as the south pins of net i, as shown in Figure 5.

When considering routing a net on M1B or M1T, the ILP assumes candidate routes with the simple structure made of a single trunk spanning the interval defined by the pins of the net and a set of branches connecting the pins to the trunk. The trunks may be located on either M1B or M1T and should be one of the available free tracks in the middle of the double-row panel. The branches are also located on M1B or M1T so they directly connect to the trunk (without need for vias). This is because M1B and M1T can support both horizontal and vertical routing. Figure 5 shows one candidate route of a net on one tier and there is another one identical to this on the other tier for the same net.

Finally, depending on the locations of north and south pins, we can sometimes make assertion that the candidate routes of two nets running on the same tier will definitely create a conflict (overlap) if selected simultaneously. Therefore the two nets may never be routed on the same tier. These conflicts are discussed in detail in Section 2.3.2, and are accounted for by the ILP.

2.3.1 ILP-Based Selection for Inter-Row Routing

Given a double-row panel P, all the nets whose pins are falling in these panels are first denoted by the set N_P.

For each net $i \in N_P$ we define three binary variables x_B^i, x_T^i and x_A^i expressing whether net i can be routed in M1B, M1T or above (referring to routing on M2 or higher layers). The ILP is formulated to maximize the number of nets which

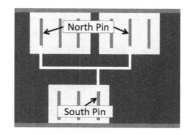

Figure 5: The single-trunk routing structure used for inter-row track routing with branches located on the same tier

may be routed on either M1T or M1B and is given below:

$$\max_{x_B, x_T, x_A} \sum_{i \in N_P} x_B^i + x_T^i$$

s.t.

$$x_B^i + x_T^i + x_A^i = 1 \qquad \forall i \in N_P \quad (1)$$
$$x_B^i + x_B^j < 1, x_T^i + x_T^j < 1 \qquad \forall \text{conflicted } i, j \in N_P \quad (2)$$
$$x_B^i, x_T^i, x_A^i \in \{0, 1\} \qquad \forall i \in N_P \quad (3)$$

The first set of constraints ensures that for each net i only one route option is selected which indicates the net may be routed on M1B or M1T or above layers.

The second set of constraints checks each pair of nets i and j which have a routing conflict and ensures they cannot get simultaneously routed on M1B or on M1T. We discuss checking for conflict for a pair of nets in Section 2.3.2.

Once the integer program is solved, all the nets with $x_B^i = 1$ may be routed in M1B and all the nets with $x_T^i = 1$ may be routed in M1T. Those nets with $x_A^i = 1$ will have to be routed in M2 or above using commercial router, since routing them in M1B or M1T will definitely cause conflict.

Please note that the objective is to maximize the number of conflict-free nets which *may* be routed on M1B or on M1T. (Alternatively it can be set to minimize the number of nets that are routed on M2 or above, i.e., sum of the x_A variables). In fact it is possible that the ILP generates a solution in which the number of nets that may be routed on a double-row panel exceeds the capacity of the panel. (By capacity we mean the number of tracks located in the middle of the double-row panel, e.g., 7 tracks in the example of Figure 3(b).) Therefore after ILP, we apply a final step to determine the nets that *can* be routed up to the panel capacity per tier. We discuss this procedure in Section 2.3.3.

2.3.2 Conflict Checking for A Pair of Nets

For two nets a and b that belong to the same double-row panel P, existence of a conflict means they cannot be routed simultaneously on M1T or M1B because their routes will overlap at some point. This is assuming the (single-trunk) routing structure as shown in Figure 5.

For net a, the x coordinates of its north and south pins are stored in two sets $\mathcal{N}(a)$ and $\mathcal{S}(a)$ as given below.

$$\mathcal{N}(a) = \{n_1^a, n_2^a, \ldots, n_{N_a}^a\}, \qquad n_1^a < \cdots < n_{N_a}^a \quad (4)$$
$$\mathcal{S}(a) = \{s_1^a, s_2^a, \ldots, s_{S_a}^a\}, \qquad s_1^a < \cdots < s_{S_a}^a \quad (5)$$

Table I is a look-up table (LUT) that we use to check if two nets a and b *do not* have a conflict based on their sets $\mathcal{N}$ and $\mathcal{S}$. In case of a conflict, a pair of constraints are created for them in the ILP as we discussed before.

Table I: Lookup table to check if nets a and b are conflict-free. Elements in sets $\mathcal{N}$ or $\mathcal{S}$ are sorted in ascending order.

Case	Net a $\mathcal{N}(a)$	Net a $\mathcal{S}(a)$	Net b $\mathcal{N}(b)$	Net b $\mathcal{S}(b)$	Conflict-Free Conditions	Examples
1	$n_1^a,\ldots,n_{N_a}^a$	$\emptyset$	$\emptyset$	$s_1^b,\ldots,s_{S_b}^b$	• No conflict exists between net a and net b.	
2	$\emptyset$	$s_1^a,\ldots,s_{S_a}^a$	$n_1^b,\ldots,n_{N_b}^b$	$\emptyset$	Similar to case 1.	
3	$n_1^a,\ldots,n_{N_a}^a$	$\emptyset$	$n_1^b,\ldots,n_{N_b}^b$	$\emptyset$	a) $\mathcal{N}(a)$ and $\mathcal{N}(b)$ do no overlap: $n_{N_a}^a < n_1^b$ OR $n_{N_b}^b < n_1^a$ OR b) north pins of net a fall between two neighboring pins in $\mathcal{N}(b)$: $\exists k$ s.t. $n_k^b < n_1^a$ AND $n_{N_a}^a < n_{k+1}^b$ OR c) north pins of net b fall between two neighboring pins in $\mathcal{N}(a)$: $\exists k$ s.t. $n_k^a < n_1^b$ AND $n_{N_b}^b < n_{k+1}^a$	(a) (b) (c)
4	$\emptyset$	$s_1^a,\ldots,s_{S_a}^a$	$\emptyset$	$s_1^b,\ldots,s_{S_b}^b$	Similar to case 3.	
5	$n_1^a,\ldots,n_{N_a}^a$	$\emptyset$	$n_1^b,\ldots,n_{N_b}^b$	$s_1^b,\ldots,s_{S_b}^b$	a) $\mathcal{N}(a)$ and $\mathcal{N}(b)$ do not overlap: $n_{N_a}^a < n_1^b$ OR $n_{N_b}^b < n_1^a$ OR b) north pins of net a fall two neighboring pins in $\mathcal{N}(b)$: $\exists k$ s.t. $n_k^b < n_1^a$ AND $n_{N_a}^a < n_{k+1}^b$	(a) (b)
6	$\emptyset$	$s_1^a,\ldots,s_{S_a}^a$	$n_1^b,\ldots,n_{N_b}^b$	$s_1^b,\ldots,s_{S_b}^b$	Similar to case 5.	
7	$n_1^a,\ldots,n_{N_a}^a$	$s_1^a,\ldots,s_{S_a}^a$	$\emptyset$	$s_1^b,\ldots,s_{S_b}^b$		
8	$n_1^a,\ldots,n_{N_a}^a$	$s_1^a,\ldots,s_{S_a}^a$	$n_1^b,\ldots,n_{N_b}^b$	$\emptyset$		
9	$n_1^a,\ldots,n_{N_a}^a$	$s_1^a,\ldots,s_{S_a}^a$	$n_1^b,\ldots,n_{N_b}^b$	$s_1^b,\ldots,s_{S_b}^b$	a) $\mathcal{N}(a)$ is to left of $\mathcal{N}(b)$ AND $\mathcal{S}(a)$ is to left of $\mathcal{S}(b)$: $n_{N_a}^a < n_1^b$ AND $s_{S_a}^a < s_1^b$ OR b) $\mathcal{N}(a)$ is to right of $\mathcal{N}(b)$ AND $\mathcal{S}(a)$ is to right of $\mathcal{S}(b)$: $n_{N_b}^b < n_1^a$ AND $s_{S_b}^b < s_1^a$	(a) (b)

Based on the north and south pins of the two nets, we first look up columns 2 to 5 to identify one of the rows (9 cases). For each case, the conflict-free condition is listed in column 6 and a graphical example of that is listed in column 7. Note when multiple conditions are listed per case, only one of them needs to be satisfied. For example consider case 3 which is identified when all pins of nets a and b are north pins. Here one of the 3 listed conditions must be satisfied which are shown in the figure to ensure they are conflict-free. If none are satisfied, then the two nets have a conflict.

2.3.3 Inter-Track Routing Using the ILP Solution

Once the lists of conflict-free nets that *may* be routed on M1B and M1T are found from the ILP solution, we try to route as many as possible up to the panel's capacity. Our procedure works on each tier independently. For example for M1T, all nets with $x_T = 1$ are first identified for the top tier. Next, these nets are sorted in ascending order, by the length of the interval defined by their left-most and right-most pins.

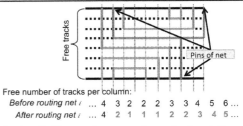

Figure 6: Available tracks per column before/after routing net i. Assume the blue nets have already been routed.

Next we attempt to route each net in the sorted order using the simple structure (one trunk connected by branches), if there exists free tracks in the middle of the panel. Specifically, we keep track of the number of free tracks per 'column' (corresponding to pin coordinates) as each net gets routed. Initially all the tracks are available per column. Once a net gets routed, the number of tracks in each column covered in the net's range is deducted by 1. Figure 6 illustrates.

Table II: Results of M1B/M1T routing

Benchmark	# nets	cell-to-cell intra-row		ILP-based inter-row				ILP information		
		routed		selected		routed		# ILPs (panels)	Ave. # constraints	Runtime (seconds)
des_perf_1	112877	1534	1.4%	37450	33.2%	37289	33.0%	112	1655.6	10.2
des_perf_a	110280	1206	1.1%	28521	25.9%	28506	25.8%	226	560.2	6.8
des_perf_b	112877	1445	1.3%	30126	26.7%	30113	26.7%	151	724.1	7.0
edit_dist_a	131133	1513	1.1%	28537	21.8%	28274	21.6%	200	611.5	6.0
fft_1	33306	237	0.7%	11008	33.1%	10880	32.7%	67	698.0	2.0
fft_2	33306	313	0.9%	10595	31.8%	10594	31.8%	86	381.0	1.6
fft_a	32087	206	0.6%	7182	22.4%	7021	21.9%	200	93.5	1.3
fft_b	32087	225	0.7%	7606	23.7%	7482	23.3%	200	108.3	1.0
matrix_mult_1	158526	1921	1.2%	51612	32.6%	51203	32.3%	137	1793.3	12.0
matrix_mult_a	154283	2217	1.4%	44784	29.0%	44761	29.0%	376	418.4	8.2
matrix_mult_b	151611	2177	1.4%	35078	23.1%	35068	23.1%	376	254.1	5.8
pci_bridge32_b	29416	1407	4.8%	8840	30.1%	8833	30.0%	200	103.7	1.5
Average	**90982.4**	**1200.0**	**1.39%**	**25111.5**	**27.76%**	**25002.0**	**27.60%**	**194.2**	**616.8**	**5.3**

3. EXPERIMENTAL RESULTS

We implemented our design flow in C++ on the 45nm ISPD 2015 [5] benchmarks. All simulations ran on a Linux machine with a 2.8GHz Intel CPU and 12GB memory.

To apply the transformation from 2D to 3DM standard rows, we assumed a 2D standard row height of 10 tracks which resulted in a 3DM row height with 7 tracks and 6 free tracks in between a pair of 3DM rows, as shown in Figure 3.

Next our framework routed as many nets as possible on M1T and M1B. Specifically it first identified and routed all nets in adjacent cells which were eligible for cell-to-cell intra-row track routing. Then, for each double-row panel, we used our ILP formulation to maximize the number of nets which *may* be routed using inter-row tracking using and selected a group of eligible nets. After the ILP, we used the technique given in Section 2.3.3 to route as many as possible from the selected nets on the free tracks in the middle of each double-row panel. We used CPLEX 12.6 [8] to solve the ILPs. We then removed the nets which were routed on M1B and M1T from the benchmarks and used the Olympus SoC global and track router [1] for the remaining nets. The detailed routing solution generated by Olympus was finally evaluated by running the 'check_drc' command.

In our experiments we make comparison between the above 3DM-based implementation and a standard implementation using 2D cells. Specifically in the 2D case, we started with the same placed design and only ran it through the Olympus SoC global and detailed router and then evaluated the generated solution for detailed routability.

Next we discuss our simulation results at different stages of our framework (i.e., M1B/M1T routing as well as M2 and above routing). We also do an experiment in which we vary the number of free tracks in the middle of a double-row panel to show the existing trade offs between area reduction and improvement in routability.

3.1 Routing on M1B/M1T

Table II shows the results of M1B/M1T routing. Columns 3 and 4 show the numbers and percentages of nets routed at the cell-to-cell intra-row routing stage. As can be seen only a small percentage (on-average 1.39%) of nets were routed at this step. This shows intra-row routing in practice is quite limited for making improvement.

Table III: Results of routing on M2 and above

Benchmark	# violated segments		# DRC errors	
	2D	3DM	2D	3DM
des_perf_1	2768	75.4%	1987	65.2%
des_perf_a	7062	30.1%	5262	22.2%
des_perf_b	307	61.6%	550	50.4%
edit_dist_a	83671	46.8%	33581	40.4%
fft_1	205	25.4%	388	-11.3%
fft_2	2584	13.1%	2577	9.8%
fft_a	1474	11.2%	1418	11.6%
fft_b	3024	15.2%	4218	1.9%
matrix_mult_1	10906	46.4%	7984	25.1%
matrix_mult_a	5141	18.0%	3348	8.7%
matrix_mult_b	9416	11.4%	7561	9.2%
pci_bridge32_b	730	2.9%	712	14.9%
Average	**10607.3**	**5968.8 (29.8%)**	**5418.0**	**3896.6 (20.7%)**

Columns 5 and 6 report the numbers and percentages of nets selected by ILP. The nets which are eventually routed in M1B/M1T using the ILP solution are reported in columns 7 and 8. As can be seen, on-average 27.76% were routed on M1B/M1T across the benchmarks which is a relatively high percentage and we show results in significant improvement in detailed routability.

The last three columns (9 to 11) report information about ILPs, which includes the number of ILP problems (i.e. the number of double-row panels), the average number of constraints per ILP and the total runtime to solve *all* the ILPs. As can be seen on-average about 194 ILPs are solved in 5.3 seconds and each include on-average 617 constraints.

3.2 Routing on M2 and Above

After routing nets in M1B/M1T, we performed global routing and track routing on the remaining nets. These nets are routed on M2 or above (i.e. M2 to M5 in the ISPD 2015 benchmarks). We used the Olympus commands 'route_global' and 'route_track' to perform global and track routing. Table III shows the comparison of detailed routing results between the 2D and 3DM cases. Recall in the 2D case, the original benchmarks containing all the nets are global and detailed routed.

Table IV: Impact of varying number of free tracks in the middle on the number of nets routed in M1B and M1T

Benchmark	# free tracks			
	6	4	2	1
des_perf_1	34.4%	33.4%	25.8%	16.4%
des_perf_a	26.9%	26.6%	22.0%	14.7%
des_perf_b	28.0%	27.6%	23.1%	15.6%
edit_dist_a	22.7%	22.4%	19.5%	14.0%
fft_1	33.4%	33.0%	26.7%	17.1%
fft_2	32.7%	32.6%	28.6%	19.3%
fft_a	22.5%	22.5%	21.1%	15.8%
fft_b	24.0%	24.0%	22.4%	16.5%
matrix_mult_1	33.5%	32.9%	26.0%	16.5%
matrix_mult_a	30.4%	30.3%	26.7%	18.2%
matrix_mult_b	24.6%	24.5%	22.3%	16.0%
pci_bridge32_b	34.8%	34.7%	32.1%	23.9%
Average	**29.00%**	**28.69%**	**24.69%**	**17.01%**

We ran the 'check_drc' command on the detailed routing DB in Olympus SoC which reported the total number of violated segments and total number of DRC errors. The total number of violated segments included errors on shorts, spacing, port shorts, cross shorts, twist shorts, diffnet shorts, diffnet spacings, samenet spacings, cut projection, cut spacing, end of line, min-area bottom, min-area, loop over port, minstep, and vias overlap.

As can be seen from the table the total number of violated segments and DRC errors were reduced on-average by 29.8% and 20.7% in the 3DM case, compared to the 2D case.

3.3 Impacts of Number of Free Tracks on the M1B/M1T Routing

Recall the transformation process of 2D to 3DM standard row results in free tracks in the middle of a double-row panel as shown in Figure 3. In this experiment we reduce the number of free tracks which translates into direct area saving in terms of reducing the height of the layout. We show the tradeoff of this reduction with fewer number of nets that were routed by our framework on M1B and M1T. Note that this step only impacts the inter-row track routing step of our framework.

Table IV reports the result when the number of free tracks vary from 6 (original) to 4, 2, and 1 tracks in the middle. As can be seen, using 6 free tracks our framework routed 29.00% of all the nets (which can also be obtained by adding the nets routed at the intra-row and inter-row stages of our framework in Table II). Using 4 and 2 free tracks our framework routed 28.69% and 24.69%, respectively. With just 1 free track, we were still able to route 17.01% of the nets on M1B/M1T. We note 1 free track translates into area saving of 5 (=6 − 1) tracks per panel for per each pair of standard rows. This is a significant reduction in the height of the layout. These results are fundamentally because many nets connect pins which are placed close to each other and located on adjacent standard rows. In future we plan to conduct experiments to measure the impact of this tradeoff at the detailed routing stage.

4. CONCLUSIONS

In this work we proposed a design flow based on translating rows of 2D standard cells into 3D monolithic standard cells. We showed that this translation resulted in on-average 20.7% reduction in the DRC errors at the detailed routing stage for the 45nm ISPD 2015 benchmarks. This was because on-average our framework was able to route 29% of the nets on the two tiers corresponding to the 3D monolithic standard cells. This shows the high promise of this technology to improve routability besides its other features. Our framework utilized a novel Integer Linear Program as well as the presence of redundant pins to maximize the number of nets that can be routed in the two tiers for the 3D monolithic cells.

5. ACKNOWLEDGEMENT

This research has been supported by award # 1608040 from the National Science Foundation, USA.

6. REFERENCES

[1] Olympus-SoC: Place and route for advanced node designs.
[2] K. Acharya, K. Chang, B. W. Ku, S. Panth, S. Sinha, B. Cline, G. Yeric, and S. K. Lim. Monolithic 3D IC design: Power, performance, and area impact at 7nm. In *International Symposium on Quality Electronic Design*, pages 41–48, 2016.
[3] K. Arabi, K. Samadi, and Y. Du. 3D VLSI: A scalable integration beyond 2d. In *International Symposium on Physical Design*, pages 1–7, 2015.
[4] O. Billoint, H. Sarhan, I. Rayane, M. Vinet, P. Batude, C. Fenouillet-Béranger, O. Rozeau, G. Cibrario, F. Deprat, O. Turkyilmaz, S. Thuries, and F. Clermidy. From 2D to monolithic 3D: Design possibilities, expectations and challenges. In *International Symposium on Physical Design*, page 127, 2015.
[5] I. S. Bustany, D. G. Chinnery, J. R. Shinnerl, and V. Yutsis. ISPD 2015 benchmarks with fence regions and routing blockages for detailed-routing-driven placement. In *International Symposium on Physical Design*, pages 157–164, 2015.
[6] N. K. Darav, A. A. Kennings, A. F. Tabrizi, D. T. Westwick, and L. Behjat. Eh?placer: A high-performance modern technology-driven placer. *ACM Trans. Design Automation Electronic Systems*, 21(3):37, 2016.
[7] C. Huang, C. Chiou, K. Tseng, and Y. Chang. Detailed-routing-driven analytical standard-cell placement. In *Asia and South Pacific Design Automation Conference*, pages 378–383, 2015.
[8] *IBM ILOG CPLEX V12.0, User's Manual for CPLEX*, 2009.
[9] Y. Lee, D. B. Limbrick, and S. K. Lim. Power benefit study for ultra-high density transistor-level monolithic 3D ICs. In *Design Automation Conference*, pages 104:1–104:10, 2013.
[10] S. Panth, K. Samadi, Y. Du, and S. K. Lim. Placement-driven partitioning for congestion mitigation in monolithic 3D IC designs. *IEEE Trans. on CAD of Integrated Circuits and Systems*, 34(4):540–553, 2015.
[11] X. Qiu and M. Marek-Sadowska. Routing challenges for designs with super high pin density. *IEEE Trans. on CAD of Integrated Circuits and Systems*, 32(9):1357–1368, 2013.
[12] D. Shi, E. Tashjian, and A. Davoodi. Dynamic planning of local congestion from varying-size vias for global routing layer assignment. In *Asia and South Pacific Design Automation Conference*, pages 372–377, 2016.
[13] Y. Wei, C. C. N. Sze, N. Viswanathan, Z. Li, C. J. Alpert, L. N. Reddy, A. D. Huber, G. E. Téllez, D. Keller, and S. S. Sapatnekar. GLARE: global and local wiring aware routability evaluation. In *Design Automation Conference*, pages 768–773, 2012.
[14] M. Wong, W. Liu, and T. Wang. Negotiation-based track assignment considering local nets. In *Asia South Pacific Design Automation Conference*, pages 378–383, 2016.
[15] V. Yutsis, I. Bustany, D. G. Chinnery, J. R. Shinnerl, and W. Liu. ISPD 2014 benchmarks with sub-45nm technology rules for detailed-routing-driven placement. In *International Symposium on Physical Design*, pages 161–168, 2014.

The Spirit of in-house CAD Achieved by the Legend of Master "Prof. Goto" and his Apprentices

Yuichi Nakamura

System Platform Research Laboratories, NEC Corp.

1753, Shimonumabe, Nakahara-ku, Kawasaki, 211-8666 Japan

+81-44-431-7192

yuichi@az.jp.nec.com

ABSTRACT

In this paper, a legend story to develop CAD algorithms and CAD/EDA tools for NEC's in-house use is described. About 30 years ago, since there are few commercial CAD tools, ICT vendors had to develop their own CAD tools to enhance the performance of their systems in a short time. Prof. Goto developed several important algorithms for CAD tools and managed to develop many excellent in-house CAD tools. The tools made by him and his apprentices have designed many VLSI/ASIC for NEC's innovative computers and communication systems to enrich our daily lives.

Keywords

CAD algorithm, Electrical Design Automation, ASIC, VLSI design of ICT systems

1. Background

From 70's, ICT vendors have been developing their proprietary systems, like as main frame computers, transmission systems, and wired/mobile communication systems. These systems needed a lot of various VLSI/ASIC, since they should achieve high performance and short developing time to overcome the competitions. In early stage of VLSI/ASIC development, VLSI/ASIC could be implemented by manual design. However, according to increasing the size of design and VLSI, an automatic design system, CAD or EDA, was required.

The legends in that era, had to make research to realize both basically algorithms and useful systems, however, there are few text books and established theories. In addition, the legends in commercial company should output the tangible results as soon as possible. Prof. Goto, who is one of pioneers in CAD research joined NEC in 1970 and worked for CAD research. He could achieve all of them, the innovative algorithms, the useful systems and the productively tangible results in a short time. Thanks to the computer and communication systems by his contributions, many ICT systems had been developed in NEC and shipped, like as the mainframe computers, the work stations, the supercomputers, the

transmission systems, and the submarine optical communication systems. Then, we have been acquired that we can pull out at ATMs in anywhere by on-line system among various banks, automatic sales and salary calculation, cheap international calls without waiting time.

Prof. Goto had left many outcomes, the innovative algorithms, and many CAD/EDA systems and the excellent his apprentices.

2. His Research and Contribution for Systems

Early stage of CAD research, the most important problem is optimizing the various combinational problems on poor and slow computers. To solve the problems, the combinational optimization research was evolved. Prof. Goto had been proposing many efficient matrix operation algorithms like as LU-decomposition. These proposed algorithms have been utilized to solve "simultaneous linear equations" which is essential for optimization problems. In addition, Prof. Goto proposed the various ideas on graph theory.

Prof. Goto also organized and led many the projects to develop CAD System. The typical projects are listed

1) The floorplan and placement layout system for the mater slice LSI(1980)

2) The logic synthesis system (1986)

3) The routing optimization system(1987)

The technical research results on these projects were presented at DAC or ICCAD. And also, they had contributed to develop NEC's many ICT systems.

The first system was based on efficient local interchange method to attack hard combinatorial problems to obtain a near optimal solution with limited computation time. This system used to design more than 5000 real chips in NEC for 15 years.

The second system is based on rule based and dynamic optimization to synthesize circuits from register transfer level description. This system had been used to design VLSI for main frame and propriety computers in NEC for 20 year. Especially, the latest version of this system contributed to design "earth simulator computer" which obtained the prize of the fastest super computer in the world from 2002 to 2004.

The third system is used efficient local interchange method to attack hard combinatorial problems to obtain a near optimal solution with limited computation time. This system is also had been designed many VLSI/ASIC in NEC.

ISPD '17, March 19-22, 2017, Portland, OR, USA .

© 2017 ACM. ISBN 978-1-4503-4696-2/17/03…$15.00.

DOI: http://dx.doi.org/10.1145/3036669.3038253

3. The Works by His Apprentices

The spirit and DNA of Prof. Goto are still in NEC laboratories. A lot of his apprentices with his spirit and DNA have contributed to CAD/EDA world. Thus his apprentices also presented many researches at DAC/ICCAD. For example, 1) one of the world's first "High level Synthesis tool" [4] 2) the novel method of a zero-skew clock wiring [5], 3) one of the first software verification systems with clock synchronization by FPGA[6]. And then, their researches also were contributed to the developments of NEC's various ICT systems like as the mobile phones, the media processing systems, and the base station of mobile systems and the super computers. Recently, the researchers in NEC labs with Prof. Goto's spirit obtained the best presentation award of design track at DAC 2016[7]. They developed the efficient computing system by using FPGA to optimize the social optimization problems.

4. Conclusion

There is no doubt that Prof. Goto is a legend master "Yoda" of CAD/EDA society from the theoretical and practical aspects. Especially, it is worthy of high praise that his research results had been contributed development for many VLSI/ASIC for a long time. And his apprentices with his spirit and DNA also achieved great contributions for VLSI/ASIC design for NEC's ICT systems. After retired from NEC, he became a professor of Waseda University and had been brought up many excellent students. They utilized many good researches in video codec area.

5. REFERENCES

[1] S. Goto, "An efficient algorithm for the two-dimensional placement problem in electrical circuit layout", pp. 11-17, ACM/IEEE Design Automation Conference (DAC) 1979.

[2] Takeshi Yoshimura and Satoshi Goto, "A Rule based and algorithm based Approach to Logic Design", International Conference on Computer Aided Design (ICCAD), pp.162-165,Nov. 1986.

[3] Satoshi Goto and Tomoyuki Fijita, "A new Knowledge based Approach to Circuit Design", ICCAD, pp.156-159, Nov. 1987.

[4] Kazutoshi Wakabayashi and Hirohito Tanaka, "Global scheduling independent of control dependencies based on condition vectors", pp.112-115, ACM/IEEE Design Automation Conference (DAC) 1992.

[5] Msato Edahiro, "An efficient zero-skew routing algorithm", pp. 375–380, ACM/IEEE Design Automation Conference (DAC) 1994.

[6] Yuichi Nakamura, Kouhei Hosokawa, Ichiro Kuroda, Ko Yoshikawa, and Takeshi Yoshimura, "A Fast Hardware/Software Co-Verification Method for System-onChip By using a C/C++ Simulator and FPGA Emulator with Shared Register Communication", pp.299-304, ACM/IEEE Design Automation Conference (DAC) 2004.

[7] Yuki Kobayashi, Takashi Takenaka, Takeo Hosomi, Yuichi Nakamura, "Accelerating an IoT Application by using FPGA tightly coupled with CPU", presented at design track, ACM/IEEE Design Automation Conference (DAC) 2016.

Generalized Force Directed Relaxation with Optimal Regions and Its Applications to Circuit Placement *

(Invited Paper: A Tribute to Professor Satoshi Goto)

Yao-Wen Chang
Graduate Institute of Electronics Engineering, National Taiwan University, Taipei 106, Taiwan
Department of Electrical Engineering, National Taiwan University, Taipei 106, Taiwan
ywchang@ntu.edu.tw

ABSTRACT

This paper introduces popular algorithmic paradigms for circuit placement, presents Goto's classical placement framework based on the generalized force directed relaxation (GFDR) method with an optimal region (OR) formulation and its impacts on modern circuit placement and applications, and provides future placement research directions based on the GFDR and OR formulations.

Keywords

Physical Design, Placement, Iterative placement, Constructive placement, Nondeterministic placement, Mixed-size placement, Mixed-cell-height placement, Simulated annealing, Force-directed relaxation, Optimal region, FPGA, Routability, Timing

1. INTRODUCTION

The placement problem is to assign circuit modules (e.g., standard cells, macros, etc.) to desired positions on the chip, such that no two modules overlap with each other and some predefined cost metric (e.g., wirelength, routability, timing) is optimized; Figure 1 illustrates a placement instance, where interconnections among circuit modules are not shown. Placement is a major step in physical design, which plays a pivotal role in determining the final quality of a circuit design. As such, placement has been studied for several decades since the early days of integrated circuit designs. Recently, it has attracted much more attention than

*This work was partially supported by AnaGlobe, MediaTek, RealTek, TSMC, MOST of Taiwan under Grant NSC 102-2221-E-002-235-MY3, NSC 102-2923-E-002-006-MY3, MoST 103-2221-E-002-259-MY3, MoST 103-2812-8-002-003, MoST 104-2221-E-002-132-MY3, and NTU under Grant NTU-ERP-105R8951.

ISPD'17, March 19-22, 2017, Portland, OR, USA
DOI: http://dx.doi.org/10.1145/3036669.3038250

ever, due mainly to the dramatic growth in design complexity and many emerging technology challenges.

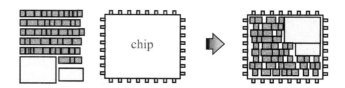

Figure 1: The circuit placement problem.

There are three major algorithmic paradigms for circuit placement [12, 15]: (1) constructive approach: once the position of a module is fixed, it is not changed anymore (for example, cluster growth, min-cut partitioning, quadratic placement, etc.), (2) iterative approach: intermediate placements are modified to improve the solution quality until some termination conditions are met (for example, force-directed method, etc.), and (3) nondeterministic approach: a placer may behave differently from run to run (say, based on a probabilistic formulation), even for the same input (for example, simulated annealing, genetic algorithm, etc.). The three types of approaches can be combined to further improve placement solutions; for example, an initial placement can be obtained by a constructive approach, followed by iterative improvement to enhance the placement, and further refined by simulated annealing to get the final placement.

Professor Satoshi Goto's 1981 paper [6] is an influential milestone work on circuit placement, which elegantly combines two algorithmic paradigms with a constructive initial placement followed by iterative improvement to obtain an effective and efficient placement framework. The initial placement, called *sub-optimum random generation (SORG)*, sequentially selects unplaced modules according to their connectivity to other modules and places them in desired positions to minimize the total wirelength. The iterative improvement, called *generalized force-directed relaxation (GFDR)*, repeatedly interchanges a set of modules to minimize the total wirelength.

Besides demonstrating an important breakthrough in placement techniques, it exemplifies a well-written, influential paper that combines both theoretical and empirical ingredients. Circuit placement is an NP-complete problem that had already been explored by many researchers in both industry and academia by 1981 [12, 15]. Professor Goto shows in his paper the then surprising theoretical finding that the *optimal region (OR)* for a module to achieve the minimum wirelength can be computed by an efficient median formulation. This is an exciting work where a solid theory and its practical benefits can be achieved simultaneously. As a result, its impacts is profound and long-lasting—the technique is not only well adopted in industry (like NEC), but is incorporated into even well-known modern placers such as FastPlace [11], mPL [1], NTUplace [3, 7], and POLAR [9].

In this article, we review Goto's OR- and GFDR-based classical placement framework and explain its impacts on modern circuit placement and applications. With their great success in modern placement, we further discuss potential future research directions based on the OR and GFDR formulations.

The rest of this paper is organized as follows: Section 2 reviews the OR formulation and the GFDR method, and also discusses their applications to modern placement. Section 3 explores future research directions based on the techniques presented in [6]. Finally, we conclude our work in Section 4.

2. OPTIMAL REGIONS AND GENERALIZED FORCE-DIRECTED RELAXATION

We first review the two key techniques presented in the pioneering work [6] and then address their applications to modern placement.

2.1 Optimal Region

For a set of nets and other modules connecting to a module m_i, the *optimal region* for m_i is defined as the region for placing m_i with the minimum total wirelength, with all the other modules being fixed. The optimal region can be found based on the median formulation proposed in [6]; see Figure 2 for an illustration. We follow the notations in [13] for easier presentation. Let $E_i = \{e_{i,1}, e_{i,2}, ..., e_{i,n_i}\}$ be the set of n_i nets connecting to m_i. Assume that pins are located in the centers of modules. For each net $e_{i,j} \in E_i$, we define the *bounding box* of $e_{i,j}$ as the minimum enclosing rectangle of all pins for $e_{i,j}$, excluding the module m_i. Let $x_{e_{i,j},l}$, $x_{e_{i,j},u}$, $y_{e_{i,j},l}$, and $y_{e_{i,j},u}$ be the respective left, right, lower, and upper boundaries of the bounding box of $e_{i,j}$. Let $\tilde{X}_i = \langle \tilde{x}_{i,1}, \tilde{x}_{i,2}, ..., \tilde{x}_{i,2n_i} \rangle$ be the sorted sequence of the x-boundaries $\{x_{e_{i,1},l}, x_{e_{i,1},u}, x_{e_{i,2},l}, x_{e_{i,2},u}, ..., x_{i,n_i,l}, x_{e_{i,n_i},u}\}$, and $\tilde{Y}_i = \langle \tilde{y}_{i,1}, \tilde{y}_{i,2}, ..., \tilde{y}_{i,2n_i} \rangle$ the sorted sequence of the y-boundaries $\{y_{e_{i,1},l}, y_{e_{i,1},u}, y_{e_{i,2},l}, y_{e_{i,2},u}, ..., y_{e_{i,n_i},l}, y_{e_{i,n_i},u}\}$. The optimal x and y coordinates of m_i can be obtained by solving the following optimization problem:

$$\min \sum_{j=1}^{2n_i} |x_i - \tilde{x}_{i,j}| + \sum_{j=1}^{2n_i} |y_i - \tilde{y}_{i,j}|. \quad (1)$$

The optimal solution for Equation (1) can be solved by finding the medians of $\tilde{X}_i$ and $\tilde{Y}_i$. Because both $\tilde{X}_i$ and $\tilde{Y}_i$ con-

tain even members, both the medians of $\tilde{X}_i$ and $\tilde{Y}_i$ can be the optimal solutions, which form the left, right, lower, and upper boundaries for the optimal region of m_i.

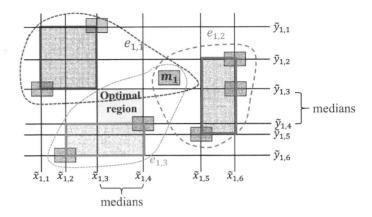

Figure 2: Optimal region computation for a module m_i, assuming that pins are located in the centers of modules.

2.2 Generalized Force Directed Relaxation

After an initial placement is obtained, the work [6] employs an iterative scheme to improve the objective based on the concepts of ϵ-neighborhood and λ-exchange. Fixing all other modules in their current positions, we can compute the optimal region for module m based on the formulation presented in Section 2.1. Suppose the optimal location of the module m is bin (s, t). Then, modules located at bin (i, j), where $|i - s| + |j - t| \leq \epsilon$, are called ϵ-neighbors of module m. For the example shown in Figure 3, the 1-neighbors of module A are $\{B, C, D, E, F\}$ if the optimal location of module A is occupied by module B.

Starting from a module m, GFDR computes the ϵ-neighbors of m, and for each ϵ-neighbor of m, GFDR further computes its ϵ-neighbors, and so on. For example, Figure 3 illustrates the exchange sequence with $\epsilon = 1$ and $\lambda = 3$ (three modules for such exchanges): $A \rightarrow B \rightarrow J \rightarrow A$ by moving module A to B's bin, module B to J's bin, and module J to A's bin. All module exchange sequences with $\epsilon = 1$ and $\lambda = 3$ are explored during the iterative improvement process, and the sequence with the minimum total wirelength is selected, or no exchange is performed if we cannot find an exchange sequence with a smaller wirelength.

2.3 Applications to Modern Placement

A modern chip could contain tens of millions of modules (standard cells). To handle this high design complexity, modern placement typically consists of three major stages: (1) global placement, (2) legalization, and (3) detailed placement. See Figure 4 for an illustration. Global placement computes the best position for each module to minimize the cost (e.g., wirelength), while ignoring module overlaps. Then, legalization places modules into desired positions and

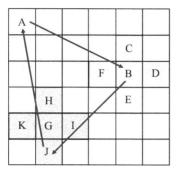

Figure 3: Trial interchange of modules with ϵ-neighborhood.

removes all overlaps among the modules. Finally, detailed placement further refines the module positions to obtain the final solution.

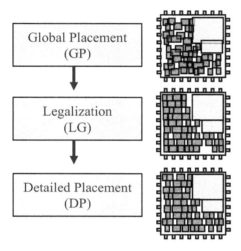

Figure 4: The modern placement flow typically consists of three stages: global placement, legalization, and detailed placement.

Even though the methods of ORs and GFDR were developed more than three decades ago, these methods are still pervasively used in modern placement algorithms. The following subsections just give several of such examples.

2.3.1 Applications of the Optimal Regions

FastPlace performs three types of module swaps to refine its placement solutions during its detailed placement stage: global swap, vertical swap, and local reordering [11]. The underlying idea of global swap is to find the optimal region for a module m_i in the placement region and swap m_i with another module m_j or a space in the optimal region to minimize the wirelength. A gain function is defined to choose the most profitable one among potential multiple modules or spaces in the optimal region.

Tseng, Chang, and Liu presented a detailed placement algorithm to handle the minimum-implant-area (MIA) con-

straint [13], where MIA-violating modules of the same threshold voltage are clustered in their optimal regions, and then an existing detailed placement algorithm is applied to deal with the cluster-based placement problem. This way the algorithm can simultaneously solve MIA violations while minimizing the wirelength. They extend the concept of the optimal region presented in [6] to placement with clusters of modules, called the *cluster-based optimal region*, to find the minimum wirelength region for a cluster. For a cluster $u_\ell = \{c_1, c_2, ..., c_{n_{u_\ell}}\}$ with n_{u_ℓ} modules, the optimization problem of finding the cluster-based optimal region is given as follows:

$$\min \ \sum_{i=1}^{n_{u_\ell}} \sum_{j=1}^{2n_i} |x_i - \tilde{x}_{i,j}| + \sum_{i=1}^{n_{u_\ell}} \sum_{j=1}^{2n_i} |y_i - \tilde{y}_{i,j}|. \qquad (2)$$

Unlike Equation (1) that determines the position of a module alone, Equation (2) contains multiple variables for both x and y coordinates for modules in a cluster. The work [13] further extends the median idea to determining the location of a seed module in a cluster and then placing the remaining modules accordingly, based on their relative positions to the seed module.

2.3.2 Applications of Generalized Force-Directed Relaxation

The work [1] presents a multilevel optimization for large-scale circuit placement, where a placement region is partitioned into a set of regular bins. At each level of refinement, this work locally permutes modules in a small subset of bins to improve the total wirelength. This work revises the ϵ-neighborhood, λ-exchange procedure as follows. Starting from a module m, the revised scheme computes its ϵ-neighbors and randomly selects one module, and for this newly selected module, this scheme further computes its ϵ-neighbors; this process is repeated until λ modules are selected. For these λ modules, the scheme tries all placement permutations and selects the permutation with the smallest wirelngth for real exchange. For example, if modules A, B, J are selected, all six permutations will be considered: no exchange, $A \leftrightarrow B$, $A \leftrightarrow J$, $B \leftrightarrow J$, $A \to B \to J \to A$, $A \to J \to B \to A$. The authors claimed to find superior solutions to those by the original work [6]. The POLAR placer also extends the GFDR framework in its density preserving refinement process [9].

3. FUTURE DIRECTIONS

Although placement is a classical problem, modern design challenges have reshaped the problem. The modern placement problem becomes very complicated mainly because of many emerging challenges with the following four aspects: (1) design scalability: handle ultra large-scale designs for modern applications; (2) multi-objective requirements: consider multiple placement constraints simultaneously, such as preplaced blockages, routability, timing, reliability, co-design with other circuit components (clock networks, power/ground networks), etc.; (3) heterogeneous circuit components: tackle standard cells of different heights, mixed-sized designs with thousands of big macros together with tens of millions of standard cells, heterogeneous circuit components in an FPGA, etc.; and (4) emerging technologies: handle 3D placement, discrete FinFET-based placement, manufacturability-aware placement, etc. As a result, modern placement problems have attracted much research attention recently. We believe that the methods of the OR and GFDR will still play an important role in modern and future placement problems. In the following subsections, we present some potential research directions for modern placement with these challenges.

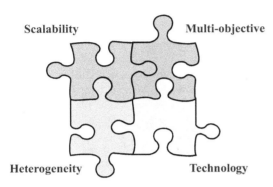

Figure 5: Major current and future circuit placement challenges.

3.1 Multi-Cell-Height Placement

For modern circuit designs, standard-cell libraries might contain cells of different heights, say, single-row-height cells, double-row-height cells, etc. Higher cells provide greater drive strengths at the cost of larger areas and power. Such mixed-cell-height cells incur complicated challenges for placement, because of the heterogeneity in cell dimensions [5, 10, 14]. As illustrated in Figure 6, mixed-cell-height placement shall consider standard cells of different cell heights and power-rail alignment as well. For an odd-row-height cell, such alignment can be achieved also by vertical cell flipping, while there are two types of an even-row-height cell with either VDD or VSS running along its top and bottom boundaries. The mixed-cell-height placement incurs new challenges for the computation of the ORs and thus force-directed relaxation, and its bin selection from ε-neighbors as well, especially when additional design constraints (e.g., the minimum implant area) need to be addressed simultaneously.

3.2 Mixed-Size Placement

A modern chip could contains thousands of big macros (due to IP modules, embedded memory modules, analog modules, etc.) and tens of millions of small standard cells, which significantly differ in both sizes and shapes. Figure 7

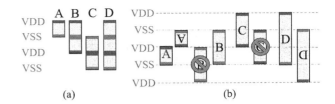

Figure 6: Mixed-cell-height placement shall consider standard cells of different heights and power-rail alignment.

shows two instances of mixed-size placements with large macros, with a single macro hierarchy (single-domain mixed-size placement in Figure 7(a)) and multiple macro hierarchies (multi-domain mixed-size placement in Figure 7(b)) with region constraints.

Pre-designed macros typically preserve multiple metal layers for interior routing, and these regions could become blockages during routing. Consequently, macros have a significant impact on chip routability. Further, the optimal regions and thus force-directed relaxation would be significantly different from a design with standard cells alone. So a modern placer should be capable of handling macro orientations and positions and capturing the interactions between big macros and small standard cells to derive accurate models for the optimal region computation and ε-neighbor selection for placement optimization.

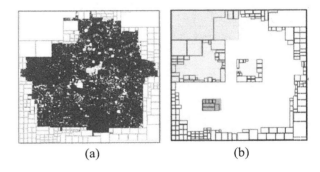

Figure 7: Mixed-size placements with large macros. (a) Single-domain mixed-size placement. (b) Multi-domain mixed-size placement with region constraints.

3.3 Routability/Timing-Driven Placement

Traditional placement relies on total wirelength minimization to obtain better circuit performance and smaller layout area. However, there is a mismatch between wirelength and congestion objectives in placement. See Figure 8 for the dramatically different behaviors with wirelength- and routability-driven placements. A wirelength-driven placer (NTUplace3 [3]) packs standard cells closer to minimize the total wirelength (see Figure 8(a)), incurring significant routing congestion violations (see Figure 8(b)). In contrast, a routability-driven placer (NTUplace4 [7]) spreads standard cells over the chip to achieve better routability at the cost of longer total wirelength (Figures 8(c) and (d)). The original OR and ϵ-neighborhood formulations are intended for wirelength optimization alone. It is thus desirable to develop a routabilty-driven OR formulation and its corresponding force-directed relaxation scheme to optimize routabilty and wirelength simultaneously.

Timing optimization during placement is critical to high-speed circuit designs. Traditional placement algorithms often try to achieve the timing goal via wirelength minimization. Nevertheless, there is a gap between wirelength and actual delay, so many methods have been proposed to overcome this challenge. Existing timing-driven placement algorithms can be classified into two major categories: (1) path-based and (2) net-based methods [2]. Net-based methods are much more popular because the prohibitive exponentially-growing number of timing paths for the path-based methods. The net-based method converts the timing constraint of each path into net weights. For a placement algorithm with the OR and ϵ-neighborhood formulation, such net weight modeling is crucial for developing a timing optimization technique with high accuracy, low complexity, and good controllability.

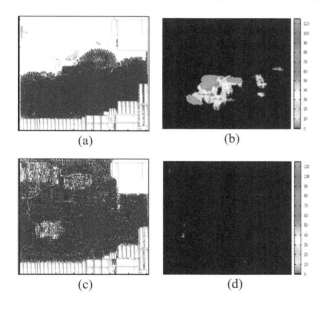

Figure 8: Dramatically different behaviors with wirelength- and routability-driven placements on the circuit sb12. (a) Wirelength-driven placed layout. (b) Congestion map for the wirelength-driven placed layout. (c) Routability-driven placed layout. (d) Congestion map for the routability-driven placed layout.

3.4 FinFET Self-Heating-Aware Placement

With their lower threshold voltage and smaller dynamic current leakage than those of traditional planar devices, Fin-FETs have emerged as a popular 3D transistor technology for circuit designs at the 22nm node and beyond [8]. The number of fins in a FinFET transistor plays a key role in

determining its circuit performance and the self-heating effect caused by fingers is getting more severe, due mainly to the low thermal conductivity of buried oxide and interlayer dielectric materials and its compacted 3D device geometry. As a result, the self heating could significantly cause performance and reliability degradation. The self-heating effect is more dominant between fins and fins than that between devices and devices [16, 17]; see Figure 9 for an illustration. So a device itself acts like a thermal source. It is thus desirable to consider placement of such thermal sources to reduce the self-heating effect for designs with the FinFET technology. To handle the self-heating-aware placement problem, it is of particular importance to develop an effective model of the thermally optimal region and incorporate such a model into an effective placement framework to achieve desired solution quality.

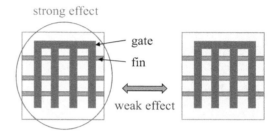

Figure 9: Self-heating effect inside a FinFET device and between two FinFET devices. The effect is more dominant between fins and fins than that between devices and devices.

3.5 FPGA Placement

A traditional symmetrical-array-based FPGA contains a two-dimensional array of configurable logic blocks (CLBs) surrounded by general routing resources and bounded by I/O blocks [4]. A modern FPGA often consists of complex heterogenous blocks, such as RAMs and DSPs, widely used to implement various circuit applications effectively. These complex blocks often contain datapath-intensive circuits. It is desirable to develop novel techniques to handle large-scale heterogeneous FPGAs placement with issues on heterogeneity, datapath regularity, and scalability. Obviously, any methods involving the ORs and force-directed relaxation would need to be revised to address the unique problems induced from the heterogeneous FPGA structures.

4. CONCLUSIONS

This article has introduced popular algorithmic paradigms for circuit placement. The classical, yet effective GFDR method and the OR formulation for finding desired placement solutions have then been presented. We have also discussed their impacts on modern placement and applications. Finally, we have further provided future placement research directions associated with the OR and GFDR formulations.

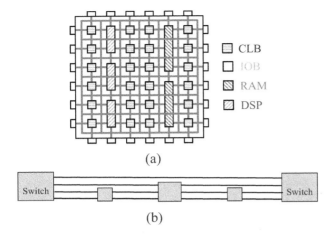

(a)

(b)

Figure 10: An FPGA architecture with heterogeneous circuit components (CLBs, IOBs, RAMs, and DSPs) and segmented routing structures.

A significant role of the OR and GFDR formulations for future placement problems is well expected.

5. REFERENCES

[1] T. F. Chan, J. Cong, T. Kong, and J. R. Shinnerl, "Multilevel optimization for large-scale circuit placement," in *Proc. IEEE/ACM Int. Conf. Computer-Aided Design*, pp. 171–176, San Jose, CA, November 2005.

[2] Y.-W. Chang, Z.-W. Jiang, and T.-C. Chen, "Essential issues in analytical placement algorithms," *IPSJ Transactions on System LSI Design Methodology*, pp. 815–835, August 2009

[3] T.-C. Chen, Z.-W. Jiang, T.-C. Hsu, H.-C. Chen, and Y.-W. Chang, "NTUplace3: An analytical placer for large-scale mixed-size designs with preplaced blocks and density constraints," *IEEE Trans. Computer-Aided Design of Integrated Circuits and Systems*, Vol. 27, No. 7, pp. 1228–1240, July 2008.

[4] Y.-C. Chen, S.-Y. Chen, and Y.-W. Chang, "Efficient and effective packing and analytical placement for large-scale heterogeneous FPGAs," in *Proc. IEEE/ACM Int. Conf. Computer-Aided Design*, San Jose, CA, November 2014.

[5] W.-K. Chow, C-.W. Pui, F.Y. Young, "Legalization algorithm for multiple-row height standard cell design," in *Proc. ACM/IEEE Design Automation Conference*, Austin, TX, June 2016.

[6] S. Goto, "An efficient algorithm for the two-dimensional placemet problem in electrical circuit layout," *IEEE Trans. Circuits and Systems*, Vol. 28, No. 1, pp. 12–18, January 1981.

[7] M.-K. Hsu, Y.-F. Chen, C.-C. Huang, S. Chou, T.-H. Lin, T.-C. Chen, and Y.-W. Chang, "NTUplace4h: A novel routability-driven placement algorithm for hierarchical mixed-size circuit designs,"

[8] D. Hisamoto, W.-C. Lee, J. Kedzierski, H. Takeuchi, K. Asano, C. Kuo, E. AAnderson, T.-J. King, J. Bokor, and C. Hu, "FinFET-a self-aligned double-gate MOSFET scalable to 20 nm," *IEEE Trans. Electron Devices*, vol. 47, No. 12, pp. 2320ạV-2325, December 2000.

[9] T. Lin, C. Chu, J. R. Shinnerl, I. Bustany, and I. Nedelchev, "POLAR: Placement based on novel rough legalization and refinement," in *Proc. IEEE/ACM Int. Conf. Computer-Aided Design*, San Jose, CA, November 2013.

[10] Y. Lin, B. Yu, X. Xu, J.-R. Gao, N. Viswanathan, W.-H. Liu, Z. Li, C. J. Alpert, and D. Z. Pan, "MrDP: Multiple-row detailed placement of heterogeneous-sized cells for advanced nodes," in *Proc. IEEE/ACM Int. Conf. Computer-Aided Design*, Austin, TX, Novvember 2016

[11] M. Pan, N. Viswanathan, and C. Chu, "An efficient and effective detailed placement algorithm," in *Proc. IEEE/ACM Int. Conf. Computer-Aided Design*, pp. 48–55, San Jose, CA, November 2005.

[12] S. M. Sait and H. Youssef, *VLSI Physical Design Automation: Theory and Practice*, World Scientific Publishing Co., 1999

[13] K.-H. Tseng, Y.-W. Chang, and C. C. C. Liu, "Minimum-implant-area-aware detailed placement with spacing constraints," in *Proc. ACM/IEEE Design Automation Conf.*, Austin, TX, June 2016.

[14] C.-H. Wang, Y.-Y. Wu, J. Chen, Y.-W. Chang, S.-Y. Kuo, W. Zhu, and G. Fan, "An effective legalization algorithm for mixed-cell-height standard cells," in *Proc. of IEEE/ACM Asia and South Pacific Design Automation Conf.*, January 2017.

[15] L. T. Wang, Y.-W. Chang, and K.-T. Cheng (Ed.), *Electronic Design Automation: Synthesis, Verification, and Test*, Morgan Kaufmann, 2009

[16] C. Xu, S. K. Kolluri, K. Endo, and K. Banerjee, "Analytical thermal model for self-heating in advanced FinFET devices with implications for design and reliability," *IEEE Trans. Computer-Aided Design of Integrated Circuits and Systems*, pp. 1045-1058, Vol. 32, No. 7, July 2013.

[17] J.-Y. Yan, Y.-J. Peng, and C. W. Liu, "TCAD simulation and analytic modeling of self-heating effects in FinFETs," *MediaTek Semi-annual Report*, June 2016.

100x Evolution of Video Codec Chips

Jinjia Zhou
Hosei University
Tokyo, Japan
jinjia.zhou.35@hosei.ac.jp

Dajiang Zhou
Waseda University
Kitakyushu, Japan
zhou@fuji.waseda.jp

Satoshi Goto
Waseda University
Kitakyushu, Japan
goto@waseda.jp

ABSTRACT

In the past two decades, there has been tremendous progress in video compression technologies. Meanwhile, the use of these technologies, along with the ever-increasing demand for emerging ultra-high-definition applications greatly challenges the design of video codec chips, with the extensive requirements on both memory (DRAM) bandwidth and computation power. Besides, the high data dependencies of video coding algorithms restrict the degree of efficient hardware parallelism and pipelining. This paper describes the techniques to realize high-performance video codec chips. Firstly, we introduce various optimization techniques to solve the DRAM traffic issue. Furthermore, the techniques to reduce the computational complexity and alleviate data dependencies are described. The proposed techniques have been implemented in several ASIC video codecs. Experiments show that the DRAM traffic and DRAM access time are reduced by 80% and 90% respectively. The performance of the video codec chips can achieve 7680x4320@120fps, which is more than 100x better than previous works.

Keywords

video coding; VLSI; UHDTV; low power; memory bandwidth

1. INTRODUCTION

In recent years, the visual experience is significantly enhanced by increasing the spatial resolution from 1920x1080 to 7680x4320 pixels per frame, and the temporal resolution from 30 to 120 frames/s. To store and transmit the huge volume of data, efficient video coding tools such as H.264/AVC and H.265/HEVC which provide excellent compression ratio (100:1 and 200:1) are utilized to encode the video data. However, their high compression ratio is at the expense of high computational complexity, high data dependencies, and huge DRAM bandwidth requirement. These three main issues make it difficult to support the increasing throughput of the video codec chips. Furthermore, since high throughput can be traded off for power savings using voltage and frequency scaling, the three problems also limit the energy efficiency.

This paper describes the techniques to solve the three issues. These techniques have been implemented in several video codec chips including the 1080p video codec (ISSCC'06[1], VLSIC'09[2]), the 2160p video decoder (VLSIC'10[3]), the 4320p video codecs (ISSCC'12[4], VLSIC'13[5], ISSCC'16[6]) and so on.

ISPD '17, March 19-22, 2017, Portland, OR, USA
© 2017 ACM. ISBN 978-1-4503-4696-2/17/03...$15.00
DOI: http://dx.doi.org/10.1145/3036669.3038252

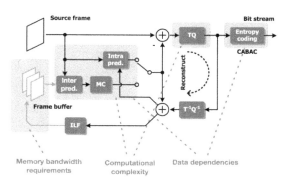

Fig. 1 Main problems in video coding

2. PROPOSED TECHNIQUES

There are three major issues we tried to solve in implementing the chips. 1) The Dynamic Random-Access Memory (DRAM) traffic issue. The off-chip DRAM is the performance bottleneck of the video codec system. For 8K UHDTV (Ultrahigh-definition television) applications, more than 100GBps bandwidth is required. Even the fastest DDR3 cannot meet this requirement. Besides, DRAM bandwidth efficiency is also a dominant factor in determining the fabrication cost and the power consumption of the whole systems [7]. 2) Computational complexity issue. Many high-complexity video coding tools such as inter prediction with large search range, are applied to improve the compression ratio. High complexity costs large power consumption, large chip area, and low processing speed. 3) Data dependency issue. Video codecs exploit all kinds of data dependencies to strengthen compression. These dependencies restrict the degree of efficient parallelism and pipelining. Fig. 1 summarizes the three challenges in video coding.

2.1 Improving DRAM Bandwidth Efficiency

In order to solve the DRAM traffic, we develop various optimization techniques to reduce the off-chip DRAM bandwidth requirement. 1) Data reusing techniques reuse the redundant data transferring between the DRAM and the encoder/decoder core. The proposed methods include the pipelined 2-D cache architecture, the partial MB reordering scheme, and the frame-parallel reference sharing scheme. 2) Data recompression techniques recompress and re-express the data stored in the DRAM to reduce the DRAM traffic. The proposed techniques include the lossless reference frame recompression architecture, the hybrid caching scheme, and the motion data recompression technique. 3) DRAM sub-system optimization techniques improve the DRAM access efficiency by combining the effects of an increment customizable bus protocol, a transaction scheduling scheme and a score-board based arbiter strategy. As a result, the bandwidth reduction ratio with the proposed techniques can be more than 80%, when comparing with the general VBSMC scheme [7].

We also propose the system-in-silicon design [1] and the 3D stacked memory design [8] to solve the DRAM traffic issue. As a result, enough memory bandwidth can be provided and the memory power can be significantly saved.

2.2 Reducing Computational Complexity and Alleviate Data Dependencies

Various techniques are applied to reduce the computation complexity and alleviate the data dependencies. 1) Inter prediction which searches the best matching blocks in the reference frames, is the most computation intensive component of a video encoder. To reduce the complexity of searching motions, we propose an alternating asymmetric search range assignment scheme, a rhombus window full search, a hierarchal search, a directional 5T12S search scheme and a low-pass truncated DCT cost function [5][9]. 2) For the Intra prediction component, it involves extensive complexity, and data dependencies of the reconstruction loop restrict hardware utilization. To solve these problems, coarse-to-fine mode decision, interlaced block reordering, and probability-based reconstruction are proposed [10]. 3) Due to the critical bin-to-bin data dependencies, context based binary arithmetic coding (CABAC) is the speed bottleneck of the video coding system. Techniques including pre-normalization, hybrid path coverage , and bypass bin splitting are proposed to alleviate the data dependencies [10]. As a result, all of the components can support real-time coding of 7680x4320 applications.

3. RESULTS

The proposed algorithms to reduce DRAM bandwidth requirement are implemented in several codec chips [2][3][4]. Fig. 2 shows the bandwidth reduction step by step when encoding a 10-frame IBBBP H.264/AVC stream of the 3840x2160 CrowdRun sequence with the QP28. The bandwidth in the figure refers to the amount of data transfer. Comparing with the general VBSMC scheme which reduced near 50% of the reference frame reading (RFR) part of bandwidth, the overall bandwidth reduction ratio after combing the proposed techniques can be more than 80%. Moreover, after further combing with the proposed DRAM subsystem optimization techniques which are applied to further reduce the DRAM access clock cycles, the total access time can be saved by 90% [7]. Fig.3 shows the performance of the video codec VLSI chips [11][4][10][12] [13][14][6]. By applying our optimization on both DRAM and codec core, a throughput of 7680x4320@120fps is achieved, which is improved by 144x.

4. ACKNOWLEDGMENTS

This work was supported in part by Regional Innovation Strategy Support Program of MEXT, Japan and NEC Corporation.

5. REFERENCES

[1] K. Kumagai *et al.*, "System-in-silicon architecture and its application to H.264/AVC motion estimation for 1080HDTV," in *2006 IEEE International Solid State Circuits Conference (ISSCC)*, 2006, pp. 1706–1715.

[2] D. Zhou *et al.*, "A 1080p@60fps multi-standard video decoder chip designed for power and cost efficiency in a system perspective," in *2009 Symposium on VLSI Circuits (VLSIC)*, 2009, pp. 262–263.

[3] D. Zhou *et al.*, "A 530Mpixels/s 4096x2160@60fps H.264/AVC high profile video decoder chip," in *2010 Symposium on VLSI Circuits (VLSIC)*, 2010, pp. 171–172.

[4] D. Zhou, J. Zhou, J. Zhu, P. Liu, and S. Goto, "A 2Gpixel/s H.264/AVC HP/MVC video decoder chip for Super Hi-Vision and 3DTV/FTV applications," in *2012 IEEE International Solid-State Circuits Conference (ISSCC)*, 2012, pp. 224–226.

[5] J. Zhou, D. Zhou, G. He, and S. Goto, "A 1.59Gpixel/s motion estimation processor with -211-to-211 search range for UHDTV video

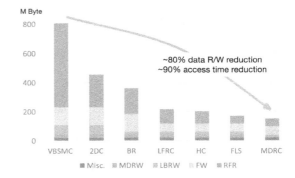

Fig. 2 Overall DRAM traffic reduction. VBSMC is the general optimization algorithm. 2DC, BR, LFRC, HC, FLS, and MDRC are the proposed schemes. [7]

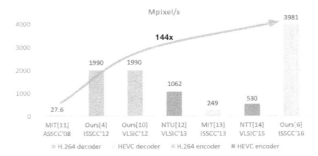

Fig. 3 Performance of codec VLSI chips

encoder," in *2013 Symposium on VLSI Circuits (VLSIC)*, 2013, pp. 286–287.

[6] D. Zhou *et al.*, "A 4Gpixel/s 8/10b H.265/HEVC video decoder chip for 8K Ultra HD applications," in *2016 IEEE International Solid-State Circuits Conference (ISSCC)*, 2016, pp. 266–268.

[7] Dajiang Zhou, "DRAM Bandwidth Optimized Design for High-Throughput Video Decoder Chips," *Dr. Thesis*, 2010.

[8] S. Zhang, J. Zhou, D. Zhou, and S. Goto, "A low power 720p motion estimation processor with 3D stacked memory," in *2014 International Conference on Very Large Scale Integration (VLSI-SoC)*, 2014, pp. 237–242.

[9] G. He, D. Zhou, Z. Chen, T. Zhang, and S. Goto, "A 995Mpixels/s 0.2nJ/pixel fractional motion estimation architecture in HEVC for Ultra-HD," in *2013 IEEE Asian Solid-State Circuits Conference (A-SSCC)*, 2013, pp. 301–304.

[10] D. Zhou, G. He, W. Fei, Z. Chen, J. Zhou, and S. Goto, "A 4320p 60fps H.264/AVC intra-frame encoder chip with 1.41Gbins/s CABAC," in *2012 Symposium on VLSI Circuits (VLSIC)*, 2012, pp. 154–155.

[11] D. F. Finchelstein, V. Sze, M. E. Sinangil, Y. Koken, and A. P. Chandrakasan, "A low-power 0.7-V H.264 720p video decoder," in *2008 IEEE Asian Solid-State Circuits Conference (A-SSCC)*, 2008, pp. 173–176.

[12] S. F. Tsai, C. T. Li, H. H. Chen, P. K. Tsung, K. Y. Chen, and L. G. Chen, "A 1062Mpixels/s 8192x4320p High Efficiency Video Coding (H.265) encoder chip," in *2013 Symposium on VLSI Circuits (VLSIC)*, 2013, pp. C188–C189.

[13] C. T. Huang, M. Tikekar, C. Juvekar, V. Sze, and A. Chandrakasan, "A 249Mpixel/s HEVC video-decoder chip for Quad Full HD applications," in *2013 IEEE International Solid-State Circuits Conference (ISSCC)*, 2013, pp. 162–163.

[14] T. Onishi *et al.*, "Single-chip 4K 60fps 4:2:2 HEVC video encoder LSI with 8K scalability," in *2015 Symposium on VLSI Circuits (VLSIC)*, 2015, pp. C54–C55.

Physical Layout after Half a Century: From Back-Board Ordering to Multi-Dimensional Placement and Beyond

Ilgweon Kang and Chung-Kuan Cheng
Computer Science and Engineering
Department
UC San Diego, La Jolla, CA
{igkang, ckcheng}@ucsd.edu

ABSTRACT

Innovations and advancements on physical design (PD) in the past half century significantly contribute to the progresses of modern VLSI designs. While "Moore's Law" and "Dennard Scaling" have become slowing down recently, physical design society encountered a set of challenges and opportunities. This article is presented at the event of the Life Time Achievement Award for Dr. Satoshi Goto by ISPD 2017. Dr. Goto's career in VLSI designs sets an exemplar role model for young engineers. Thus, we use his contributions as a thread to describe our personal view of physical layout from early back-board ordering to recent multi-dimensional placement and the future.

1. INTRODUCTION

In the past half-century, semiconductor technologies have dramatically advanced the modern society and led entire industry to a more automated world with sophisticated integrated circuits. Physical design (PD) deserves significant credits on the reduction of design gaps of VLSI designs. For the past half-century by virtue of PD community the performance of integrated circuits (ICs) has been extremely advanced, the industry has been profitable, and the global semiconductor market size has shown an upward climbing for many decades.

While "Moore's Law" and "Dennard Scaling" have shown the correction of slowing down, the hardware design cost increases rapidly and the cost per gate trend reverses from decreasing toward the direction of upward rising after 20nm technology node. Figure 1 shows the hardware design cost per technology node in bar chart and the cost per gate trend in a curved line. In other words, the cost reduction by scal-

ISPD '17, March 19–22, 2017, Portland, OR, USA.
© 2017 ACM. ISBN 978-1-4503-4696-2/17/03...$15.00
DOI: http://dx.doi.org/10.1145/3036669.3038251

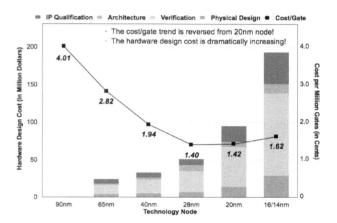

Figure 1: Distribution of hardware design cost per technology node (bar chart) and the cost per gate trend (line) [58]. Hardware design cost at 90nm technology node is not available from the reference [58].

ing becomes harder or no longer available. In the meantime, the growth rate of IC industry revenue has stagnated. Therefore, the industrial environment looks for higher efficiency on design optimization/automation/innovation for cost reduction and performance improvement. Moreover, we have concerns about the momentum to continue our innovations as recent publication submissions shrink quantitatively, as shown from the record of ISPD and ICCAD in last 12 years.

On the time scale of half a century, the challenges and opportunities we face today are actually the extension of, and in the same context as what we encountered before in the perspective of semiconductor history. The integrated circuit industry has grown by research and development. With this in mind, we describe the current challenges on physical design and present opportunities that enable us to drive new growth engine. Then we suggest that the career path of physical design automation should participate into the ongoing and upcoming innovations.

The remainder of this paper is organized as follows. In section 2, we review researches and progresses on VLSI physical layout. Section 3 describes recent academic activities on physical design field. Section 4 introduces new opportunities on physical design with reference to the International Technology Roadmap for Semiconductors (ITRS). In section 5, we reflect upon Dr. Goto's career path at the event of the Life Time Achievement Award, ISPD 2017 with aspiration for young generations of physical design researchers and engineers.

2. RESEARCHES ON PHYSICAL LAYOUT

Physical layout formulation is based on the VLSI technologies. On the other hand, physical layout enables the technologies, reduces design gaps, and extends the reach of the design capability. In this section, we summarize researches and progresses on physical layout designs.

2.1 Back-Board Ordering

The placement paper published at the first Design Automation Conference (DAC 1964) [50] is about back board ordering. At the very early days of physical layout design, most design complexity occurs at board and system levels. Placement of back boards was formulated as a one-dimensional ordering problem. We arrange circuit boards on a backplane in a linear order to minimize the wiring requirement of the backplane. Clearly, the quality of the placement causes a direct impact on the cost and performance of the system. Thus, the importance of physical layout optimization/automation is recognized in the early time of circuit designs.

Dr. Goto [10] is one of the pioneers who researched on the back-board ordering problem. In [10], he devised graphs to represent the placement process and thus used graph theory and Dijkstra algorithm to search for the optimal solutions. This work is one of the early attempts to use graph theory and mathematical algorithms for physical layout design automation.

2.2 Two-Dimensional Physical Layout Design

For IC chip designs, we treat the placement as a two-dimensional (2D) problem. In the transition between 1970s and 1980s, as the on-die circuit complexity increased, the need of placement tools became evident: layout designers could no longer handle hundreds of objects to produce high quality results in short turnaround. Dr. Goto made notable progresses on two-dimensional placement in collaborated with many of academy- and industry-leading researchers [11–14]. In 1978 [11], he first took advantage of previous works on one-dimensional ordering to improve the two-dimensional placement by rows or by columns iteratively. Then in 1979 [12], he performed a two-dimensional placement with a tree search approach (Fig. 2). His study selected the depth and width of the trees (Fig. 2(a)) and experimented for the best placement outcomes (Fig. 2(b)). After the investigation, his team at NEC implemented a place-and-route system (termed *LAMBDA*) [14] which became a leading industrial layout tool.

As the circuit complexity kept growing, we observed several breakthroughs in placement algorithms to tackle the design gaps. With interconnect dominance, placement solution plays a significant role on system performance. IC design-

ers allocate heavy efforts to improve the placement quality. We have seen the innovations via netlist/graph partitioning methods, combinatorial algorithms, and hierarchical approaches. In the 1980s when the placement sizes are less than a hundred thousand components, annealing-based methods produced excellent results [41]. However, as the problem sizes grew, the scalability of the iterative methods became a bottleneck. Partitioning-based placement methods could reduce the complexity using hierarchical methodologies at the expenses of quality loss due to suboptimal partitioning results.

As the placement problem size approached million components, major placement tools started with analytical algorithms using quadratic or nonlinear optimization. The analytical methods were proposed in the late 1970s [4, 16, 40, 51]. Throughout the years, many innovations made the method efficient and effective. 1. The sparsity of the circuit was exploited with a quadratic formulation [9]. 2. The linear wire length metric was approximated with nonlinear equations. 3. The cell density was enforced by partitioning, pulling anchors or local repulsive forces [7–9, 22, 25, 27, 49]. 4. Recently in ePlace [30, 31], the density was treated as electronic charges. The balance of the electrostatic system was modelled as classic Poisson equations. The global repulsive force could then be derived using Fast Fourier transform with $O(n log n)$ complexity where n is the size of the problem.

At the architecture level, floorplanning is a useful tool for physical layout [19, 34, 37, 38, 44, 52]. In [15], Dr. Goto's team used a hierarchical quadtree to represent the topology of the floorplan. Thus, they could apply algebraic operations and iterative improvement to optimize the design. Later in [17], they included the bus routing in the formulation of the problem.

2.3 Multi-Dimensional Physical Layout Design: 3D, Potentially 4D and Beyond

The extension to three-dimensional placement was initiated for the mapping of the dynamic FPGA (field-programmable gate array). Physical layout becomes a compiler tool for the high performance reconfigurable computing. Since the same space can be time shared by various functions, time domain becomes the third dimension for the placement. In this case,

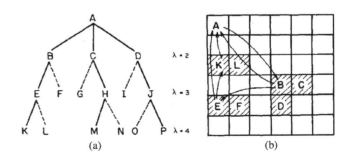

(a)   (b)

Figure 2: (a) A search tree to find the minimum-cost solution [12]. (b) Trial interchanges of modules based on Figure 2(a) [12].

the turnaround time for the placement became even more critical since compilation is part of user experiences.

Recently, as three-dimensional IC technologies emerged as a promising option for the "more-than-Moore" strategy, three-dimensional layout became one key piece of the puzzle to enable the technology. We have found that with the addition of the third dimension, the floorplan topologies are much more complicated and the problem appears intriguing [39]. On top of three-dimensional physical space, we can add time as an extra dimension to make layout four-dimensional. Potentially, the number of dimensions can increase with extra factors such as energy, thermal, security and etc.

3. ACADEMIC ACTIVITIES

The academic activities have blossomed following the original mission started by the SHARE committee half a century ago. The SHARE committee was formed in 1955 with the purpose of "Share to Help Avoid Redundant Effort". In 1964, the committee organized the first design automation conference (DAC) to provide a medium whereby people can interchange ideas, techniques, experience, and even specific programs on a regular basis.[1] Later, International Conference on Computer-Aided Design was started in 1981 and then ISPD in 1997 after several years of workshop as a predecessor.

3.1 Recent PD Research Trends

The role of physical design is to execute the physical implementation flow, which carries the system design process: Physical design is one corner stone of a reliable, predictable implementation fabric [20] that enables system-level signoff. Due to the important role in the IC implementation steps, placement is one crucial subject. Thus, we should push the edge to further improve the solution quality and reduce the design gaps. Layout designers must consider all design aspects together with various nontrivial design constraints. Thus, we have seen in placement articles, the key words such as timing driven [32], routability driven [18], clock aware, datapath aware, signal integrity aware, power aware and etc [3,33].

Recently, low power became one target objective for IC designs [3, 57]. The effort is to reduce packaging cost, increase battery life, and achieve high performance without thermal stress. Still, to produce low power design with tight constraints is nontrivial.

Mixed-size placement needs further improvement [33,53]. In mixed-size designs, large modules can block routing space and enforce detours on critical interconnect. Thus, manual intervention is still wanted to place, refine, and align large modules.

For three-dimensional placement, we need detailed formulations and methodologies. Physical design engineers must address the challenging issues such as 3D thermal distribution, floorplanning, clock tree synthesis, power distribu-

tion network, stacking methods by using through-silicon via (TSV) or monolithic inter-tier via (MIV) and etc.

Tighter vertical integration in the design flow is important for the system performance. For example, interactions and convergences among physical design procedures frequently occur to reduce cost and improve solution quality: interactions between placement and gate sizing, buffer insertion, design for manufacturing; interface with logic synthesis, clock tree synthesis and engineering change order. Thus, PD designers must consider more design aspects than before.

3.2 Publication Trend in Quantitative View

For publication trend, we use the data of ISPD and ICCAD for discussion. Figure 3 illustrates the quantitative trends of academic researches on (a) ISPD and (b) ICCAD, respectively, in terms of the number of submissions and acceptances. In the past decade, the two conferences remain very competitive in terms of acceptance rate. However, the submission rates decreased for both conferences. In reality, physical layout problems have become larger and more complicated. Thus, we are deeply concerned about the momentum to continue our innovations. The shrinkage of the submission may reflect the interests of the people or the funding opportunities from government and industry. The trend also implies the reduction of new graduates into the force of physical design automation. It is important for us to overcome the negative feedback loop to maintain our momentum to solve the design issues and to grow the IC industry. A recent publication [21] gives a couple of interesting data points/correlations with respect to design automation research, design automation research outputs (papers, patents, and EDA companies), and funding program.

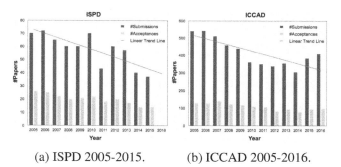

(a) ISPD 2005-2015.　　　(b) ICCAD 2005-2016.

Figure 3: The number of submitted (blue bars) and accepted (yellow bars) papers in the past 12 years at ISPD and ICCAD. Red line depicts the linear trend. ISPD 2016 information is not available from ACM online library.

3.3 Benchmarks

The release of the benchmarks enables the researchers to measure the algorithms on a common platform, and makes the research relevant to practice. Therefore, many innovations can be incorporated into EDA tools for applications in a faster pace. Table 1 lists classic and modern placement benchmark suites while Figure 4 depicts the trend. Up to the mid-2000, circuit sizes increased. From 2006, we saw

---

[1]The first three DACs (i.e., DAC'64-DAC'66) were called as the SHARE design automation workshop.

Table 1: Placement benchmark suites, from classic to modern benchmarks.

Benchmark	Description
Steinberg [42]	Steinberg back-board placement
Illiac IV [43]	Board-level design for supercomputer
MCNC [5]	General purpose benchmarks for design automation
ISPD98 [2]	Physical design applications, e.g., partitioning and placement
ISPD-2005 [36]	Placement (also applicable to floorplanning and routing)
ISPD-2006 [35]	Placement with target density per benchmark
MMS [53]	Large-scale modern mixed-size (MMS) placement
ISPD-2011 [48]	(Global) Routability-driven placement
DAC-2012 [46]	(Global) Routability-driven placement
ICCAD-2012 [47]	Design hierarchy aware (global) routability-driven placement
ICCAD-2013 [26]	Placement finishing – detailed placement and legalization
ISPD-2014 [55]	Detailed routing-driven placement
ICCAD-2014 [23]	Incremental timing-driven placement
ISPD-2015 [6]	Blockage-aware detailed routing-driven placement
ICCAD-2015 [24]	Incremental timing-driven placement
ISPD-2016 [54]	Routability-driven FPGA placement
ISPD-2017 [56]	Clock-aware FPGA placement

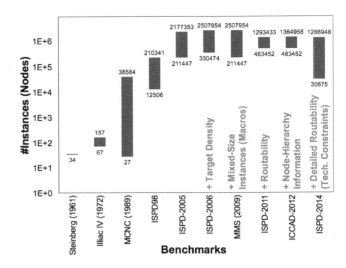

Figure 4: The benchmarks plotted with ranges of instances (displayed in log scale). Benchmarks are selectively chosen from Table 1. The minimum and maximum instances are displayed at the bottom and top of each bar, respectively. The number of instances saturates after 2005. Additional design features, e.g. density and routability, contribute to design complexity.

more features, e.g. target density, mixed size instances, and routability [18]. In the meanwhile, the saturated circuit size calls a necessity of benchmarks with even larger number of instances since the size of circuits does matter on the choice of methods and quality of results, e.g. using distributed computation and memory management.

4. NEW OPPORTUNITIES ON PHYSICAL DESIGN

In this section, we introduce new opportunities on physical design in three aspects: (i) the international technology roadmap for semiconductors (ITRS) shows that technology is going through divergence and evolution, which calls for new physical layout researches; (ii) paradigm-shifting design methodologies and innovative algorithmic techniques can improve design automation tools, and (iii) the semiconductor market and economy forecast show potential returns for further investments from the government and the industry.

4.1 Physical Design and ITRS

The latest ITRS [57] report suggests numerous challenging research topics, introduced by innovations on semiconductor integration technology [20]. Figure 5 illustrates the transistor structures for logic devices. For 10nm technology, the transistor structure use finFET and the technology node will advance to 7nm for mass production soon. As shown in Figure 6, the extensions to the existing FDSOI and finFET will sustain for two or three technology nodes until 2020 [57]. Beyond 2020 a transition to gate-all-around and potentially to vertical nanowires devices will be needed, providing new research topics.

From 20nm and below, we observed that the gap between device pitch and metal pitch becomes wider, i.e. routing resources per cell area is diminishing. The number of fins on the standard cells has dropped from 12 tracks to 9/8 tracks, and even to 5 tracks. Thus, pin accessibility and design rule conflicts became serious issues for detailed placement and routing [1], which call for new methodologies and innovations.

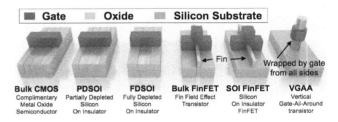

Figure 5: Shrink scenarios for logic devices [59]. In the current market (January 2017), the state-of-the-art transistor structure is finFET with 10nm technology.

4.2 New Techniques

Emerging algorithmic techniques from outside fields provide potential methods to solve some physical design bottlenecks. Attempts to apply artificial intelligence and deep learning techniques present progresses to predict potential congestion during placement and to detect data paths from netlist or design-hierarchy information. Massively parallel computing gives new chances to try distributed algorithms which can drastically improve our computation and memory capacity.

4.3 New Markets for IC Design

Historically, the EDA industry grew from solving new design problems and the industry grew by expanding the market demand. From the mid-90s, the internet revolution has led the skyrocketing growth of the information technology. The advancement of semiconductor enabled portable and powerful devices with more functionality. Eventually, billions of electronic devices will be connected through the internet (so called the Internet of Things (IoT), Figure 7).

Year of Production	2015	2017	2019	2021	2024	2027	2030
Technology Node (nm)	16/14	11/10	8/7	6/5	4/3	3/2.5	2/1.5
Transistor Structure							
Fully Depleted SOI (FDSOI)							
FinFET							
Lateral Gate-All-Around (LGAA)							
Vertical Gate-All-Around (VGAA)							
Monolithic 3D							

Figure 6: Transistor structure roadmap [57].

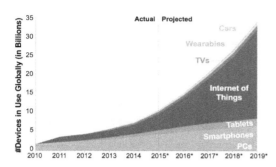

Figure 7: Internet of Things (IoT): The explosively growing internet device market [45].

The trend inevitably results in "small quantity batch production" of ICs ensuring low power application, by very cost-effective design and manufacturing. The new market will enable a new growth engine to our industry with new opportunities.[2]

5. CAREER PATH OF PHYSICAL DESIGN AUTOMATION

In physical design automation community, we have observed many leading pioneers as illustrated by previous ISPD Lifetime Achievement Awardees, and have found new generations of talented researchers and engineers. Dr. Goto's career is one illuminating example for us to aspire since his profession covers many aspects: research, engineering, management and academia.

1. Dr. Goto values scholarship, inspiration and wisdom by expressing deep appreciation to his advisors. He described his view of their advising as follows. Prof. Hiroshi Hirayama at Waseda University is my thesis advisor. He taught me how to enjoy the life, not only research but life itself. Prof. Ernest S. Kuh is considered to be my second advisor. He taught me a lot on my research and career as a professional. Without their help, I don't think that I can be successful in Academic and Business Society.

2. Dr. Goto strived to contribute to industry by translating research results into product advancement and innovation. While at NEC, Dr. Goto made important technical contributions in the electronic design automation (EDA) area by leading a team that developed one of the first layout design automation systems in the world in the late 1970s. Dr. Goto

---

[2]Management consulting companies and market survey companies estimate the potential economic impact of IoT technology to be over a dozen trillion dollars within ten years [45].

was at NEC for 33 years and was vice president and general manager of C&C media research [28]. Note that during Dr. Goto's leadership at NEC Corporation, the company held a major market share of semiconductor industry in the world.

3. Dr. Goto provided services, mentorship and feedback to the community. He served as Technical Program Chair and General Chair of IEEE/ACM ICCAD (1988-89), Technical Program Chair of ACM/IEEE DAC (1992), ad General Chair of ASPDAC 2001. As a manager and general manager at NEC, Dr. Goto encouraged his colleagues to advance their careers by visiting research laboratory at UC Berkeley. Among the young researchers, Takeshi Yashimura took the opportunity to publish the classic Yashimura and Kuh channel router. During his tenure at NEC, the company made NEC C&C Prize awards to EDA field twice: Once for computer-aided design tools for circuit simulation at transistor level (SPICE), and the second for simulation into the manufacturing process for semiconductor devices.

6. CONCLUSION

In this article, we briefly review the previous paths and challenges that we are facing. Then, we introduce and summarize new opportunities of physical design related researches. Lastly, we present the career path in physical design field with highlights of Dr. Satoshi Goto's contributions.

7. ACKNOWLEDGEMENT

This work was supported in part by the National Science Foundation (Grant CCF-1564302).

8. REFERENCES

[1] R. Aitken, G. Yeric, B. Cline, S. Sinha, L. Shifren, I. Iqbal and V. Chandra, "Physical Design and FinFETs", *Proc. ISPD*, 2014, pp. 65-68.

[2] C. J. Alpert, "The ISPD98 Circuit Benchmark Suite", *Proc. ISPD*, 1998, pp. 80-85.

[3] C. Alpert, Z. Li, G.-J. Nam, C. N. Sze, N. Viswanathan and S. I. Ward, "Placement: How or Not?", *Proc. ICCAD*, 2012, pp. 283-290.

[4] K.J. Antreich, F.M. Johnnes, and F.H. Kirsch, "A New Approach for Solving the Placement Problem using Force Models," IEEE Int. Symp. Circuits and Systems, 1982, pp. 481-486.

[5] F. Brglez, D. Bryan and K. Kozminski, "Combinational Profiles of Sequential Benchmark Circuits", *Proc. ISCAS*, 1989, pp. 1929-1934.

[6] I. S. Bustany, D. Chinnery, J. R. Shinnerl and V. Yutsis, "ISPD 2015 Benchmarks with Fence Regions and Routing Blockages for Detailed-Routing-Driven Placement", *Proc. ISPD*, 2015, pp. 157-164.

[7] T. F. Chan, J. Cong, M. Romesis, J. R. Shinnerl, K. Sze and M. Xie, "mPL6: A Robust Multilevel Mixed-Size Placement Engine", *Proc. ISPD*, 2005, pp. 227-229.

[8] T.-C. Chen, Z.-W. Jiang, T.-C. Hsu, H.-C. Chen and Y.-W. Chang, "NTUplace3: An Analytical Placer for Large-Scale Mixed-Size Designs with Preplaced Blocks and Density Constraints", *Trans. on CAD*, 27(7), 2008, pp. 1228-1240.

[9] C.-K. Cheng and E. S. Kuh, "Module Placement Based on Resistive Network Optimization", *Trans. on CAD*, 3(3), 1984, pp. 218-225.

[10] S. Goto, I. Cederbaum and B. S. Ting, "Suboptimum Solution of the Back-Board Ordering with Channel Capacity Constraint", *IEEE Trans. on CAS* CAS-24(11), 1977, pp. 645-652.

[11] S. Goto and E. S. Kuh, "An Approach to the Two-Dimensional Placement Problem in Circuit Layout", *IEEE Trans. on CAS* CAS-25(4), 1978, pp. 208-217.

[12] S. Goto, "A Two-Dimensional Placement Algorithm for the Master Slice LSI Layout Problem", *Proc. DAC*, 1979, pp. 11-17.

[13] S. Goto, "An Efficient Algorithm for the Two-Dimensional Placement Problem in Electrical Circuit Layout", *IEEE Trans. on CAS* CAS-28(1), 1981, pp. 12-18.

[14] S. Goto, T. Matsuda, K. Takamizawa, T. Fujita, H. Mizumura, H. Nakamura and F. Kitajima, "LAMBDA, an Integrated Master-Slice LSI CAD System", *Integration, the VLSI Journal* 1(1), 1983, Elsevier, pp. 53-69.

[15] O. He, S. Dong, J. Bian, S. Goto and C.-K. Cheng, "A Novel Fixed-Outline Floorplanner with Zero Deadspace for Hierarchical Design", *Proc. ICCAD*, 2008, pp. 16-23.

[16] T.C. Hu and E.S. Kuh, VLSI Circuit Layout Theory and Design, IEEE Press, 1985.

[17] O. He, S. Dong, J. Bian, S. Goto and C.-K. Cheng, "Bus Via Reduction Based on Floorplan Revising", *Proc. GLSVLSI*, 2010, pp. 9-14.

[18] X. He, T. Huang, L. Xiao, H. Tian, G. Cui and E. F. Y. Young, "Ripple: An Effective Routability-Driven Placer by Iterative Cell Movement", *Proc. ICCAD*, 2011, pp. 74-79.

[19] X. Hong, G. Huang, Y. Cai, J. Gu, S. Dong, C.-K. Cheng and J. Gu, "Corner Block List: An Effective and Efficient Topological Representation of Non-Slicing Floorplan", *Proc. ICCAD*, 2000, pp. 8-12.

[20] A. B. Kahng, "A Roadmap and Vision for Physical Design", *Proc. ISPD*, 2002, pp. 112-117.

[21] A. B. Kahng, M. Luo, G.-J. Nam, S. Nath, D. Z. Pan and G. Robins, "Toward Metrics of Design Automation Research Impact", *Proc. ICCAD*, 2015, pp. 263-270.

[22] A. B. Kahng, S. Reda and Q. Wang, "APlace: A General Analytic Placement Framework", *Proc. ISPD*, 2005, pp. 233-235.

[23] M.-C. Kim, J. Hu and N. Viswanathan, "ICCAD-2014 CAD Contest in Incremental Timing-Driven Placement and Benchmark Suite", *Proc. ICCAD*, 2014, pp. 361-366.

[24] M.-C. Kim, J. Hu, J. Li and N. Viswanathan, "ICCAD-2015 CAD Contest in Incremental Timing-Driven Placement and Benchmark Suite", *Proc. ICCAD*, 2015, pp. 921-926.

[25] M.-C. Kim, D.-J. Lee and I. L. Markov, "SimPL: An Effective Placement Algorithm", *Trans. on CAD*, 31(1), 2012, pp. 50-60.

[26] M.-C. Kim, N. Viswanathan, Z. Li and C. Alpert, "ICCAD-2013 CAD contest in Placement Finishing and Benchmark Suite", *Proc. ICCAD*, 2013, pp. 268-270.

[27] J. M. Kleinhans, G. Sigl, F. M. Johannes and K. J. Antreich, "GORDIAN: VLSI Placement by Quadratic Programming and Slicing Optimization", *Trans. on CAD*, 10(3), 1991, pp. 356-365.

[28] E. S. Kuh, Quote from a Recommendation Letter, *Personal Communication*.

[29] J. Liu, S. Dong, X. Hong and S. Goto, "Floorplanning with Constraint Extraction based on Interconnecting Information Analysis", *Proc. ASICON*, 2007, pp. 1084-1087.

[30] J. Lu, P. Chen, C.-C. Chang, L. Sha, D. Huang, C.-C. Teng and C.-K. Cheng, "ePlace: Electrostatics based Placement using Fast Fourier Transform and Nesterov's Method", *Trans. on DAES* 20(2), 2015, article 17.

[31] J. Lu, H. Zhang, P. Chen H. Chang, C.-C. Chang, Y.-C. Wong, L. Sha, D. Huang, Y. Luo, C.-C. Teng and C.-K. Cheng, "ePlace-MS: Electrostatics-Based Placement for Mixed-Size Circuits", *IEEE Trans. on CAD* 34(5), 2015, pp. 685-698.

[32] M. Marek-Sadowska and S. P. Lin, "Timing Driven Placement", *Proc. ICCAD*, 1989, pp. 94-97.

[33] I. L. Markov, J. Hu and M.-C. Kim, "Progress and Challenges in VLSI Placement Research", *Proc. ICCAD*, 2012, pp. 275-282.

[34] H. Murata, K. Fujiyoshi, S. Nakatake and Y. Kajitani, "VLSI Module Placement Based on Rectangle-Packing by the Sequence-Pair", *Trans. on CAD*, 15(12), 1996, pp. 1518-1524.

[35] G.-J. Nam, "ISPD 2006 Placement Contest: Benchmark Suite and Results", *Proc. ISPD*, 2006, pp. 167.

[36] G.-J. Nam, C. J. Alpert, P. Villarrubia, B. Winter and M. Yildiz, "The ISPD2005 Placement Contest and Benchmark Suite", *Proc. ISPD*, 2005, pp. 216-220.

[37] R. H. J. M. Otten, "Automatic Floorplan Design", *Proc. DAC*, 1982, pp. 261-267.

[38] B. T. Preas and W. M. van Cleemput, "Placement Algorithms for Arbitrarily Shaped Blocks", *Proc. DAC*, 1979, pp. 474-480.

[39] F. Qiao, I. Kang, D. Kane, E. F. Y. Young, C.-K. Cheng and R. Graham, "3D Floorplan Representations: Corner Links and Partial Order", *Proc. 3DIC*, 2016, to appear.

[40] N. Quinn and M. Breuer, "A Forced Directed Component Placement Procedure for Printed Circuit Boards", *IEEE Trans. on CAS*, 26(6), 1979, pp. 377-388.

[41] C. Sechen and A. Sangiovanni-Vincentelli, "The TimberWolf Placement and Routing Package", *IEEE Journal of SSC*, 20(2), 1985, pp. 510-522.

[42] L. Steinberg, "The Backboard Wiring Problem: A Placement Algorithm," *SIAM Review* 3(1), 1961, pp. 37-50.

[43] J. E. Stevens, "Fast Heuristic Techniques for Placing and Wiring Printed Circuit Boards", *Ph. D. dissertation*, University of Illinois at Urbana-Champaign, 1972.

[44] X. Tang and D. F. Wong, "FAST-SP: A Fast Algorithm for Block Placement Based on Sequence Pair", *Proc. ASP-DAC*, 2001, pp. 521-526.

[45] A. Thierer and A. Castillo, "Projecting the Growth and Economic Impact of the Internet of Things", *Technology Policy, Policy Briefing, Mercatus Center at George Mason University*, June 15, 2015, https://www.mercatus.org/system/files/IoT-EP-v3.pdf.

[46] N. Viswanathan, C. J. Alpert, C. N. Sze, Z. Li and Y. Wei, "The DAC 2012 Routability-driven Placement Contest and Benchmark Suite", *Proc. DAC*, 2012, pp. 774-782.

[47] N. Viswanathan, C. J. Alpert, C. N. Sze, Z. Li and Y. Wei, "ICCAD-2012 CAD Contest in Design Hierarchy Aware Routability-Driven Placement and Benchmark Suite", *Proc. ICCAD*, 2012, pp. 345-348.

[48] N. Viswanathan, C. J. Alpert, C. N. Sze, Z. Li, G.-J. Nam and J. A. Roy, "The ISPD-2011 Routability-Driven Placement Contest and Benchmark Suite", *Proc. ISPD*, 2011, pp. 141-146.

[49] N. Viswanathan, M. Pan and C. Chu, "FastPlace 3.0: A Fast Multilevel Quadratic Placement Algorithm with Placement Congestion Control", *Proc. ASP-DAC*, 2007, pp. 135-140.

[50] M. B. Weindling, "A Method for the Best Geometric Placement of Units on a Plane", *Proc. DAC*, 1964, pp. 5.1-5.54.

[51] G. J. Wipfler, M. Wiesel and D. A. Mlynski, "A combined force and cut algorithm for hierarchical VLSI layout" *Proc. DAC*, 1982, pp. 671-677.

[52] D. F. M. Wong and C.-L. Liu "A New Algorithm for Floorplan Design", *Proc. DAC*, 1986, pp. 101-107.

[53] J. Z. Yan, N. Viswanathan and C. Chu, "Handling Complexities in Modern Large-Scale Mixed-Size Placement", *Proc. DAC*, 2009, pp. 436-441.

[54] S. Yang, A. Gayasen, C. Mulpuri, S. Reddy and R. Aggarwal, "Routability-Driven FPGA Placement Contest", *Proc. ISPD*, 2016, pp. 139-143.

[55] V. Yutsis, I. S. Bustany, D. Chinnery, J. Shinnerl and W.-H. Liu, "ISPD 2014 Benchmarks with Sub-45nm Technology Rules for Detailed-Routing-Driven Placement", *Proc. ISPD*, 2014, pp. 161-168.

[56] ISPD-2017 Contest, http://www.ispd.cc/contests/17/.

[57] ITRS Report 2015 Edition, http://www.semiconductors.org/main/2015_international_technology_roadmap_for_semiconductors_itrs/.

[58] Hardware Design Cost: Faster, Cooler, Simpler, could FD-SOI be Cheaper too?, https://www.semiwiki.com/forum/content/2991-faster-cooler-simpler-could-fd-soi-cheaper-too.html.

[59] Many Ways to Shrink: The Right Moves to 10 Nanometer and Beyond, https://staticwww.asml.com/doclib/investor/asml_3_Investor_Day-Many_ways_to_shrink_MvdBrink1.pdf.

Past, Present and Future of the Research

Satoshi Goto
Waseda University
Japan
goto@waseda.jp

Biography

Satoshi Goto received the B.E. and the M.E. Degrees in Electronics and Communication Engineering from Waseda University in 1968 and 1970 respectively. He also received the Dr. of Engineering from the same University in 1978. He joined NEC Laboratories in 1970 where he worked for LSI design, Multimedia system and Software as GM and Vice President. Since 2002, he has been Professor, at Graduate School of Information, Production and Systems of Waseda University at Kitakyushu and now Emeritus Professor at Waseda University, Japan. He served as GC of ICCAD, ASPDAC, VLSI-SOC, ASICON and ISOCC and was a board member of IEEE CAS society. He is IEEE Life Fellow and IEICE Fellow. He is Visiting Professor at Shanghai Jiao Tang University, Sun Yat-sen University and Tsinghua University of China and Member of Science Council of Japan.

Research Overview

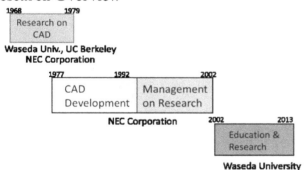

Figure 1. Research Overview.

ISPD '17, March 19-22, 2017, Portland, OR, USA
© 2017 ACM. ISBN 978-1-4503-4696-2/17/03…$15.00
DOI: http://dx.doi.org/10.1145/3036669.3038254

Research on CAD

Graph Algorithm:
    Shortest path problem
    Simplex method in LP and Path & Cut set problem
    Heuristic method for NP-hard problem

CAD algorithm
    Back-board ordering
    2-dimestional placement
    Building Block routing
    Knowledge-based routing/Logic design

2-dimensional placement algorithm was based on efficient local interchange method to attack hard combinatorial problems to obtain a near optimal solution with the limit of computation time. (DAC1979, IEEE Trans.CAS,1981). This algorithm has been implemented in CAD System developed by the author and had been used to design more than 5000 real chips in NEC Corporation for 15 year.

CAD Development

CAD for Printed Circuit board
P&R for Gate Array LSI and Standard Cell LSI
Interactive system for LSI Layout Design
Logic Synthesis and Verification
Workstation based LSI design system
Knowledge-based Routing   System

The knowledge based EDA System was first developed in early 1980. A lot of expert system had been developed in 1980's based on so called "Artificial Intelligence Approach". The author and his group introduced a rule-based approach for routing problem in EDA System, and logic circuit optimization problem (ICCAD1986, 1987). Based on these artificial intelligence approach, the EDA system has been developed, and been used by adding more sophisticated rules for 10 years to design real circuit design in NEC.

At ICCAD 1987, a panel ,"On the future of CAD" was held. Fig.3 shows the author's presentation slides. By the year of 2000, his prediction is that Physical design will be fully automatically designed by computer, and Logic design will be 80%. Also, there was a battle between vendor tools and in-house tools in the company. The specific EDA tools and advanced tools only had been developed and used inside the company.

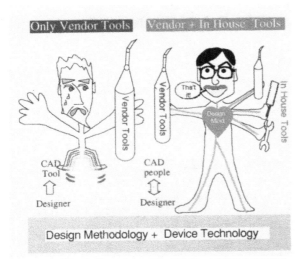

Fig.2 Panel on the CAD at ICCAD1985
In-house tool vs Vendor tool

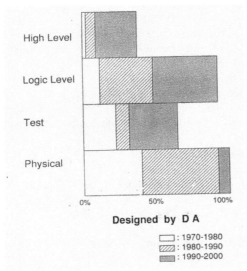

Designed by D A

☐ : 1970-1980
▨ : 1980-1990
▨ : 1990-2000

Fig.3 Panel on the future of CAD
(ICCAD1987)

Management on Research

As GM and VP of NEC Reseach Labs., several important projects had to been managed by the author to create and develop a new business.

- C-Based design tool

- Highly Parallel Computer/ Super Computer Automatic Translation Machine (English ↔Japanese)

- Finger print recognition/ Face recognition

- Video and Audio Codec system and chip

- Cryptographic system and chip

- Artificial Intelligence & Expert System

Education and Research

After moving from industry to academia in 2002, education and research for multimedia system is the main interesting subjects. 30 students got Ph.D degree and 80 got ME degree for 12 years.

The number of published papers was increased drastically; 10 times and more than the ones in industries, even though the research budget was decreased to 1/10.

Number of Published Technical Papers

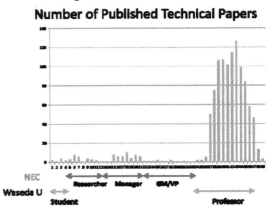

Figure 4 Number of Published papers

The main projects in universities are as follows:
Video Encoder/Decoder algorithms and chip design
Error Correction Code (LDPC) algorithm
and chip design
Low power design for Media Processing
Human or object detection algorithm and System
Cypher algorithms and circuit design

The research in a laboratory of university is used to be done by each student independently. But, in the author's laboratory, each student not only focused on his/her specific subject, but also work together to design a chip by implementing his own idea. 15 real chips were fabricated within 12 years. The students would be so much satisfied with their designed chips by testing and operating the chips and got a real world feeling.

The typical chips are as follows:

H.264 2K Video Encoder chip (VLSI2007)
H.264 4K Video Decoder chip (VLSI2010)
H.264 8K Video Decoder chip (ISSCC2012)
HEVC 8K Video Decoder chip (ISSCC2015)
WPAN LDPC Decoder chip (VLSI-DAT2011)
AES with DPA attack countermeasure (ISLPED2010)
32-Core Vector Processor (ISLPED2011)

The author is so grateful to his advisors and mentors to conduct the research, particularly, Prof. Hiroshi Hirayama, Prof. Tatsuo Ohtsuki, Prof. Ernest Kuh and Prof. Chung Laung Liu and to all my colleagues of NEC and students of Waseda University for the collaboration.

Interesting Problems in Physical Synthesis

Pei-Hsin Ho
Synopsys, Inc.
Hillsboro, Oregon
pho@synopsys.com

ABSTRACT

It is a misperception that the Chinese have the same word for crisis as opportunity. Despite that, a technical crisis does present opportunities for researchers and practitioners to solve interesting problems. In this talk we point out two crises: interconnect and runtime, we enumerate interesting physical-synthesis problems arising from these crises, and we discuss the possibility of employing machine learning and hardware acceleration techniques to attack those problems.

Keywords

Physical synthesis; CPU performance; machine learning; hardware acceleration.

1. INTRODUCTION

In 2011 Intel announced FinFET transistors that greatly improved the performance and power efficiency of the cells, but unfortunately not the wires. To speed up at least some of the wires to marry the much faster cells, Intel and foundries like TSMC and Samsung decided to create a large spread in resistance across the metal stack, in which a few higher metal layers are more than 10X less resistive than the lower metal layers. The greater variation in resistance across different metal layers increases the error in resistance estimation prior to detailed routing, which makes it hard for physical synthesis prior to detailed routing to achieve good quality of result (QoR) in timing, power and area.

Furthermore, multiple patterning techniques used in 14/16nm technology nodes and beyond introduce many more constraints to routing, pin access and cell placement, which makes it hard for physical synthesis prior to detailed routing to accurately predict or optimize for routability. These challenges constitute the interconnect crisis. We will discuss the possibility of employing statistical analysis and machine learning techniques "trained" separately for each process technology node to solve these physical-synthesis problems.

Since 2004, when Intel canceled its 3 GHz Tejas project due to an overheating problem, CPU clock frequency has gotten stuck at around 3 GHz in the last 13 years. In contrast, in the 10 years prior to 2004, Intel increased the clock frequency of its CPUs by around 60X (from 50 MHz to around 3 GHz).

Although our algorithms no longer automatically run faster every 18 months, the number of cores in each processor has been increasing. For instance, state-of-the-art Intel Xeon processors now have 72 cores running at 1.5 GHz. Therefore, in the last decade, EDA companies have carefully multi-threaded most of the physical-synthesis algorithms to take the runtime advantage of multi-core CPUs. But many physical-synthesis algorithms, whose speedup on multi-core CPUs plateaus out at between 8 to 64 cores. Therefore, running 72 (or more) cores at the same (or lower) clock frequency will not further improve runtime, whereas the complexity of the physical-synthesis problems has not stopped growing. Consequently, we are facing a runtime crisis in physical synthesis.

Algorithms that perform the same calculations on large arrays of normal integer or floating-point data can utilize more than 72 cores. For example, since around 2009, GPUs with thousands (close to 5000) of cores supporting efficient SIMD (Single Instruction Multiple Data) computations have sped up deep neural networks by more than two orders of magnitude compared to CPUs and thus enabled machine learning to become effective for many different applications. Recently, AWS (Amazon Web Service) and Tencent (a Chinese cloud provider) started to "preview" cloud servers equipped with one or multiple FPGAs to support customizable hardware accelerations to software. We will discuss the usage of GPU and FPGA based hardware acceleration of physical-synthesis algorithms to handle the ever-increasing problem complexity without sacrificing QoR. We will also discuss the challenges in high-level synthesis and physical synthesis to support software developers, as opposed to chip designers, to utilize FPGA-based hardware acceleration in the cloud.

ISPD'17, March 19–22, 2017, Portland, OR, USA.
ACM. ISBN 978-1-4503-4696-2/17/03.
DOI: http://dx.doi.org/10.1145/3036669.3038245

Pin Accessibility-Driven Detailed Placement Refinement

Yixiao Ding
Department of Electrical and
Computer Engineering
Iowa State University
Ames, IA, 50011, USA
yxding@cadence.com

Chris Chu
Department of Electrical and
Computer Engineering
Iowa State University
Ames, IA, 50011, USA
cnchu@iastate.edu

Wai-Kei Mak
Department of Computer
Science
National Tsing Hua University
Hsinchu, Taiwan 30013
wkmak@cs.nthu.edu.tw

ABSTRACT

The significantly increased number of routing design rules at sub-20nm nodes has made pin access one of the most critical challenges in detailed routing. Resolving pin access issues in detailed routing stage may be too late due to the fixed pin locations, especially in the area with high pin density. In placement stage when cell movement is allowed, the consideration of pin access has more flexibility. We propose a refinement stage after detailed placement to improve pin access. To respect the given placement solution, the refinement techniques are restricted to cell flipping, same-row adjacent cell swap, and cell shifting. A cost function is presented to model pin access for each pin-to-pin connection. Based on the cost function, two phases are proposed to improve pin access for all the connections simultaneously. In the first phase, we refine the placement by cell flipping and same-row adjacent cell swap. The problem is solved by dynamic programming row by row. In the second phase, only cell shifting is used, and a linear program is formulated to further refine the placement. Experimental results demonstrate that the proposed detailed placement refinement can improve pin access and reduce unroutable nets by about 33% in the detailed routing stage.

1. INTRODUCTION

With increasing number of design rules in advanced technology nodes, detailed routing (DR) is becoming more and more difficult. Pin access is one of the most critical problems [1, 2]. To alleviate pin access difficulty, the choice of tapping point is important during DR. Fig. 1 shows the pin access issue for a standard cell containing three pins a, b, and c. Each pin has several tapping points for via insertion to connect to a metal 2 wire segment. Suppose pins a, b, and c belong to nets A, B, and C respectively, and connection direction for each pin is pre-determined by global routing (GR) or steiner tree. DR is performed in the order of $A \rightarrow B \rightarrow C$. In Fig. 1(b), after routing nets A and B, all tapping points of pin c are blocked by other routes. There is no way to connect pin c to a metal 2 wire segment, which

ISPD '17, March 19-22, 2017, Portland, OR, USA
© 2017 ACM. ISBN 978-1-4503-4696-2/17/03. . . $15.00
DOI: http://dx.doi.org/10.1145/3036669.3036679

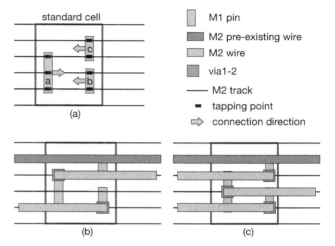

Figure 1: Detailed routing around pins in a standard cell. (a) A standard cell with three pins. (b) Pin C cannot be accessed because all its tapping points are blocked. (c) A wise choice of tapping points makes all pins accessible.

leads to a pin access failure. With a wise choice of tapping points as shown in Fig. 1(c), all three pins can be accessed in DR.

However, choosing tapping points wisely during DR is not always sufficient due to the fixed cell placement. In the area with high pin density, pin access may still be impossible even with a careful choice of tapping points. As shown in Fig. 2(a), the standard cell SC_a is placed abutting to the left boundary of standard cell SC_b. Thus, pins are very close to each other, especially for pins D and E, which potentially increase pin access difficulty. Fig. 2(b) shows DR around the two standard cells. Both of pin E's tapping points are blocked by metal 2 wire segments, which used to access pin D and pin E. As a result, pin access for pin E is not possible.

To further improve pin accessibility, we propose a refinement stage after the detailed placement (DP) stage, in which small perturbation of a given DP is allowed. Fig. 3 shows the three possible options of refining the placement to improve pin access. In Fig. 3(a), cell SC_b shifts to the right to make some space between SC_a and SC_b. Then, a via can be inserted at the top tapping point of pin D, and there is enough space to form a metal 2 wire segment from the tapping point. By utilizing both metal 2 and metal 3 wire segments, pin access for pin D is not the bottleneck

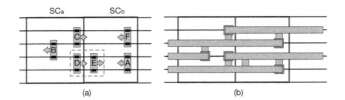

Figure 2: Enhance pin accessibility in DR. (a) Pin access becomes harder within area with high pin density. (b) Pin E cannot be accessed even with careful choice of tapping points

in DR anymore. In Fig. 3(b), cell SC_b is flipped, and all pins can be easily accessed during DR. Finally, in Fig. 3(c), two cells are swapped, and pins are better distributed with more space in between than in Fig. 2(a). Thus, pin access becomes easier and DR can be completed with less efforts. From the examples above, we observe pin access can be effectively improved by cell shifting, cell flipping, and adjacent cell swap. Thus, we propose a detailed placement refinement stage which directly targets at pin accessibility enhancement

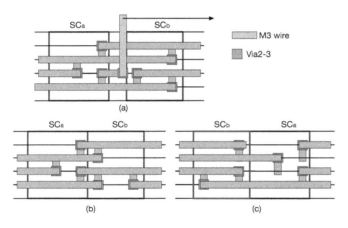

Figure 3: Three approaches to enhance pin accessibility in DP (a) Cell shifting. (b) Cell flipping. (c) Adjacent cell swap.

Pin access is considered in DR stage [3, 4, 5, 6, 7, 8]. [3, 4, 5, 6] proposed standard cell-level pin access planning under SADP lithography constraints. [7] addressed offgrid or gridless pin access while [8] tackled escape routing for a dense pin cluster. Pin access is also considered in the GR stage in the form of local routing congestion estimation [9, 10, 11]. However, they only took into account pin information, like pin count, pin shape, and pin's Steiner tree length, which fails to capture the real pin access scenario during DR. Furthermore, in both GR and DR stages, cell placement cannot be changed and all pin locations are fixed. Even with the proposed techniques in works above, pin access may still be impossible which leads to failed connection. To overcome such limitation, detailed routing is considered during placement. The recent ISPD placement contest [12] demonstrates that physical data, like pin geometries, is important, and needs to be considered in placement to improve routability in DR. Furthermore, routing congestion is con-

sidered during DP [13, 14, 15]. The models to estimate congestion in [13, 14] are very rough, especially for local routing congestion, and pin access problem is not directly addressed. [15] included pin information in the cost function to guide detailed placement. However, the pin information are not enough to model pin access in DR accurately.

Our major contributions are summarized as follows:
- It is the first work to directly consider pin access issue in detailed placement stage.
- We propose an accurate model to capture the pin access scenario during detailed routing. A cost function is used to guide the detailed placement refinement.
- The placement refinement operations are limited to cell flipping, adjacent cell swap, and cell shifting. Meanwhile, the proposed algorithm is dynamic programing and linear programing based. Thus, our DP refinement ensures a fast runtime without a big perturbation of the given legalized placement.
- The experimental results demonstrate that by applying the DP refinement, unroutable nets can be significantly reduced in DR. Moveover, the total cell displacement is kept in control and overheads in total wirelength, via count and runtime are low.

The rest of the paper is organized as follows. Section 2 presents some preliminaries. Section 3 is the problem formulation. The overall flow and details of our proposed algorithm are presented in Section 4. Section 5 shows ours experimental results, and finally Section 6 concludes the paper.

2. PRELIMINARIES

2.1 Assumptions

In the following, we present our DP refinement approach under a few assumptions. Note that our approach is general and is not limited to these assumptions. It can be easily extended to handle different assumptions.

In typical designs, the majority of pins occur on metal 1 layer, where the available routing resources are extremely limited. Meanwhile, 1D gridded design has become the mainstream in advanced technology nodes [16]. Each metal layer has a routing direction, either horizontal or vertical. Without loss of generality, we assume metal 1 layer is not allowed for routing, metal 2 has horizontal routing direction, metal 3 has vertical routing direction, and so on. We also assume each pin in the cell is either a rectangle strip or a rectilinear shape spanning one or more metal 2 tracks. A tapping point (TP) is defined as the overlap of a metal 2 track and the pin shape, where a via can be inserted to connect the pin to a metal 2 wire segment.

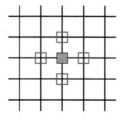

Figure 4: The minimum center-to-center spacing rule in via design rules.

In 1D gridded design, changing the routing direction means switching to another metal layer and via insertion between the layers. Thus, maintaining via design rules in DR is critical to both routing solution quality and layout manufacturing. For example, the minimum center-to-center via spacing is one of the major via design rules [17]. In this paper, the minimum center-to-center via spacing is assumed to be more than one routing pitch, and it is enforced for every via layer. As shown in Fig. 4, an via is inserted on the via layer between metal 1 and metal 2. Thus, the four via locations on the same via layer represented by purple empty squares are forbidden. Note that the assumed via design rules can be easily extended to other complex via design rules, e.g., multiple patterning constraints on via layer pattern [18].

2.2 Pin access region

Pin access is to select a tapping point as the via insertion location to connect the pin to a wire segment on metal 2. The wire segment is preferred to extend in the connection direction in order to move closer to the other pin of this connection. We define a pin access region (PAR) for each pin-to-pin connection of each pin. It is a bounding box, whose height is same as the pin shape and width is same as the horizontal distance between the two connected pins. PAR_{AB} denotes the PAR of connection AB of pin A, and $w_{PAR_{AB}}$ is the width of the PAR_{AB}. Fig. 5 shows totally four PARs of two pin-to-pin connections. The connection AB connects two pins from cells in a same standard cell row, we call it same-row pin-to-pin connection. On the other hand, connection CD is a different-row pin-to-pin connection since the two pins are from cells in different standard cell rows.

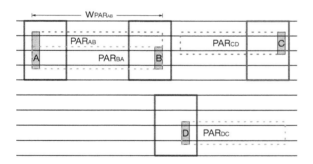

Figure 5: A PAR is defined for each pin-to-pin connection of each pin. Connection AB is a same-row connection while connection CD is a different-row connection.

2.3 Pin access penalty

If the PAR of a connection of a pin is obstructed by an object (e.g., blockage or metal 2 wire segment), the pin access to the pin in this connection is affected negatively. We use a penalty function to quantify the impact on the pin access, which is shown in Fig. 6. In penalty function $f_w(dist)$, input $dist$ is the horizontal distance between the pin and the object, and parameter w is the width of the PAR. For a same-row connection, e.g., connection AB in Fig. 5, it is desirable to have a single metal 2 wire segment to connect the two pins in DR. Fig. 6(a) shows the penalty function for this case. It always outputs the maximum penalty, namely 1, to

penalize any object within the PAR, i.e., when $dist$ value is smaller than w. When $dist$ is larger than w, i.e., the PAR does not intersect with the object, the output value of penalty function is zero. For a different-row connection, e.g., connection CD in Fig. 5, a router has the flexibility to choose a turning point within PAR to switch to metal 3 in DR. Fig. 6(b) shows the corresponding penalty function where min_l is the minimum length value for a metal 2 wire segment. When $dist$ is less than min_l, the space to form a metal 2 wire segment for pin access is occupied by the object. Thus, the penalty function outputs the maximum penalty 1. The penalty decreases with increasing $dist$ since the DR will then has more flexibility in pin access. Mathematically, when $dist \leq w$, $f_w(dist)$ is in the form of $\frac{\alpha}{dist} + \beta$, where parameters α and β are set so that $f_w(min_l) = 1$ and $f_w(u$
w, tl
$f_w(d$

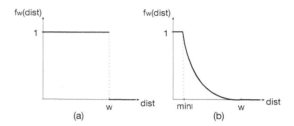

Figure 6: Penalty function $f_w(dist)$ for (a) same-row connection, and (b) different-row connection.

Given a connection of a pin, the pin access penalty (PAP) is a cost imposed on the connection to reflect the impact of an object on the pin access of the connection. The computation of PAP depends on the type of object and how the PAR of the connection intersects with the object. As shown in Fig. 7, there are totally four scenarios. Let's firstly consider the simplest scenario which is shown in Fig. 7(a). The $PAR_{AA'}$ of a connection AA' of pin A is intersected with a metal 2 blockage B. We say that connection AA' is in conflict with blockage B. $dist_{A.B}$ denotes the horizontal distance between pin A and blockage B. A conflict tapping point (CTP) is a TP on a metal 2 track which is obstructed by the blockage B. TP_A denotes the number of TPs of pin A. $CTP_{AA'.B}$ denotes the number of CTPs of pin A when connection AA' is in conflict with blockage B. In Fig. 7(a), $CTP_{AA'.B} = 2$, and they are highlighted with red color. In the first scenario, the pin access to pin A becomes harder since the routing resources used for pin access are occupied by blockage B. $PAP_{AA'}^B$ is the PAP cost imposed on connection AA' to model the increase in the hardness to access pin A.

$$PAP_{AA'}^B = \frac{CTP_{AA'.B}}{TP_A} \times f_{w_{PAR_{AA'}}}(dist_{A.B}) \quad (1)$$

$PAP_{AA'}^B = 0$ if access to pin A in the connection AA' is completely free from the impact of blockage B. $PAP_{AA'}^B = 1$ if the pin access is impossible through all pin A's TPs. $PAP_{AA'}^B$ consists of two components. One is the probability of the occupied routing resource will actually affect pin access, which is $\frac{CTP_{AA'.B}}{TP_A}$. The other is the penalty function to determine the negative impact on pin access, which is

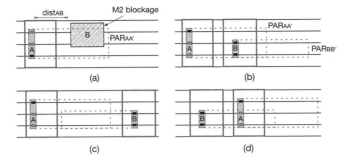

Figure 7: PAP in four scenarios. (a) 1st scenario. (b) 2nd scenario. (c) 3rd scenario. (d) 4th scenario.

$f_{w_{PAR_{AA'}}}(dist_{A.B})$. The penalty function used in the computation of $PAP_{AA'}^B$ depends on whether connection AA' is a same-row connection or a different-row connection as described earlier.

In other scenarios, the PAP cost is imposed on the connection AA' when its PAR intersects with the PAR of another connection. As shown in Fig. 7(b)(c)(d), there are three kinds of intersection which lead to the other three scenarios. Suppose the $PAR_{AA'}$ of connection AA' of pin A is intersected with the PAR of connection BB' of pin B. We say that connection AA' is in conflict with the connection BB'. The second scenario is when the connection directions of pin A and pin B are right and pin A is on the left side of pin B, or connection direction of pin A and pin B are left and pin A is on the right side of pin B. The third scenario is when the connection directions of pin A and pin B are different. The fourth scenario is when the connection directions of pin A and pin B are right and pin A is on the right side of pin B, or connection directions of pin A and pin B are left and pin A is on the left side of pin B. $PAP_{AA'}^{BB'}$ is the PAP cost imposed on connection AA' due to conflicting connection BB'. $PAP_{AA'}^{BB'}$ for the three scenarios are shown as follows.

$$PAP_{AA'}^{BB'} = \frac{CTP_{AA'.BB'}}{TP_A \times TP_B} f_{w_{PAR_{AA'}}}(dist_{A.B}) \quad (2)$$

$$PAP_{AA'}^{BB'} = \frac{CTP_{AA'.BB'}}{TP_A \times TP_B} f_{w_{PAR_{AA'}}} \left(\frac{w_{PAR_{AA'}}}{w_{PAR_{AA'}} + w_{PAR_{BB'}}} dist_{A.B} \right) \quad (3)$$

$$PAP_{AA'}^{BB'} = \frac{CTP_{AA'.BB'}}{TP_A \times TP_B} f_{w_{PAR_{BB'}}}(dist_{A.B}) \quad (4)$$

Similar to $PAP_{AA'}^B$, $PAP_{AA'}^{BB'}$ is a product of a probability term and a penalty function. The penalty function used in the computation also depends on the type of connection AA'.

The PAP function computes the PAP cost imposed on a connection due to a conflicting blockage or connection. For each connection AA', we can compute its total PAP cost $PAP_{AA'}$ imposed by all conflicting blockages and connections as follows.

$$PAP_{AA'} = \sum_{block \in CB} PAP_{AA'}^{block} + \sum_{conn \in CC} PAP_{AA'}^{conn} \quad (5)$$

where CB is the set of conflicting blockages with AA' and CC is the set of conflicting connections with AA'. Furthermore, we define $CPAP_c$ for each cell c as the total PAP cost

imposed on all the connections of all the pins in c.

$$CPAP_c = \sum_{A \in Pin_c} \sum_{AA' \in Conn_A} PAP_{AA'} \quad (6)$$

where $Conn_A$ denotes all the connections of pin A and Pin_c denotes all the pins in c. $CPAP_c$ reflects the pin accessibility for all the connections of all the pins in the cell c. It can be used to evaluate if the cell placement is good in terms of pin access. We are trying to refine the cell placement to improve pin access for all the connections. Thus, we define total cell pin access penalty (TCPAP) as the total PAP cost computed for all the connections in the placement.

$$TCPAP = \sum_{c \in All\_Cells} CPAP_c \quad (7)$$

3. PROBLEM FORMULATION

The TCPAP can be used to evaluate the pin accessibility of a detailed placement. Our proposed DP refinement is targeted to improve pin access by minimizing the TCPAP. Below is our formal problem statement.

Given an legalized placement solution, we try to refine the placement solution to enhance pin accessibility and improve routability during detailed routing stage. The refinement techniques are limited to cell flipping, cell shifting, and adjacent cell swap. The objective is to minimize TCPAP while DP perturbation during refinement is kept minimal. Furthermore, the quality of detailed routing solution in terms of total wirelength and via count for refined placement solution should be good. The constraint is the placement solution should still be legal after refinement.

4. PROPOSED REFINEMENT ALGORITHM

4.1 Algorithm framework

Fig. 8 shows the framework of our pin accessibility-driven detailed placement refinement. The input is a legalized detailed placement solution, we target to improve pin access in DR by refining the placement. To keep the detailed placement perturbation minimal, we limit our refinement techniques to cell flipping, same-row adjacent cell swap, and cell shifting. Our DP refinement has two phases. In the first phase, we refine the placement by cell flipping and same-row adjacent cell swap. It is solved by dynamic programming row by row. In the second phase, we further refine placement by cell shifting. It is solved by linear programming. The output is the refined and legalized placement. It is ready for routing, and expected to have better pin access in DR.

4.2 Phase 1: Cell flipping and adjacent cell swap

In this phase, we try to refine an initial placement by cell flipping and adjacent cell swap to minimize TCPAP. To compute $PAP_{AA'}$ for a connection AA' of a pin A from cell c, we make an assumption that the PAP due to the connections conflicting with AA' but not containing a pin in cell c or a cell adjacent to c is not significantly affected by cell flipping and adjacent cell swap. By ignoring those conflicting connections, $PAP_{AA'}$ can be approximated as follows:

$$PAP_{AA'} \approx \sum_{block \in CB} PAP_{AA'}^{block} + \sum_{conn \in CC'} PAP_{AA'}^{conn} \quad (8)$$

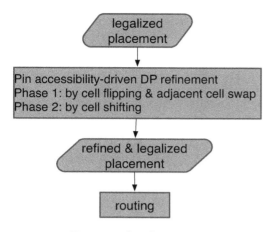

Figure 8: Our framework

where CB is the set of the conflicting blockages with AA', and CC' is the set of conflicting connections with AA' which contain a pin in cell c or a cell adjacent to c. Based on the above approximation, we can solve the problem by dynamic programming row by row. For each row, the dynamic programming helps to find the optimal cell placement to minimize $\sum_{c \in C_{row}} CPAP_c$ where C_{row} denotes the set of all cells in the row. Given $TCPAP = \sum_{row \in All\_Rows} \sum_{c \in C_{row}} CPAP_c$, TCPAP can be minimized. In the following paragraph, we will discuss how an optimal cell placement for a given row of cells is found by dynamic programming.

Given a placement row with n placed cells, we denote the cells as c_1 to c_n according to their order in the original placement. We use c'_k to denote the flipped version of c_k. We use dynamic programming to compute the optimal refined prefix placement of length k for $k = 1, 2, ..., n$ where refinement by cell flipping and adjacent cell swap is allowed. Let $sol_k(\gamma)$ denotes the optimal refined prefix placement of length k when the cell in the k-th position is γ. Since we only allow cell flipping and adjacent cell swap in this phase, the cell γ in $sol_k(\gamma)$ is either c_k, c'_k, c_{k-1}, c'_{k-1}, c_{k+1}, or c'_{k+1}. Let $P_k(\gamma)$ denotes the total CPAP of cells in $sol_k(\gamma)$. To construct $sol_{k+1}(\theta)$, we append a cell θ to the end of $sol_k(\gamma)$, and use $\Delta P(\gamma, \theta)$ to denote the change of total CPAP. Observe that to construct all $sol_{k+1}(\theta)$ where θ could be c_{k+1}, c'_{k+1}, c_k, c'_k, c_{k+2}, and c'_{k+2}, six solutions are required including $sol_k(c_k)$, $sol_k(c'_k)$, $sol_k(c_{k-1})$, $sol_k(c'_{k-1})$, $sol_k(c_{k+1})$, and $sol_k(c'_{k+1})$. Specifically, for each case of $sol_{k+1}(\theta)$, we find the corresponding solution above and compute total CPAP after appending θ to the end of solution. The newly constructed solution with minimum total CPAP value is $sol_{k+1}(\theta)$.

Here is an example of how to construct intermediate solutions containing refined prefix placement of length k when $k = 5$. Firstly, to construct $sol_5(c_5)$, we append c_5 at the end of $sol_4(c_4)$, $sol_4(c'_4)$, $sol_4(c_3)$, and $sol_4(c'_3)$, respectively. Then, we compute $P_4(c_4) + \Delta P(c_4, c_5)$, $P_4(c'_4) + \Delta P(c'_4, c_5)$, $P_4(c_3) + \Delta P(c_3, c_5)$, and $P_4(c'_3) + \Delta P(c'_3, c_5)$ for all the newly constructed solutions. The $P_5(c_5)$ is the minimum of the above values, and the newly constructed solution with the minimum of the above values is $sol_5(c_5)$. Similarly, other refined prefix placement of length 5, which could be $sol_5(c'_5)$, $sol_5(c_4)$, $sol_5(c'_4)$, $sol_5(c_6)$, and $sol_5(c'_6)$, can be constructed.

The base cases and recursive formulas of our dynamic program are shown as follows.

Base cases:
$$\{P_1(c_1), \ P_1(c'_1), \ P_1(c_2), \ P_1(c'_2)\}$$
where each case is obtained by computing total CPAP for initial solutions $sol_1(c_1)$, $sol_1(c_{1'})$, $sol_1(c_2)$, and $sol_1(c_{2'})$.

Recursive formulas:
$$P_k(c_k) = min \ \{ \ P_{k-1}(c_{k-1}) + \Delta P(c_{k-1}, c_k),$$
$$P_{k-1}(c'_{k-1}) + \Delta P(c'_{k-1}, c_k),$$
$$P_{k-1}(c_{k-2}) + \Delta P(c_{k-2}, c_k),$$
$$P_{k-1}(c'_{k-2}) + \Delta P(c'_{k-2}, c_k) \ \}$$

$$P_k(c'_k) = min \ \{ \ P_{k-1}(c_{k-1}) + \Delta P(c_{k-1}, c_{k'}),$$
$$P_{k-1}(c'_{k-1}) + \Delta P(c'_{k-1}, c_{k'}),$$
$$P_{k-1}(c_{k-2}) + \Delta P(c_{k-2}, c_{k'}),$$
$$P_{k-1}(c'_{k-2}) + \Delta P(c'_{k-2}, c_{k'}) \ \}$$

$$P_k(c_{k-1}) = min \ \{ \ P_{k-1}(c_k) + \Delta P(c_k, c_{k-1}),$$
$$P_{k-1}(c'_k) + \Delta P(c'_k, c_{k-1}) \ \}$$

$$P_k(c'_{k-1}) = min \ \{ \ P_{k-1}(c_k) + \Delta P((c_k, c'_{k-1}),$$
$$P_{k-1}(c'_k) + \Delta P(c'_k, c'_{k-1}) \ \}$$

$$P_k(c_{k+1}) = min \ \{ \ P_{k-1}(c_{k-1}) + \Delta P(c_{k-1}, c_{k+1}),$$
$$P_{k-1}(c'_{k-1}) + \Delta P(c'_{k-1}, c_{k+1}),$$
$$P_{k-1}(c_{k-2}) + \Delta P(c_{k-2}, c_{k+1}),$$
$$P_{k-1}(c'_{k-2}) + \Delta P(c'_{k-2}, c_{k+1}) \ \}$$

$$P_k(c'_{k+1}) = min \ \{ \ P_{k-1}(c_{k-1}) + \Delta P(c_{k-1}, c'_{k+1}),$$
$$P_{k-1}(c'_{k-1}) + \Delta P(c'_{k-1}, c'_{k+1}),$$
$$P_{k-1}(c_{k-2}) + \Delta P(c_{k-2}, c'_{k+1}),$$
$$P_{k-1}(c'_{k-2}) + \Delta P(c'_{k-2}, c'_{k+1}) \ \}$$

Finally, we construct $sol_n(c_n)$, $sol_n(c'_n)$, $sol_n(c_{n-1})$, and $sol_n(c'_{n-1})$, and compute their corresponding $P_n(c_n)$, $P_n(c'_n)$, $P_n(c_{n-1})$, and $P_n(c'_{n-1})$ for the given row. The minimum value of $\sum_{c \in C_{row}} CPAP_c$ is equal to $min\{ P_n(c_n), P_n(c'_n), P_n(c_{n-1}), P_n(c'_{n-1}) \}$. The optimal refined cell placement for the given row is the solution with the minimum value of $\sum_{c \in C_{row}} CPAP_c$.

4.3 Phase 2: Cell shifting

In this phase, we try to further refine the placement by cell shifting. As mentioned before, cell shifting helps to redistribute the space between the cells, which will potentially improve pin access in DR. We continue to use the proposed PAP function to guide the refinement. However, we need to keep the cell displacement in control to avoid big perturbation of the given legalized placement. We solve this problem by formulating a linear program (LP). Given the refined placement after phase 1, we label all the cells in the i-th row from left to right as $cell_{i1}$, $cell_{i2}$, ..., $cell_{in}$. For $cell_{ij}$, let L_{ij} denote the x coordinate of its bottom left corner, and W_{ij} denote its width. In addition, let LL and RR be the x coordinates of the left and right boundaries of the placement region, respectively. Suppose a pin A in $cell_{ij}$ has a connection AA'. Let bk denote a block which is in conflict with connection AA'. $dist_{A.bk}$ is the distance between A and bk. Similarly, let BB' denote a connection of pin B which is in conflict with connection AA'. $dist_{A.B}$ is the distance between A and B. We use a continuous variable δ_{ij} to represent the shift amount for $cell_{ij}$. To avoid a big amount of shift, we set ΔS as the maximum shift distance for every cell. For the connection AA', the width of its PAR changes by δ_{ij} during the cell shifting. Meanwhile, both $dist_{A.bk}$ and $dist_{A.B}$ also change by δ_{ij}. Other parameters in the equations (1)(2)(3)(4) in Section 2.3 to compute PAP remain the same. Hence, the equations to compute PAP become functions of δ_{ij} during cell shifting.

However, the PAP function is non-linear when AA' is a different-row connection. To formulate the problem as a LP, we use linear approximation to approximate the new penalty cost computed by the PAP functions after cell shifting. The linear functions of δ_{ij} used to approximate the PAP functions for connection AA' during cell shifting are shown as follows.

$$\widetilde{PAP}_{AA'}^{bk}(\delta_{ij}) = \alpha \times \delta_{ij} + \beta \qquad (9)$$

where $\alpha = \frac{\partial \widetilde{PAP}_{AA'}^{bk}}{\partial \delta_{ij}}|_{\delta_{ij}=0}$ and $\beta = \widetilde{PAP}_{AA'}^{bk}|_{\delta_{ij}=0}$.

$$\widetilde{PAP}_{AA'}^{BB'}(\delta_{ij}) = \alpha\prime \times \delta_{ij} + \beta\prime \qquad (10)$$

where $\alpha\prime = \frac{\partial \widetilde{PAP}_{AA'}^{BB'}}{\partial \delta_{ij}}|_{\delta_{ij}=0}$ and $\beta\prime = \widetilde{PAP}_{AA'}^{BB'}|_{\delta_{ij}=0}$. The δ_{ij} is controlled by ΔS which is usually small in practice (several routing pitches). The approximation is usually accurate enough to be used to compute PAP during cell shifting. Thus, we can approximate TCPAP by a linear function $\sum_{AA'\in C}(\sum_{bk\in CB}\widetilde{PAP}_{AA'}^{bk} + \sum_{BB'\in CC}\widetilde{PAP}_{AA'}^{BB'})$, where CB is a set of blockages in conflict with AA', CC is a set of connections in conflict with AA', and C contains all the connections of all the pins in all the cells in the placement. Below is the LP formulation for refinement phase 2.

Objective:

$$Min \sum_{AA'\in C}(\sum_{bk\in CB}\widetilde{PAP}_{AA'}^{bk} + \sum_{BB'\in CC}\widetilde{PAP}_{AA'}^{BB'})$$

Constraints:

C1: For the leftmost cell c_{i1} in row_i,

$$L_{i1} + \delta_{i1} \geq LL$$

C2: For the rightmost cell c_{in} in row_i,

$$L_{in} + \delta_{in} + W_{in} \leq RR$$

C3: For two adjacent cells c_{ij} and $c_{i(j+1)}$ in row_i,

$$L_{ij} + \delta_{ij} + W_{ij} \leq L_{i(j+1)} + \delta_{i(j+1)}$$

C4: For each c_{ij},

$$\delta_{ij} \leq \Delta S \text{ and } \delta_{ij} \geq -\Delta S$$

C1 (C2) ensures that the leftmost (rightmost) cell in each row is not shifted out of left (right) boundary. C3 ensures that no two adjacent cells in the same row are overlapped after cell shifting. Finally, C4 makes sure each cell cannot shift more than the pre-set threshold.

5. EXPERIMENTAL RESULTS

We implemented our pin accessibility-driven detailed placement refinement by C++ programming language. All experiments are performed on a machine with 2.4 GHz Intel Core i5 and 8GB memory. Gurobi 6.0.5 is called to solve the LP in refinement phase 2. As mentioned before, this is the first work to directly consider pin access in DP stage. We derive

our benchmarks based on the netlist and placement information that the authors of [5] used to construct their detailed routing benchmarks. Every net with m pins is decomposed into $m-1$ pin-to-pin connections. Meanwhile, the connection direction of the pin in each connection are determined. In a few standard cells, we found that some pins from metal 1 have only a single TP, and the distance between these TPs is less than the required assumed minimum center-to-center via spacing. Thus, pin access is impossible for these pins due to the constraint of via design rules. Thus, we elongate these pins to increase their TP counts. Table I shows the statistics for each benchmark, including cell count, the number of pin-to-pin connections, and average TP count of all the pins.

Table 1: Statistics of benchmarks

Benchmark	ecc	efc	ctl	alu	div	top
#Cells	1302	1197	1715	1802	3260	12576
#Connections	1615	2872	3308	3261	5847	18618
ave. #TPs	3.02	3.21	3.39	3.28	3.27	3.03

Table II shows the results of our pin accessibility-driven detailed placement refinement. TCPAP is computed for the given legalized placement, placement after refinement phase 1, and placement after refinement phases 1 and 2 respectively. Note that only one iteration of dynamic programming is performed in phase 1 and one iteration of LP is performed in phase 2. Compared with the given placement, the refinement phase 1 can reduce TCPAP by 15% on average over all the benchmarks. In refinement phase 2, we set ΔS to $3 \times p$ in the LP formulation, where p is the pitch size of metal 1 vertical tracks. It can further reduce the TCPAP by another 3%. One of the objectives for our DP refinement is to keep the change of the given placement small. To measure the difference between refined placement and given placement, we also report the average cell displacement and the flipped cell count, which are represented as "Ave. Disp." and "#FCs" in Table II. The average cell displacement is defined as $\frac{\sum_{c_i \in Cells}|x_i-x_i'|}{Cell|\times p}$, where $Cells$ denotes the set of all the cells in the given placement, x_i' denotes c_i's x coordinate in the given placement, x_i is c_i's x coordinate after refinement. In phase 1, the cell displacement is due to adjacent cell swap, and on average cells are displaced from their original location by 5.04 metal 1 pitch size. Meanwhile, on average 33.56% of all the cells are flipped after refinement phase 1. After refinement phases 1 and 2, on average, cells are displaced from the original placement by 6.73 metal 1 pitch size. As shown in Table II, our DP refinement is very fast and takes only 13.14 seconds on average over all the benchmarks.

Next we will demonstrate that our pin accessibility-driven DP refinement really improves pin access and reduces unroutable nets in DR. Table III compares the detailed routing solutions for the given placement, the placement after refinement phase 1, and the placement after refinement phases 1 and 2. The state-of-the-art SID-type SADP-aware detailed router from [19] is applied to route each placement. There are totally four layers, where metal 1 layer is not allowed for routing, metal 2 and metal 4 has horizontal routing direction, metal 3 has vertical routing direction. We report in Table III total wirelength, via count, the number of unroutable nets (#UNs), and detailed routing runtime. Com-

Table 2: Comparison between the given placement and the placements after refinement

	Given placement	After refinement phase 1				After refinement phases 1 and 2		
Benchmark	TCPAP	TCPAP	Ave. Disp.	#FCs (pct %)	CPU(s)	TCPAP	Ave. Disp.	CPU(s)
ecc	2469.41	2108.51	5.65	500 (38.40)	4.25	2070.43	7.40	5.01
efc	3926.39	3472.32	5.20	438 (36.59)	5.66	3419.43	7.04	6.56
ctl	3327.58	2912.31	5.33	557 (32.48)	6.04	2874.78	7.18	7.00
alu	3409.91	2848.64	3.59	549 (30.47)	5.55	2849.36	5.14	5.80
div	7044.60	6659.68	5.40	1059 (32.48)	11.13	6119.21	6.99	12.48
top	18909.70	15236.80	5.08	3892 (30.95)	39.68	14823.90	6.61	41.96
Ave.	6514.60	5539.71	5.04	1165.83 (33.56)	12.05	5359.52	6.73	13.14
Nor.	1.00	0.85	1.00		1.00	0.82	1.33	1.09

Table 3: Comparison of the detailed routing results for the given and the refined placements.

	Given placement				Placement after refinement phase 1				Placement after refinement phases 1 and 2			
Benchmark	WL	#Vias	#UNs	CPU(s)	WL	#Vias	#UNs	CPU(s)	WL	#Vias	#UNs	CPU(s)
ecc	104016	10710	158	109.67	113015	11041	120	163.09	118717	11305	84	123.99
efc	85030	11446	162	106.26	95256	11719	102	87.09	101314	11852	92	84.17
ctl	111746	12936	139	109.39	121619	13501	104	134.08	127986	13668	89	98.58
alu	92117	12807	177	91.47	96823	12854	141	107.31	103084	13318	150	149.16
div	180061	23865	258	261.12	199196	24573	218	251.41	209648	25056	202	360.94
top	808978	73058	899	1181.68	855856	74521	743	1220.30	892590	76171	588	1314.92
Ave.	230324.67	24137.00	298.83	309.93	246960.83	24701.50	238.00	327.21	25889.83	25228.33	200.83	355.29
Nor.	1.00	1.00	1.00	1.00	1.07	1.02	0.80	1.06	1.12	1.05	0.67	1.15

pared with the routing for the given placement, the number of unroutable nets can be reduced by 20% on average in DR for placement with refinement phase 1. Meanwhile, the wirelength, via count, and runtime are increased by 7%, 2%, and 6%, respectively. Note that part of the increase is due to the increase in number of routable nets in DR for placement with refinement phase 1. With our DP refinement phases 1 and 2, the number of unroutable nets can be reduced by 33% on average in DR. The wirelength, via count, and runtime are increased by 12%, 5%, and 15%, respectively. In conclusion, the TCPAP used to evaluate the pin accessibility in DP stage is accurate. Our dynamic programming and linear programming based refinement techniques can effectively improve pin access and reduce the number of unroutable nets in DR.

6. CONCLUSION

In this paper, we propose a detailed placement refinement stage after detailed placement. It directly targets to improve pin accessibility during detailed routing stage. One of the future works is to extend our pin accessibility-driven detailed placement refinement to handle standard cells with different row heights for wider industrial applications.

7. REFERENCES

[1] Xiang Qiu and Malgorzata Marek-Sadowska. Can pin access limit the footprint scaling. In *Proc. of DAC*, June 2012.

[2] M. Hsu, N. Katta, H. Lin, K. Lin, K. Tam, and K. Wang. Design and manufacturing process co-optimization in nano-technology. In *Proc. of ICCAD*, November 2014.

[3] X. Xu, G. Yeric B. Cline, B. Yu, and D. Pan. Self-aligned double patterning aware pin access and standard cell layout co-optimization. In *Proc. of ISPD*, March 2014.

[4] X. Xu, G. Yeric B. Cline, B. Yu, and D. Pan. Self-aligned double patterning aware pin access and standard cell layout co-optimization. *IEEE Trans. Computer-Aided Design Integrated Circuits Systems*, 34, 2015.

[5] X. Xu, B. Yu, J. Gao, C. Hsu, and D. Pan. PARR: Pin access planning and regular routing for self-aligned double patterning. In *Proc. of DAC*, June 2015.

[6] X. Xu, B. Yu, J. Gao, C. Hsu, and D. Pan. PARR: Pin access planning and regular routing for self-aligned double patterning. *ACM Transactions on Design Automation of Electronic Systems*, 21, 2016.

[7] Tim Nieberg. Gridless pin access in detailed routing. In *Proc. of DAC*, June 2011.

[8] Muhammet Ozdal. Detailed-routing algorithms for dense pin clusters in integrated circuits. *IEEE Transactions on Computer-Aided Design of Integrated Circuits and Systems*, 28, 2009.

[9] C.J. Alpert, Z. Li, C.N. Sze, and Y. Wei. Consideration of local routing and pin access during vlsi global routing, April 9 2013. US Patent 8,418,113.

[10] Z. Qi, Y. Cai, and Q. Zhou. Accurate prediction of detailed routing congestion using supervised data learning. In *Proc. of ICCAD*, March 2014.

[11] Y. Wei, C. Sze, N.Viswanathan, Z. Li, C. Alpert, L. Reddy, A. Huber, G. Tellez, D. Keller, and S.Sapatnekar. GLARE: Global and local wiring aware routability evaluation. In *Proc. of DAC*, Jun 2012.

[12] V. Yutsis, I. Bustany, D. Chinnery, J. Shinnerl, and W. Liu. ISPD 2014 benchmarks with sub-45nm technology rules for detailed-routing-driven placement. In *Proc. of ISPD*, March 2014.

[13] Yanheng Zhang and Chris Chu. CROP: Fast and effective congestion refinement of placement. In *Proc. of ICCAD*, March 2009.

[14] W.H. Liu, C. Koh, and Y. Li. Optimization of placement solutions for routability. In *Proc. of DAC*,

June 2013.

[15] T. Taghavi, C. Alpert, A.Huber, G. Nam Z. Li, and S. Ramji. New placement prediction and mitigation techniques for local routing congestion. In *Proc. of ICCAD*, March 2010.

[16] Y. Ding, C. Chu, and W.K. Mak. Throughput optimization for SADP and e-beam based manufacturing of 1d layout. In *Proc. of DAC*, June 2014.

[17] J. Cong, J. Fang, and K.Y. Khoo. Via design rule consideration in multilayer maze routing algorithms. *ACM Transactions on Design Automation of Electronic Systems*, 9, 2000.

[18] Y. Ding, C. Chu, and W.K. Mak. Self-aligned double patterning-aware detailed routing with double via insertion and via manufacturability consideration. In *Proc. of DAC*, June 2016.

[19] Y. Ding, C. Chu, and W. K. Mak. Self-aligned double patterning lithography aware detailed routing with color pre-assignment. *IEEE Transactions on Computer-Aided Design of Integrated Circuits and Systems*, 2016.

A Fast, Robust Network Flow-based Standard-Cell Legalization Method for Minimizing Maximum Movement

Nima Karimpour Darav
University of Calgary
nkarimpo@ucalgary.ca

Ismail S. Bustany
Mentor Graphics Corporation
ismail_bustany@mentor.com

Andrew Kennings
University of Waterloo
akenning@uwaterloo.ca

Laleh Behjat
University of Calgary
laleh@ucalgary.ca

ABSTRACT

The standard-cell placement legalization problem has become critical due to increasing design rule complexity and design utilization at 16nm and lower technology nodes. An ideal legalization approach should preserve the quality of the input placement in terms of routability and timing, as well as effectively manage white space availability and have low runtime. In this work, we present a robust legalization algorithm for standard cell placement that minimizes maximum cell movements fast and effectively based on a novel network-flow approach. The idea is inspired by path augmentation but with important differences. In contrast to the classical path augmentation approaches, we resolve bin overflows by finding several candidate paths that guarantee realizable (legal) flow solutions. In addition, we show how the proposed algorithm can be seamlessly extended to handle relevant cell edge spacing design rules. Our experimental results on the ISPD 2014 benchmarks illustrate that our proposed method yields 2.5x and 3.3x less maximum and average cell movement, respectively, and the runtime is significantly (18x) lower compared to best-in-class academic legalizers.

Keywords

Placement; Network flows; Legalization

1. INTRODUCTION

The standard-cell placement legalization problem has become more challenging because of complicated design rules and design utilization at 16nm and lower technology nodes. An ideal legalization method should remove all overlaps while satisfying delicate and complicated design rules with preserving the quality of the given placement provided by global placement or timing optimization steps. In other words, during the legalization step, not only the average cell movement but also maximum cell movement should be minimized. In

ISPD '17, March 19–22, 2017, Portland, OR, USA.
© 2017 ACM. ISBN 978-1-4503-4696-2/17/03. . . $15.00
DOI: http://dx.doi.org/10.1145/3036669.3036680

addition, the process must be fast and robust to handle the sheer number of cells in the state-of-the-art designs [1].

Available legalization methods are mainly categorized as: (i) heuristic algorithms and (ii) formal approaches. Most legalization methods [2–6] fall into the first group that resolve violations (such as cell overlaps) by exploiting a greedy search for moving cells located in violated areas to appropriate locations. Heuristic methods may lead to unnecessarily-large cell movement for designs with blockages or high utilization since they try to locally resolve violations instead of using a global approach.

On the other hand, formal approaches formulate the legalization problem as a mathematical model such as network flow [7, 8] or diffusion [9]. However, the resulting placement may still have overlaps and need another legalization step. In flow-based methods, legalization is modeled as a minimum-cost flow problem [10] where cells (flow) are moved between source and sink nodes for resolving overflowed bins while minimizing cell movement. The problem can be solved in polynomial time if all cells have the same size [7]. However, in practice, most designs have cells with different sizes for which the time complexity of the problem converts to NP-hard. In [7], in order to solve the problem using network flows, every cell is shredded into partial cells with a size equal to a unit, then the network flow formulation is solved. Afterward, the flow realization step is performed if cells need to move partially. If this step fails, a history learning approach is used to avoid the same flow in the next iterations. However, according the results reported in [7], on average the approach is more than 13 times slower than FastPlace [6] and is not appropriate to be used in an iterative process such as timing optimization. In BonnPlaceLegal [8], a modified version of the successive shortest path algorithm is presented. The algorithm iteratively computes shortest paths from source (overflowed) bins to sink bins using a variant of Dijkstra's algorithm [11]. At each augmentation, a shortest path is selected such that the path is able to sink all extra partial cells in the overflowed bin. The cost from one bin to another is computed as the total cost of moving partial cells from the source bin to the destination bin measured by the quadratic displacement. According to the results reported in [8], BonnPlaceLegal is competitive with other legalizers. However, it suffers from two main issues. First, BonnPlaceLegal may fail if there are some blockages or the placement has local areas with more than 100% utilization [1] because BonnPlaceLegal tries to resolve any overflowed bin through moving extra (partial) cells along only one path while no single path may exist to sink all extra partial cells. The authors in [8] have not reported any experiment on designs that have local areas with more than 100% uitization. Second, BonnPlaceLegal does not consider maximum cell movement for finding a shortest path because the cost is computed as the total quadratic displacement of the partial cells to be moved from a bin to another and the original positions of cells are not taken into account. Even if the cost is based on the original positions of cells, the issue will not be resolved because the algorithm works based on the total cost of cell movements for finding a shortest path and not the best possible paths leading to minimum maximum cell movement. In other words, there may be some solutions with higher cost (meaning that more cells are involved) but resulting in lower maximum cell displacement.

In this paper, we propose a flow-based approach for standard cell legalization inspired by path augmentation but with key differences. We iteratively resolve overflowed bins by finding several candidate paths for each overflowed bin and then moving (partial) cells along the identified paths. We consider maximum cell movement as a constraint in finding candidate paths since minimizing maximum cell movement is difficult to achieve during legalization. At each iteration, each candidate path satisfies the maximum movement value computed at that iteration. Using multiple paths in resolving an overflowed bin ensures that all extra partial cells in the bin can be moved along those paths. Our proposed approach offers several advantages compared with available legalization methods:

- The proposed algorithm can legalize complex designs, without facing any deadlock as all bins are connected to each other and there is at least one path from any bin to any other bin in the design.

- The proposed algorithm results in less maximum cell movement compared to available legalization methods because it directly considers maximum cell movement value for finding paths and moving cells along paths.

- The proposed algorithm results in less average cell movement because the proposed approach for realizing flow identifies candidate paths over which moving cells resolves overflowed bins. Therefore, it avoids cell movements that do not help to resolve overfilled bins.

- The proposed algorithm is able to legalize designs with high cell densities or designs having regions with high utilization (e.g. created after timing optimization during a place-and-route flow).

- The proposed algorithm can be used in iterative processes including timing optimization as the proposed approach is fast and applies the least perturbation on designs to resolve overfilled bins.

The rest of this paper is organized as follows: In Section 2, preliminaries related to legalization and network flow are presented. In Section 3, the proposed techniques are discussed. Experimental validations are presented in Section 4, and conclusions are provided in Section 5.

---

[1] After timing optimization, some local areas with more than 100% utilization may be created because of buffer sizing and inserting steps.

2. PRELIMINARIES

We assume that a chip is divided into horizontal partitions called rows with the same height h_r. The height of a standard-cell is equal to the height of a row. Let a segment s be the widest part of a row with no blockages. A row r may be divided into several segments segregated by blockages. Each segment is divided into smaller areas called bins V. A set $\Gamma(v)$ of (partial) cells can be assigned to a bin v. Each cell assigned to v is denoted by a pair $(c_\gamma, \delta_\gamma)$ of cell c_γ and a number $\delta_\gamma \in (0, 1]$. The number δ_γ determines what portion of cell c_γ is assigned to the bin. If $\delta_\gamma = 1$, it means that c_γ is completely assigned to the bin. In our algorithm, a cell may be partially assigned to two bins, if two bins are horizontally adjacent while a cell is not shared between two bins from two different rows. Let the width of a cell c_γ be width(c_γ). Hence, the total width of (partial) cells in a bin v is computed as $width(\Gamma(v)) = \sum_{\gamma \in \Gamma(v)} width(c_\gamma) * \delta_\gamma$. Let supply$(v) = max\{0, width(\Gamma(v)) - width(v)\}$ and demand$(v) = max\{0, width(v) - width(\Gamma(v))\}$. For a given bin v, if supply$(v) > 0$, the bin is overflowed and it is considered as a supply (source) bin. If demand$(v) > 0$, the bin is considered as a sink bin. Resolving all overflowed bins is the main objective of our proposed algorithm subject to several constraints that are described further in next sections.

3. PROPOSED ALGORITHM

The idea behind our proposed algorithm is inspired by the successive shortest path algorithm [10]. However, instead of minimizing maximum cell movement which is difficult to achieve, maximum cell movement θ is considered as an upper bound for moving cells. All candidate paths are identified under this upper bound at each iteration of our proposed algorithm. Hence, any cell move along a candidate path is applied if it satisfies the maximum cell movement constraint. Using the fact that the cost (distance) of every two bins are fixed, a modified version of Breadth-Search First (BFS) algorithm [12] is exploited to identify candidate paths satisfying the computed upper bound of cell movement instead of using Dijkstra's algorithm [11].

3.1 Algorithm Outline

The outline of our proposed legalization method is presented in Algorithm 1. First, all movable standard cells C are collected (line 1). In lines 2 and 3, the chip area is divided into a grid of bins V and bins are connected to each other through a set of edges E. Bins V are built upon the same method introduced in [8] with some modifications. Since a design may have some blockages, there are some bins with no connection to the right, left, top, or bottom sides; this can cause serious issues and the algorithm may fail. In order to cope with this issue, if a bin v has no connection in any direction because of blockages, the closest bin to bin v on the blocked direction is connected to the bin using an edge e. In contrast to BonnPlaceLegal [8], our method in connecting bins allows any possibility of flows and prevents deadlocks that may be caused by blockages.

In line 4, all movable cells C are assigned to bins V based on the closest Manhattan distance to the original positions of cells. If a cell is located on a blockage or outside of the chip area, it is assigned to a bin with the minimum Manhattan distance from the original position of the cell. If a cell overlaps with two bins, it is partially assigned to both bins.

Algorithm 1 Standard-Cell Legalization

Require: The circuit N is loaded into the memory.
1: $C = \text{collectStandardCells}(N)$
2: $V = \text{extractBins}(N)$
3: $E = \text{connectBins}(V)$
4: $\text{assignCellsToBins}(C, V)$
5: $iter = 0$
6: **repeat**
7:    $\theta = \text{computeMaxDisplacement}(iter)$
8:    $\Lambda = \text{identifyOverflowedBins}(V)$
9:    **for** each bin $v \in \Lambda$ **do**
10:       $P = $ identify candidate paths using Algorithm 2
11:       **for** each $p \in P$ **do**
12:          **if** $\text{supply}(v) > 0$ **then**
13:             Move cells over path p using Algorithm 3
14:          **end if**
15:       **end for**
16:    **end for**
17:    $iter = iter + 1$
18: **until** Λ is empty
19: **for** each $v \in V$ **do**
20:    $\text{removeCellOverlapsInBin}(v)$
21: **end for**
22: $S = \text{extractPlacementSegments}(N)$
23: $\text{assignCellsToSegments}(C, S)$
24: **for** each $s \in S$ **do**
25:    $\text{removeCellOverlapsInSegment}(s)$
26: **end for**

A cell cannot overlap with more than two bins as the width of any cell in the design is less than the width of any bin.

In lines 6-18, an iterative process is performed to compute maximum displacement and to identify and resolve all overflowed bins. In line 7, the upper bound for maximum cell movement is computed using the following linear equation:

$$\theta = max(\alpha * w_b + \beta * iter * w_b, h_b); \qquad (1)$$

where w_b and h_b in turn indicate the width and height of bins. $iter$ is the number of the current iteration. The parameters α and β are two constants which are set to 0.6 and 0.05 in our algorithm, respectively [2]. For computing θ, any non-decreasing function can be used. It can also be defined using a learning process based on the successful rate of each iteration. Regardless of the chosen function, the choice of θ at each iteration is a trade off between runtime and cell movement. If the rate of increasing θ is small, the runtime will increase because fewer candidate paths are identified, and hence, fewer overflowed bins are resolved at each iteration. On the contrary, if the rate of increasing θ is large, the quality of the solution degrades as more candidate paths are identified. Consequently, more cells are allowed to move.

In line 8, all overflowed bins are collected and saved into Λ. In contrast to BonnPlaceLegal [8], the quality of the final solution is mostly independent of the order of resolving overflowed bins because cell movements are limited by θ. After identifying overflowed bins, for each overflowed bin v, first a set of candidate paths P is realized and for each identified path p, cells are moved along the path p until bin v is no longer overfilled (lines 9-16). Details of lines 10 and 13 are in turn described in Sections 3.2 and 3.3. After resolving all overflowed bins, for each bin v, overlaps between cells assigned to bin v are removed using the graph-based approach introduced in [13] and the cell positions are updated (lines 19-21). Since there are some cells shared

---

Algorithm 2 Path Augmentation

Require: Set B of all bins, set E of all network flow edges, overflowed bin v, and maximum movement θ are given.
1: $demand_T = 0$
2: **for** each $b_i \in B$ **do**
3:    $\text{visited}(b_i) = $ false
4: **end for**
5: $\text{visited}(v) = $ true
6: Insert v into an empty path p
7: $\text{lastFlow}(p) = \min(\text{avgW}(v), \text{supply}(v))$
8: Insert path p into an empty queue Q
9: **repeat**
10:    dequeue path p from queue Q
11:    $b_{src} = $ the tail of path p
12:    $completePath = $ true
13:    **for** each bin b_i connected to bin b_{src} **do**
14:       **if** $\text{visited}(b_i) \; != $ true **then**
15:          $outFlow = \text{computeFlow}(b_{src}, b_i, \text{lastFlow}(p), \theta)$
16:          **if** $outFlow > 0$ **then**
17:             Create a copy p_i of path p
18:             $\text{lastFlow}(p_i) = outFlow$
19:             Insert bin b_i into path p_i
20:             **if** $\text{demand}(b_i) < outFlow$ **then**
21:                $addedCap = 0$
22:             **else**
23:                $addedCap = outFlow$
24:             **end if**
25:             **if** $completePath == $ true **then**
26:                $completePath = $ false
27:                $\text{cap}(p_i) = \text{cap}(p) + addedCap$
28:             **else**
29:                $\text{cap}(p_i) = addedCap$
30:             **end if**
31:             Insert path p_i into queue Q
32:             $demand_T = demand_T + addedCap$
33:             $\text{visited}(b_i) = $ true
34:          **end if**
35:       **end if**
36:    **end for**
37:    **if** $completePath == $ true **and** $\text{cap}(p) > 0$ **then**
38:       Insert p into the set P
39:    **end if**
40: **until** Q is empty **or** $\text{supply}(v) <= demand_T$
41: **for** each $p \in Q$ **do**
42:    **if** $\text{cap}(p) > 0$ **then**
43:       Insert p into the set P
44:    **end if**
45: **end for**

between two neighboring bins and need to be shifted based on the location of cells inside the bins, bins V are merged into placement segments, and then for each segment, cell overlaps are removed (lines 22-26).

3.2 Path Augmentation Algorithm

Algorithm 2 is the core of our proposed standard-cell legalization approach. It is inspired by path augmentation used in successive shortest path algorithm [10]. However, Algorithm 2 identifies multiple paths subject to three constraints: (i) any cell movement along the identified paths must be less than or equal to the computed maximum movement θ; (ii) there is at least one cell in each bin that can be moved to the next bin along the identified paths while satisfying the first constraint [3]; and (iii) the identified paths include bins with demand values greater than zero (there is some white space

---

[2] The values for α and β are determined empirically.

[3] In our algorithm, if the second constraint is not satisfied for a bin on path p, the path will no longer be allowed to grow and other candidate paths are explored.

along the path). The first constraint guarantees that no cell move leads to unnecessarily-long displacement while the second constraint avoids paths leading to a deadlock. Finally, the third constraint ensures that the entire or a portion of supply of the overflowed bin can be sunk along the identified paths.

In line 1 of Algorithm 2, $demand_T$, which is the total capacity of all identified paths, is set to zero. In Algorithm 2, each bin cannot be traversed more than once. Therefore, if a bin b_i is already visited (visited(b_i) == true), it will be ignored for the next steps. In lines 2-5, for each bin b_i, visited(b_i) is initialized. The overflowed bin v is inserted to an empty path p in line 6. Each path in Algorithm 2 is a queue of bins, whose first element is the overflowed bin v. For each path p, lastFlow(p) is used to save the flow between two last consecutive bins in the path. In line 7, lastFlow(p) is set to the minimum value of supply(v) and average width of cells assigned to bin v (avgW(v)) as there is only one element on the path.

Instead of using Dijkstra's algorithm, in Algorithm 2, a variant of BFS algorithm [12] is used to find candidate paths as the cost (distance) between every two bins is fixed during the process. For this reason, any partial path is saved into a queue Q. Lines 9-40 are repeated until the total demand ($demand_T$) provided by the traversed paths can sink supply(v). The last bin b_{src} of path p on the head of queue Q is determined in lines 10-11. For each bin b_i connected to bin b_{src}, a partial path p_i is created and inserted into queue Q if the new path p_i satisfies the three constraints and bin b_{src} is not already visited (lines 13-36). In line 15, the flow $outFlow$ of moving cells from b_{src} to b_i is computed based on maximum cell movement θ, lastFlow(p), and available white space in bin b_{src} (demand(b_{src})). For a certain flow (lastFlow(p)) into b_{src}, an amount of flow out of b_{src} to b_i is computed. In computeFlow, if lastFlow(p) is completely sunk by b_{src}, it will return zero and bin b_i is ignored in line 16 of Algorithm 2. Otherwise, all cells in b_{src} are sorted in order of ascending distance of the original positions of cells from the center of bin b_i. Any cell with a distance greater than θ is removed from the sorted list. Then, a set of (partial) cells Γ_i with minimum total width is found such that the following constraint is satisfied to ensure that no new overflowed bin is created:

$$width(\Gamma_i) >= lastFlow(p) - demand(b_{src}) \qquad (2)$$

In lines 20-24, if the computed flow $outFlow$ can be completely sunk by bin b_i, $outFlow$ will be considered as the available capacity of bin b_i along path p_i. Otherwise, no capacity is considered for bin b_i because path p_i cannot sink all flow. If path p is a partial path of multiple paths, the capacity of path p is ignored for the current path p_i (lines 25-30) because we do not want to overestimate the available capacity on each path. In lines 37-39, if path p does not lead to any new path and its capacity is greater than zero, it will be added into the set P as one of the candidate paths.

Finally, any path p left in queue Q is considered as one of the candidate paths if it's capacity is greater than zero (lines 41-45).

3.3 Moving Cells Along Paths

Cells are moved along a path p using Algorithm 3. In lines 1-12 of Algorithm 3, for every two consecutive bins b_{src} and b_{sink} along path p, the possible flow(b_{src},b_{sink}) is

---

Algorithm 3 Cell Move
***
Require: Set B of all bins, set E of all network flow edges, path p and the maximum movement θ are given.
1: dequeue bin b_{src} from path p
2: lastFlow(p)=min(avgW(b_{src}), supply(b_{src}))
3: Insert bin b_{src} into a stack Z
4: **while** p is not empty **do**
5:     dequeue bin b_{sink} from path p
6:     flow(b_{src},b_{sink}) = computeFlow(b_{src}, b_{sink}, lastFlow(p), θ)
7:     **if** flow(b_{src},b_{sink}) == 0 **then**
8:         **break**
9:     **end if**
10:     $b_{src} = b_{sink}$
11:     Insert bin b_{sink} into stack Z
12: **end while**
13: Pop bin b_{sink} from stack Z
14: **while** Z is not empty **do**
15:     Pop bin b_{src} from stack Z
16:     Sort cells in bin b_{src} in order of the closest to bin b_{sink}
17:     **if** Partial cell moves are available **then**
18:         Move sorted cells (partial cells) one-by-one from b_{src} to b_{sink} such that the flow is equal to flow(b_{src},b_{sink})
19:     **else**
20:         Move sorted cells one-by-one from b_{src} to b_{sink} such that the flow is less than or equal to flow(b_{src},b_{sink})
21:     **end if**
22:     $b_{sink} = b_{src}$
23: **end while**

---

recomputed as it might have been changed by moving cells along other candidate paths sharing some partial paths with path p. In addition, the order of traversing the path is reversed using a stack Z. Then, cells are moved along path p using lines 14-23. If two bins b_{src} and b_{sink} are horizontally adjacent (line 17), cells are fractionally moved (line 18). Otherwise, moving cells from b_{src} to b_{sink} is performed such that the total width of the moved cells is less than or equal to flow(b_{src},b_{sink}). In line 20, for vertical moves, if a partial cell c_γ is decided to move to b_{sink}, the entirety of the cell is moved, and all other partial cells composing cell c_γ are removed from other horizontally-adjacent bins.

3.4 Illustrative Example

In order to illustrate how the proposed algorithm works, an example is presented in Figure 1. In Figure 1(a), a region of a standard-cell global placement solution is illustrated along with the arrangement of cells. The amount of available white space for each bin is presented in Figure 1(b). Bins (colored in pink) with negative values inside are overflowed. Bins shown in green are sink bins with white space.

In this example, the overflow of the bin located in $[1, 2]$ (row 1, column 2) is to be resolved. For better illustration, the cells inside this bin are colored in orange. In Figure 1(c), the cells subject to move in neighboring bins are shown in blue and purple. In Figure 1(d), the candidate paths ($\uparrow$) and invalid paths ($\top$) after running our proposed path augmentation algorithm (see Section 3.2) for resolving the overflow of bin $[1, 2]$ are illustrated. In Figure 2, the tree made by our proposed method (see Algorithm 2) in finding candidate paths is shown. Three candidate paths identified in this tree are shown by green arrows while invalid paths are illustrated by black arrows. In Figure 1(e), the new arrangement of cells after moving cells (see Section 3.3) on all candidate paths is illustrated. It should be mentioned that cells can be fractionally moved between two horizontally-

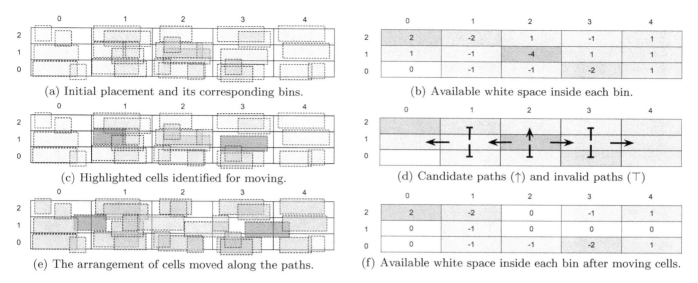

(a) Initial placement and its corresponding bins.

(b) Available white space inside each bin.

(c) Highlighted cells identified for moving.

(d) Candidate paths (↑) and invalid paths (⊤)

(e) The arrangement of cells moved along the paths.

(f) Available white space inside each bin after moving cells.

Figure 1: An example of an initial placement, bins, candidate paths, and a solution for the bin [1,2].

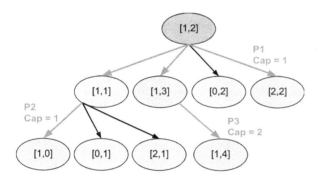

Figure 2: The traversed tree for identifying candidate paths for bin [2,1] in Figure 1.

adjacent bins while the entirety of a cell has to be moved between two vertically-adjacent bins (see Figure 1(e)). In Figure 1(f), the overflowed bins are shown. It can be seen that the bin [1,2] is no longer overflowed. In addition, no new overflowed bin is created or no increase supply in the overflowed bins occurs.

It is important to mention that for this example, BonnPlaceLegal [8] cannot find a solution for resolving bin located in [1,2] as it is based on a variant of Dijkstra's algorithm for finding a shortest path to sink the supply bin while no single shortest path can sink the entire supply of the bin.

3.5 Cell Edge Spacing Rules

Our proposed algorithm keeps track of the order of cells inside bins and cells between horizontally-adjacent bins in order to satisfy cell edge spacing constraints defined in modern technologies [14–16]. Cell edge spacing constraints in modern technologies ensure that no short happens for two neighboring cells during detailed routing. Two pins of two adjacent cells on either the same layer or two different layers may cause a short during detailed routing, if the two cells are placed too close to each other.

Cells inside each bin are maintained in a sorted order based on their original x-coordinates using a balanced bi-

nary tree such as a Red-Black tree [12]. This allows fast insertion and removal (with logarithmic time complexity) as cells are moved between bins. Maintaining cells sorted is essential to compute the space necessary to meet edge spacing requirements. The total space $\Phi(v)$ required for edge spacing rules in bin v is computed as the following:

$$\Phi(v) = \phi(c_r, c_l) + \sum_{c_i \in \Gamma(v)} \phi(c_i, c_{i+1}) \qquad (3)$$

where $\phi(c_i, c_{i+1})$ is the minimum horizontal gap required between two consecutive cells in bin v. $\phi(c_r, c_l)$ is the minimum gap between the most right cell c_r in the left bin v_l neighboring with bin v and the most left cell c_l in bin v. If there is a cell overlapping with both bins v_l and v, $\phi(c_r, c_l)$ is set to zero because the required gap is already considered in bin v_l or v using $\sum_{c_i \in \Gamma(v)} \phi(c_i, c_{i+1})$ in Equation 3. In order to avoid evaluating Equation 3 every time a cell is inserted or removed, Equations 4 and 5 are in turn used to compute the updated value of the gap $\Phi(v)$ when a cell c_j is inserted to and removed from a bin v:

$$\Phi(v) = \Phi(v) + \phi(c_{j-1}, c_j) + \phi(c_j, c_{j+1}) - \phi(c_{j-1}, c_{j+1}) \quad (4)$$

$$\Phi(v) = \Phi(v) + \phi(c_{j-1}, c_{j+1}) - \phi(c_{j-1}, c_j) - \phi(c_j, c_{j+1}) \quad (5)$$

where c_{j-1} and c_{j+1} in turn are the cells on the left and right of cell c_j after inserting (before removing) cell c_j to (from) bin v in Equation 4 (5). Gap $\Phi(v)$ required by edge spacing rules is added to the total width of (partial) cells inside bin v to determine if the bin is overflowed or not. Our empirical experiments illustrate that a better solution is achieved if edge spacing rules are incrementally applied in Algorithm 1. In other words, first all overflowed bins are resolved without considering edge spacing rules (for each bin v, $\Phi(v) = 0$ in lines 5-18 of Algorithm 1). Afterwards, edge spacing rules are enabled and overflowed bins are resolved again.

4. EXPERIMENTAL RESULTS

Our legalizer has been developed in C++ and compiled by gcc version 4.8.5. All experiments were conducted on a CentOS (release 7.0) server with two Intel Xeon E5-2620 proces-

Table 1: Circuit characteristics for the ISPD 2006 and 2014 benchmarks [14, 17].

ISPD 2006	Cells	Fixed	RowH	AvgW	MaxW	DD
newblue3	482833	11178	12	18.37	104	0.26
newblue4	642717	3422	12	12.78	106	0.46
newblue5	1228177	4881	12	11.01	104	0.50
newblue6	1248150	6889	12	13.24	104	0.39
newblue7	2481372	26582	12	11.70	104	0.49
ISPD 2014	Cells	Fixed	RowH	AvgW	MaxW	DD
des_perf_1	112644	0	2000	794.38	1600	0.91
des_perf_2	112644	0	2000	794.38	1600	0.85
edit_dist_1	130661	0	2000	798.54	51200	0.40
edit_dist_2	130661	0	2000	798.54	51200	0.43
fft	32281	0	2000	905.33	1600	0.84
matrix_mult	155325	0	2000	781.39	1600	0.80
pci_bridge32_1	30675	0	2000	829.65	1600	0.84
pci_bridge32_2	30675	0	2000	829.65	1600	0.86
superblue11	925616	1458	900	1196.39	5300	0.41
superblue12	1286948	89	900	870.69	5300	0.44
superblue16	680450	419	900	1013.58	5300	0.46

sors running at 2.00 GHz and 64 GB of RAM. Circuits from the ISPD 2014 detailed routability driven placement contest [14] and the ISPD 2006 placement contest [17] are used. The ISPD 2015 benchmarks [15] are not used as they include fence regions and are originally derived from the 2014 ISPD benchmarks. In additions, circuits from ISPD 2006 that include movable macro cells are also excluded from the experiments. The legalization of circuits with movable macros and more design rules such as fence regions will be part of our future work. Details of the benchmarks used in the experiments are presented in Table 1. In this table, columns 1 to 7 represent the names of circuits, the number of movable cells (Cells), the number of fixed cells including macro blocks (Fixed), the height of rows in the design (RowH), the average width of movable cells (avgW), the maximum width of movable cells (maxW), and the design density (DD), respectively. To show the efficacy of the proposed algorithms, several sets of experiments were conducted.

The first set of experiments were performed on the ISPD 2014 benchmarks. These benchmarks are in LEF/DEF exchange format [18] and we were able to gain two external legalizers (Eh?Placer [3] and RippleDP [5]) which are able to handle this format. All global placements were generated using Eh?Placer [3] that achieved first place and second place in the ISPD 2014 and 2015 contests, respectively [19, 20].

In many cases (e.g, after timing optimization), some local areas can have cell utilization more than 100%. To be able to simulate this type of situations, the generated global placements have some local areas with cell utilization up to 120%. Two examples of this are illustrated in Figures 3(a) and 3(b). In Figure 3(a), the histogram of cell utilization for circuit des_perf_1 is shown. This circuit has a design density of 91% while 85 and 42 local areas with cell utilization around 100% and more, respectively. On the other hand, circuit edit_dist_1 has a design density of 40% (much lower than des_perf_1); but has 26 and 26 local areas with cell utilization around 100% and more, respectively, as shown in Figure 3(b). Moreover, design rules such as pin shorts, pin access, and cell edge spacing [16] were removed from the benchmarks to have apple-to-apple comparisons with the available legalizers.

In Table 2, the results for the HPWL increase (HPWL ↑), average movement (Avg. Disp), maximum cell movement (Max. Disp) and runtime for three legalizers: Rip-

pleDP (RDP), Eh?Placer (EP) and the proposed algorithm (Ours), are demonstrated. In column 2, HPWL after global placement is presented. The increase in HPWL for the three legalizers are shown in columns 3 to 5. In columns 6 to 8, the average cell movement for the three legalizers are listed while maximum cell movements are given in columns 9 to 11. Finally, runtimes for the three algorithms are compared in columns 12 to 14. It should be mentioned that maximum and average cell movements are normalized by the row height. The dash in any column entry indicates that the placer crashed during legalization. Considering RippleDP, it should be mentioned that RippleDP receives the maximum cell movement as an input and performs a detailed placement step after legalization which we could not disable. In addition, we set maximum movement to 10 rows for RippleDP since any value less than 10 rows leads to unacceptable runtime (more than 12 hours) for RippleDP. As shown in Table 2, RippleDP crashed for some of the benchmarks no matters what value is given as the maximum movement.

The results in Table 2 illustrate that the proposed algorithm achieved on average 2.5 and 2.7 times less maximum movement and 3.3 and 4.6 times less average movement compared to Eh?Placer and RippleDP, respectively. At the same time, HPWL increase is 2.5 times more for Eh?Placer compared to our proposed technique, while ours on average remains the same compared to RippleDP, even though RippleDP performs a detailed placement step whereas we do not perform detailed placement. Therefore, we can also conclude that our legalizer preserves more of the quality of the global placement while minimizing cell movement.

Most importantly, the runtime for the proposed algorithm is 18.7 times less than the runtime for Eh?Placer and 31.1 times less than the runtime for RippleDP. Since Eh?Placer uses parallel computations, in order to make the runtime comparisons fair, all three legalizers were run on the same machine, restricted to one CPU core.

In the second set of experiments, cell edge spacing rules were enabled for the same global placements used in the first set of experiments. The results for these experiments are included in Table 3. According to our observation, RippleDP does not consider edge spacing and hence is not included in the comparison. In addition, edge spacing rules were not violated for circuits superblue 11, 12 and 16 in the first set of experiments. Hence, the results for these circuits are not repeated in this table.

The results in Table 3 indicate that the proposed algorithm yields on average 3.4 times less maximum movement and 1.4 times less average movement compared to Eh?Placer. HPWL increase is 2.1 times more for Eh?Placer compared to our proposed technique while runtime of our algorithm is 2.8 times less than runtime of Eh?Placer even though the results for superblue11, superblue12, and superblue16 are not included in Table 3.

The last set of experiments was conducted on the 2006 ISPD benchmarks which are in the bookshelf format to give us the ability to compare our method with FastPlace [6] in order to make an indirect comparison with other legalizers since others have also been compared to FastPlace (e.g., [8,9])[4]. For these benchmarks, global placements were generated by POLAR [21] with the target utilization set to

---

[4]The binary of BonnPlaceLegal was not available at the time of writing this paper.

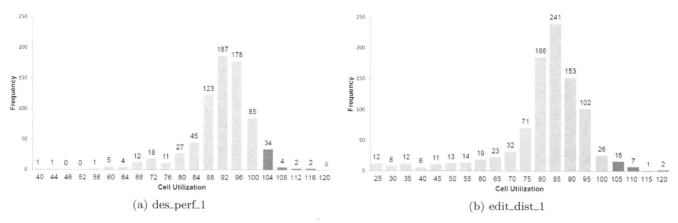

(a) des_perf_1   (b) edit_dist_1

Figure 3: Histogram of cell utilization of global placements for two circuits from the ISPD 2014 benchmarks.

Table 2: Comparison on the results of our legalization method (Ours) with other available legalizers for the ISPD 2014 benchmarks.

Design	GP HPWL (e+9)	HPWL↑ (%)			Avg. Disp (rows)			Max. Disp (rows)			Runtime(sec)		
		RDP	EP	Ours	RDP	EP	Ours	RDP	EP	Ours	RDP	EP	Ours
des_perf_1	1.2	**5.4**	14.2	6.1	3.6	1.3	**0.8**	10.0	11.1	**4.3**	89.1	5.5	**2.5**
des_perf_2	1.2	**4.9**	12.7	5.9	3.6	1.2	**0.8**	10.0	13.2	**3.7**	80.1	5.1	**2.1**
edit_dist_1	3.2	–	5.8	**3.3**	–	1.2	**1.1**	–	17.8	**8.3**	–	5.9	**1.0**
edit_dist_2	3.1	–	5.7	**3.4**	–	1.2	**1.1**	–	12.2	**7.8**	–	6.1	**1.1**
fft	0.4	10.4	17.5	**8.5**	3.8	1.3	**0.9**	10.0	17.9	**3.9**	10.9	1.2	**0.4**
matrix_mult	2.1	9.2	15.0	**7.9**	3.8	1.2	**0.8**	10.0	12.5	**3.8**	52.8	7.8	**3.0**
pci_bridge32_1	0.2	**12.3**	25.2	12.7	4.0	1.2	**0.8**	10.0	8.7	**3.0**	17.8	0.9	**0.3**
pci_bridge32_2	0.2	**10.4**	23.9	12.5	4.1	1.1	**0.8**	10.0	8.2	**3.8**	17.1	0.8	**0.3**
superblue11	33.1	–	32.4	**4.7**	–	21.2	**3.0**	–	951.6	**388.6**	–	3088.1	**154.7**
superblue12	25.4	–	26.6	**5.2**	–	6.6	**1.9**	–	428.0	**180.6**	–	1537.5	**112.1**
superblue16	23.4	–	18.1	**4.2**	–	10.6	**2.6**	–	666.9	**259.0**	–	2123.9	**85.5**
Norm.	–	**1.0**	2.5	**1.0**	4.6	3.3	**1.0**	2.7	2.5	**1.0**	31.1	18.7	**1.0**

Table 3: Comparison on the results of our legalization method (Ours) with Eh?Placer (EP) [3] when edge spacing rules are enabled.

Design	EP				Ours			
	Max. Disp (rows)	Avg. Disp (rows)	HPWL↑ %	Runtime (sec)	Max. Disp (rows)	Avg. Disp (rows)	HPWL↑ %	Runtime (sec)
des_perf_1	14.1	1.3	14.7	5.4	**4.3**	**0.9**	**6.2**	**2.5**
des_perf_2	10.1	1.2	13.0	5.2	**3.7**	**1.0**	**6.0**	**2.2**
edit_dist_1	19.0	1.5	7.9	5.9	**8.9**	**1.3**	**4.2**	**1.9**
edit_dist_2	13.9	1.4	7.5	6.0	**9.2**	**1.3**	**4.1**	**1.4**
fft	54.3	1.7	23.6	2.6	**4.9**	**1.0**	**10.0**	**0.6**
matrix_mult	12.5	1.2	16.0	8.8	**3.8**	**0.8**	**8.1**	**3.4**
pci_bridge32_1	8.6	1.3	27.1	0.9	**3.4**	**0.9**	**13.3**	**0.5**
pci_bridge32_2	8.8	1.2	25.5	0.8	**3.8**	**0.8**	**12.9**	**0.4**
Norm.	3.4	1.4	2.1	2.8	**1.0**	**1.0**	**1.0**	**1.0**

100%. In order to have fair comparisons, the detailed placement step of FastPlace was disabled.

The results of these experiments are demonstrated in Table 4. It should be mentioned that for these comparisons, only the circuits that did not include movable macros were used. From this table, it can be seen that with no exception, our proposed algorithms achieves better results for all four metrics compared to the results of FastPlace. All these three sets of experiments illustrate the efficacy and effectiveness of our proposed algorithms in terms of average and maximum

movement and HPWL while the runtime is notably lower than other methods.

5. CONCLUSIONS

In this paper, we have proposed a fast and effective legalization approach for standard-cell placement. The contributions of the proposed approach include minimizing maximum movement, the ability to effectively handle regions with high cell density, and significant low runtimes. The porposed approach is based on a novel implementation of

Table 4: Comparison on the results of our legalization method (Ours) with FastPlace [6] for the ISDP 2006 circuits with no movable macro cells.

Design	GP HPWL (e+8)	FastPlace				Ours			
		Max. Disp (rows)	Avg. Disp (rows)	HPWL↑ %	Runtime (sec)	Max. Disp (rows)	Avg. Disp (rows)	HPWL↑ %	Runtime (sec)
newblue3	2.68	1162.9	3.7	2.8	20.2	**196.9**	**2.1**	**2.7**	**9.4**
newblue4	2.45	644.4	4.6	6.2	38.9	**69.9**	**1.8**	**2.9**	**9.8**
newblue5	4.13	630.3	3.5	4.4	83.5	**55.2**	**1.7**	**3.2**	**23.7**
newblue6	4.79	847.6	3.8	5.6	69.0	**46.0**	**1.7**	**2.8**	**18.0**
newblue7	10.01	545.0	3.6	4.7	194.4	**211.7**	**1.6**	**2.1**	**43.1**
Norm.	−	6.6	2.2	1.8	3.9	**1.0**	**1.0**	**1.0**	**1.0**

the path augmentation algorithm where bin overflows are resolved by finding several candidate paths to guarantee a legal solution. This is in sharp contrast with other network flow based algorithms.

The impact of the proposed legalization technique is its ability to preserve the timing and routability obtained during global placement. Future work will include extending the algorithm to legalize designs with multi-deck cells, to apply more design rules such as fence regions, and to exploit parallel computation methods for parts of the algorithm to achieve even better runtime for extremely large circuits.

6. ACKNOWLEDGMENTS

This work has been supported by Natural Sciences and Engineering Council of Canada (NSERC), Alberta Innovates-Technology Futures (AITF), and Mentor Graphics Corporation. In addition, computing resources for this work have been provided by Compute/Calcul Canada and the Canadian Microelectronics Corporation (CMC).

7. REFERENCES

[1] M. C. Kim, N. Viswanathan, Z. Li, and C. Alpert. ICCAD-2013 CAD contest in placement finishing and benchmark suite. In *Proc. of ICCAD*, pages 268–270, Nov 2013.

[2] D. Hill. Method and system for high speed detailed placement of cells within an integrated circuit design, April 9 2002. US Patent 6,370,673.

[3] N. Karimpour Darav, A. Kennings, A. Fakheri Tabrizi, D. Westwick, and L. Behjat. Eh?placer: A high-performance modern technology-driven placer. *ACM TODAES*, 21(3):37:1–37:27, April 2016.

[4] P. Spindler, U. Schlichtmann, and F. M. Johannes. Abacus: Fast legalization of standard cell circuits with minimal movement. In *Proc. of ISPD*, pages 47–53, 2008.

[5] W.-K. Chow, J. Kuang, X. He, W. Cai, and Evangeline F.Y. Young. Cell density-driven detailed placement with displacement constraint. In *Proc. of ISPD*, pages 3–10, 2014.

[6] N. Viswanathan, Min Pan, and C. Chu. Fastplace 3.0: A fast multilevel quadratic placement algorithm with placement congestion control. In *Proc. of ASP-DAC*, pages 135–140, Washington, DC, USA, 2007.

[7] M. Cho, H. Ren, H. Xiang, and R. Puri. History-based VLSI legalization using network flow. In *Proc. of DAC*, pages 286–291, 2010.

[8] U. Brenner. Bonnplace legalization: Minimizing movement by iterative augmentation. *IEEE TCAD*, 32(8):1215–1227, August 2013.

[9] H. Ren, D. Z. Pan, C. J. Alpert, and P. Villarrubia. Diffusion-based placement migration. In *Proc. of DAC*, pages 515–520, 2005.

[10] R. K. Ahuja, T. L. Magnanti, and J. B. Orlin. *Network Flows: Theory, Algorithms, and Applications*. Prentice-Hall, Inc., Upper Saddle River, NJ, USA, 1993.

[11] E. W. Dijkstra. A note on two problems in connexion with graphs. *Numer. Math.*, 1(1):269–271, December 1959.

[12] S. S. Skiena. *The Algorithm Design Manual*. Springer Publishing Company, Incorporated, 2nd edition, 2008.

[13] Andrew B. Kahng, Igor L. Markov, and Sherief Reda. On legalization of row-based placements. In *Proc. of GLSVLSI*, pages 214–219, 2004.

[14] V. Yutsis, I. S. Bustany, D. Chinnery, J. R. Shinnerl, and W.-H. Liu. ISPD 2014 benchmarks with sub-45nm technology rules for detailed-routing-driven placement. In *Proc. of ISPD*, pages 161–168, 2014.

[15] I. S. Bustany, D. Chinnery, J. R. Shinnerl, and V. Yutsi. ISPD 2015 benchmarks with fence regions and routing blockages for detailed-routing-driven placement. In *Proc. of ISPD*, pages 157–164, 2015.

[16] A. Kennings, N.. Karimpour Darav, and L. Behjat. Detailed placement accounting for technology constraints. In *Proc. of VLSI-SoC*, pages 1–6, 2014.

[17] G. J. Nam. ISPD 2006 placement contest: Benchmark suite and results. In *Proc. of ISPD*, pages 167–167, 2006.

[18] Cadence, Inc. LEF/DEF version 5.3-5.7 exchange format. http://si2.org/openeda.si2.org/projects/lefdef. Accessed: 2015-01-29.

[19] ISPD 2014 detailed routing-driven placement contest. http://www.ispd.cc/contests/14/ispd2014_contest.html. Accessed: 2016-10-03.

[20] ISPD 2015 blockage-aware detailed routing-driven placement contest. http://www.ispd.cc/contests/15/ispd2015_contest.html. Accessed: 2016-10-03.

[21] T. Lin, C. Chu, J.R. Shinnerl, I. Bustany, and I. Nedelchev. POLAR: A high performance mixed-size wirelengh-driven placer with density constraints. *IEEE TCAD*, 34(3):447–459, 2015.

CAD Opportunities with Hyper-Pipelining

Mahesh A. Iyer
Intel Corporation
mahesh.iyer@intel.com

ABSTRACT

Hyper-pipelining is a design technique that results in significant performance and throughput improvements in latency-insensitive designs. Modern FPGA architectures like Intel's Stratix®10 feature a revolutionary register-rich HyperFlex™ core fabric architecture that make it amenable for hyper-pipelining. Design implementation CAD tools can provide insights into performance bottlenecks and how hyper-pipelining can result in improved performance, that can then be implemented using well-known techniques like retiming.

Retiming was first introduced as a powerful sequential design optimization technique three decades ago, yet gained limited popularity in the ASIC industry. In recent years, retiming has gained tremendous popularity in the FPGA industry. This talk will discuss why this is the case, and provide insights into some of the interesting opportunities it presents for design implementation, analysis, and verification CAD tools. Impacts of hyper-pipelining on the physical design CAD flow and timing closure will also be discussed.

Author Keywords

Pipelining; retiming; CAD; EDA; FPGA; physical design; timing closure

BIOGRAPHY

Mahesh A. Iyer is an Intel Fellow and the chief architect and technologist for electronic design automation (EDA) in the Programmable Solutions Group at Intel Corporation. He is responsible for defining and carrying out the technical vision and direction for the Quartus compiler organization and its products, a role that encompasses logic synthesis, placement, clock allocation, physical synthesis, clustering, routing, timing analysis, flow convergence and design verification. Iyer collaborates with global teams of software engineers and architects focused on architecture, integrated circuit design and design automation to advance design implementation tools and next-generation field-programmable gate array (FPGA) architectures.

A recognized EDA industry expert, Iyer joined Intel in 2015 with the acquisition of Altera Corp., where he had held similar responsibilities since 2013. Before joining Altera, Iyer accrued 17 years of experience at Synopsys Inc., a leader in the EDA industry. He served as the software architect for some of Synopsys' most successful EDA products, including Design Compiler, IC Compiler and VCS. During his Synopsys career, Iyer invented and developed numerous algorithms for logic synthesis, physical synthesis, design implementation flows and test-bench automation. In 2010, he was named Synopsys' Inventor of the Year. Iyer began his professional career in the early 1990s at AT&T Bell Laboratories, where he researched and invented seminal algorithms for hardware test automation.

Iyer earned a bachelor's degree in electronics from the University of Bombay in India and a master's degree and Ph.D. in electrical engineering from the Illinois Institute of Technology, which honored him with a Distinguished Alumni Professional Achievement Award in 2010. He has published more than 20 papers on various EDA topics and has 75 issued or pending patents in related fields. He was named a Synopsys Fellow in 2006, an Altera Fellow in 2013 and an Intel Fellow in 2016.

Permission to make digital or hard copies of part or all of this work for personal or classroom use is granted without fee provided that copies are not made or distributed for profit or commercial advantage and that copies bear this notice and the full citation on the first page. Copyrights for third-party components of this work must be honored. For all other uses, contact the Owner/Author(s). Copyright is held by the owner/author(s). © 2015 Intel Corporation.

ISPD '17, March 19–22, 2017, Portland, OR, USA.
ACM. ISBN 978-1-4503-4696-2/17/03.
DOI: http://dx.doi.org/10.1145/3036669.3044804

An Effective Timing-Driven Detailed Placement Algorithm for FPGAs

Shounak Dhar
University of Texas at Austin

Mahesh A. Iyer
Intel Corporation

Saurabh Adya
Intel Corporation

Love Singhal
Intel Corporation

Nikolay Rubanov
Intel Corporation

David Z. Pan
University of Texas at Austin

ABSTRACT

In this paper, we propose a new timing-driven detailed placement technique for FPGAs based on optimizing critical paths. Our approach extends well beyond the previously known critical path optimization approaches and explores a significantly larger solution space. It is also complementary to single-net based timing optimization approaches. The new algorithm models the detailed placement improvement problem as a shortest path optimization problem, and optimizes the placement of all elements in the entire timing critical path simultaneously, while minimizing the costs of adjusting the placement of adjacent non-critical elements. Experimental results on industrial circuits using a modern FPGA device show an average placement clock frequency improvement of 4.5%.

1. INTRODUCTION

In deep sub-micron technology nodes, Application-Specific Integrated Circuits (ASICs) are becoming prohibitively expensive to design and manufacture. For this reason Field-Programmable Gate Arrays (FPGAs) which are general-purpose and flexible programmable hardware are gaining more design wins in lower geometries. Modern FPGAs are becoming popular in high performance data analytics, search engines, autonomous cars, communication and networking applications. These design applications mapped onto the FPGA demand high maximum achievable clock frequency (Fmax).

The FPGA CAD flow is similar in spirit to an ASIC CAD flow with a few differences. The FPGA CAD flow consists of key engines like logic synthesis, global placement, clustering, detailed placement, routing, timing analysis, and physical synthesis. Most of these engines concurrently optimize for various metrics like Fmax, wiring usage, logic utilization, and routing congestion.

A key stage in the FPGA CAD flow is detailed placement that optimizes the placement of the design taking into account all the legality rules of the underlying FPGA target

ISPD '17, March 19–22, 2017, Portland, OR, USA.

© 2017 Copyright held by the owner/author(s). Publication rights licensed to ACM.
ISBN 978-1-4503-4696-2/17/03...$15.00

DOI: http://dx.doi.org/3036669.3036682

architecture. In this paper, we propose a new algorithm for detailed placement in an FPGA CAD flow.

1.1 FPGA Architecture and CAD Flow

Modern FPGA devices typically consist of a grid of different types of blocks like logic array blocks (LABs), digital signal processors (DSPs), RAMs and IOs along with routing resources. LABs internally consist of lookup tables (LUTs), flip-flops (FFs), multiplexers (MUXes) and routing resources. The first step in the CAD flow is mapping the synthesized netlist to LUTs and FFs. The LUTs and FFs are subsequently packed into LABs following some complex packing rules. Pre-placement may also be performed to assist packing. Next, global placement and legalization are performed to place the packed netlist on the FPGA grid, followed by a local refinement phase or detailed placement for optimizing metrics like wirelength, Fmax and routability which are hard to model accurately during global placement and packing. Finally, routing is performed to realize all the nets using actual routing resources followed by signoff timing analysis.

Although timing-driven placement and packing for FPGAs is similar in many aspects to that for ASICs, there are a few important differences:

- LABs in FPGAs have many more pins ($\sim$60) compared to standard cells in ASICs (2-5)

- LABs in FPGAs have multiple output pins, hence can be start-points of multiple timing paths whereas standard cells usually have one output and have fewer number of different output paths (depends only on fanout of the output net)

- Routing resources in an FPGA are fixed. Hence, wirelength and delay estimation for a net cannot be done by simple steiner routes but have to take routing resources in the underlying FPGA target device into account

1.2 Previous work on Timing-driven Placement

Timing-driven placement has two aspects - (i)the objective function or 'metric' that we are directly trying to optimize (ii)how we explore our solution space. The objective function can be loosely classified as net-based ([1],[3],[4],[5],[13]), path-based ([9],[6],[10],[11]) or a hybrid of the two ([2],[8]). The general theme of net-based objective functions is to run timing analysis, generate slacks and criticalities for nets and use those values to generate net weights (more critical nets get higher weights). Then, placement is performed to minimize weighted wirelength. They do not optimize critical paths explicitly. In a linear weighted model, nets with higher weights dominate nets with lower weights. This necessitates the use of constraints on length or delay or slack for nets ([15],[16]). Some algorithms count the number of critical paths passing through a net and use this information for generating net weights [3]. Net-based approaches work well in a global perspective. They tend to saturate when the placement is close enough to optimal from the global perspective. They leave significant room for improvement as they do not optimize the most critical paths and may create new critical paths while trying to reduce delays of other nets.

Path-based optimization algorithms try to model exact delays for the most critical paths and optimize them. Many of them use linear programming or lagrangian relaxation formulations. Some approaches use simulated annealing. Linear programs scale poorly, especially for FPGAs where LABs can have ~60 pins and moving one LAB can affect a large number of critical paths. Simulated annealing also has scalability problems and it cannot maintain the same solution quality with similar runtime for increasingly larger modern designs.

A variety of ideas have been proposed for solution space exploration or the actual 'placement'. The most common ones are greedy swaps or moves or shifting of cells ([1],[6]). Some works extend the greedy approaches to tunnel through barriers or use hill-climbing moves like simulated annealing ([3],[5],[8]). Many of the techniques prevalent in popular literature concentrate on minimizing their objective function first to generate a placement that can have possible overlaps and legalize afterwards ([2],[9]). Some approaches which use linear or integer programming also incorporate the legalization into the LP or IP. [11] proposes a discrete optimization technique based on choosing candidate locations but the authors try to address all affected critical paths together which is infeasible for FPGAs. Also, they choose disjoint sets of candidate locations for different nodes on a critical path, which restricts the solution space.

1.3 Motivation

We briefly describe state-of-the-art timing-driven detailed placement techniques, as well as their limitations and areas for improvement, especially with respect to FPGAs.

- Traditional net-based timing optimization tends to saturate at some distance from the global optimum. Further, they tend to oscillate. The output of net-based detailed placement has a large scope for improvement.

- Linear programming (LP) based critical path optimizations are not good for FPGAs since LABs in FPGAs have a large number of pins and moving one LAB affects many critical paths leading to a large number of constraints for LP.

- The discrete optimization of critical paths in [11] attempts to minimize the maximum delay of all the critical paths incident on a set of nodes. This is infeasible for FPGAs due to the large number of paths per node (LAB)

- [11] uses a branch-and bound algorithm. We need a

faster algorithm that can cope with large modern designs.

- Critical path optimization techniques which move one path node at a time are highly susceptible to getting stuck in local minima. Therefore, we need to optimize all the critical path nodes concurrently.

1.4 Our Contributions

The key contributions of our work are as follows:

- We propose a new timing-driven placement algorithm which is tailored towards high connectivity netlists like those for FPGAs

- We propose an algorithm to optimize critical paths where the path nodes are allowed to move to a set of candidate locations which may overlap with candidate locations of other path nodes. This gives more freedom for movement than [11]

- We formulate our optimization problem as a shortest path problem on a layered network of candidate locations for each path node

- We use hard delay limits for nets which prevents degradation in the worst slack. This is an effective way of controlling side (non-critical) paths rather than minimizing the maximum delay for a set of paths.

- Our formulation enables us to use breadth-first traversal (similar to timing analysis) to solve for the shortest path, whereas [11] uses branch-and-bound.

- Timing improvements from our algorithm stack up on conventional net-based detailed placement algorithms, thus augmenting their capabilities.

- Our algorithm has negligible effect on wirelength and congestion and has a small runtime overhead

The rest of the paper is organized as follows: Section 2 presents the basic concepts and the problem formulation. Section 3 presents the algorithms used in our technique. Section 4 presents complexity analyses for these agorithms. Section 5 discusses the slack allocation algorithm. Section 6 discusses parallelization and speedup techniques. Section 7 discusses various schemes related to applying our algorithm to the whole chip. Section 8 presents our experimental results and Section 9 concludes our paper.

2. PROBLEM FORMULATION

2.1 Timing Model

We introduce virtual 2-pin nets called tnets for each source-sink pair in each net. Tnets represent timing arcs. They capture routing information of the corresponding net segments and hence provide accurate information for timing calculation. Delay between any two locations on the FPGA grid is modelled in a lookup-table fashion for fast access. The lookup tables are sufficiently small as the regular routing architecture in FPGAs leads to uniform delays. This delay depends on current cell placement and can be easily modified for incremental changes. We skip the details of the delay computation. Since we would be moving a very small fraction of the cells (and therefore, nets), the routing information and congestion maps would be practically undisturbed during the course of our algorithm.

2.2 Setting up the Optimization Problem for a Critical Path

Let's consider the example shown in Figure 1. It shows a portion of the FPGA grid with different types of sites. In this grid, A-B-C-D-E is a critical path that we expect to optimize. We pick some candidate locations for each of the nodes A,B,C,D,E that are in close proximity to the path (shown in Figure 2). For example B can move to B1, B2, etc. and C can move to C1, etc. B and C can also move to BC1, BC2, etc. with the constraint that both of them should not end up in the same location. Legality is also taken into account while choosing candidate locations. The set of these candidate locations is called 'neighborhood' of the path. (Details on how the neighborhood is selected is discussed later). The set of candidate locations for a single path node is called a 'sub-neighborhood'. Candidate locations for two consecutive path nodes may overlap (ex: B and C can go to BC1, BC2, etc and D and E can go to DE1, DE2, etc.) but candidate locations for two nodes that are not adjacent in our chosen path may not overlap (ex: AC, AD, BD etc. are not allowed). We stress the importance of our 'chosen' path. There could be another net (which may branch into or out of the current path) from A to C making A and C adjacent, but we only have the edges A-B, B-C, C-D, D-E in our chosen path. We will discuss how we tackle side paths like A-C shortly. We ensure that original locations of the path nodes are also in the candidate location set.

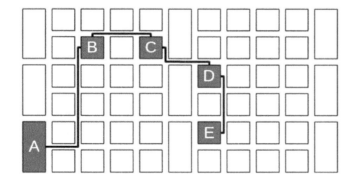

Figure 1: FPGA grid with a critical path

Candidate locations for path nodes can be empty or occupied by some other object (LAB, RAM, DSP, etc.). If a candidate location is empty, we may allow the corresponding path node to move there. If they are occupied by some other object, we may swap the object with the corresponding path node. For example, in Figure 3, assume that B1 is an empty site and B4 is occupied. In this case, B could move to B1 or B4. If B moves to B4, the cell that is currently at B4 must move to B's original site.

2.3 Classification of Tnets

We now consider the set of all tnets connected to the critical path nodes and the neighborhood nodes. They can be classified into the following 10 types (illustrated in Figure 4):

- **Type 1:** tnets in the critical path (one path node to the next or previous node)

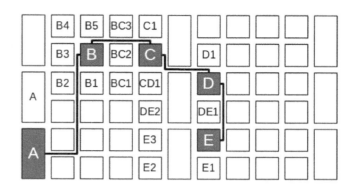

Figure 2: Neighborhood chosen around a critical path

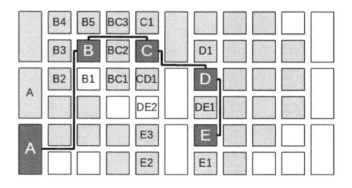

Figure 3: Placement of other cells in the neighborhood

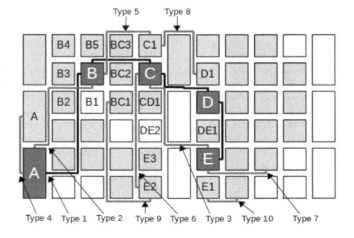

Figure 4: Classification of tnets

- **Type 2:** tnets between consecutive path nodes that are not in the current critical path

- **Type 3:** tnets from one path node to another path node at distance 2 or more in the critical path

- **Type 4:** tnets from a path node to its neighbor

- **Type 5:** tnets from one path node to the neighbors assigned to the next or previous path node

- **Type 6:** tnets from one path node to neighbors assigned to path nodes at distance 2 or more in the critical path

- **Type 7:** tnets from a path node to outside the neighborhood

- **Type 8:** tnets between neighbors assigned to consecutive path nodes

- **Type 9:** tnets between neighbors assigned to path nodes at a distance 2 or more apart in the critical path

- **Type 10:** tnets from a neighborhood node to a node outside the neighborhood

When a neighbor is assigned to 2 path nodes like BC1, DE1, etc. the types of some tnets may vary depending on the context. For example, when we are finding new locations of tnet pins by swapping BC1 with B, we will treat BC1 as B's neighbor and not C's neighbor. Similarly, when we consider swapping BC1 with C, we will treat BC1 as C's neighbor and not B's neighbor.

2.4 Shortest Path Problem

Our objective is to achieve minimum delay for the path A-B-C-D-E while ensuring that other paths do not become more critical than the one which is currently most critical. To achieve this, we formulate a shortest path problem with certain constraints on tnet delays. The maximum delay that can be allowed on a tnet is denoted by $delay\_limit_{tnet}$. These delay limits are calculated by a slack allocation algorithm right after each timing analysis (discussed later).

Let there be N nodes on the critical path. This implies there are N-1 tnets on the critical path. Each path node has a choice of some candidate locations. We construct a graph as follows: The graph has N layers, one for each node in the critical path. Each layer has nodes corresponding to the candidate locations for that path node. For example, in Figure 5, the layer for B has nodes B1 to B5 and BC1 to BC3. We add an edge for each feasible pair of locations of adjacent nodes in the critical path. For example, two adjacent nodes, B and C have a feasible pair of locations B5, C1 if B can move to B5 and C can move to C1. The edge represents the delay between B and C after the movement. Also, observe that all BCs in B's layer have outgoing edges to all Cs, BCs and CDs in C's layer except the corresponding BC. This exclusion is necessary to prevent nodes from overlapping. BC2 in B's layer does not have an edge to BC2 in C's layer as that could potentially lead us to choose both BC2s implying that B and C both go to site BC2. The edges essentially model the delays of the type 1 tnets defined above. For example, the edge from B1 to C1 in the graph represents the delay of the tnet B-C when B is moved to B1 and C is moved to C1.

We want to find locations for the path nodes such that the delay of the critical path (which is the sum of the delays represented by these edges) corresponding to the node locations is minimized.

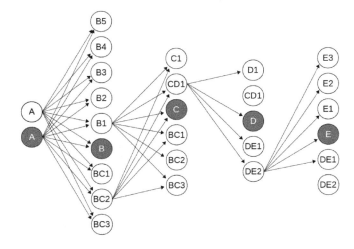

Figure 5: Shortest path problem; All outgoing edges for only some of the nodes are shown. Note that BC2 in B's layer does not have an edge to BC2 in C's layer. This is necessary to prevent overlaps. Similar case with CD1 and DE2

When we move or swap nodes, the delays of tnets connected to the nodes being moved will change. These tnets can be classified into the following types:

- Case (i): delay independent of any other move or swap

- Case (ii): delay dependent on move or swap of adjacent path node

- Case (iii): delay dependent on move or swap of a path node at a distance of 2 or more in the critical path

Case (i) consists of tnet types 4, 7 and 10. Case (ii) consists of tnet types 1, 2, 5 and 8. Case (iii) consists of types 3, 6 and 9.

As stated earlier, each tnet has a delay limit. Some placements in the chosen candidate locations may violate the delay limits of some tnet connected to the nodes being moved. If such a case occurs, we remove that candidate location from our graph.

Tnet delays in case (i) can be computed for each candidate location with the current placement information of the other nodes in the netlist. If we find a candidate location that violates the delay limit of some tnet, we remove that location from our graph. Tnet delays for case (ii) are computed by considering pairs of location assignments for consecutive path nodes. If any pair of location assignments causes a tnet delay limit violation, we remove the corresponding edge from the graph. For case (iii), we compute tet delays based on the current placement of nodes and we update the delays when we reach the corresponding path node downstream while finding the shortest path. We remove the edge to the corresponding node from the graph if there is a delay limit violation.

3. ALGORITHMS

3.1 Finding the Shortest Path

Once we have built the graph, we can find the shortest path from any node in the first layer to any node in the last layer. We do this using breadth-first traversal on layers which runs in $\Theta(E)$ time on a layered graph like ours, where E is the number of edges. We do not need an elaborate algorithm like Dijkstra's due to the layered nature of our network. The delay for a node in layer i can be calculated from the delays for layer $i-1$ and the delays of the edges between the two layers.

We initialize delays of all nodes in the graph except the first layer to infinity. The nodes in the first layer are assigned delay value 0. We proceed layer by layer. At step i, we compute the outgoing delays for each node in layer $i-1$ by adding the previously computed delay for that node to the delay of the outgoing tnet. Thus, we get a set of delay values for each node in layer i corresponding to the incoming tnets for that node. We set the delay for that node to the minimum of all its incoming delays. We also keep a pointer to the incoming tnet which led to the minimum delay for each node. This is useful for tracing the optimal location assignment for the critical path nodes.

The cost(cumulative delay) for a node v in the graph is given by:

$$cost(v) = \min_{u \in input(v)} \{cost(u) + edge\_cost(u,v)\} \quad (1)$$

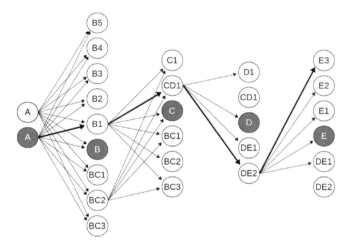

Figure 6: A solution to the shortest path problem

When we have chosen a tnet with minimum cumulative incoming delay for a node in level i, we also store the locations of the nodes in levels before i that affect the case (iii) tnets. Thus we will have accurate placement information when computing tnet delays for layer $i+1$.

Once we have found the shortest path, we change the node locations to reflect the same. Figure 6 shows a possible shortest path. Here, the shortest path goes through A's originl location, B1, CD1, DE2 and E3. So, we choose A's original location for A, B1 for B, CD1 for C (and move the object previously at CD1 to C's original location), DE2 for D and E3 for E (and move the object previously at E3 to E's original location), as shown in Figure 7.

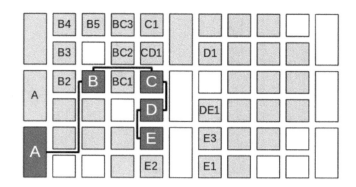

Figure 7: Changing placement to reflect the shortest path

3.2 Selecting a Critical Path

We store the delay and slack values obtained from timing analysis in the tnets. For each tnet, we compute a parameter called *criticality* ($\in [0,1]$), according to [5]:

$$criticality_{tnet} = 1 - \frac{slack_{tnet} - worst\_slack}{D_{max}} \quad (2)$$

Where D_{max} is the critical path delay (maximum of arrival times of all sinks for the corresponding clock) and $slack_{tnet}$ is the difference between the required and arrival times of the tnet's load pin.

We pick all the nets with criticality greater than a certain threshold c. We have empirically determined the best value of c to be 0.98. We extract critical paths from these selected tnets based on connectivity information from the netlist. Note that a tnet can belong to more than one critical path.

Critical paths are extracted by the following algorithm: Initialize a critical path consisting of only one tnet. The path is grown by successively adding tnets to the front and back of our current critical path. For the starting node of the critical path, we go through all the tnets that drive the tnet connected to this node and find the one with the highest criticality (this criticality value will be same as the criticality of all the tnets in the current critical path) and add that tnet to critical path. Ties in criticality value are broken arbitrarily, but such cases are highly unlikely. For the ending node of the critical path, we similarly go through all the tnets that are driven by the tnet connected to this node and find the one with the highest criticality and add it to the critical path. Propagation stops when we reach timing start/end points.

The *criticality* metric normalizes the slack of a tnet to the longest path delay for the corresponding clock. This allows us to distinguish between similar slack tnets, weighting ones with a higher longest path delay to be more critical.

3.3 Neighborhood Extraction

We extract candidate locations for each node in the critical path from within a square of size d centered at that path node. For example, Figure 8 shows a critical path A-B-C and three squares of side length 5 centered at A, B and C respectively. It is highly likely that these squares would overlap, and we have to decide which location to assign to which node or pair of nodes adjacent in the critical path. For this, we first check the legality of placing a critical path node in all the locations lying within its square. Illegal locations would not be considered henceforth.

After this, we compute the distances of each of the locations lying within some square from the corresponding critical path nodes (shown in Figure 8). We assign each location to the critical path node which is closest to it (Figure 9). We can also add a second node that is adjacent to the chosen node in the critical path. Consider the example in Figure 9. The black location AB is closest to A. So, we assign it to A first. The next closest path node is C, but C is not adjacent to A in the critical path. So, we assign it to B. The case with the black location(s) C is similar. They are closest to C, so we assign them to C first. The next closest path node is A, but A is not adjacent to C in the critical path, so we cannot assign it to A. They are not in B's box, se we cannot assign them to B either. We are left with C only.

It may so happen that some path nodes in the middle of the path are assigned too few sites due to conflict with other path nodes. In such cases, we adjust the site assignment by borrowing sites from adjacent path nodes so that each node has sufficient chance to move. If we want to assign more locations to a particular critical path node, we traverse the locations within its box that are assigned to some other node(s) one by one and keep assigning them to this node subject to the condition that the resultant number of locations assigned to the node from which we are borrowing should not be less than that for the current node. If we assign a location to 2 nodes, we ensure that they are adjacent in the critical path.

The nodes in the middle of the critical path are connected to two tnets which are likely to be in different directions. However, the starting and ending nodes have only one tnet each from the critical path. Hence we give a higher priority to the starting and ending nodes in the critical path in case of ties as these nodes have a definite direction of movement which could shorten the path.

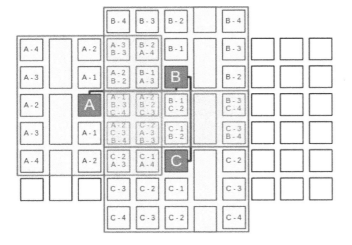

Figure 8: Extracting neighborhood around a critical path

4. COMPLEXITY ANALYSIS

We assume that the average length of a critical path is N, the average size of sub-neighborhood for each path node

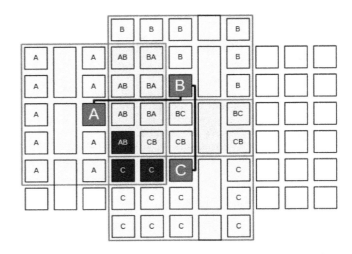

Figure 9: Assignment of locations to critical path nodes

is M ($=d^2$) and the average no. of pins per node (CLB or DSP or RAM) is p.

Extracting the critical path from a tnet: Path extraction involves forward and backward propagation for the seed tnet. At each step, we go through all the incoming or outgoing tnets for a node that share a combinational path with the seed tnet and choose the one with the highest criticality. The amortized no. of tnets that we go through per node is p. We do this for at most N nodes. Hence, the complexity for extracting a path is pN.

Extracting the neighborhood from a path: The average number of sites that we consider for each path node is M. We have to compute distances from each path node to all sites within its box. This will require a total of MN operations. Assigning the sites to nodes will take a constant multiple of MN time.

Generating the graph given the neighborhood: Time complexity here is dominated by edge costs. There are $(N-1)M^2$ edges in the graph. We have to iterate over at most $2p$ tnets for each edge. Hence, edge cost computation requires $2p(N-1)M^2$ time. Cost computation for case (i) tnets takes an additional pNM time.

Solving for shortest path: We iterate over the incoming edges for each node at each level and store the minimum cost. We have to go through at most M incoming edges for each node starting from the second layer. There are a total of $M(N-1)$ such nodes. Hence the total time taken is $(N-1)M^2$.

We see that the overall complexity is dominated by complexity of graph generation, which is $\mathcal{O}(pNM^2)$

5. SLACK ALLOCATION

The simplest way of allocating slack while preserving the worst slack is to assign the minimum possible marginal delay increase for each tnet. We get slack values for each tnet from timing analysis. Assuming there are no combinational cycles in the logic, we can count the number of distinct timing paths passing through each tnet. These are paths with respect to different timing end points. We also compute the length of the longest timing path (number of tnets on that path) passing through each tnet by forward propagation. This can be done only once as the netlist is not being changed. Now, we can set delay_limit for a tnet as follows (extending the concepts from [3] and [16]):

$$delay\_limit_{tnet} = delay_{tnet} + \frac{slack_{tnet} - worst\_slack}{longest\_path\_length_{tnet}} \quad (3)$$

This slack allocation scheme ensures that even if all tnets increase in delay to be at their upper bound limits, the total delay of the worst path through these tnets would not be any worse than that of the original worst critical path. However, note that this is not the optimal slack allocation. We have pessimistically limited the maximum delay for some tnets but they could go even higher without affecting the worst slack. [12] discusses the slack allocation problem in detail. Optimal slack allocation is generally achieved by solving linear programs, but that would be too slow for our purpose. In our work, we use a simple slack allocation algorithm similar to the idea described above.

6. PARALLELIZATION SCHEMES

The most widely used method of speeding up an optimization procedure is to divide the problem into subproblems with little or no interaction and solve them in parallel. In out context, this would mean optimizing different critical paths in parallel. We are thus forced to ensure that the neighborhoods that we choose for different paths are disjoint and that there is no tnet connecting these neighborhoods. Also, critical paths are not spread uniformly over the chip but tend to form clusters at a few spots. Many different critical paths can share a LAB. Therefore, these paths cannot be optimized in parallel. Instead, we look at ways to speed up our algorithm for a single critical path.

Consider our shortest path problem. While computing the cost for each edge in the graph, we have to iterate over all the tnets under case (ii) incident on the two path nodes corresponding to that edge. We have already seen that the complexity for computing the edge costs is $\mathcal{O}(pNM^2)$, which is high. Hence we would like to speed up this part of our algorithm.

Observation 1: The cost of each edge in the graph that we form is independent of the cost of other edges.

Using this observation, we can compute all the edge costs in parallel. A similar observation shows that delays for tnets under case (i) can also be computed in parallel.

Observation 2: Each node within a single layer of our graph (for finding shortest path) is independent of the other nodes in the same layer.

Each node only depends on the nodes on the previous layer which have outgoing edges to that node. Since we solve for shortest path dynamically layer-by-layer, we can parallelize the computation at each layer. This is similar to parallelization of timing analysis where the computations for different timing end-points are independent.

None of the above parallelization schemes affect the placement or Fmax results. They only change runtime.

7. OPTIMIZATION SCHEMES FOR THE WHOLE CHIP

We run a fixed number of iterations of our critical path optimization algorithm. At each iteration, we select all tnets with criticality ≥ 0.98. We extract critical paths from all of these tnets, limiting each tnet to be in at most one critical path. We extract neighborhoods and solve the shortest path problem for each critical path. After this, we update timing. We keep track of those paths which do not improve.

If certain paths are not improving even after a few iterations, we iterate over those paths one by one. For each such path, we attempt to move the nodes connected to the path nodes closer to the path without violating the delay limit of any tnet. We then run our shortest path algorithm on the path.

It may so happen than a critical path cannot be optimized as it disturbs other critical paths connected to it. In such a case, we follow a recursive approach. We first identify the path with higher criticality and make all its nodes fixed. We then apply shortest path algorithm to other critical side-paths of this path to help create more delay budget on these side-paths. Then, we free the fixed path nodes and optimize the original critical path.

8. RESULTS

We tested our algorithm on an industrial benchmark set.

Table 1: Benchmark set details

Design size	# LABs, RAMs and DSPs
Minimum	4156
Maximum	40889
Average	14850
Number of designs	86

The industrial benchmark set details are given in Table 1. Logic utilizations for all designs are shown in Figure 10. Our base flow consists of an industrial strength timing-driven global placer followed by a legalizer followed by the net-based timing-driven detailed placement from [18]. In our new flow, we run our critical path based detailed placer after the net based detailed placer. We set the value of d to 5. In all the data presented in this subsection, we report the geometric average across all benchmarks that have high statistical confidence.

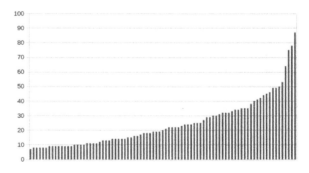

Figure 10: % Logic utilization (y-axis) for all designs

We compare our results with the net-based detailed placement algorithm in [18]. On the average, our algorithm improves the maximum clock frequency (Fmax) at placement stage by 4.5% on top of the net-based placer in [18], while degrading wirelength by only 0.2%. Our runtime overhead is 7.5% of placement and packing runtime.

We have thus confirmed our hypothesis that we need both net-based and path based optimization for achieving better timing. Also, we verified that net based approaches work better earlier in the flow and path-based approaches work well towards the end.

Table 2: Results for our Algorithm

ΔFmax(%)	ΔWirelength(%)	ΔRuntime(%)
4.5	0.2	7.5

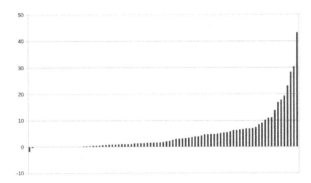

Figure 11: % Fmax change (y-axis) for all designs

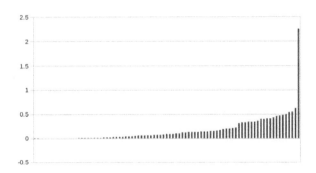

Figure 12: % Wirelength change (y-axis) for all designs

The Fmax and wirelength histograms for all designs are shown in Figures 11 and 12 respectively. We observe that the majority of the Fmax changes are within 10% but there are some extremely good outliers. The variance in the Fmax changes are due to factors like the structure of the design, congestion, etc. Two designs have a negative Fmax change, which may be due to our relaxation of delay limits slightly beyond the worst slack. Most of the wirelength changes are within 0.5%. The negligible impact on wirelength is expected as our algorithm only works on a few critical paths and leaves most of the nets undisturbed.

9. CONCLUSION

In this paper, we discuss the challenges in timing-driven detailed placement for modern FPGAs and propose a new critical path optimization technique to address them. Two enhancements to critical path optimization have been proposed, of which one is using a shortest path formulation and the other is using hard limits on delays for each net to prevent timing degradation in other non-critical paths. We also proposed parallelization schemes related to our algorithm. Experimental results on industrial-scale benchmarks demonstrate that our algorithm achieves good improvement in Fmax with negligible wirelength and runtime penalty.

10. REFERENCES

[1] Chrystian Guth, Vinicius Livramento, Renan Netto, Renan Fonseca, Jose Luis Guntzel, Luiz Santos, *"Timing-Driven Placement Based on Dynamic Net-Weighting for Efficient Slack Histogram Compression"*, International Symposium on Physical Design, 2015

[2] Amit Chowdhary, Karthik Rajagopal, Satish Venkatesan, Tung Cao, Vladimir Tiourin, Yegna Parasuram, Bill Halpin, *"How Accurately Can We Model Timing In A Placement Engine?"*, Design Automation Conference, 2005

[3] Tim Kong, *"A novel net weighting algorithm for timing-driven placement"*, International Conference on Computer Aided Design, 2002.

[4] Haoxing Ren, David Z. Pan, David S. Kung, *"Sensitivity guided net weighting for placement-driven synthesis"*, IEEE Transactions on Computer Aided Design of Integrated Circuits and Systems, 2005.

[5] Alexander Marquardt, Vaughn Betz, Jonathan Rose, *"Timing-Driven Placement for FPGAs"*, International Symposium on Field Programmable Gate Arrays, 2000

[6] Haoxing Ren, David Z. Pan, Charles J. Alpert, Gi-Joon Nam, Paul Villarrubia, *"Hippocrates: First-Do-No-Harm Detailed Placement"*, Asia and South Pacific Design Automation Conference, 2007

[7] Huimin Bian, Andrew C. Ling, Alexander Choong, Jianwen Zhu, *"Towards scalable placement for FPGAs"*, International Symposium on Field Programmable Gate Arrays, 2010

[8] Natarajan Viswanathan, Gi-Joon Nam, Jarrod A. Roy, Zhuo Li, Charles J. Alpert, Shyam Ramji, Chris Chu, *"ITOP: Integrating Timing Optimization within Placement"*, International Symposium on Physical Design 2010

[9] Tao Luo, David Newmark, David Z. Pan, *"A New LP Based Incremental Timing Driven Placement for High Performance Designs"*, Design Automation Conference, 2006

[10] Andrew B. Kahng , Stefanus Mantik, Igor L. Markov, *"Min-Max Placement for Large-Scale Timing Optimization"*, International Symposium on Physical Design, 2002

[11] Michael D. Moffitt, David A. Papa, Zhuo Li, Charles J. Alpert, *"Path Smoothing via Discrete Optimization"*, Design Automation Conference, 2008

[12] Siddharth Joshi, Stephen Boyd, *"An Efficient Method for Large-Scale Slack Allocation"*, 2008

[13] Ken Eguro, Scott Hauck, *"Enhancing Timing-Driven FPGA Placement for Pipelined Netlists"*, Design Automation Conference, 2008

[14] Chao Chris Wang, Guy G. F. Lemieux, *"Scalable and Deterministic Timing-Driven Parallel Placement for FPGAs"*, International Symposium on Field Programmable Gate Arrays, 2011

[15] Mei-Fang Chiang, Takumi Okamoto, Takeshi Yoshimura, *"Register Placement for High-performance Circuits"*, Design Automation and Test in Europe, 2009

[16] Bill Halpin, C. Y. Roger Chen, Naresh Sehgal, *"Detailed Placement with Net Length Constraints"*, International Workshop on System On Chip, 2003

[17] Igor L. Markov, Jin Hu, Myung-Chul Kim, *"Progress and Challenges in VLSI Placement Research"*, International Conference on Computer Aided Design, 2012

[18] Shounak Dhar, Saurabh Adya, Love Singhal, Mahesh A. Iyer, David Z. Pan, *"Detailed Placement for Modern FPGAs using 2D Dynamic Programming"*, International Conference on Computer Aided Design, 2016

Clock-Aware FPGA Placement Contest

Stephen Yang, Chandra Mulpuri, Sainath Reddy, Meghraj Kalase,
Srinivasan Dasasathyan, Mehrdad E. Dehkordi, Marvin Tom, Rajat Aggarwal

Xilinx Inc. 2100 Logic Drive   San Jose, CA 95124

{stepheny,chandim,sainath,meghraj,sda,mehrdad,marvint,rajata}@xilinx.com

ABSTRACT

Modern FPGA device contains complex clocking architecture on top of FPGA logic fabric. To best utilize FPGA clocking architecture, both FPGA designers and EDA tool developers need to understand the clocking architecture and design best methodology/algorithm for various design styles. Clock legalization and clock aware placement become one of the key factors in FPGA design flow. They can greatly influence FPGA design performance and routability. FPGA placement problem can get very difficult with clock legalization constraints. This year's contest is a continuous challenge based on last year's routability driven placement. Contestants need to design best-in-class clock aware placement approach to excel in the contest.

Keywords

FPGA; Placement; Clock; Legalization; Routability

1. INTRODUCTION

As modern FPGA architectures continue to evolve and designs become more complex, FPGA placement remains to be one of the most challenging problems in FPGA design flow [1]. Today's FPGA architecture imposes complicated layout rules during placement stage. The benefit is that designers can ignore the layout details and focus on logical and functional aspect. The tool developers, however, need to improve placement, routing and optimization algorithms to best achieve design goals while meeting architecture constraints. Clock legalization rule, among all the architectural constrains, has major impact on layout quality including design timing performance and routability.

Routability-driven FPGA placement contest held in ISPD 2016 [2] successfully attracted attention from academic research groups. 19 teams registered for the contest and 12 teams submitted final version of the FPGA placement tool. FPGA placement problem was well studied. New algorithms were tested on academic format benchmarks based on modern FPGA architecture. A number of FPGA placement papers have been published [8][9][10][11].

The contest of this year is an extension of ISPD 2016 contest. The introduction of clock-aware concept gives placement problem a new challenge. The best placement algorithm needs to find the balance between getting the appropriate clock legalization constraints and optimizing the basic placement quality.

2. FPGA ARCHITECTURE
2.1 FPGA Programmable Blocks

Xilinx FPGAs [3], an example of which is illustrated in Figure 1, consist of an array of programmable blocks of different types, including general logic (CLB), memory (BRAM) and multiplier (DSP) blocks, surrounded by a programmable routing fabric (interconnect) that allows these blocks to be connected via horizontal and vertical routing channels. This array is surrounded by programmable input/output blocks (IO) that interface the chip to the outside world.

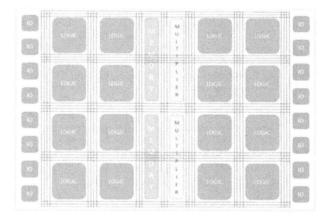

Figure 1. Example of Xilinx FPGA Architecture

This array has a configuration memory (SRAM) beneath it, which, when loaded with appropriate bits, programs the blocks and the interconnects to behave a certain way, as illustrated in Figure 2.

Given a logic design that the user wants to implement on the FPGA, the Xilinx Implementation Tool flow (Vivado) converts the design into the appropriate set of configuration bits (bitstream) which is loaded onto the SRAM to make the FPGA behave as the design. There are usually multiple steps involved in this tool flow, the main ones being, Synthesis, Placement, Routing, and Bitstream generation.

ISPD'17, March 19–22, 2017, Portland, OR, USA.
© 2017 ACM. ISBN 978-1-4503-4696-2/17/03...$15.00.
DOI: http://dx.doi.org/10.1145/3036669.3038241

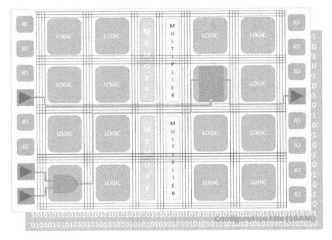

Figure 2. Example of Programming the Xilinx FPGA

Synthesis tool infers the design logic in terms of the logic blocks available within the FPGA. Placement tool places these inferred logic blocks on the various sites of physical logic blocks present in the FPGA. Routing tool connects up the pins of these physical logic blocks using the programmable interconnect routing structures in the FPGA. Bitstream generation tool then proceeds to generate the set of configuration bits that program these logic blocks and interconnect routing structures to behave as the design intended.

The general logic block (also referred to as the configurable logic block, or CLB), is the main resource for implementing general-purpose combinatorial and sequential circuits. The CLB is made up of the logic elements themselves, which are grouped together into a slice. These logic elements are of the type lookup tables (LUTs) or sequential elements (FFs). Each CLB contains one slice. Each slice provides sixteen LUTs and sixteen flip-flops. The slices and their CLBs are arranged in columns throughout the device. There are, however, certain restrictions pertaining to how these LUTs and FFs can be used within each slice. These are explained in detail in the "Placement Evaluation Flow" section under "Legalization Rules" subsection.

In the specific Xilinx FPGA we're targeting for this contest, the XCVU095-ffva2104-es2 device, we have 67,200 CLB/SLICE locations, 880 usable IO locations, 770 DSP locations, and 1730 BRAM locations. More information on this device, and the architecture in general, can be obtained from [5].

2.2 Clocking Architecture

Xilinx UltraScale Architecture introduces a new ASIC-like clocking architecture to the FPGA world. One main feature of this new architecture is the abundance of clocking resources. For example, the biggest device can accommodate more than 600 total clocking buffers. The architecture also introduces a mesh-like routing structure for routing clocks from clock sources all the way to all loads. Such routing structure allows the software tools to make smart choices of how the clocks are placed and routed in a way that have not been feasible in any other FPGA architecture.

The clock placement problem can be stated as the problem of assigning clocking components of a design to compatible clocking resources on a device. In the simplest form, clocking components consist of clock sources and clock loads. Clock sources are

components that generate clock signals and/or derive dedicated clock nets using dedicated clocking trees. Clock loads are sequential components that capture data with respect to the input clock signal.

Clock source placement is usually done early in the placement flow along with general IO placement, and it heavily depends on architectural rules imposed by the device constraints. Clock load placement, specifically for non-IO clock loads, is taken care by the general placement flow. This usually starts with a global placement of all placeable components, where an approximate location is found for each component. This is followed by a detailed placement, where a legal placement is created and each component is assigned to a physical site on the device. At early stages in the global placement flow, the clock loads are partitioned based on their placement at the time. The Clock load partitioning is driven by clocking architectural constraints. Without a correct clock load partitioning the final placement solution could be illegal, i.e., no routing solution would be available.

The clock placement and partitioning approach explained above is independent of the how the clocks are routed. But this approach is not enough to create legal clocking solutions. A clock partitioning solution that combines the problems of clock partitioning and clock routing, is needed to produce legal clocking solution and optimize clocking network for better skew, hold requirement, and insertion delay.

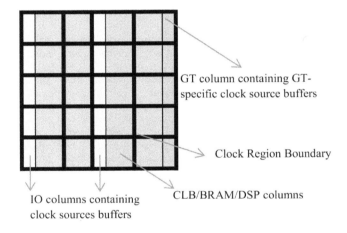

Figure 3. Clock Region Boundaries in an UltraScale device

Each FPGA device in this architecture is divided into multiple clock regions. A clock region includes all synchronous elements-- Configurable Logic Block (CLB), I/O, high speed transceivers (GT), DSP, block RAM, and so on-- in an area spanning one I/O bank, with a horizontal clock row (HROW) in its center. Figure 3 shows clock region divisions for one of the UltraScale devices.

This particular device is divided into a 4x5 rectangular grid of 20 clock regions. Note that some clock regions may contain an IO bank or a GT quad. Clock source buffers are inside the IO and GT columns. So clocks can only be sourced from such clock regions.

The clock routing structure consists of a two-layer network of routing tracks as detailed below:

- A routing network consisting of 24 horizontal and 24 vertical tracks

o There is a one-to-one bidirectional connection between any two horizontal routing and vertical routing tracks in each clock region. For example, for a clock using horizontal routing track 0, it can switch to vertical routing track 0 at their intersection in one clock region and back to horizontal routing track 0 in another clock region.

o There is no vertical routing track in IO or GT columns.

• A distribution network, also consisting of 24 horizontal and 24 vertical tracks

o There is a one-to-one unidirectional connection (from vertical to horizontal) between any two horizontal distribution and vertical distribution tracks in each clock region. For example, for a clock using vertical distribution track 0, it can switch to horizontal distribution track 0 at any possible intersection.

o There is no vertical distribution track in GT columns.

There is no path from distribution back to routing tracks. So once a clock is on the distribution network it can only go to the leaf level nodes. From routing (horizontal or vertical) to distribution network clocks need to hop onto vertical distribution first. There is a one-to-one connection from every routing (horizontal or vertical) to its corresponding vertical distribution track.

The clock can be distributed from the sources in one of two ways. They can go onto routing tracks which take the clock to a particular sub-region without going to any loads and then go onto the distribution tracks. This is used to move the root for all the loads to be at a location beneficial from a skew perspective. Alternatively, they can go straight onto the distribution tracks. This would be to reduce insertion delay or that point being the root is most beneficial for skew. Once on the distribution tracks, the clock travels vertically and taps off at various horizontal segments. Before driving the horizontal segment it would go through a programmable delay and clock enable circuit. From the horizontal distribution it can feed the leaf clocks.

Each clock segment can be driven at either end or by a driver within the segment. Each of those drivers therefore would be tri-stable. This allows the clock network to be segmented at each fabric sub-region boundary. By having the clock only use segments as needed, it allows the tracks to be reused.

The clock routing structure consists of a two-layer network of routing tracks as detailed below:

• A routing network consisting of 24 horizontal and 24 vertical tracks

• A distribution network, also consisting of 24 horizontal and 24 vertical tracks

• Each clock region has 24 horizontal routing (HR) and 24 vertical routing (VR) tracks

• Each clock region has 24 horizontal distribution (HD) and 24 vertical distribution (VD) tracks

• There is a one-to-one bidirectional connection between any two HR and VR tracks in each clock region. For example, for a clock using HR track 0, it can switch to VR track 0 at their intersection in one clock region and back to HR track 0 in another clock region

• There is a one-to-one unidirectional connection from VD to HD in each clock region. For example, for a clock using VD track 0, it can switch HD track 0

• Once on HD, clock only drives HD tracks on neighboring clock regions or clock loads in that region. There is no way back on HR/VR/VD tracks

• From HR/VR to distribution network clocks need to hop onto VD first. There is a one-to-one connection from every routing (horizontal or vertical) to its corresponding VD track

• All tracks are segmented at clock region boundaries, therefore two clocks can use the same track provided that their loads are in non-intersecting rectangular clock region areas

• Each clock net should use a single clock track and a single clock root

• Each global clock buffer has a dedicated clock track that can only be driven by that clock buffer. The Y coordinate of the site where the clock buffer is placed at can be used to specify the track number for that given site. So for BUFGCE_XmYn the clock track number will be n%24

• Within a clock region, global clock buffer locations can be changed without affecting design legality

2.3 Clock Placement Problem

Place all clock sources and clock loads and partition the clock loads into partitions containing one or more clock regions, such that

• Number of global clocks in each clock region is at most 24 clocks.

• Within each clock region, each half column has at most 12 clocks.

• Each clock region has enough resources to accommodate all clock loads assigned to that region.

• If needed, all loads of each clock should be constrained to a continuous rectangular area consisting of one or more clock regions.

3. BENCHMARKS

The benchmarks for ISPD 2017 clock placement contest have been generated using an internal netlist-generation tool based on Generate NetList (GNL [7]). The tool allows us to create netlists which varies in features such as number of components, interconnection, number of control sets, number of clocks. Additionally, it provides control over the type of components (primitives) used in the netlist. For ISPD 2017 benchmarks, we have restricted the primitives to be Look-Up-Tables (LUTs), Flip-Flops (FFs), DSP blocks (DSFs),

Design Name	#Luts (Util)	#Flops (Util)	#RAMB36	#DSPs	#IOs	Rent	#Clocks
design5	215K(40%)	236K(22%)	170(10%)	75(10%)	300	0.6	30
design6	242K(45%)	270K(25%)	255(15%)	112(15%)	300	0.6	33
design7	268K(50%)	300K928%)	340(20%)	150(20%)	300	0.6	36
design8	295K(55%)	325K(30%)	425(25%)	187(25%)	300	0.6	39
design9	322K(60%)	354K(33%)	510(30%)	225(30%)	400	0.63	42
design10	350K(65%)	384K(36%)	595(35%)	262(35%)	400	0.63	45
design11	376K(70%)	414K(38%)	680(40%)	300(40%)	400	0.63	48
design12	392K(73%)	431K(40%)	765(45%)	337(45%)	400	0.63	51
design13	408K(76%)	449K(42%)	850(50%)	375(50%)	400	0.63	54
design14	424K(79%)	450K(43%)	900(53%)	397(53%)	400	0.63	55
design15	440K(82%)	484K(45%)	950(56%)	420(56%)	400	0.63	56
design16	456K(85%)	503K(47%)	1000(59%)	442(59%)	400	0.63	57

Table 1. Benchmark statistics

*Number in parenthesis indicates the utilization as percentage of available resources in the FPGA [6]

and Block RAMs (BRAMs). We have varied number of primitives of different types, interconnection complexity, number of clocks to create netlist of varied complexity. The target device chosen was xcvu095, part of the Virtex UltraScale [4] family.

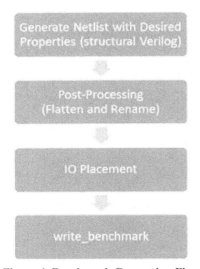

Figure 4. Benchmark Generation Flow

The following properties of the netlist were varied among the ISPD benchmarks.

- Number of instance: We have created benchmarks that utilize between 40% and 85% of the available LUTs. Proportionally we have also varied the number of DSPs, BRAMs, and FFs to create medium to highly utilized designs.

- Rent exponent: Interconnection complexity were varied to create netlists of different Rent exponents. This is important to test the routability aspect of the placement solution.

- Number of clock: Further complex designs were created by varying the number of clocks from 30 to 57.

- Number of Resets: FPGA architecture limits the number of unique reset nets per Slice. By varying the number of resets we test how well the placer can support such restrictions.

Figure 4 explains the flow used for generating these benchmarks. First, we generate structural Verilog using our netlist-generation tool. The input to this tool is a configuration file, which specifies the desired parameters in the netlist. The structural Verilog file is post-processed to create a flattened design, without any hierarchies. Along with dissolving hierarchies, we also rename the instances and nets in this step. Next, we run Vivado placer to place IO ports of the design. Finally, we write the benchmark in Bookshelf format. The Bookshelf format list the instances in the design in a ".nodes" file and their interconnection in a ".nets" file. It also writes IO placement in a ".pl" file. Library cells are separately listed in a "*.lib" file.

4. PLACEMENT EVALUATION

The placement evaluation flow is similar to ISPD 2016 contest [2]. The major difference is on the clock legalization check. Total wirelength is the main evaluation metric. Clock skew and timing are not part of the metrics in this contest.

4.1 Placement Interface

Contestants are expected to write the output of their placement tool in a specific (.pl) file format. Placer's output placement file should contain locations of all the instances in the design. The location of an instance has three fields: x-coord, y-coord (to determine the SITE) and BEL (index within the SITE). Figure 5 shows the BEL number for LUTs/FFs placed inside a SLICE SITE.

For BRAM and DSP instances, since there are no BELs within a SITE, the BEL index remains 0.

Figure 5. BEL offsets within a SLICE

The placement output (.pl) file, will be given as an input to Xilinx Vivado tool using the flow.tcl file, which is available as part of each benchmarks archive. Vivado Placer will then read these instance placements, and check for legal placement on every instance. In case of illegal placement, Vivado Placer will error out with a reason behind the illegality for each instance. If the placement is legal, Vivado router starts and completes routing, or report unroutable design. If routing completes successfully, the following message indicates total routed wirelength: "Total Routed Wirelength: xxxxx (Vertical xxxx, Horizontal xxxx)". In case of unroutable placement, the following message shows up: "CRITICAL WARNING: [Route 35-162] xxxx signals failed to route due to routing congestion."

4.2 Legalization Rules

Each SLICE site provides sixteen LUTs and sixteen FFs. There are, however, certain restrictions pertaining to how these LUTs and FFs can be used within each SLICE.

4.2.1 Clock Legalization Rules

- Number of global clocks in each clock region is at most 24 clocks.
- Within each clock region, each half column has at most 12 clocks.
- Each clock region has enough resources to accommodate all clock loads assigned to that region.

4.2.2 Using LUTs in a SLICE:

- The 16 LUTs within SLICE are conceptual LUTs that can only be fully used under certain conditions:

- When implementing a 6-input LUT with one output, one can only use LUT 1 (leaving LUT 0 unused) or LUT 3 (leaving LUT 2 unused) or ... or LUT 15 (leaving LUT 14 unused)
- When implementing two 5-input LUTs with separate outputs but common inputs, one can use {LUT 0, LUT 1} or {LUT 2, LUT 3} or ... or {LUT 14, LUT 15}
- The above rule of coming LUTs with separate outputs but common inputs, holds good for 5-input LUTs (as mentioned above) or fewer input LUTs as well
- When implementing two 3-input (or fewer input) LUTs together (irrespective of common inputs), one can use {LUT 0, LUT 1} or {LUT 2, LUT 3} or ... or {LUT 14, LUT 15}

4.2.3 Using FFs in a SLICE:

- There are 16 FFs per SLICE (two per LUT pair), and all can be used fully under certain conditions:
- All FFs can take independent inputs from outside the SLICE, or outputs of their corresponding LUT pair (FF 0 can take LUT 0 or LUT 1 output as input, ..., FF 15 can take LUT 14 or LUT 15 output as input)
- All can be configured as either edge-triggered D-type flip-flops or level-sensitive latches. The latch option is by top or bottom half of the SLICE (0 to 7, and 8 to 15). If the latch option is selected on a FF, all eight FFs in that half must be either used as latches or left unused. When configured as a latch, the latch is transparent when the clock input (CLK) is high.
- There are two clock inputs (CLK) and two set/reset inputs (SR) to every SLICE for the FFs. Each clock or set/reset input is dedicated to eight of the sixteen FFs, split by top and bottom halves (0 to 7, and 8 to 15). FF pairs ({0,1} or {2,3} or ... or {14,15}) share the same clock and set/reset signals. The clock and set/reset signals have programmable polarity at their slice inputs, allowing any inversion to be automatically absorbed into the CLB.
- There are four clock enables (CE) per SLICE. The clock enables are split both by top and bottom halves, and by the two FFs per LUT-pair. Thus, the CEs are independent for: {FF 0, FF 2, FF 4, FF 6}, {FF 1, FF 3, FF 5, FF 7}, {FF 8, FF 10, FF 12, FF 14}, {FF 9, FF 11, FF 13, FF 15}. When one storage element has CE enabled, the other three storage elements in the group must also have CE enabled. The CE is always active High at the slice, but can be inverted in the source logic.
- The two SR set/reset inputs to a SLICE can be programmed to be synchronous or asynchronous. The set/reset signal can be programmed to be a set or reset, but not both, for any individual FF. The configuration options for the SR set and reset functionality of a register or latch are: No set or reset, Synchronous set (FDSE primitive), Synchronous reset (FDRE primitive), Asynchronous set (preset) (FDPE primitive), Asynchronous reset (clear) (FDCE primitive). The SR set/reset input can be ignored for groups of four flip-flops (the same groups as controlled by the CE inputs). When one FF has SR enabled, the other three FFs in the group must also have SR enabled.
- The choice of set or reset can be controlled individually for each FF in a SLICE. The choice of synchronous (SYNC) or asynchronous (ASYNC) set/reset (SYNC_ATTR) is

controlled in groups of eight FFs, individually for the two separate SR inputs.

Some of these FF Packing rules are illustrated in Figure 6.

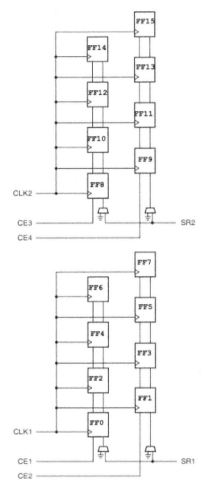

Figure 6. Flip Flop control signals connectivity within a SLICE

More information on the CLB composition can be obtained from [5]

4.3 Evaluation Metrics

- For each design in the benchmark suite, the placers will be ranked based on the contest evaluation metric. The final rank for a placer will be the sum of the individual ranks on all the circuits. The placer with the smallest total rank wins the contest.
- The placement runtime must be 12 hours or shorter.
- The placement must be legal in terms of logic legalization.
- The placement must be legal in terms of clock legalization rules described in Section 2.
- The placement has to be routed by Vivado router, and the router has to complete the job within 12 hours. Routing is regarded as failed if it takes more than 12 hours to complete.

- PlacementScore=RoutedWirelength*(1 + Runtime_Factor)
  - o Vivado router reports total routed wirelength. This is the base of the score.
  - o Total placement and routing runtime will be used in computing P&R_Runtime_Factor;
  - o Runtime_Factor= -(Runtime - Median_Runtime) / 10.0
  - o Runtime factor is between -10% and +10%
- The failed place/route job will get the lowest rank on this design. In the presence of failures on multiple placers, the break-tie factors are (in order): placer failure, logic legalization failure, clock legalization failure, router failure.

5. ACKNOWLEDGMENTS
The authors would like to thank Dr. Sudip Nag, Dr. Padmini Gopalakrishnan and Dr. Sabya Das for their support.

6. REFERENCES
[1] R. Aggarwal, FPGA Place and Route Challenges, *International Symposium on Physical Design. 2014*

[2] S. Yang, A. Gayasen, C. Mulpuri, S. Reddy, and R. Aggarwal, Routability-Driven FPGA Placement Contest, *International Symposium on Physical Design, 2016*

[3] Xilinx, "UltraScale Architecture", http://www.xilinx.com/products/technology/ultrascale.html

[4] Xilinx, "Virtex UltraScale FPGAs", http://www.xilinx.com/publications/prod_mktg/ultrascalevirtex-product-table

[5] Xilinx, "UltraScale Architecture Configurable Logic Block User Guide", http://www.xilinx.com/support/documentation/user_guides/ug574-ultrascale-clb.pdf

[6] Xilinx, "UltraScale Architecture and Product Overview", http://www.xilinx.com/support/documentation/data_sheets/ds890-ultrascale-overview.pdf

[7] GNL: http://users.elis.ugent.be/~dstrooba/gnl/

[8] W. Li, S. Dhah, and D. Z. Pan, "UTPlaceF: A Routability-Driven FPGA Placer with Physical and Congestion Aware Packing", *International Conference on Computer-Aided Design (ICCAD), 2016*

[9] C.W. Pui, G. Chen, W.K. Chow, K.C. Lam, J. Kuang, P. Tu, H. Zhang, F.Y. Young, B. Yu, "RippleFPGA: A Routability-Driven Placement for Large-Scale Heterogeneous FPGAs", *International Conference on Computer-Aided Design (ICCAD), 2016*

[10] R. Pattison, Z. Abuowaimer, S. Areibi, G. Grewal, A. Vannelli, "GPlace – A Congestion-aware Placement tool for UltraScale FPGAs ", *International Conference on Computer-Aided Design (ICCAD), 2016*

[11] S. Dhah, S. Adya, L. Singhal, M. A. Iyer and D. Z. Pan "Detailed Placement for Modern FPGAs using 2D Dynamic Programming", *International Conference on Computer-Aided Design (ICCAD), 2016*

Author Index